BENJAMIN'S LIBRARY

signale

modern german letters, cultures, and thought

Series editor: Peter Uwe Hohendahl, Cornell University

Signale: Modern German Letters, Cultures, and Thought publishes new English-language books in literary studies, criticism, cultural studies, and intellectual history pertaining to the German-speaking world, as well as translations of important German-language works. *Signale* construes "modern" in the broadest terms: the series covers topics ranging from the early modern period to the present. *Signale* books are published under a joint imprint of Cornell University Press and Cornell University Library in electronic and print formats. Please see http://signale.cornell.edu/.

BENJAMIN'S LIBRARY

Modernity, Nation, and the Baroque

JANE O. NEWMAN

A Signale Book

CORNELL UNIVERSITY PRESS AND CORNELL UNIVERSITY LIBRARY
ITHACA, NEW YORK

Cornell University Press and Cornell University Library gratefully
acknowledge the support of The Andrew W. Mellon Foundation for the
publication of this volume.

First published 2011 by Cornell University Press and Cornell University Library

Printed in the United States of America

Library of Congress Cataloging-in-Publication Data

Newman, Jane O.
    Benjamin's library : modernity, nation, and the Baroque / Jane O. Newman.
        p. cm. — (Signale : modern German letters, cultures, and thought)
    Includes bibliographical references and index.
    ISBN 978-0-8014-7659-4 (pbk. : alk. paper)
    1. Benjamin, Walter, 1892–1940—Criticism and interpretation.
2. Benjamin, Walter, 1892–1940—Contributions in criticism.   3. German
literature—Early modern, 1500–1700—History and criticism.   4. Baroque
literature—History and criticism.   5. Germany—Intellectual life.
I. Title.   II. Series: Signale (Ithaca, N.Y.)
    PT2603.E455Z7934 2011
    838'91209—dc23   2011026074

Paperback printing   10 9 8 7 6 5 4 3 2 1

For Jordan, who grew up with this book

Contents

PREFACE

In his famous essay "Literaturgeschichte und Literaturwissenschaft" (Literary History and the Study of Literature) (1931), Walter Benjamin describes the methods of contemporary literary historians as akin to the clumsy acts of a platoon of mercenaries, who, entering into a beautiful house full of treasures and claiming to admire its spectacular contents, in fact "do not give a damn for the order and inventory of the house. They have moved in because it is strategically situated and because it is a convenient vantage point from which to bombard a railway or bridgehead whose defense is important in the civil war" (Benjamin, *Selected Writings* 2: 461–62). As David Bathrick, Jeffrey Grossman, and Detlev Schöttker ("Walter Benjamin und seine Rezeption") have shown, the historiography of Benjamin studies could be described in similar terms. Bathrick and Grossman chart the opportunistic intrusion on the corpus of Benjamin's publications and surviving manuscripts by various scholars, beginning with Theodor W. Adorno and Gershom Scholem and extending up into GDR/DDR-based struggles and deconstructive receptions, respectively. The battle lines they describe are as clear as they are everywhere debated: the early versus the late Benjamin, the messianic-theological versus the Marxist-materialist Benjamin, a "reader's" Benjamin versus the "historical" Benjamin (Nägele 8–9), and so on. Schöttker argues that the proliferation of these often opposing receptions is the natural result of the nearly impossibly varied genres of those of Benjamin's writings that were published during his lifetime—literary and cultural criticism, academic writing and book reviews, translations, and much more. The fragmentary state of much of the posthumously published work, and especially of the "torso" of the Arcades Project (Wolin xl), has provoked similar contests over its meaning.

Benjamin's *Ursprung des deutschen Trauerspiels* (The Origin of the German Tragic Drama) has been subjected by cultural, intellectual, and literary historians, critics, and theorists to any number of occupations over the years in ways not unlike those that have characterized the reception of his entire oeuvre. The *Tragic Drama* book has been variously seen as the "tragic" beginning of the end of the possibility of an academic career (Lindner, "Habilitationsakte Benjamin"; Brodersen, *Spinne im eigenen Netz*), as an early articulation of Benjamin's "avant garde theory" and of his "micrological" thinking and "messianic" philosophy of history (Jäger, Kany, and Pizer), and, finally, as a performance of his theories of allegory (Menninghaus) and "constructivism" (Schöttker, *Konstruktiver Fragmentarismus*). The *Tragic Drama* book has nevertheless seldom been read—even by scholars who call for an investigation of its "complex intellectual debts to |a| rich network of competing intellectual traditions" in the early twentieth century, among them Neoplatonism, neo-Kantianism, Surrealism, Marxism (Richter 23), and Schmittian "construction|s| of sovereignty" (Koepnick 280)—for the purchase the book provides on the vexed politico-historiographic status of the Baroque, the period and concept whose texts are Benjamin's direct object of concern there.

The title of the *Tragic Drama* book, with the mysterious "mourning play," or tragic drama (*Trauerspiel*), at its center, refers not to the genre of tragedy writ large, for example, but to a very specific corpus of German-language drama by the authors known as the Second Silesian school (Zweite Schlesische Schule) of the seventeenth century; theirs were the plays that were the textual objects with which Benjamin—either "for opportunistic reasons" or not (*Briefe* 1: 304)—was primarily concerned when he undertook his postdoctoral thesis, or *Habilitation*. He probably read many of these plays, as well as the numerous other Baroque texts from which he quotes, in the Prussian State Library on Unter den Linden in Berlin. It was there that he copied onto note cards the "600 citations," all "well organized for getting an overview" (*Gesammelte Schriften* 1.3: 875), that he then took with him to the island of Capri in 1924 to draft the thesis there. At the time, however, the sometimes scandalous and always extravagant historical plays of the Second Silesian school were not "dusty volumes of plays long unread," or "bastardized" texts of a lost period that had deservedly "long been consigned to the dusty attic of literary failures" (Gilloch 63 and 15).[1] Rather, they belonged to a complex network

---

1. The names of some of the most well-known German Baroque playwrights and poets are nevertheless for the most part less well-known today than in Benjamin's time. Among them are the Silesians, Martin Opitz (1597–1639), Andreas Gryphius (1616–64), Daniel Casper von Lohenstein (1635–83), and Johann Christian Hallmann (c. 1640–1704), as well as other authors curiously included by Benjamin in this tradition, such as the Viennese Josef Anton Stranitzky (c. 1676–1726) and the Nuremberg poets Georg Philipp Harsdörffer (1607–58), Sigmund von Birken (1626–81), and Johann Klaj (1616–56).

of texts and ideological positions associated with a period very much at the center of contemporary debates about nationalism and modernity. We need to know at least as much as Benjamin did about these texts—or be able to contextualize their place in the debates about the Baroque being conducted before and as he began his work—if we want to understand the dense book he wrote about them as a historical document written at a specific moment and in a specific place. Lutz Koepnick usefully interrogates the ways in which the *Tragic Drama* book "projects onto the seventeenth century a political matrix deeply rooted in the cultural climate after the end of [the] World War," suggesting that Benjamin "simultaneously reads the baroque through the lenses of Weimar and mirrors Weimar in the baroque" (281–82). *Benjamin's Library* takes such quasi-mimetic claims one step further in the direction of historical specificity by engaging with the construction of the Baroque as the origin of a peculiarly German modernity both before and during the Weimar years. When he embarked on his study of the Baroque, Benjamin stepped onto a hazardous ideological minefield, in other words. Rather than providing readings of historically Baroque texts, my purpose here is to reconstruct the debates about the Baroque that raged around the author of the *Tragic Drama* book as he wrote it, debates that can thus be understood as constituting the book's "enabling conditions."[2] Put somewhat differently, this is a book about Benjamin's "libraries," the holdings of which we can study as a way of understanding the often heavily overdetermined vocabularies in which he embeds his reflections on the nation's modernity in discussions of a wide range of Baroque texts.

Benjamin himself of course "resisted all attempts . . . to annex him and his writings for a cause" (Jennings, *Dialectical Images* 91). His thinking was opposed to any "theoretical and political attempts to usurp it" (Brodersen, *Walter Benjamin* 31) for a specific end. Schöttker is thus correct to declare "Benjamin" a "phenomenon of reception history" ("Walter Benjamin und seine Rezeption" 268), a Foucauldian "author function" rather than an author in the traditional sense. Grossman agrees, arguing somewhat more modestly that the man and his writings operate as "signs which various discourses attempt to rewrite according to their own model" (414). In all of these cases, "Benjamin" emerges as a thinker and writer who is constructed anew each time his work is "filtered" (Gilloch 235) by a new microcommunity of scholars, each of which is engaged in legacy management of some kind. Ironically, the greatest cultural capital seems to have been gained from stabilizing one particularly dark version of his work and life, namely Benjamin's role as a martyred German-Jewish intellectual and academic outsider. The efficacy of this particular "myth" (Jennings, *Dialectical Images* 1; Schöttker, *Konstruktiver Fragmentarismus* 126–29) is obvious in the sheer number of positions it has buttressed over the years

---

2. I am indebted to one of the anonymous readers of this book for Cornell University Press for the phrase "enabling conditions," which accurately captures the nature of the textual and historical contexts in which Benjamin produced his book and that I assemble here.

on the fraught ideological battlefields of an academy that Benjamin never joined.[3] When myth, or the sign, is used in this way, it works opportunistically, as Roland Barthes explained already some years ago, "abolishing the complexity of human acts" in order to create "a world which is without contradictions because it is without depth" (143). Such a "draining out" of the complexities of history from myth only opens the myth up to further appropriations, according to Barthes (118–19), and thus continues to ignore (to return to Benjamin's original image) the abundant and, in the case of Benjamin's own oeuvre, nearly impossibly cluttered and incongruous inventory of the house overrun by the various groups in the first place. In the case of the *Tragic Drama* book, this "house" was originally furnished in elaborate fashion with early twentieth-century period pieces testifying to the earnestness with which discussions about the Baroque were pursued. These are the discussions I investigate here.

Mythologization has also led to the peculiar position Benjamin occupies in a number of periodization schemes, most of which likewise characteristically disappear from view the very Baroque that was one of his main orientation points. I return in the introduction to the issue of periodization studies and its relevance for writing a book about the Baroque in the early twentieth century, as Benjamin did, as well as for reading my book about it in the twenty-first century. Here, I need only note the impact that Benjamin's induction into the pantheon of postmodern thinkers, alongside Jacques Derrida and Paul de Man, for example, has had on the (in)visibility of his own period claims. (It is interesting that the *grand récit* created by collocating this particular band of "anticlassical" brothers is not unlike those used in the mid- to late 1920s to celebrate the Baroque, one of the more heterodox periods of German literary history, as integral to the national "spirit.")[4] Unlike their postmodernizing fellows, scholars such as Susan Buck-Morss, Michael Jennings, and Richard Wolin have devoted welcome attention to Benjamin's position within a narrative of modernity (rather than of the *post*modern). Yet they too find Benjamin's stance on the modern "nihilistic," suggesting that his work is characteristically prescient about the catastrophe that was to come.[5] Common to both receptions is thus the absence of the *early* modern period, which is so much at the center of

3. This myth has also functioned as an organizing trope around which to market any number of "extracurricular" cultural events, such as art installations and concerts as well as film series. See the 2004–5 exhibit at Haus am Waldsee, Berlin, Germany, and associated film and performance events at the 2006 "NOW—Das Jetzt der Erkennbarkeit: Orte Walter Benjamins in Kultur, Kunst und Wissenschaft" (JETZT—The Now of Recognizability: Sites of Engagement; Walter Benjamin in the History of Culture, the Arts, and Sciences), a "festival" organized by the Zentrum für Literaturforschung, Berlin.

4. See Link-Heer, "Zur Kanonisierung antiklassischer Stile," on the canonization of the "anticlassical."

5. Benjamin of course himself claimed to be skeptical of such progressive historiographies in general; his "conception of history" was, as he wrote in 1931, decisively "against the possibility of an evolutionary and universal[izing] component in history" (*Gesammelte Schriften* 6: 442–43).

the *Tragic Drama* book that even its author could not overlook the traces it had left there. "In the meantime what surprises me above all," Benjamin wrote to Scholem in December 1924, "is that, if you will, what I have written is composed almost entirely of citations" (*Gesammelte Schriften* 1.3: 881). As I show here, many of these citations derive from Baroque texts and from the debates about the sixteenth and seventeenth centuries that were central in defining the origins of a uniquely German modernity at the time.

For Benjamin and his age, literal citation of a tradition of specifically German Baroque texts was not difficult. It was a literary-historical period that was materially present in and to the early twentieth century in numerous ways. Some of these belonged to the realm of technical academic practice, such as the production of critical editions of Baroque plays by individual seventeenth-century playwrights, including Andreas Gryphius and Daniel Casper von Lohenstein, from which Benjamin quotes; many of the editions he used were based on ideologically loaded text-editing principles, as I explain. Benjamin also read and cites plays after versions contained in anthologies of a longer history of German-language theater, anthologies full of equally as pointed messages about the continuities of a "national" culture. The "German" Baroque was also present to Benjamin in other, more figurative ways, as in his discussion of works by originally non-German playwrights of the same period, among them Shakespeare and Calderón. The apparently odd presence of English and Spanish drama in a book about the German tradition is nevertheless not all that surprising, because, for one thing, it is clear from his notes that Benjamin read the English and Spanish plays in German-language translations heavy with politically inflected commentary of a particular sort. By the early twentieth century, there was, moreover, a well-developed German-language school of Shakespeare criticism that identified the Bard not only as German, but also as Baroque. Benjamin was familiar with this scholarship, and his understanding in the *Tragic Drama* book of Shakespeare's role in the German cultural and political imaginary can be read as at least partially based on it.

Even though important work has been done on the centrality of Benjamin's "philological work" (Jennings, *Dialectical Images* 92–93; see also Weigel) in his theorization of the "natural history" of a text, the political and ideological agendas behind the actual philological products he used also need to be considered, especially in conversations regarding the *Tragic Drama* book that see the Baroque as having an "affinity . . . with the immediate post-war period."[6] That such conversations have not yet occurred is due, I suspect, to the reputation that philology has gained in the contemporary division of scholarly labor, which for the most part bans such technical issues from the realm of "high theory" with which Benjamin is commonly

---

6. See Koepnick 281–82 and 282 n. 29, where he refers to Buck-Morss. In both cases, the Baroque nevertheless merely "mirrors" what are assumed to be Benjamin's actual interests, rather than being understood as his primary concern.

said to have been concerned. Roger Chartier famously counters this trend by noting that in "the order of books," "meanings are dependent upon the forms through which they are received and appropriated by their readers (or hearers)." "Forms" are understood here to refer not to "abstract or ideal texts detached from all materiality," but to "objects" (3); "to read is to read something" (5), Chartier explains. Understanding which versions of the German Baroque were quite literally available to Benjamin in the books that he read, and what their material nature reveals about the various narratives of the "modern" German nation in which they were implicated, are thus crucial next steps.[7]

One last observation: associating the figure and work of Walter Benjamin with the interrogation of the Baroque as implicated in the narration of nation and modernity may seem counterintuitive, even perverse, to some. After all, he died as a result of persecution by a National Socialist regime hugely invested in the production of thoroughly rationalizing scripts of all kinds, including one of a continuous history of Ur-German literary and cultural periods culminating in a present-day "Third Reich," which I discuss in the conclusion. It thus seems implausible that Benjamin would have been concerned with how the "modern" German nation got to be what it had so tragically become. And yet the question of which version of Germany's identity was the true one was of ongoing concern to him, and at no time so urgently as during the volatile wartime and immediate post–World War I years. In the very midst of writing the *Tragic Drama* book, the severe nature of the political and economic circumstances that had engulfed the nation caused Benjamin to reflect at length on the history and nature of the crises afflicting the "present situation of Germanness" (gegenwärtige Lage des Deutschtums) in a letter to Florens Christian Rang in 1925 (*Briefe* 1: 309–13). As late as 1936, in his book *Deutsche Menschen* (German Men and Women), Benjamin was still trying to understand the nature of a German tradition worth defending, even as the project of that nation took its dismal turn for the worst. It must thus have seemed quite logical to him to undertake a full genealogy of the German literary and cultural tradition somewhat earlier, during and immediately after the Great War, when the bewildering

---

7. It may well be the case that the way the *Tragic Drama* book has entered Chartier's "order" has made it difficult for professional students of Benjamin to see the importance of the German Baroque in the text. In the commentary volume (1.3) of the Frankfurt edition of Benjamin's works, published by Suhrkamp, on which most scholars rely, for example, the editors have included a huge variety of useful materials. Even notes, such as those that Benjamin jotted down on the back of the "narrow slips of paper" that were the book checkout slips from the State Library (1.3: 919–20), are included. Yet evidence that he actually read either the Silesian plays or any other Baroque texts, not to mention contemporary scholarship on them, is left out—even when it exists. The editors write, for example: "Finally, a handwritten page has survived that contains the schematic listing of the appearance of a variety of motifs from the Baroque tragic drama" (920). Yet, "we have decided against reproducing this list" (920). Such elisions offer unbidden support to Benjamin's odd claim that the materials that he must have had before him on the tables of the State Library were "remote," "very [*sic*] missing" (sehr verschollen), and even "unlocatable," as he writes to Scholem in December 1924 and February 1925 (883, 881). Access to Benjamin's Baroque is in any case blocked here.

tangle of what Martin Jay calls the "desperate hope and looming catastrophe, [the] experimental ebullience and cynical disillusionment" of the intellectual class, show-cased the weaknesses of the modern nation in ways that made those weaknesses just as visible (if not more visible) as they were to become just a few years hence (vii).[8] It may not have been by chance, in other words, that the focus of what Bea-trice Hanssen calls Benjamin's "German period" (26), beginning "after the Treaty of Versailles" (nach dem Friedensschluß) and extending up through his work on the *Tragic Drama* book, concerned the origins of a "modern" German tradition that—as Benjamin himself points out in one of the last versions of his curriculum vitae (1939–40) that survives (*Gesammelte Schriften* 6: 226)—was to be celebrated, but also feared, not because it had "*fail[ed]* to live up to the possibilities it ha[d] made available" (Koepnick 278, emphasis added), but rather, precisely because it *had* lived up to them in spades.

What I mean by this is the following: Benjamin's interest in early modernity signals his awareness that the "origin" of the "pathogenesis of the modern age" lay in the Baroque era, as Koepnick suggests (278). But we must remember that it was also a specifically German version of this early modernity that Benjamin took as his theme. It is surely no accident, for example, that the legacy of Lutheranism looms large in the *Tragic Drama* book. Indeed, if Benjamin sought to understand the rela-tionship of the German nation to a secular "European" modernity that, following Jacob Burckhardt, had its beginning in the Renaissance in Italy, he must surely have contemplated the consequences of Germany having had the Reformation in-stead of a Renaissance. Could Germany be modern, he might well have asked?[9] If so, what was the role of the peculiar modernity of the Protestant Baroque about which he wrote in the production of the "cultural and political predicament" that Germany was in (Koepnick 278)? What was the relation not merely of spirituality in the abstract, in other words, but of the historically confessionalized religions in Germany to the "modern" situation the nation faced? Such questions were not idle ones in a book "conceptualized," as Benjamin famously writes on the dedicatory page, in 1916, at the low point of a war fought under the banner of the Lutheran "war theology" (*Kriegstheologie*) that I discuss in chapter 3, and "completed" in 1925 on the heels of the hunger years following Germany's resounding defeat in 1918.[10]

---

8. In a much later letter to Scholem, Benjamin emphasizes the specifically German context of his interest in the Baroque: "Just as the tragic drama book interrogated the seventeenth century from the point of view of Germany, so [will the Arcades book] consider the nineteenth century from the point of view of France" (*Briefe* 2: 654).

9. Ernst Troeltsch, for example, thought not. See his *Protestantism and Progress: The Significance of Protestantism for the Rise of the Modern World* (1912), in which he writes, not too much before Benjamin began interrogating these very same issues, that unlike Calvinism, Lutheranism was "favorable to abso-lutism" and thus "essentially conservative" (qtd. in Brady, "'Confessionalization'" 3).

10. Although it is not the subject of this book, the analogues between these Germany-specific ques-tions about nationalism, and the particularist-nationalist versus humanist-universalist debates about early Zionism in circles with which Benjamin was familiar, should not be overlooked. See Piterberg 3.

They are no less pressing in our own time, when the terms of political theology are being upended. Whereas it was once self-understood that "all significant concepts of the modern theory of state [were] secularized theological concepts" (Schmitt 36), now it is sacred logics and timetables that are said to govern the actions of a not insignificant number of established states and aspiring world-political actors.

In *Benjamin's Library,* I argue that Benjamin's work on the Baroque emerged out of and in conversation with some of the dominant narratives of German literary and cultural history circulating at the time, narratives that had fundamental questions about modernity and the nation at their core. The *Tragic Drama* book intersects with and documents debates such as these as much as it intersects with and documents other, now perhaps better-known discussions. I am by no means proposing that these other debates and their representatives, including Theodor W. Adorno, Hermann Cohen, Martin Heidegger, Franz Rosenzweig, and Gerhard Scholem, were not important in the formation of Benjamin's ideas about the Baroque, nor in fact that they were unrelated to them.[11] Rather, I suggest that *The Origin of the German Tragic Drama* represents more than a series of fragmentary claims of relevance to everything other than the Baroque, by showing the ways in which it offers a complex theorization of that period as a moment of (re)birth for the German nation. Reading the *Tragic Drama* book as a witness to the ideologically inflected ways in which period logic circulated in the early twentieth century helps shed some clarifying light on the arguments made in this most difficult of texts.

---

11. See Newman, "Rosenzweig and the 'Modern' Baroque State."

ACKNOWLEDGMENTS

While this book had its beginning and its end in Benjamin's city of Berlin, no book is ever really written in one place. Rather, it emerges in the extended conversations with the people with whom one works and lives, on the one hand, and in the encounters with the books, projects, and institutions that one has as one writes, on the other.

In the case of *Benjamin's Library,* many of these conversations and encounters of course did occur in Berlin, and I am indebted to both individuals and institutions there for the material and intellectual help they have afforded me over the years. In particular, I would like to thank Peter-André Alt and Hans Feger of the Freie Universität, Conrad Wiedemann of the Technische Universität, and also my long-time friend, Wilfried Barner of the Universität Göttingen, who was the one who got me interested in the Baroque to begin with and who was generous enough to meet with me when he was in Berlin. I also first met Uwe Steiner (Rice University) in Berlin many years ago and have admired his work on Benjamin since. Another longtime friend, Ulrich Joost (Universität Darmstadt), made time to see me whenever we intersected in Berlin, and also never complained when I shot off an e-mail asking him to help me with locating arcane books and information (and also never disappointed me in finding out what I needed to know). Ursula Marx and Erdmut Wizisla of the Walter Benjamin Archiv, Akademie der Künste, Berlin, and the staff of the Preußische Staatsbibliothek at both Unter den Linden and Potsdamer

Strasse, Berlin, especially Robert Giel and Eva Rothkirch of the Abteilung Historische Drücke, were more than helpful in locating many of the materials used in this book, as were the librarians at the Herzog August Bibliothek (Wolfenbüttel), who even went so far as to get several volumes of Ulrici's Shakespeare edition out of a display case in an exhibit so that I could check some quotes. Not to be forgotten are the many intellectually generous and energetic colleagues at the Zentrum für Kultur- und Literaturforschung in Berlin, including Sigrid Weigel, Carlo Barck, Daniel Weidner, and last, but not at all least, Martin Treml. Finally, it goes without saying that this book could not have been written in Berlin or at all if it had not been for the hospitality of Klaus Burghard and Jutta Beversdorff-Burghard, who opened up their home and their lives to me and my family any number of times.

On the other side of the pond: I engaged in much of the thinking and writing of this book in both southern and northern California at the University of California, Irvine, and during a guest semester at the University of California, Berkeley. At Irvine, it is difficult to know whom to thank first, and thus I simply list alphabetically the names of colleagues (some of whom have since moved on to other institutions) who were crucial in helping me puzzle through Benjamin and the conundrums of academe over the years, including Kai Evers, Alex Gelley, Susan Jarratt, Adriana Johnson, Ketu Katrak, Karen Lawrence, Steve Mailloux, Ngugi wa Thiong'o, David Pan, Jim Porter, Mark Poster, Amy Powell, Leslie Rabine, Nasrin Rahimieh, Annette Schlichter, Vicky Silver, and Uli Strasser. My friend and colleague Julia Lupton is in a category of her own; her intellectual elegance, deep fund of canny insights into the cultures of the present and the past, and seemingly limitless energy provide inspiration in abundance. And my life and work and thought would not be anything without the intellectual, moral, and emotional support offered by my colleague and partner in most things, John H. Smith. Our son, Julian, whose intelligence and kindness prove that the next generation will always be the better one, has been and continues to be a gift and endless source of amazement and delight.

My semester teaching at Berkeley represented a real watershed in my thinking. For the invitation to do so, I thank Eric Naiman and Kathy McCarthy. For providing the conditions of great intellectual excitement and a cohort of deeply learned friends at Berkeley both before and during that semester and since, I thank especially Tim Hampton, Vicky Kahn, and Jonathan Sheehan, learned colleagues and friends all, as well as Tom Brady, Tony Cascardi, and Niklaus Largier. As in Berlin, so too in Berkeley, finally, it's where you live that matters. Linda Williams and Paul Fitzgerald were generous hosts, stimulating intellectual roommates, and good cooks.

Other colleagues in Europe and the United States have contributed to my thinking about the issues I address in this book in any number of different ways. They are Kathleen Biddick (Temple University), Hall Bjornstad (Indiana University, Bloomington), Chris Braider (University of Colorado), Dan and Mária Brewer

(University of Minnesota), David Damrosch (Harvard University), Page duBois (UC San Diego), Marty Elsky (CUNY Graduate Center), Sander Gilman (Emory University), Sabine Gölz (University of Iowa), Tony Grafton (Princeton University), Graham Hammill (SUNY Buffalo), Peter Uwe Hohendahl (Cornell University), Katherine Ibbett (University of London), Michael Jennings (Princeton University), John Lyons (University of Virginia), Hélène Merlin (Paris 3—Nouvelle Sorbonne), Andy Rabinbach (Princeton University), David Sabean (UCLA), Gerhild Scholz-Williams (Washington University, St. Louis), Peter Schwartz (Boston University), Sonia Velazquez (Princeton University), Martin Vialon (Yediteppe University, Istanbul), Sam Weber (Northwestern University), Christopher Wild (University of Chicago), and Irving Wohlfahrt. Thanks to you all.

Finally, I am grateful to a generation or two of graduate students (some now colleagues) in my seminars at UC Irvine and Berkeley for their commitment to helping me follow through on the links Benjamin saw between the early modern period and his own time. These students and colleagues include but are not limited to Matt Ancell, Francie Crebs, C. J. Gordon, Elizabeth Kuehn, Nichole Miller, Glenn Odom, Jen Rust, Melissa Sanchez, Gina Shaffer, Robin Stewart, Jeff Wilson, and Catherine Winiarski. Several talented undergraduates (most now engaged in and completing graduate study) accompanied me on this journey as well, including Jamie Carter, Katie Farrar, Jessie Henry, Kristine Noone, Catherine Nguyen, Rachel Schaffer, Alana Shilling, Jenny Sohn, and Martin Vega.

For financial support that allowed me time to engage in the bibliographic sleuthing central to this project as well as time to write, I acknowledge the Fulbright Foundation, the Humboldt Stiftung, the Simon Guggenheim Foundation, and the University of California, Irvine School of Humanities Committee on Research and Travel and the Humanities Center/Humanities Collective. Rivka Plesser and Ety Alagem of the Jewish National and University Library, The Hebrew University, Jerusalem, and the staff of the Interlibrary Loan Department, Langson Library, UC Irvine, were heroic in their efforts to help me find various editions of texts. Claudia Wedepohl of the Warburg Institute Archives at the Warburg Institute in London was a knowledgeable guide through some very difficult-to-decipher materials written in Warburg's difficult hand.

As is the case in any book a long time in the making, some parts have been published in earlier versions. Parts of the preface and chapter 1 appeared in "Periodization, Modernity, Nation: Benjamin between Renaissance and Baroque," *Journal of the Northern Renaissance* 1.1 (2009): 27–41. Parts of chapter 3 appeared in "'Hamlet ist auch Saturnkind': Citationality, Lutheranism, and German Identity in Walter Benjamin's *Ursprung des deutschen Trauerspiels*," *Benjamin Studien* 1 (2008): 171–88; and in "Enchantment in Times of War: Aby Warburg, Walter Benjamin, and the Secularization Thesis," *Representations* 105 (2009): 133–67. Parts of the conclusion appeared in "Baroque Legacies: National Socialism's Benjamin," *Nazi Germany and the Humanities,* ed. Anson Rabinbach and Wolfgang Bialas (Oxford: Oneworld

Press, 2007), 238–66. All reappear here with permission. The final product came to fruition thanks to the good stewardship of Kizer Walker (Cornell University), managing editor of the *Signale* series, and Marian Rogers, whose editing skills saved me from numerous infelicities. I would also like to thank Kate Mertes for preparing the index.

Quite a number of years ago in Berlin, my daughter, Jordan, was picked up by a friend's father who was going to take her and her friend to the movies. He asked why she was living in Berlin for a year, and she replied (I am told): "I'm here with my parents. My dad is a philosopher, and my mother is writing a book about some guy named Benjamin." Here's the book, Jordan. It's for you.

Textual Note

When quoting from the texts of Walter Benjamin that have not been translated, I refer to the Frankfurt edition, *Gesammelte Schriften,* published by Suhrkamp Verlag, by volume and page. In cases where translations are available, I refer to *Selected Writings,* published by Harvard University Press, by volume and page.

The translations from Benjamin, *Ursprung des deutschen Trauerspiels* (Origin of the German Tragic Drama) that appear here are my own. Nevertheless, although my translations differ in some places from John Osborne's in his *The Origin of the German Tragic Drama* (London and New York: Verso, 1996), I include page references to Osborne's translation as E (English), with page number following, after the page references to the Frankfurt edition, as G (German), with volume and page number following, for those who have access to Osborne's translation.

The majority of the late nineteenth- and early twentieth-century German texts cited here have not been translated previously. The translations here are my own unless otherwise indicated.

BENJAMIN'S LIBRARY

INTRODUCTION

Benjamin's Baroque: A Lost Object?

The history of this period and its taste is still very obscure.

—Johann Friedrich Herder, on the Baroque

One may compare [the critic] to a paleographer in front of a parchment whose faded text is covered by the lineaments of a more powerful script which refers to that text. As the paleographer would have to begin by reading the latter script, the critic would have to begin with commentary.

—Walter Benjamin, "Goethe's Elective Affinities"

Critical Periodization Studies

Herder's claim already more than two hundred years ago that the history of the Baroque is "obscure" is just as accurate in the early twenty-first century as it was in his day, this in spite of the enormous amount of attention devoted by literary, art historical, and art theoretical scholars to both the period (c. 1550–1700) and its styles in the intervening years.[1] *Benjamin's Library* thus engages in a "critical" task in the sense in which Benjamin uses that term in his "Elective Affinities" essay, taking as

---

1. "Die Geschichte dieser Zeit und dieses Geschmacks liegt noch sehr im Dunkeln" (qtd. in Benjamin, G: 1.1: 344; E: 167).

its subject the Baroque that becomes visible in a careful reading of the "commentary" on it provided in Benjamin's famously arcane *The Origin of the German Tragic Drama,* which he in fact often referred to as his "Baroque book" (*Briefe* 1: 374).[2] The *Tragic Drama* book has provoked discussion far, far beyond the borders of Baroque studies, the field to which much of its textual analysis is devoted. Indeed, it might be fair to say that because both the Baroque and Benjamin's understanding of its significance have been overwritten by so much later commentary, they have become nearly as invisible as Benjamin is visible, as unknown as he and the complexities of his thought are known—or at least assumed to be—today. And yet, Benjamin was just one of the many scholars engaged in the debates about the Baroque that were conducted with particular intensity beginning in the last decades of the nineteenth century and continuing on into the early part of the twentieth century. The project of this book is to rescue these discussions and Benjamin's role in them from the obscurity into which they have "faded" by focusing on the important role the Baroque played in theorizations of the European modernity that exploded onto the world stage over the course of these very years, the same modernity that took both promising and destructive forms in Benjamin's Germany in particular, both before and up through World War I.

As animated as debates about the Baroque were in the late nineteenth and early twentieth centuries in German-speaking central Europe, however, most Anglophone and Anglo-American scholars today will be unfamiliar with even their broad outlines. This is so for a variety of reasons, among them that, although such conversations in some cases survived World War II by "immigrating" into the English-speaking world of the United States along with their German-Jewish scholar-authors, they had originally emerged out of specifically European discussions of the role of literature and art in the development of the modern nation-state and could thus take root in their new home only after they were translated (both literally and figuratively) into a new vocabulary and period logic more appropriate to the Cold War "New World."[3] Probably because the Baroque was often associated in the popular mind with a bizarre aesthetics, and with the age of absolutism by scholars, it was neither well understood nor approved of by more than a handful of Americans. Thus, after appearing briefly alongside metaphysical poetry, for example, as a field of study in departments of English and Comparative Literature in the 1960s and early 1970s, the Baroque gradually ceded pride of place to another early modern period, namely the Renaissance, which was the discursively and ideologically more congenial period of the two because it signified the "rebirth" of a vaguely democratic "classicism" with which the collegiate intelligentsia of an

---

2. For the "Elective Affinities" essay, see Benjamin, *Selected Writings* 1: 297–98.

3. Both discussions were ideologically weighted, if in different ways. For one example of how these European ideas were "translated" into U.S. terms, see Newman, "'The Present Confusion Concerning the Renaissance.'"

America *triumphans* could identify more easily in their new postwar role as cus-
todians of the culture and achievements of a "West" that Europe could no longer
defend. By the late 1970s and early 1980s, the Baroque had all but disappeared from
the U.S. academic stage in most disciplines (except for Art History), jostled aside
first by the relentlessly upbeat field of Renaissance studies and then by the innovative and interdisciplinary field of early modern studies, which joined forces with
Renaissance studies to consign the Baroque to its academic grave.[4] If and when it is
referenced in Anglophone scholarship today, the term is associated primarily with
the Latin American neo-Baroque (see Beverley), and occasionally with a more or
less generically postmodern aesthetic and often characterized by a counter- or anti-
hegemonic Deleuzian twist.[5]

In the late nineteenth and early twentieth centuries in Europe, however, the
study of the Baroque had unfolded in dialogue with the heavily ideological interrogation of period study writ large; in such discussions, the Renaissance was often
understood not necessarily as the Baroque's adversary, but rather as a kind of historiographic twin. Below I take up the ease with which both periods were in fact read
as addressing questions of specifically national modernities at the time. Because
the terms *Renaissance* and *early modern* continue to dominate the always weighted
categories of period nomenclature that organize academic discourse about the late
fifteenth through the early seventeenth century, it is important to consider first the
politics of periodization theory in our own post– or (perhaps merely somewhat
differently configured) neo–Cold War world. To what end do we continue to periodize using the categories of Renaissance and early modern rather than Baroque?
Indeed, what are the stakes of our persistent need to periodize at all? It is under the
aegis of critical periodization theory that we can best pose such questions.

Theories of periodization have been the object of renewed critical attention.
Michel de Certeau argues, for example, that historiography creates periods by
"select[ing] between what can be *understood* and what must be *forgotten* in order
to obtain ... intelligibility" (4). When periods are produced in this highly selective
way, they become "reified" and "self-evident"; both the conditions under which
they come into being and the ideological work of elision that the act of periodization performs are forgotten in turn (K. Davis 10). De Certeau notes that there are
nevertheless always "shards created by the selection" process, "remainders left aside
by explication," which "surviv[e]" and "come back" to "discretely perturb ... [the]
system of interpretation" constructed by their repression (4). The production of
the "Middle Ages" is a particularly useful case of the process that de Certeau describes. Scholars have pondered, for example, the ways in which the "periodizing
operation" has over and over again found in the medieval a counterpoint to the

---

4. Renaissance and early modern studies are often thought to be antithetical to one another; see
Marcus. Some scholars have learned to see the "darker sides" of the European Renaissance; see Mignolo.
5. See Deleuze.

tempos and concerns of an Enlightened "modernity" that characteristically uses its forgetting of a 'devout' Middle Ages to identify itself as marching ever forward in a "telic" trajectory of rational and thus implicitly secular progress (K. Davis 1–2 and 84). This kind of "medievalization" is often deployed in civilizational terms when the project is to reduce one's adversaries and their agendas to a state of political nonage. Those who would not "advance" to "our" version of "democracy" are labeled "primitive," "pre-modern," and "feudal" and can thus be cast in the role of needing (often strong-armed) assistance in order to "develop" in the right way (Holsinger, *Neomedievalism*).

According to medievalist Bruce Holsinger, the invocation of the medieval nevertheless functioned somewhat differently for the avant-garde French theorists at the forefront of the charge to define the postmodern in the post–World War II period. Their project was, rather, to divest the present of such putative "advances," of the "baggage of humanism, capitalism, . . . and triumphalist individualism" all in one, by reaching back over the demon Enlightenment to find in the Middle Ages the origins of a postmodern "now" free of an instrumentalizing modernity's downsides (Holsinger, *Pre-Modern Condition* 197; K. Davis 5–6). As much as the progressive narrative of "forgetting" the Middle Ages may seem to be challenged by this second set of moves, the medieval is nevertheless still the main ghost in the forward-thrusting periodization machine. By embracing the Middle Ages as "modernity['s] most consistently abjected . . . temporal other," this iteration of the postmodern found in the medieval premodern a panoply of "transformative" and energizing ways to (re)invent itself as the new guardian and defender of redemptive forms of mysticism, eroticism, and irrationalism inherited from a past previously silenced, but now "reborn" (Holsinger, *Pre-Modern Condition* 5). The medieval past is neither "simply inherited" nor "patiently reconstructed" when it is "translated" into the present in either of these ways. Instead, in both cases, it is "summoned," as a "relic" "from another place," to become the sacred centerpiece of a "whole system of thought" that, whether modern or postmodern, consumes and replaces it (202, 4) in progressivist ways.

As revealing as such innovative historiography has been of the stakes involved in the role that the Middle Ages have been asked to play in the story of period evolution, it has not yet addressed the full range of dyads in whose toils the medieval as the origin of the unmodern has classically been caught. Nor has the role of situation, nation, and place been sufficiently assessed in relation to these pairs.[6] One of the most salient examples of why it is necessary to think period and place together in fact involves the well-known claim that it was the Renaissance (rather than an Enlightened "modernity") that first broke with the Middle Ages and, in so doing,

6. Holsinger (*Neomedievalism, Neoconservatism*) nevertheless does focus on the use by the "West" writ large of neomedievalizing logics to reduce its "others" to a primitive state, with the United States as a central player in this periodizing game.

became what Jacob Burckhardt already in 1860 so famously called the "mother" of "our" "civilization" (1). Cannily taking a step backward in order to progress beyond the medieval by fulfilling the promise of antiquity in its inauguration of a new and modern age, this "filiational" Renaissance—with its almost "biological link [that] binds us to the Renaissance, especially to the Renaissance in Italy"—has characteristically driven the narrative of modernity just as much as (yet also in tandem with) the Enlightenment (Mohlo 133). When understood in this way, it is a specifically *European* Renaissance that participates in what Julia Reinhard Lupton has called the logic of "typology" that is "one of the foundational principles of modern periodization" theory, a logic based on a hermeneutics of imitation, emulation, and figuration (23). Just as the New Testament and Christianity are said to both repeat and complete—and thus contain, supersede, and cancel out—the Old Testament and Judaism (23), specific *national* Renaissances are said to resurrect, repeat, and replace antiquity in the context of the evolving "modern" vernacular nation-state. In this sense, there is always a sacralizing element implicit in what we assume to be the secular periodicity of historiographic work, a sense that one period and place can "fulfill" the promise of another and be both whole and wholly present unto itself. When particular nations adopt this logic, the implications are clear.

The link between period and nation is important in several ways that I discuss in this book. My specific example is Benjamin's interest in the *German* Baroque. But a critical inquiry into this nexus deserves attention beyond the discipline of Germanics. The study of the European Renaissance in general is characteristically "nationalized," for example, when it is pursued in departments and seminars of English, French, or Italian, or as the subject of lectures at specialized conferences that nearly always tend to list in the direction of one or the other of the "great" modern nation-states. Even in our globalized world, well-patrolled borders thus continue to (de) limit both the production and the transmission of specialized knowledge. Museum collections are frequently displayed according to a similar logic, such that visitors may witness the beginnings of a national tradition in the state's "early modern" (indeed, sometimes actually pre-nation-state) period (e.g., "Italian Renaissance") and its rise to prominence thereafter. The result is a narrative of the emergence from political and confessional particularism and heterogeneity of an organically unified "nation," a story that of course obscures the ways in which internal difference must always be eliminated on the way to "national" identity. Citizen-students are interpellated, or hailed, into such disciplinarily and institutionally concretized accounts of the "golden age" of the national Renaissances when they are asked to study the period—with both its glittering history and its colonializing "dark sides"—in this way. As a result, the period becomes part of an evolutionary tale in which all forms of civilizational progress and cultural production are pressed into the service of narratives of national (self) overcoming and contemporary fulfillment similar to the one Lupton describes. When studied and taught in this way, the Renaissance comes to play the same kind of sanctifying role for today's secular states as the one with which many sixteenth- and seventeenth-century theorists of the European vernaculars had originally invested their "mother tongues" when they identified them with the Adamic language capable of signifying the world with an accuracy bestowed by God (Borst).

When the Renaissance is deployed as an institutionally and historiographically circumscribed and homogeneous "national" period in these ways, it is used to mark the beginnings of the accession of the sovereign state to its "modern" maturity, with the rights, responsibilities, and duties to both defend a single version of its cultural past and expand its literal borders as it sees fit. The modern state so designated thus becomes far more than just the sum of its literal parts, far more than the merely geographical or even geopolitical entity we commonly associate with the term. Even the clear fictionality of this outsized, imagined form of itself cannot prevent the actions of any individual state from also becoming terribly concrete under ideational banners such as "freedom" and "democracy," which it seeks to impose on both its own citizenry and other polities in the name of civilizational progress. In the face of these kinds of celebratory stories, post-"modern" and postcolonial critics can easily dismiss the study of the historical Renaissance as coincident with the cascading period logic and progressivist ideologies of both modernity and the self-aggrandizing imperial states that medievalist and theorist Kathleen Biddick calls "supersessionary" (2). While it is certainly worth asking whether it was not some version of precisely this kind of supersessionary Renaissance that became the banner under which both the nineteenth- and early twentieth-century European nation-states and the Cold War United States marched when they endorsed the study of the Renaissance with such enthusiasm, such moves did not stop there. Indeed, it bears observing that many subnational world-cultural traditions—such as the Harlem and the Maori Renaissances, as well as the continent-spanning "African" Renaissance—may also have used the idea of cultural "rebirth" as a way of finding a seat at the table of "modernity" (Schildgen et al.; Ngugi).[7] When a postcolonial culture enters upon its "Renaissance," we must ask: What will come next?

But what about the Baroque? As most art historians know, Burckhardt's "modern" Renaissance in Europe was originally joined at the hip with another period in addition to the medieval, namely the Baroque, which played its own, if somewhat differently configured, supersessionary role at the time. Both Burckhardt himself and his student and friend Heinrich Wölfflin were central participants in this debate, the latter most famously in his *Renaissance und Barock* (1888); I discuss Wölfflin's foundational claims about the period in chapter 1. In the context of the forms

---

7. The emergence of the term in such contexts is not surprising. Historian of nationalism Anthony D. Smith explains that frequently there are "cultural and literary renascences associated with nationalist movements," movements that rely precisely upon tropes of "cultural gestation" cultivated by "'humanistic' intellectuals" who are in fact "disproportionately represented in nationalist movements and revivals" (6–7).

of critical periodization theory under examination here, it is important to note that scholars have often argued (incorrectly, I think) that in the Renaissance-Baroque relation, Wölfflin set the former above, over, and against the latter by characterizing the Baroque as the Renaissance's "decay," in the process creating the "unmodern" "historiographical monstrosity" that the Baroque has become (Hampton 1). It is—somewhat counterintuitively—precisely this limping version of the Baroque, seen as an alternative to the modernity associated with the periods said to have both preceded and followed it (namely the Renaissance and the Enlightenment), that has been aligned with and seen as an origin of the "Renaissance" of the neo-Baroque in the Latin American and Caribbean "margins," as noted above. Here, like the Renaissance, the Baroque functions in a supersessionary way, allowing the periphery to become the center in clever ways. When the Baroque plays this role in the contemporary world, it is nevertheless operating in ways that are historically true to form, picking up where it left off at its very birth moment as a historiographic category in and around the time when Benjamin's "Baroque book" was under way. Indeed, at the time, the period that he was studying was actually ideologically never all that far from the "modern" Renaissance that Burckhardt described because of its articulation as a "national" form, an articulation that demanded from the Baroque that it participate in a filiational narrative of its own. Already some time ago, René Wellek claimed that discussions of the Baroque were always "frankly ideological" (92). He was certainly correct in terms of the debates about the German Baroque that I discuss here.

The Baroque that we encounter in Benjamin's thought had its roots in decisively "telic" (K. Davis 84) assumptions variously associated with the period at the time. Indeed, part of what we might call the Renaissance of the Baroque in late nineteenth and early twentieth-century Germany was specifically devoted to celebrating the period as a privileged moment of national literary-historical rebirth. The Baroque was aligned with the Middle Ages, Romanticism, and Expressionism/Surrealism all in one in the creation of a phalanx-like series of antihumanist aesthetics and *Weltanschauungen* perhaps opposed to classicism of any sort, but nevertheless the origin of a countertradition of a continuous German culture reaching its fulfillment in the present of the recently consolidated nation-state.[8] Petra Boden's work is helpful in describing the implication of this logic in the deeply nationalistic reform programs in *Geistesgeschichte* more broadly and in the study of any number of specific "national" cultural periods after approximately 1890 as well (Boden,

---

8. On the "canonization" of the Baroque as an anticlassical period, see Link-Heer, whose work is nevertheless premised on a problematic collapsing of the Baroque and the allegedly "deviant" style of Mannerism into one and the same thing in a way that obscures what was actually the rather more traditional role that the Baroque as a nondeviant period of German literature and culture was asked to play in an ideology of the modern nation. On the "positive" consideration of the Baroque in connection with a problematically "anti-humanistic" German *Volkstum,* see Honold 99.

"Stamm—Geist—Gesellschaft"). The previously much-maligned Baroque was one of the eras that benefited most from these new and integrative "impulses," as Boden shows (219). The contest to define the relation between the Renaissance and the Baroque during the late nineteenth and early twentieth centuries, a contest in which the *Tragic Drama* book was also engaged, was thus undertaken *within* the confines of the tradition of national "literary history" that Benjamin so famously distinguished from the "literary criticism" he is often said to have preferred. The latter was the "modern" and "mortifying" analysis of individual artifacts and texts, the former their "traditional" integration into narratives about the flows of national literary and cultural history.[9] The Renaissance-Baroque periodization debate that Benjamin privileges in the *Tragic Drama* book in fact belonged to this more "traditional" field. A close reading of his arguments about it thus allows us to catch a glimpse of Benjamin as a line worker in a powerful rhetorical economy working overtime in the early twentieth century to construct a more centered and orthodox national patrimony on behalf of the German *Kulturnation*.

Evolutionary logics about the German literary tradition are everywhere at work in the *Tragic Drama* book. Benjamin yokes together the passion plays of the Middle Ages and the Baroque tragic drama, for example, and links medieval to Baroque Christology, Baroque to Romantic theories of allegory, and Baroque to Expressionist art. It could even be argued that his messianic thinking and what Samuel Weber sees as the very project of defining "origin" (*Ursprung*) as the "rethinking" of the "concepts of history, tradition, and all they entail" ("Genealogy of Modernity" 467) are themselves part and parcel of developing a supremely integrative "anticlassical" tradition of German national culture. The several clear patterns of "rhythm" that characterize the treatment of German literary history in the *Tragic Drama* book suggest the centrality of periodicity to Benjamin's notion of origin, which he himself designates as a regulative theory of "periodization" (*Gesammelte Schriften* 1.3: 935). While perhaps reminiscent of Nietzsche's theory of eternal recurrence, which attempts to disrupt "progressive" history, as Richard Wolin suggests (xxv), then, Benjamin's theory of origin may also be understood in the context of theories of cultural continuity designed both rhetorically and substantively to create a place for German literature and culture writ large in the narratives of a coming national modernity that were widespread at the time. Finally, it is important to note that the allegedly deeply antithetical dynamics of the Renaissance-Baroque paradigm, which it has become traditional to claim (although not in association with Benjamin's ideas) began in the late nineteenth century and coalesced into the standoff between a "classicizing" Renaissance versus and above a "maverick" and perhaps even avant-garde Baroque during the very years during which Benjamin was at

---

9. See, again, "Literary History and the Study of Literature" (1931), in Benjamin, *Selected Writings* 2: 459–65. On the "mortification" of works by criticism, see the *Tragic Drama* book (G: 1.1: 357; E: 182).

work on the *Tragic Drama* book, had not yet done so at the time. Rather, precisely at the moment of what Marc Fumaroli (10) has called the "launching in Germany" of debates about the Baroque, Benjamin and other periodization theorists had yet to nail down—if he or they ever wanted to or could—whether and, if so, exactly how it differed from the Renaissance and where the historical or aesthetic dividing lines lay. The concept of origin as Benjamin defines it guarantees that this narrative will remain "incomplete" ("[u]nvollendet"; "[u]nabgeschlossen"; G: 1.1: 226; E: 45), part of the project of thinking the nation's modernity by engaging in periodization debates, a project that was unfinished at the time that he wrote.

That theorizing the Baroque as part of a specifically German narrative of nation was ideologically loaded during these years is expressed in the most compact of ways by the eminent literary historian Karl Borinski, who makes clear in 1919 that there had not yet been any grand settlement about the relation of Burckhardt's Renaissance, identified primarily with Italy, to the German context, and to the Reformation and the German Lutheran tradition above all, which Borinski, citing a whole host of scholars, explicitly identifies as the period of "German rebirth" (*deutsche Wiedergeburt*, 6). The political and ideological message and influence of a confession and church that in 1917—and thus at one of the most destructive moments of World War I both abroad and on the home front—had celebrated its quadricentennial jubilee nevertheless made a narrative of joyful rebirth difficult to align with the here and now of defeat at the end of this most brutal of modern wars. In this context, the much underestimated importance of Benjamin's interest in the *Tragic Drama* book in Baroque playwrights whom he explicitly identifies as "Lutheran" (G: 1.1: 317; E: 138) must be taken into account (this although at least some of the Silesians were in all likelihood crypto-Calvinists). Which version of the origins of modernity was the Baroque—as the afterlife of the Reformation (rather than of the Renaissance)—supposed to represent in Germany and for whom, and how could individual artworks be understood when measured against the very abstract categories generated by such highly politicized debates? What, finally, were the consequences of institutionalizing a version of the nation's cultural history that respected conventional confessionalized categories and terms when precisely that confession, namely Lutheranism, had been the sponsor of a devastating war? Benjamin later referred to the wartime and postwar debates as occurring during a "transitional and re-evaluating period of scholarship" (*Gesammelte Schriften* 3: 191). For him, as for others, the project of what a German modernity with origins in the early modern Baroque was to be in the aftermath of a war often conducted in Protestant terms was unfinished as well.

Given that the debates about a specifically German Baroque were ongoing when Benjamin was writing the *Tragic Drama* book, it would be foolish to say that he came down clearly on one side or the other of the tussles over nation and periodization by the time of the book's publication in 1928. Indeed, he appears to have continued to rethink the positions he had outlined there in the years that followed in ways that have been little remarked on. In the "supplemental work on the tragic drama book" notes he apparently made for a possible second edition (*Gesammelte Schriften* 1.3: 953–55), for example, Benjamin lists among the texts he needs to consult titles by a future member of the Institute for Social Research, K. A. Wittfogel. The reference to Wittfogel indicates that Benjamin may have already been on the way to developing a historiographically more traditional, materialist understanding of a different kind of "origin |*Genesis*| of the Baroque tragic drama," perhaps as a matter of the historical unfolding of class conflict about which he writes in his review of Hans Heckel's *Geschichte der deutschen Literatur in Schlesien* (History of German Literature in Silesia), the year after the *Tragic Drama* book appeared (3: 193). Elsewhere and not too much later, Benjamin nevertheless also ponders the possibility of extending his analysis into a more authentically figural approach not unlike the one often associated with his earlier "messianic" period; the theory of "origin" he developed in his "work on the tragic drama" may well be related to Franz Rosenzweig's more religiously inflected concept of "revelation" (*Offenbarung*) (6: 207), Benjamin writes. Here, the Baroque might function in the more typological sense described above. Finally, sometime after 1930, we see Benjamin returning to his "theory of the afterlife of works" (Lehre vom Fortleben der Werke), which is crucial to the *Tragic Drama* book, positing that such a theory might be best understood when correlated with "Adorno's theory of '*Schrumpfung*,'" or "diminution" (6: 174). These post-1928 references all represent very different directions of method and thought that Benjamin continued to entertain; they are as various as the several historical, art historical, and literary-historical and critical versions of the Baroque with which his Baroque went on to intersect after 1933, debates I describe in the conclusion.

Burkhardt Lindner has usefully portrayed Benjamin's writings as less of a "synthesis of a |single| theoretical position" than an "explosive mix of seismographic intellectual and historical experiences" ("*Links hatte noch alles sich zu enträtseln*" 7). The description is apt for his reading of the Baroque too. The *Tragic Drama* book illuminates not only what Benjamin thought about Romanticism, neo-Kantianism, and messianism, then, but also how he understood the complex "mix" of periodization debates under way at the time. The terms "modernity," "the modern," and "modernism" of course do not all mean the same thing, and the mistaken confusion, yet also serendipitous intersection, of these terms with one another has led them to lead vexed lives in studies of Benjamin's ideas. While I argue here that the question of "the modern" was prominent in discussions of the Baroque when Benjamin wrote, also in close association with debates about the genealogy and significance of any number of narratives of national evolution and continuity in the history of the German *Kulturnation,* I am not suggesting that Benjamin set out to write a "nationalist" literary history. That he abhorred such approaches is clear in his review of Max Kommerell's *Der Dichter als Führer in der deutschen Klassik* (The Poet as Leader in German Classicism) (1928), for example, which was published in the journal *Die literarische Welt* in 1930, but written in 1929, just one year after the *Tragic Drama* book appeared (*Gesammelte Schriften* 3: 252–59). But writing about literary-historical periods in these years involved one in debates about national culture in highly scripted ways. It is this kind of involvement that I investigate here.

Texts as Witnesses

Benjamin's Arcades Project was, as he wrote to Gershom Scholem in 1935 (*Briefe* 2: 653–54), the second installment of the approach he had taken in the *Tragic Drama* book some years before. Both works belonged to the virtual industry of archeologies of the modern that flourished in the early twentieth century. Taking place within the very halls of academe from which Benjamin was eventually excluded, but which he still hoped to enter as he wrote the book, the debates about the role of the Baroque in this modernity have for the most part been barred from consideration in connection with his work, almost as if to take revenge on the offending institutions on his behalf. These debates infiltrate the *Tragic Drama* book in some of the extremely visible ways to which I now turn. Benjamin shares a canon of Baroque texts with disciplinarily recognized discussions of their vexed periodization such as Paul Stachel's *Seneca und das deutsche Renaissancedrama* (Seneca and German Renaissance Drama) (1907), for example; he may even have borrowed the notion of the "ruin" as crucial to the Baroque from Karl Borinski's famous *Die Antike in Poetik und Kunsttheorie von Ausgang des klassischen Altertums bis auf Goethe und Wilhelm von Humboldt* (Antiquity in Poetological and Art Theory from the End of the Classical Period to Goethe and Wilhelm von Humboldt) (1914), where it appears prominently. My purpose here is nevertheless not to dissect *The Origin of the German Tragic Drama* via "source study" as traditionally and entirely too simply understood. Rather, my aim is to explain how to "re-source" the book such that the contours of contemporary debates about the Baroque become visible. Medievalist Bruce Holsinger describes *ressourcement* as the "rediscovery or redeployment" of previously marginalized or forgotten sources in the service of "contemporary reform."[10] Benjamin endorses this kind of work in the *Tragic Drama* book when he recommends "open[ing oneself]... up to the source texts" (G: 1.1: 376; E: 201). Re-sourcing the Baroque as it existed when Benjamin wrote about it is thus not a question of tracking the details of the "influences" of prior scholarship on his ideas. As Benjamin himself famously explained, "It is primarily the lethargic [scholar] who is 'influenced'; anyone who is an [active] learner sooner or later succeeds in mastering whatever becomes useful to him in pre-existing [foreign] work and makes it part of

---

10. Holsinger's prime example is the mid-twentieth-century *ressourcement* by reformist French Catholic Henri de Lubac in association with the radical reforms of Vatican II (*Pre-Modern Condition* 163–67). Holsinger himself "re-sources" avant-garde and postmodern theory by attending to an alternative canon of texts with which it intersects; see Holsinger 1–25.

his |own| work as a matter of technique" (*Gesammelte Schriften* 4.1: 507). Rather, we must learn to see the ways Benjamin "open|ed himself| up to" the numerous theories of the Baroque circulating at the time.

One way of embarking on the mission of re-sourcing is to consider the libraries Benjamin used when writing his book. In literal terms, one of these was the Prussian State Library on Unter den Linden in Berlin, which had extensive holdings of both Baroque-era texts and secondary studies of the period. Benjamin did much of his research for the *Tragic Drama* book at the Prussian State Library, and its collection contained most of the texts to which he refers. Another more figurative "library" that he consulted was the greater archive of books and journals in which the discussions of the Baroque that he engages in the *Tragic Drama* book were conducted. The holdings of both of these libraries are clearly indicated in the citations and references that clutter both the body of Benjamin's text and the extensive notes that accompany it. Reconstructing representative dialogues between his "Baroque book" and the works present in these collections reveals how difficult it would have been for Benjamin *not* to adopt the premises of debates about the Baroque as a period of national rebirth circulating at the time, while also raising the possibility that his recalcitrant theory of origin may well have been developed in response to them. The possibility of overhearing the conversations in which Benjamin was involved as he wrote, and understanding them as more than just "fictive" dialogues with texts about or associated with the Baroque, has existed for quite some time.[11] He was exceedingly fastidious about his reading habits, for example; the sequential list of books that he read beginning in 1916–17 and up to the end of his life is available in volume 7 of the Frankfurt edition of his works.[12] Benjamin also gives precise indications in the notes to the *Tragic Drama* book about where in existing scholarship expanded treatments of the arguments with which he has engaged may be found.[13]

---

11. See Kemp, "Fernbilder" 224. I do agree with Kemp's claim of the importance of understanding Benjamin as involved in a process of "taking" (*Nehmen*), "reworking" (*Verarbeiten*), and "developing further" (*Weiterentwickeln*), however.

12. Benjamin's letters are full of discussions of the books he purchased and read; in the letters he often delivers even harsher assessments of some of the books whose titles clutter the footnotes of the *Tragic Drama* book, where he is somewhat more diplomatic.

13. The "philological worries" about gathering further "references and facts acceptable to current scholarship" about the history of Greek tragedy, for example, about which he writes to his friend Florens Christian Rang in 1924 (*Gesammelte Schriften* 1.3: 892; *Briefe* 1: 332–34), are thus everywhere audible, as is his desire to be in step (albeit in a somewhat arrhythmic kind of way) with a broader academic discussion about the Baroque. In 1926, Benjamin claims to be concerned, for example, about how "official scholarship" will receive the book (*Briefe* 1: 438). Later, he writes in a letter to Hofmannsthal in 1928 of his hope not just that the Warburg circle will take note of the book (see Weigel), but also that it will be reviewed by Richard Alewyn, the up-and-coming young star of Baroque studies during these years (*Gesammelte Schriften* 1.3: 909). That Benjamin thought, finally, that he had successfully inserted himself into the academic guild of those working in the field is tragically evident as late as 1938 in his statement in a French-language curriculum vitae that the *Tragic Drama* book "was reviewed very favorably by literary critics as well as by academics" (6: 222–23). Steiner ("Allegorie und Allergie") has shown that the book was in fact more widely reviewed even in Germany than had initially been thought.

To begin the task of reading Benjamin's *Origin of the German Tragic Drama* for the evidence it provides about some of the volumes that made up his libraries is thus not a difficult task. Doing so confirms Pierre Macherey's claim—to which the title of this book refers—that "every book contains in itself the labyrinth of a library" (49). Reading a book with its library means calling the texts of a book's library as witnesses, allowing the complex and often self-contradictory "mental tools" (Macherey thought of them as "the conditions of a work's possibility"; cf. Eagleton 13, qtd. in Sprinker x) of a particular period and set of discursive systems out of which the book arose to emerge into view. The notion of calling "texts as witnesses," as I understand it, is derived from the work of the early twentieth-century Annales school historians Marc Bloch and Lucien Febvre, who found that the questions "How can we explain . . .?" and "Was it possible that . . .?" rather than "Is it true that . . .?" were the most important questions to be posed in the pursuit of historical understanding (Febvre, *Problem of Unbelief* 16). Such questions could best be answered, they claimed, by examining as wide a variety of "evidence" as possible. The complex nature of Annales school methodology as articulated by its founding fathers, Bloch and Febvre, during the very same years that Benjamin was writing his book is a vast subject that has been ably discussed by Stuart Clark, Carlo Ginzburg, and Ulrich Raulff. The nuanced way in which Bloch and Febvre dealt with texts as witnesses suggests how re-sourcing Benjamin can begin.

Sometime between 1939 and 1941, after his Jewish ancestry had barred him from occupying his professorship at the Sorbonne, medievalist Marc Bloch, who, along with Febvre, founded the *Annales d'histoire économique et sociale* (Annals of Economic and Social History), made notes for a brief and poignant little book, the *Apologie pour l'histoire; ou, Métier d'historien* (The Historian's Craft). Bloch never published—or even finished—what can be seen as his own calling to account of his life's work (cf. Bloch 4). Active in the French Resistance, he was captured and executed by the Germans in 1944, just four years after Benjamin took his own life. Both men opposed the notion that history could or should be told through the lens of what Bloch calls the "idol of origins" (29).[14] As interesting as a comparison of Bloch's and Benjamin's persons and explicit theories of history might be, it is nevertheless Bloch's nuanced examination of the question of historical evidence in his book in which I am interested here because it serves as a model for the kind of historical work in which I am engaged in this book. According to his colleague Febvre, who undertook the "delicate task" of preparing the "unfinished manuscript for publication" (cf. Bloch xiii), *The Historian's Craft* was to be a "manifesto" of a new historiographic method for the "younger generation," the central point of which was to be an understanding of the status of the "observed fact" (32, 54). If an

---

14. Benjamin's comment that he was interested less in issues of "beginnings" (*Entstehung*) than in those of "origin" (*Ursprung*) (G: 1.1: 226; E: 45) in the *Tragic Drama* book resonates here.

examination of some of the "facts" that can be "observed" in Benjamin's book on the Baroque is not to lead to the same kind of opportunistic "occupation" as that described in the quote at the beginning of the preface to this book, it must define carefully both the status of texts as witnesses to history and the methods of "cross-examination" to be employed when assessing them.

As both Raulff (184–217) and Ginzburg have shown, Bloch had been committed to developing a "critique of witnessing" ever since his short essay of 1914, "Critique historique et critique du témoignage" (Historical Criticism and a Critique of Witnessing). Although it is tempting to claim that he did so in open wartime rejection of what is so often dismissed as the "nationalist" tradition of "German positivism," Bloch was also clearly in dialogue in this essay with the equally as important and clearly German-identified method of *Geistesgeschichte* and with Karl Lamprecht's "universal" cultural history in particular, both of which had actually been attacked in Germany for their "unpatriotic" failure to be "political" enough (see Werner 126–32). Directed primarily against what was in fact the French tradition of positivist history (Schulin 199), Bloch's articulation of a critical theory of witnessing in *The Historian's Craft* grew out of this mix.

Early on in *The Historian's Craft*, Bloch offers an example of the difficulty, but also the rewards, of considering the "observed fact" in nonreductive ways:

> In the tenth century a.d., a deep gulf, the Zwin, indented the Flemish coast. It was later blocked up with sand. To what department of knowledge does the study of this phenomenon belong? At first sight, anyone would suggest geology. The action of alluvial deposit, the operation of ocean currents, or, perhaps, the changes in sea level: was not geology invented and put on earth to deal with just such as these? Of course. But at close range, the matter is not quite so simple. Is there not first a question of investigating the origin of the transformation? Immediately, the geologist is forced to ask questions that are no longer strictly within his jurisdiction. For there is no doubt that the silting of the gulf was at least assisted by dike construction, changing the direction of the channel, and drainage—all activities of man, founded in collective needs and made possible only by a certain social structure. At the other end of the chain there is a new problem: the consequences. At a little distance from the end of the gulf, and communicating with it by a short river passage, rose a town. This was Bruges. By the waters of the Zwin it imported and exported the greatest part of the merchandise which made of it, relatively speaking, the London or New York of that day. Then came, every day more apparent, the advance of the sand. As the water receded, Bruges vainly extended its docks and harbor further toward the mouth of the river. Little by little, its quays fell asleep. To be sure, this was not the sole cause of its decline. . . . But this was certainly at least one of the most efficacious of the links in the causal chain. (23–24)

Bloch's example suggests that historical knowledge projects necessarily transgress disciplinary and methodological borders; here, the "fact" of the accumulation of sand must be embedded in a complex network of diverse causes and effects. Such projects thus begin with an assessment of the famous "detail" so important to Warburg. But for understanding, they then go far beyond surface empiricism into the realm of the pre- and posthistory of the "deep gulf" of the Zwin. What seems like an assumption of the "progressive intelligibility" of the data that Bloch's unpacking of his example reveals (10) nevertheless ultimately unmasks itself as producing a kind of "history" that has no clean lines. From alluvial deposits to quays to the rise and fall of Bruges's commercial class, and thus of the city's historical fortunes, and back again: these are the diverse, yet linked, heterogeneous, yet not hierarchically organized "tracks"—Bloch attributes the term to François Simiand (55)—of the "vast chaos of reality" (22) that both produces and is produced by the historian's "data."

In the 1914 version of these ideas, Bloch had suggested the similarity of historical and scientific investigation. One can come close to probable, if not absolute, conclusions about "wie es eigentlich gewesen [ist]" via comparative study, he seems to claim, assessing the reliability of historical evidence and testimony by juxtaposing a wide range of sources. A witness's account of his heroic crossing of a flooded river can be assessed in light of statistics about the less than spectacular heights reached by floodwaters in the same year, in other words. The illustration is Bloch's (see Ginzburg 129–31). But within ten years and as a result of his observations of the disorientation and trauma of soldiers in the trenches of World War I, who could not testify accurately even about what they had themselves seen and done, Bloch began to understand that inaccuracies, even deliberate errors, were also part of history and should not be understood as mistakes. Indeed, "errors" are important "witnesses" themselves. For Bloch, historical investigation was thus a "laboratory" rather than a "tribunal" (Raulff 193). The historian's task is one of interrogation, to be sure, but interrogation as undertaken by a "teaching judge" (*juge d'instruction*) who investigates, rather than by the judge as an official who adjudicates and decides between the false and the true (Bloch 138–40). By the early 1940s, and in explicit dialogue with the changes in "mental climate" brought on by "Einstein's mechanics" and "quantum theory" (17), Bloch is thus able to claim that history can have the "dignity of a science," even as he cautions against expecting closure in its practice. Only the complexly interwoven set of factors involved in the grand "experiment" of history can be observed in their concrete "residues" (54), he writes; the phenomena themselves ultimately remain "inaccessible" (55). Bloch was thus not naive about the impossibility of ever getting to a Rankean "things as they really happened, 'wie es eigentlich gewesen'" (138). Indeed, in a phrase that sounds uncannily like Benjamin in his *Theses on the Philosophy of History,* Bloch is clear that the processes by which evidence is transmitted, the vagaries of what survives and what perishes, owe much to "the goddess Catastrophe" (73), who often intervenes in cataclysmic fashion in our access to the past. Benjamin's *Tragic Drama* book is a phenomenon, or "fact," along these kinds of Blochian lines. It cannot be reduced to its "sources" or required to illustrate what Benjamin may or may not have "gotten wrong" (or right) about the Baroque. Rather, it provides evidence that helps explain what a thesis on the Baroque could have meant at the time that he wrote.

Texts themselves are mediating as well as mediated events. It was Lucien Febvre, Bloch's colleague and fellow Annalist, who understood and exploited the
function of books as historical witnesses of these several kinds. Unlike Benjamin
and Bloch, Febvre survived the war. Historian Natalie Zemon Davis characterizes
Febvre's famous work on Rabelais, *The Problem of Unbelief in the Sixteenth Century: The Religion of Rabelais* (1942), which was written and published in occupied
Paris, as a book written "at a time of secrecy and veiled meanings . . . *about* secrecy
and veiled meanings" (4), and thus itself evidence about how to survive. By considering a huge array of treatises and polemics, scientific, medical, and theological
tracts, popular broadsheets, poetry, and contemporary manuals of language use as
"testimony and witnesses" of what men of the sixteenth century would have been
"capable of hearing and comprehending" (*Problem of Unbelief* 16, 5), Febvre came
to the conclusion that it would not have been possible, in the sixteenth century, for
Rabelais to have been the "atheist" that Abel Lefranc, against whom Febvre wrote
his book, had claimed he was. According to Davis, Febvre was nevertheless more
timid in the 1940s than Rabelais had been in the 1540s and for obvious reasons
avoided introducing into his discussion of the "possibilities" of religious thought
in the Renaissance the additional evidence of the Jewish thought that Davis claims
is so important for understanding Rabelais. In support of her argument, Davis adduces several fourteenth-century manuscripts by "Provençal rabbis" that by the
sixteenth century were printed in Italy (19); her mimicry, yet also supplementa-
tion, of Febvre's method displays how working with texts is a way of looking "not
for certainties, but for possibilities." Both Febvre and Davis thus move "outward"
from a specific text, namely Rabelais' *Gargantua et Pantagruel,* "into the collective
mental and affective world of the time" (8). Both begin with a discrete question
about what and how a specific set of terms and texts could be understood, and
end by setting the several periods with which they intersect into motion. Benjamin
might have recognized in this method his own fundamental principle that literature is "a set of principles for the analysis of history" (*Gesammelte Schriften* 3: 290).
In *Benjamin's Library,* I follow Bloch's, Febvre's, and Davis's models by beginning
with the evidence the *Tragic Drama* book itself provides, using it as a witness to the
times when the Baroque was the subject at hand. Here it is important to remember,
with Febvre, that the "history of the sciences and the history of thought are made
up of fragments of violently contrasting designs and colors, a series of theories and
attitudes that not only are distinct from one another but oppose and contradict one
another" (*Problem of Unbelief* 354). "Cross-examining" *The Origin of the German
Tragic Drama* in this way thus opens up only more—and not fewer—ways of reading Benjamin with the Baroque.

The juxtaposition of Benjamin's work with the methodologies of the early and
extremely interdisciplinary phases of the Annales School, which nearly coincided
with it, is a novel one. Indeed, even though he came from a different disciplinary
location, Marc Bloch's observation of the conundrum that telling history presented

during these difficult times reflects well on Benjamin's concerns. In 1953, Joseph Strayer writes of Bloch's *The Historian's Craft,* which was written around 1940, the year Benjamin took his own life:

> The more history we write, the more we worry about the value and nature of history. The increase in the number of books on historiography and historical methodology is proportionally far greater than the number of historians. Such books have been especially numerous in the last ten or fifteen years, for obvious reasons. (vii)

What these "reasons" were is alluded to by Annales historian Fernand Braudel in his nearly contemporary retrospective lecture, "The Situation of History in 1950":

> "History is the child of its time . . ." And should its methods, its projects, those answers that only yesterday seemed so rigorous and dependable, should all its concepts suddenly collapse, it would be from the weight of our own thinking, our own study, and, most of all, the experiences we have undergone. Now, over the past forty years those experiences have been particularly harsh for all of us . . . why should the fragile art of writing history escape from the general crisis of our age? (6)

The coincidence in the early twentieth century between the methods of the Annales scholars and Benjamin's philosophy and theory of history and his method of reading suggests that, as "children of their time," he and they were responding to a common need to try to make sense of the multiple crises facing Europe in those years. Bloch's and Febvre's firm commitment to probing the inconclusive "possibilities" of the past in their examination of diverse data serves well as a guide to examining the testimony that Benjamin's *Tragic Drama* book provides about the status of the Baroque as part of this response. Elsewhere Febvre dismisses what he calls "aristocratic history," which works by taking a sounding of an epoch on the basis only of the "great events," "great proceedings," and "great men," and then forging this evidence into "one of those great chains of distinct, homogeneous facts" ("History and Psychology" 2). This is the history of what Alain Boureau, in his study of another German Jew interested in the premodern origins of the modern, Ernst Kantorowicz, calls "known realit[ies]." They must be joined, Boureau claims in Annales-like fashion, to thicker descriptions of "supplementary microcontexts" that take seriously "the virtual embedded in the possible" (xix). "Unpacking" Benjamin's library in the *Tragic Drama* book is part of this same project.

Reading Benjamin/Reading the Baroque

In the chapters that follow, I retrieve the importance of the Baroque for Benjamin's articulation of the conundrum of German modernity by placing the *Tragic Drama* book in conversation with the debates about the Baroque being conducted at the end of the nineteenth and the beginning of the twentieth centuries. The first section of chapter 1 considers the ways in which Benjamin read the Silesian plays precisely *not* as the "tragic dramas" of Osborne's English-language translation, but rather as "mourning-play" texts that differed significantly from ancient tragedy in Benjamin's mind. According to much criticism of the genre at the time, the "rebirth" of antiquity was said to be visible in the reappearance of ancient tragedy on the Renaissance stage; German Baroque plays could be "redeemed" by inserting them into this tradition. Both established and up-and-coming scholars, such as Paul Stachel and Herbert Cysarz, were heavily invested in this narrative about the Baroque, which allowed them to include it in their versions of a continuous national literary tradition that had culminated in Weimar Classicism. According to Benjamin, Stachel's and Cysarz's versions of the period nevertheless fall short of their stated goal precisely because they ensnare the period, its plays, and thus the very idea of the Baroque in a backward-looking web of criteria and terms. Benjamin's renaming of the genre of the plays as modern "tragic dramas," or "mourning plays," thus engages in a focused polemic. While he too seeks to insert the seventeenth-century German texts in an evolutionary periodization scheme, he does so in order to free them from dependency on the ancient and foreign norms that set the standard in Stachel's work above all. The Baroque plays thus become "modern" in a new kind of way. Benjamin's understanding of how and why to define the period in this way was not coincidentally tied to challenges that the controversial historian Konrad Burdach had offered to conventional definitions of the Renaissance proper as a moment of "rebirth," as I also show in this section. Benjamin cites Burdach's recuperation of a more spiritual and, indeed, "northern" Renaissance in the (in)famously mystifying parts of the "Epistemo-Critical Prologue" that concern his ideational theory. Yoking his theory of the origin of the Baroque to Burdach's thesis about the beginnings of a new national sensibility in premodern and early modern times seems to have allowed Benjamin to offer his version of the Baroque as an alternative to Stachel's and Cysarz's versions, thus permitting him to define the period as a new kind of Renaissance in specifically German terms.

Benjamin's double-barreled gesture of refusing to define the Baroque as a latter-day Renaissance even as he argues for a Renaissance of the German Baroque was not unlike the definitions of the Baroque endorsed by the art historians and art theorists Heinrich Wölfflin and Alois Riegl, whose work on the Baroque was so influential for definitions of the period. Both Wölfflin and Riegl were concerned to describe the Baroque as something other than an eternally "decaying" Renaissance in ways not adequately addressed by criticism to date. As in the case of Benjamin, so too with Riegl and Wölfflin, the ability of the Baroque to serve as a *better* beginning of modernity than the Renaissance involved the period in a re-birthing moment of national significance that located it at not such a very great distance from the Renaissance, as its historiographic twin. In the second section of chapter 1, I examine these art historical debates and how they articulated a new periodicity of style that involved the collectivity of the nation in important ways. In the third section of the chapter, I turn to contemporary definitions of a specifically *literary* German Baroque by critics Fritz Strich and Arthur Hübscher, whose work relied on Wölfflin's. Benjamin cites Strich's and Hübscher's versions of the period throughout the *Tragic Drama* book. Their discussions mirrored the art historical conversations by striving to locate the essence of a German literary tradition in an autonomous national sensibility and canon of forms. In both cases, the existence of a "modern"—and specifically "northern" and German—Baroque was crucial in providing categories with which to construct this tradition as an alternative to a "foreign" ("southern" and hence Burckhardtian) Renaissance endlessly indebted to the past. Benjamin's Baroque dipped into and was part of these several discussions of the Baroque as a "heroic" national age.[15]

The pattern of quotations in the *Tragic Drama* book from both the Silesian plays of the seventeenth century and the other dramatic texts that are its central concern also reveals the importance of associating the origin of the tragic drama with a very specific "modern" version of the Baroque. These dramatic texts and their links to an ideology of nation are the subject of chapter 2. The literal production of the tradition of Baroque plays that Benjamin cites can be witnessed particularly clearly in a late nineteenth-century nationalist edition of the plays of one of the seventeenth-century Silesian playwrights he discusses, namely Andreas Gryphius. Benjamin appears to have owned this volume, which was edited by Hermann Palm.[16] I discuss the Palm Gryphius in the first section of chapter 2. In the second section, I place Palm's version of the Baroque in dialogue with, first, several Baroque and "Enlightenment" editions of plays by two other seventeenth-century Silesian playwrights, Daniel Casper von Lohenstein and Johann Christian Hallmann, which Benjamin appears to have used in the State Library, and then with the longer tradition of German theater that Benjamin also discovered there. It was in anthologies of dramatic texts edited by men whose work is little known today, such as the mid-nineteenth-century scholars Karl Weiß and Franz Josef Mone, for example, and the early twentieth-century Rudolf Payer von Thurn, that Benjamin claims to have found the origin of a fully German dramatic tradition; his work with their texts tells us quite a bit about the genre in which he was interested in the *Tragic Drama* book. Benjamin also investigated another and somewhat odd set of plays in his book. These other plays, *Hamlet* and *Life Is a Dream,* are of course not in and of themselves odd. Nor were they by German Baroque playwrights or by Germans at all, but rather by the Englishman Shakespeare and the Golden Age Spanish playwright Calderón. In the *Tragic Drama* book, Benjamin reads them not only as Baroque, but also as part of an argument about the need to understand

---

15. On the "heroic" stage of Baroque studies in the early twentieth century, see Voßkamp 687–89, and below, chapter 1.

16. See *Briefe* 1: 140.

the "mourning play" as "nationally determined" (*nationell bedingt*) (G: 1.1: 265; E: 86). What is particularly striking about the plays of Calderón and Shakespeare in Benjamin's argument is not only that they are cited as "tragic dramas" instead of as tragedies, but also that he designates them as the best exemplars, "the complete and perfected form" of the "baroque mourning play" (G: 1.1: 260; E: 81). How a non-German playwright like Shakespeare could belong to a "modern" German Baroque is the subject of the final section of chapter 2.

There is, finally, another specifically German, but far less celebratory Baroque in which Benjamin is interested in the *Tragic Drama* book. It is at the center of his concern in some of the most esoteric and mystifying parts of his study, namely the sections on melancholy and on the allegorical emblematics of the texts that he describes as having been written by specifically "Lutheran" playwrights. These aspects are the focus of chapter 3, which calls attention to the commentary that the "Baroque book" offers on the afterlives of the Lutheran Reformation in both the seventeenth century and in Benjamin's own time. The political theology of German *melancholia* as it was associated with a "Lutheran" dramatic tradition was addressed in a popular short story about Shakespeare's Hamlet by the nineteenth-century Protestant literary historian Rochus von Liliencron, as well as in Liliencron's late nineteenth-century edition of the works of the seventeenth-century Jesuit theorist of melancholy Aegidius Albertinus. Benjamin cites both of these texts in the *Tragic Drama* book, and I analyze the greater context of their confessional politics in the first section of chapter 3. Benjamin's complex claims about melancholy, martyrdom, and creatureliness, on the one hand, and the allegorical nature of representation, language, and staging in what he claims are the "Lutheran" emblematic texts of the Baroque, on the other, locate them within the vexed narrative of modern Germany's cultural and political continuity with the world of Luther's Reformation, a narrative deeply embedded in the literal and ideological strife of the late nineteenth- and early twentieth-century "battle for civilization" (*Kulturkampf*) between the confessions and in the politically inflected versions of Protestant "war theology" (*Kriegstheologie*) that arose during World War I. Liliencron's work offers a window onto these issues as they emerged out of the culture of the sixteenth century and spilled into modern Germany; Benjamin's seventeenth century extends and completes and yet also pauses before the implications of this legacy.

"Allegory," Benjamin explains in several of the versions of his curriculum vitae that have been preserved, was an "art form" "related" (*verwandt*) to the tragic drama (*Gesammelte Schriften* 6: 226) and more often than not was associated with the spectacular emblem books that poured out of the presses of Europe throughout the late sixteenth and seventeenth centuries. Although of great interest to libraries and private collectors alike, these volumes have been as historiographically lost and misunderstood as the Baroque plays themselves in Benjamin criticism. In claiming that the allegorical logic dominant in these texts was also peculiarly Lutheran, Benjamin was nevertheless following a pattern of claims that had already been made in earlier twentieth-century work on the "afterlives" of classical and late medieval mythology, theology, and humoral psychology in the Reformation era by the scholars of the so-called Warburg school, such as Erwin Panofsky and Fritz Saxl, as well as by Aby Warburg himself. This work and Benjamin's response to it are the focus of the second section of chapter 3. The work of the Warburg scholars focused on the tensions that disputes about astrology, faith, and action had created among the German Reformers; the specific object of interest was the famous image of melancholy depicted by the sixteenth-century German artist Albrecht Dürer. Benjamin had seen Dürer's *Melencolia I*, which he calls an "inexpressibly deep and expressive print," for the first time in 1913 (*Briefe* 1: 76). Warburg had endorsed understanding the image as a meditation on the impact of a version of war-theological "heroic" Lutheranism on both Dürer and the modern German state. It is in explicit dialogue with Warburg's claims that Benjamin's significantly more downbeat position on a "Lutheran" Baroque allegory must be understood.

The final section of chapter 3 is the only part of *Benjamin's Library* that takes a historically Baroque text as its focus. It does so as a way of understanding Benjamin's reading of Andreas Gryphius's shockingly literal allegorical play, *Catharina von Georgien Oder Bewehrete Beständigkeit* (Catharine of Georgia; or, Constancy Defended) (1657), in the context of the confessional stew created by Benjamin's contestation of Warburg scholarship, and explains his understanding of the horrific consequences for life in the "creaturely" world of the Lutheran allegorical logic he thinks informs the play. Benjamin's description of the "brutal stage" (*rohe Bühne*) of the Baroque tragic drama was accurate, as the emblematic poetics that drives Gryphius's play makes clear. In the links Benjamin sees between this brutality and the autonomy of the secular world when it is unleashed from its ethical and spiritual moorings according to the Lutheran model, he finds a way to problematize the literary and art historical narratives about the "heroic age" of a modernity built on this particular version of a confessionalized German state. The events of Gryphius's play may explain why Benjamin found it necessary to try to distinguish between ancient tragedy and the "modern" tragic dramas in the first place. The "allegedly . . . post-tragic idioms" of the tragic drama seem nevertheless to have collapsed back into "complicity" with tragedy (Koepnick 279) under a Lutheran sky. Pointing out how this occurred during the Baroque was the first step to declaring the project of German modernity incomplete in the immediate post–World War I years.

The German Baroque that emerges out of the intricate arguments of Benjamin's *Tragic Drama* book had several significant afterlives, none of which Benjamin himself lived to experience. They nevertheless shine as bright a light on his version of the period as his version sheds on theirs. One particularly disturbing example is the subject of the conclusion: the astonishing resonance of Benjamin's ideas about the Baroque in National Socialist literary histories. The dislocating effect of linking Benjamin to the Nazis nevertheless captures his theory of the afterlife of the work exquisitely and helps diagnose the problems involved in telling history in a clear-cut or monodirectional way, with "good" and "bad" legacies and the national or counternational traditions they create antiseptically disentangled from one another and leading to different goals. The project of mapping national modernities onto the body of the Baroque in the present study begins, then, with what Katie King has called the "citational community" of the *Tragic Drama* book, in which the texts—primary and secondary, critical and philosophical, literary and art historical—from which Benjamin quotes jostle for visibility as "witnesses" to a series of moments in the late nineteenth and early twentieth centuries when a variety of questions about the role of nationalism and culture, of modernity and tradition, clustered around the terms and texts in which the history and aesthetics of the Baroque were debated. This study ends by citing a particularly perverse afterlife, suggesting that we can never be sure what the famous "eddy" of "becoming" that is "origin" as an "thoroughly historical category" (G: 1.1: 226; E: 45) will bring. The image that results is what Benjamin might have called a "representation" of the Baroque as viewed from a series of "stations of observation," at which one stops and periodically tries to "catch . . . one's breath" (*Atemholen*) (208; 28).

Not all of the texts that may have been in Benjamin's several libraries are dealt with in what follows. Rather, I focus primarily on those in which questions about the Baroque are posed both directly and indirectly as inquiries into the origins of modernity and the characteristics of a specifically German tradition. The anxiety associated with addressing such topics at all is palpable in the astoundingly diverse array of books that Benjamin cites, as well as in the multiple contradictions in which the argument becomes entangled as he struggles to whittle out a place and position for both his subject and himself in these debates. In Germany during these years such questions were, again, not casual ones. As Anson Rabinbach has argued, the "catastrophe" of World War I challenged many of the progressive narratives about the inheritance of the past and the prognosis for the future of individuals, nation-states, and "civilization" as a whole in fundamental ways. The aftermath of decisions made in Versailles could be felt in the military, political, and economic crises that came to a head in Germany as Benjamin was completing his book, and his letters from this period testify to the ideological and existential crises besetting both him and the nation in these years (e.g., *Briefe* 1: 311). Re-sourcing *The Origin of the German Tragic Drama* reveals the ways such issues were embedded in debates about the Baroque at a time when only an "ambivalent narration of progress" could be told (Koepnick 279). Unearthing these issues is an exercise in what Lucien Goldmann, in nearly Annales-like terms, called the science of "découpage," the "circumscription" of the evidence, not in order to solve, but rather to "explain" the problem not of "what," but of "how" the German Baroque could have signified at the time (99). The jumble in Benjamin's book of critical voices and disciplinary debates testifies to the cacophony of the times. The afterlives of his Baroque in the 1930s and 1940s in Germany offer us a platform from which we may, in turn, consider the implications of our own periodization work in more critical ways.

1

Inventing the Baroque

A Critical History of Nineteenth- and Early Twentieth-Century Debates

In 1935, just seven years after Benjamin's book on the German tragic drama appeared, the Paris publishing house Gallimard released a slim volume entitled *Du baroque* (On the Baroque) by the Spanish philosopher and man of letters Eugenio d'Ors. Midway through the book, d'Ors indicates, in an idiosyncratic chart entitled "Genre: *Barocchus*" (161), that the Baroque is far more than an "oddly shaped pearl" or "the fourth mode of the second figure in the scholastic nomenclature of syllogisms" that René Wellek would famously cite, but then reject, as possible definitions some ten years later in his "The Concept of Baroque in Literary Scholarship" (1946). Rather, d'Ors's Baroque spills out over the borders of the categories discussed by Wellek and repeated more recently by Walter Moser (578–79), appearing as the "Barocchus macedonicus" and the "Barocchus romanus," the "Barocchus buddhicus" and the "Barocchus tridentius, sive romanus, sive jesuiticus" in turn. According to d'Ors's chart, there have been no fewer than twenty-two "species" of the Baroque since the "prehistoric" "Barocchus pristinus" "among the savages" (162). The historically most recent Baroque is version 20, the "Barocchus posteabellicus" of d'Ors's—and Benjamin's—own immediate wartime and post–World War I past.

The Baroque that d'Ors finds, or invents (from *invenio,* "to find"), in the early twentieth century appears to be less a specific moment in time than a "constant of culture" (99). The description is reminiscent of Friedrich Nietzsche's identification of "Baroque style" as a "timeless phenomenon that periodically recurs," in his *Menschliches, Allzumenschliches* (Human, All Too Human) of 1879 (see Barner, "Nietzsches literarischer Barockbegriff" 569). Both versions are typical of one of the ways the Baroque is said to have been defined in the late nineteenth and early twentieth centuries as a strictly stylistic category; often offered as the most prominent example of this kind of deracinated metaphysics of the aesthetic is Heinrich Wölfflin's definition of the Baroque in his famous *Kunstgeschichtliche Grundbegriffe* (Principles of Art History) (1915); there the art historian is said to have distinguished the Baroque from the Renaissance in primarily formal terms. Even though both Wellek and Ernst Robert Curtius, for example, rebelled against this account early on and in firm ways, the subsequent historiography of the period has been consistent.[1] According to this narrative, formalist periodization theory developed in the early twentieth century in explicit counterpoint to—and thus as an alternative to—the heavily ideological mid- to late nineteenth-century linear and historicist versions of individual national cultural histories, the task of which had been to describe the gradual emergence of art and literature from the unified "spirit" of any given *Volk*. D'Ors's chart would seem to reflect at least one part of this nonlinear and implicitly antinationalizing story when it celebrates the self-forming and self-(re)generating power of style.

Upon closer examination, however, it is difficult to see how d'Ors's chart uncouples theorizations of period from place. In fact, the table problematizes the claim that situatedness and style are distinct from one another, and thus also the assertion that an interest in matters of form challenged cultural-historical—what we today might call ideological and identitarian—approaches to period study at the time. Its wit is lodged, for example, in its production of the Baroque not only as an insistently recurring style, but also as a combination of style with historical specificity and site. The best example is the cascade of adjectives—Jesuit, Roman, and Tridentine—that d'Ors associates with the sixteenth-century moment often singled out as the historical Baroque of record; here, local theological and political histories collaborate to anchor the period type in a place in a completely overdetermined way. D'Ors's chart thus suggests that the task of inventing the Baroque was much more than a question of sheer form in the early twentieth century. Rather, many arguments about the period—and about its allegedly antithetical twin, the Renaissance—rooted questions of style in specific cultural sites and in nations above all. In this chapter, I argue that such period definitions emerged with particular complexity in Germany during the time d'Ors refers to as the "Barocchus posteabellicus," the post–World War I Baroque, which was the time of Benjamin's Baroque too.

---

1. For Curtius's suggestion in 1948 in his *Europäische Literatur und lateinisches Mittelalter* (European Literature and the Latin Middle Ages) to dispense with the concept of the Baroque in favor of the category Mannerism, see Link-Heer, "Zur Kanonisierung antiklassischer Stile" 160–61. Although dated, Wellek's 1946 article is still useful in giving a detailed account of the explosion of work on the literary Baroque in particular, beginning, Wellek claims, in 1921–22 (79). The dates are slightly misleading, as this upsurge was based on work that began at the end of the nineteenth century. See also Moser.

The conventional claim—that, in the contest between theories of culture that pitted aesthetic autonomy and formal criticism against the historical functionalization and interpretation of art, it was the former that "won," because they resisted ideological instrumentalization—obscures the ease with which the stylistic argument was itself pressed into the service of a widespread set of narratives about how the history of national modernities and of the modern German *Kulturnation* in particular could be told. It is in conversation with this aspect of debates about periodization that it is important to understand a further aspect of the context of Benjamin's argument about the German Baroque—that is, as different as the methodological assumptions were in the work of the various scholars that he cites in his *Tragic Drama* book, all contributed to a constellation of discourses that *celebrated* the Baroque, finding in it *not* an "obscure" or degenerate period and style, *not* the marginal and heterodox "border region" of academic concern that many students of Benjamin—and sometimes Benjamin himself—would have had it be.[2] Rather, for Benjamin, as for others, the Baroque was a privileged, and even "fashionable,"[3] object of study in a field that was in the midst of its "heroic" phase (Voßkamp 684) and "golden years" (Alewyn, Vorwort 9) at the time. As often as not, this Baroque was also claimed by many to be firmly rooted in a specific place, namely the German "north," as I show below. While Benjamin admits in a letter to Florens Christian Rang that he was not always "gripped" by his work on his thesis and occasionally had to "force" himself to work on it (*Briefe* 1: 326), the "dégout" that he appears sometimes to have felt for his project (327) may have resulted from a combination of the pressures on him to complete it quickly, on the one hand, and the real existential anxieties by which he was beset at the time, on the other—rather than from an aversion to the period and its peculiar texts. In the "Epistemo-Critical Prologue" of the *Tragic Drama* book, Benjamin identifies the celebration of the Baroque with the "if not also mostly sentimental, then certainly positive obsession" with the period (G: 1.1: 234; E: 54) common at the time. This observation sheds light on how it was possible for him to have considered it a legitimate object of study in the first place.[4]

---

2. Benjamin's interest in the "border regions," or marginal areas, of art history is articulated in his "Strenge Kunstwissenschaft" essay, which I discuss below; the status of his claim to see examples of "times of decay" in both the Baroque and Expressionism is also addressed. For an early and more clear-eyed assessment of the "heroic" age of Baroque studies as something of a desperate fad among younger scholars in a crisis-ridden time, see Milch's 1940 article (131), published, interestingly, in the U.S. Germanics journal *German Quarterly*, rather than in Germany.

3. Walzel, "Shakespeares dramatische Baukunst" 317. Walzel is referring to the application of the "fashionable term" (*Modewort*) Baroque to the work of Shakespeare; he had of course himself used the term in this way in 1916 in his famous essay "Shakespeares dramatische Baukunst"; a revised version of the essay was published in 1926. See chapter 2.

4. Voßkamp (688–89) sees a critical stance toward this "metaphysicalization of the concept of the Baroque" emerging already in the 1920s, and suggests that sociological methods were proposed as a corrective to it by scholars such as Erika Voigt and Arnold Hirsch. Voigt's and Hirsch's books were published in 1932 and 1933, respectively, however, only after Benjamin had completed work on the *Tragic Drama* book.

Scholarship by Wilhelm Voßkamp and Petra Boden ("Stamm—Geist—Gesellschaft") on the history of literary and cultural studies in Germany in the post-1871 era has linked the spike in interest in the Baroque to the more general methodological debates that came to a head around 1890 in the new and antipositivist approach of *Geistesgeschichte*. Trends in the sociological study of literature, on the one hand, and the struggle to align the so-called humanistic disciplines with "scientific" (*naturwissenschaftlich*) approaches via reference to various systematic models, on the other, may also have played a role in crafting a science of periodization that would celebrate all epochs of the new nation's cultural achievement in equal measure. Such debates informed literary and art historical studies alike, as they struggled to understand the relation of the Renaissance and the Baroque as two periods that were often caught in the sometimes confusing crossfire of disputes about the relationship between the *formal* differences that scholars and critics saw in the heterogeneous styles of the two eras and a *literary-historical* narrative of cultural continuity organized as a celebration of their common origins in a specific cultural and spiritual collectivity, nation, and race. It is this second aspect of the argument about period that is of particular interest in connection with Benjamin's *Tragic Drama* book.

Wilfried Barner ("Das europäische 17. Jahrhundert") has noted that beginning already in the eighteenth century the Baroque had been celebrated as much for its commitment to a kind of linguistic nationalism, in the form of massive translation projects and the production of vernacular dictionaries, for example, as for the eccentricities of style also associated with it. This "patriotic" conservation of an ancient "German (Teutonic) inheritance" (405) trespassed on yet also trumped and replaced the reputation of an Italianate Renaissance famous for the glorious rediscovery of a Romance antiquity with the equally as significant achievements of a specifically northern Baroque twin. To identify a German national Baroque as the rival to a Pan-European Renaissance, yet also as a fellow traveler in supersessionary efforts to reanimate the nation's modernity by calling forth "ancient" forms, thus did not necessarily distinguish the periods cleanly from one another, at least in terms of their ideological thrust. As noted above, Jacob Burckhardt's discussion of the Renaissance provided one of the most salient examples of the figurative logic subtending this kind of modernization talk. His well-known claim that the Italian Renaissance was the birth moment and "mother" of "our" "civilization" (Burckhardt 1), the Renaissance man of Italy the high-achieving "first-born [son] among the sons of Europe today" (87), still hung in the air in the 1910s and 1920s as the unanswered question about the exact relation of those beginnings to the here and now. Indeed, as Lionel Gossman and others have shown, the scary legacy for modernity of Burckhardt's more or less ruthlessly individualistic Renaissance man, as well as of the irresponsibly extravagant and politically opportunistic secularized culture that produced him, was still very much a topic. At stake was what exactly it was that had been "reborn" in the Renaissance and was now coming to fruition in the European nations of more modern times. Was the story of the period that of a model age of glorious achievement endlessly indebted to an ancient past, or a horrific cautionary tale of a thoroughly integrated historical culture within which no one escaped the clutches of a brutally "progressive" age?[5] Such questions in turn generated the dilemma of how to understand the alleged successor culture of the Renaissance, namely the Baroque. Did it continue or alter, prolong or replace, this potentially problematic Renaissance with a compensatory or alternative origin of the "modern" sensibility that was more appropriate—and potentially also more beneficial—to the here and now?[6] Moreover, how was the Baroque to be understood as the afterlife of the end of the (Italian) Renaissance in the (rest of the European) modern world, and especially in the recently created German nation? Theorizations of the German Baroque during the late nineteenth and early twentieth centuries may well have seen the period as an alternative to the Renaissance. But they understood the Baroque as doing essentially the same ideological work as the Renaissance.

This chapter examines, first, the ways in which contemporary debates about the relationship between period, modernity, and place are audible in the sections of the notoriously difficult "Epistemo-Critical Prologue" of the *Tragic Drama* book that deal explicitly with questions about whether or not, and, if so, how, the German Baroque should be understood as part of a "Renaissance" of the nation. Benjamin's citation and rejection of arguments made to this effect by Paul Stachel and Herbert Cysarz, two well-known scholars of the German Baroque, are placed in conversation with arguments he derives from the medievalist Konrad Burdach, arguments about German literary-historical periodization that Benjamin then substitutes for Stachel's and Cysarz's claims. In the second section, I turn to exemplary articulations of contemporary discussions of the Baroque in the field most often aligned with it, namely art history; noting their centrality in Benjamin's essay "Strenge Kunstwissenschaft" (On the Rigorous Study of Art) (1933), I discuss art historians and art theorists Heinrich Wölfflin and Alois Riegl, whose legacies are crucial to understanding the claims that were being made about the Renaissance-to-Baroque

---

5. The best example of this second kind of critical examination of the Renaissance is Alfred von Martin's *Soziologie der Renaissance* (Sociology of the Renaissance) (1932). In the *Tragic Drama* book Benjamin cites an earlier von Martin work on Coluccio Salutati in which essentially the same points are made.

6. Art historians, including Hauser, Gombrich, and Ackerman, have suggested that the debate about the Renaissance and the Baroque in art history in the early twentieth century was part of an "evolutionary" "Hegelian art history" that valued periods that promoted "change" (Ackerman 319). Honold suggests within the context of his discussion of questions of literary-historical continuity and periodization during these years that the understanding of the German Baroque as rooted in the chaos of the Thirty Years' War, for example, helped make it attractive to scholars during World War I and the interwar years who saw themselves and their own period mirrored in the chaos of the earlier period (102–3). Such parallels would also have made it difficult to see the differences between the periods only as a matter of style.

relation at the time. Observing the much underestimated importance of place in their theories helps us see how Benjamin's citation of their work creates the basis of a new argument about the Baroque as a moment of national cultural rebirth. In the final section, I examine the work of two of the literary scholars whom Benjamin cites over and over again in the *Tragic Drama* book, Arthur Hübscher and Fritz Strich. Traditionally, both of these men's work about the Baroque has been read (when it is read at all) as contributing only to stylistic debates. Returning to them to see what they say about the national collectivity and the power of place in connection with periodization theory sheds light on Benjamin's definition of the "origin" of the Baroque German tragic drama in his book. Understanding how contemporary debates about the Baroque can be witnessed in his project to redeem the period and its texts makes clear that his project was neither idiosyncratic nor eccentric. Rather, *The Origin of the German Tragic Drama* was caught in a reeling network of arguments that used the Renaissance-Baroque dyad to pose questions about period and style, modernity and progress, and the cultural identity of the German nation.

The Renaissance of the German Baroque in the "Epistemo-Critical Prologue"

As opaque as the first twenty pages of the *Tragic Drama* book are—Benjamin himself was in all likelihood referring to them when he wrote to Gershom Scholem on 19 February 1925 that parts of the "Prologue" were "an outrageous Chutzpah" (*Briefe* 1: 372)—they were not the reason university officials in Frankfurt recommended that Benjamin withdraw the work from consideration as his *Habilitation*. In fact, like the fictional foreword that Benjamin wrote *after* the withdrawal, the pages that we now read as the opening salvo of his theoretical argument were not handed in with the rest of the study; rather, they appeared only later in the version of the book published in 1928.[7] Without them, Benjamin's "Baroque book" actually begins, in the section identified by the running head "The Dismissal and Misunderstanding of Baroque Tragedy" (*Gesammelte Schriften* 1.1: 229–31), with an overview of existing criticism, entitled "History of the Study of the German Literary Baroque" (G: 1.1: 228–37; E: 48–56); such overviews were a common way of opening a German academic exercise, both at the time and since. The strategic (mis)use

---

7. See *Briefe* 1: 372. This is not to say that Benjamin was not concerned with the "epistemological" aspects of his thesis before this date. He writes to Scholem from Capri on 13 June 1924 (*Briefe* 1: 346–47), for example, of the difficulties he is having clarifying these aspects of his work for himself, and refers on 16 September 1924 (*Briefe* 1: 353–54) to some part of the "epistemological introduction to the work" as complete. By 22 December 1924, he has decided, however, to "hold back" those parts, including the introduction, that have to do with methodology, so that he might finally finish the thesis (*Briefe* 1: 365). In the February letter (372), he indicates that a "large part" of the introduction, which he identifies as the "theory of ideas" (*Ideenlehre*), had not yet been written.

of the term "tragedy" in the head to explain existing misinterpretations of what Benjamin insists is not "tragedy," but rather the Baroque "tragic drama" (*Trauerspiel*), or mourning play, in fact points to one of his main complaints in this section about the prior scholarship, namely its failure to distinguish the imitative culture of the Renaissance, with its relationship of indebtedness to ancient tragedy, from the new and modern forms of the Baroque *Trauerspiel*.[8] While Benjamin may have sought later to differentiate himself from the tribe of academics who chose not to accept him, the periodization debates in which he engages in these more traditional, or "profane," parts of the "Prologue" suggest that this most complex of texts may profitably be read in dialogue with work about the Baroque being published at the time.[9]

Benjamin's more or less workmanly overview of recent scholarship begins by noting the considerable barriers erected in the grand narratives of nineteenth-century German literary history to an objective assessment of the period (G: 1.1: 228–30; E: 48–49). Without going into detail, he notes the suspicion on the part of the proto-Romantic and nationalist "philologists of the Grimm and Lachmannian schools" vis-à-vis the dramatic texts authored by the "learned civil-servant class," to which the Silesian authors Martin Opitz, Andreas Gryphius, and Daniel Casper von Lohenstein, among others, belonged (229; 48); these texts, Benjamin explains, were deemed by mid- to late nineteenth-century scholarship not to have been sufficiently devoted to excavating the achievements of the German *Volk* to serve as models for a coming German nation. Because "Baroque drama" was interested in neither "German legend" nor "German history" (229; 48), it was considered an affront to this kind of "pious and piety-provoking" work (Jaumann, *Die deutsche Barockliteratur* 226). The names and titles that Benjamin does not supply here would nevertheless have been so well known as not to require listing; they included Wilhelm Wackernagel's *Geschichte der deutschen Litteratur: Ein Handbuch* (History of German Literature: A Handbook) (1848), Carl Lemcke's *Geschichte der deutschen Dichtung neuerer Zeit* (History of German Poetry of Modern Times) (1871), and, most famously, Wilhelm Scherer's *Geschichte der deutschen Literatur* (History of German Literature) (1880–83) (see Voßkamp), all tomes that belonged

---

8. The fullest outline of Benjamin's thesis that survives (the Frankfurt editors date it to sometime after November 1923) is just as traditional; it lays out an organizational scheme that calls for sections that treat literary history, the tradition of historical aesthetics and the history of styles, and cultural history of the period (here, especially the role of Protestantism) (*Gesammelte Schriften* 1.3: 915–18); the separate steps suggest the various disciplinary locations where the Baroque was under debate at the time. Both Hofmannsthal's (*Gesammelte Schriften* 1.3: 903) and others' claims and Benjamin's subsequent self-representation as an outsider within the "halls of academe," as he wrote in an unpublished foreword to the *Tragic Drama* book (902), notwithstanding, it may have been the more mundane existential concerns that Benjamin had at the time (*Briefe* 1: 339) that motivated his fairly conventional approach to this academic task. See his sadly mistaken comment to Scholem in 1923 that in its present form the *Habilitation* should be acceptable to the authorities at Frankfurt (*Briefe* 1: 319).

9. On the "profane" parts of the "Prologue," see Hanssen 45.

to the standard equipment of students of German literary history in the early years of the twentieth century, when Benjamin wrote.

The work of one of the major figures in the academic study of German literature at the time, Erich Schmidt, was a direct legacy of this literary-historical school and still dominated university circles in Benjamin's Berlin.[10] Schmidt had only recently died (1913) when Benjamin read his first Baroque tragic drama in 1917 (see *Briefe* 1: 140); the search for a successor to Schmidt at Berlin lasted the length of World War I and suggests the contentious nature of debates about the relation of literary-historical methodology to the nation during these years (Höppner, "Eine Institution wehrt sich"). Julius Petersen was finally named to take over Schmidt's university chair in 1920, just a few years before Benjamin began his research, practically next door, in the Prussian State Library. While more diplomatic than Schmidt in his tolerance of a wide range of approaches, as Boden ("Zur Entwicklung") and Alexander Honold have shown, Petersen, whose work Benjamin knew and cites in the *Tragic Drama* book, was still more or less respectful of the older traditions and offered his famous seminar on Baroque literature in Berlin in the winter semester of 1927–28, just as Benjamin's *Habilitation* was finally going to press. The work of seminar participants—much of which touched on many of the same issues in which Benjamin was interested, including Baroque language theory and the analysis of style—set the agenda for German Baroque studies up through and even after the next war.[11]

Benjamin claims in the "Epistemo-Critical Prologue" that the literary histories whose legacies surrounded him in Berlin blocked an "objective" understanding of the Baroque (G: 1.1: 232; E: 51), since they saw it as the primary duty of the "German Poet" to "administer" the nation's indigenous "cultural capital" on behalf of the *Volk* (Fohrmann, "Das Bild des 17. Jahrhunderts" 586). Benjamin correctly captures the centrality of such sentiments when he points out Scherer et al.'s allergies to the highly complex and learned texts of the Baroque and to their non-"völkisch"

---

10. For a detailed and evenhanded discussion of the "völkisch" elements of Schmidt's work, also as the head of German literary studies in Berlin during Benjamin's own student years, which he spent in Berlin as well in other German university towns, see Höppner, "Die Gründung des Germanischen Seminars."

11. Benjamin cites (albeit dismissively) Petersen's well-known essay "Der Aufbau der Literaturgeschichte" (The Structure of Literary History) (1914) in the "Prologue." On the work of the participants in Petersen's famous "Barock-Seminar," see Boden ("Julius Petersen") and Honold as well as Trunz's memoirs of the seminar ("Erinnerungen an Julius Petersens Seminar"). Much of this work, including Wolfgang Kayser's seminar report on Baroque language theory, for example, which became his 1932 book, *Die Klangmalerei bei Harsdörffer: Ein Beitrag zur Geschichte der Literatur, Poetik, und Sprachtheorie der Barockzeit* (Onomatopoeia in Harsdörffer: A Study of the History of Literature, Poetics, and Language Theory in the Baroque) dealt with topics in which Benjamin was also interested. In his book, Kayser cites the same work on Baroque language theory that Benjamin cites, suggesting the parallels of the *Tragic Drama* book with scholarship contemporary with it.

and cosmopolitan authors. Benjamin goes on to argue, however, that both the German Romantics and these more recent exponents of nationalist philology incorrectly dismissed Baroque drama as irrelevant to the literary-historical politics of "renewal" (*Erneuerung*) and to the celebration of "folk" tradition that this kind of work had so famously undertaken in its studies of Shakespeare, for example (G: 1.1: 229; E: 48). The actual "services" (229; 48) performed by the German Baroque authors on behalf of both the nation and the national language must be noted, he claims. The irony of this last point is important enough to Benjamin for him to circle back to it again at the end of the chapter, where he argues—in defense of the "men of letters" (Opitz, Gryphius, and Lohenstein in particular)—that, unlike their modern counterparts, they were in fact successful servants of the state (236; 56). According to Benjamin, "literature ... in Germany of the seventeenth century" was central to the more or less patriotic "rebirth" (*Neugeburt*) of "the nation"— even if no such nation existed at the time (236; 56). The rhetoric that emerges in Benjamin's rather unadventurous review of the scholarship here thus characterizes the Baroque as a kind of substitute Renaissance, especially in the field of vernacular language theory. The indirect effect is to begin a kind of counterattack on the prejudices of a tradition of nationalist philology that would exclude the Baroque, doing so by means of an argument that highlights, rather, the period's proto-patriotic achievements. Both here and later in the second part of the second chapter, Benjamin in fact writes of the "blossoming" and "vital energy" of the German dialects as evidenced in the texts of the period (379; 204).

Benjamin's endorsement of the Baroque's contribution to the literary and linguistic Renaissance of the German nation in the seventeenth century thus represents a decided turn *away* from the downbeat assessments of the period and its texts standard in what he refers to as the "older research" (G: 1.1: 230; E: 49). In this, he was not unique, as Herbert Jaumann has shown. As early as 1894, Rudolf Fürst had already called for leaving behind the traditionally "deprecatory assessments" of the Baroque, in the first number of what was to become the highly respected journal *Euphorion* (Jaumann, "Der Barockbegriff" 625). The need to reject this older tradition went on to produce several waves of scholarship that moved beyond the pieties of Lemcke, Scherer, et al. In the "Prologue" Benjamin makes clear that he is familiar with these innovations, yet he goes on to refute them too. Such apologetic scholarship likewise fails in its task, he asserts, precisely because it denies the Baroque a role in the revitalization of modernity, particularly when it openly and deliberately falls back into a critical vocabulary associated with the historical Renaissance. Benjamin shrewdly notes that this move cannot help but identify the age that followed it as a "clumsy Renaissance" (G: 1.1: 230; E: 50) in turn. Any scholarship that binds the Baroque to the Renaissance in this way thus disallows the former a proper historical afterlife, which he calls a "historical echo" (229; 48). Such scholarship is of no use in charting the direction of future research, which in his estimation can be undertaken only if it recognizes the contemporary "relevance" of the Baroque (235; 55).[12] Benjamin's project is thus to enable an "afterlife" (*Nachleben*) for the Baroque as a way of challenging existing literary-historical periodization practices. It does so, however, in a traditional academic way that serves the very same kind of supersessionary narrative in which the idea of the Renaissance itself had classically been embedded, a narrative that claims that the Baroque actually does the Renaissance one better because it provides an authentically new foundation on which a future national modernity can be built.

In this section of the "Epistemo-Critical Prologue," Benjamin goes on to name names, taking aim at scholars who defend the German Baroque only ineptly when they make it an extension of the Renaissance. Representative of this literary-historical and literary-critical trend is the well-known *Seneca und das deutsche Renaissancedrama* (Seneca and German Renaissance Drama) (1907) by the Germanist Paul Stachel (1880–1919), which had been one of the first close studies of the texts of the Silesian playwrights to have been published in the modern period. Benjamin submits Stachel's work to a searing critique (G: 1.1: 231; E: 50) here and does the same for the much more recent *Deutsche Barockdichtung: Renaissance, Barock, Rokoko* (German Baroque Poetry: Renaissance, Baroque, Rococo) (1924) by Herbert Cysarz (1896–1985) (G: 1.1: 233; E: 52).[13] These two books bracket the decades during which Baroque studies was in its prime. Even though Benjamin dismisses them together here, Stachel's and Cysarz's approaches were as methodologically different from one another as were their authors. Parts of Stachel's book had been written in 1904 as his doctoral dissertation in Berlin under Erich Schmidt (1853–1913), the student of Scherer's mentioned above and master of the old-style philology that

---

12. Arguments for the "timeliness" of the Baroque were all the rage in Germany in both scholarly and more popular work of the early twentieth century for a number of reasons, including parallels that were claimed to exist between the chaos of the Thirty Years' War and the Great War, as well as between the early modern and modern forms of grandiose cultural projects associated with absolutism and the national state. See H.-H. Müller, "Die Übertragung des Barockbegriffs" 95–96; Warnke, "Die Entstehung des Barockbegriffs." Benjamin's claims sometimes contradict one another in this respect. Here, for example, the argument against the identification of the Baroque with the Renaissance explains his later approval of Manheimer's 1904 claim that the "Baroque literature of the seventeenth century" shows parallels with "artistic sensibility of our own time," which precedes the claim for the importance of its contemporary "relevance." Just before the Manheimer quote, however, Benjamin had argued against this kind of identificatory logic based on "empathy" and "substitution," which fails to consider the historical alterity of the period and its texts. See G: 1.1: 234–35; E: 53–54.

13. Benjamin appears to have owned a copy of Cysarz's book, which had only just appeared, and to have either taken it with him to Capri or asked someone to send it to him there. See Benjamin's letter to Scholem of 16 September 1924 (*Briefe* 1: 353–59; on Cysarz, 354). As much as he critiques both Stachel and Cysarz, it is important to note that Benjamin cites their work throughout the *Tragic Drama* book in both acknowledged and unacknowledged ways. As suggested above, it may have been in Stachel's appendix, "Beilage I" (Stachel 351–53), for example, where German plays in which ghosts appear are listed, that Benjamin was able to witness the prominence of such features, to which he then calls attention in turn (G: 1.1: 313–14 and 370; E: 134–35, 193). Benjamin also actively relies on Stachel in his description of the martyrdom scenes of the Baroque plays (392; 218). In the case of Cysarz, we can also see a broad common interest in the allegory-symbol distinction ("Vom Geist" 261) as well as in the role of Cartesianism (260).

Benjamin and others condemned.[14] By contrast, twenty years later, Cysarz had just completed his doctoral work in Vienna under the guidance of Walter Brecht. (Ironically, Brecht later served as the liaison between Benjamin and Hugo von Hofmannsthal in arranging for the publication of the third section of the second chapter of the *Tragic Drama* book in Hofmannsthal's *Neue deutsche Beiträge* in 1927.)[15] That Cysarz's 1924 book, on which Benjamin comments dismissively here, was the former's own successfully completed *Habilitation* is a poignant reminder that the soon-to-be goose-stepping Cysarz had a successful academic career under the National Socialist regime that led to Benjamin's death.[16] As different as they were, however, what Stachel and Cysarz shared is clear from the titles of the books that Benjamin cites, namely a belief that the best defense of the texts of the German Baroque was a good offense—that is, the alignment of the period with several versions of the Renaissance—which was precisely the stance that Benjamin rejects.

Stachel's *Seneca and German Renaissance Drama* defends the Baroque by yoking its texts to the lineage of Senecan tragedy that extends from the plays of the Roman master through the French and Dutch humanist school drama of the fifteenth and sixteenth centuries. Stachel includes in this "Renaissance" tradition plays by the "father of German poetry," Martin Opitz (Garber, *Martin Opitz*), and by the later playwrights Gryphius and Lohenstein, of the Second Silesian school, on the one hand, and texts of the mid- to late seventeenth-century Nuremberg poets Georg Philipp Harsdörffer, Sigmund von Birken, and Johann Klaj and the Silesian "epigones" Johann Christian Hallmann and August Adolph von Haugwitz, on the other. This genealogical scenario is a familiar one that animates the fundamentally countertypological narratives of the vernacular Renaissances in general, finding legitimacy in the work of the moderns only insofar as they looked back to the ancients. Stachel apologizes that it is the "unnatural monster" (2) of the ancient, Seneca, whose work is the decisive factor in linking the Germans to this lofty past. His opening statement nevertheless claims that, in their dependency, the Germans achieved a kind of modern legitimacy in the same way that prior critics had shown

---

14. See Höppner, "Die Gründung des Germanischen Seminars," on Scherer and Schmidt.

15. Cf. *Gesammelte Schriften* 1.3: 903–4. Hofmannsthal saw his own time and work as contemporary successors to the Baroque (see Schoolfield). Benjamin's review of Hofmannsthal's play *Der Turm*, which was based on a work by the Spanish Baroque playwright Calderón, was published in the same year as the *Tragic Drama* book; compare Benjamin's description of the "Baroqueness" of Hofmannsthal's play (3: 98–101).

16. Cysarz's improbably deep erudition and his breathless pronouncements on the Baroque were already known, although not universally praised, even before his thesis was complete, because of the appearance of his essay "Vom Geist des deutschen Literatur-Barocks" in the inaugural volume of the reputable journal *Deutsche Vierteljahresschrift*, vol. 1.2 (1923), the year before the publication of *Deutsche Barockdichtung*. In his review of Cysarz's 1924 book, Körner (459) implies that it is highly unlikely that Cysarz actually read all the texts to which he refers. Cysarz's subsequent career can and should be read as a perverse twin of Benjamin's own. See the conclusion.

the Elizabethan as well as the French and Dutch playwrights of the sixteenth and seventeenth centuries to have done, namely by demonstrating their imitative side. Indeed, the more the German tragic dramas can be said to resemble not just the plays of Seneca and Sophocles, but those of Shakespeare, Vondel, Corneille, and de Mairet as well, the more legitimately they testify to a German "rebirth." In Stachel's argument, although latecomers, the Germans thus attain the stature due a "modern" culture not merely by mimicking the ancients, but also by joining the ranks of prior inheritor cultures. The argument of course not only fails to identify what is actually modern about the German plays, but also collaborates in the production of a lineage for them that falls far short of identifying what it is about them that, for Benjamin, is "specifically German" (G: 1.1: 260; E: 81). Correcting both of these errors was Benjamin's task.

The literary-historical (mis)application of Renaissance categories to Baroque plays in Stachel's book bleeds into stylistic arguments that are equally problematic and that Benjamin also rejects. As the author of the first vernacular poetics in German (1624), Martin Opitz is said to have brought "the classicistic Renaissance" (180) to Germany with his translation of Seneca's *Trojan Women* into German in 1636, for example: All that is "Roman" is thereby "teutonified" (*germanisiert*), "the ancient world view replaced by the modern" national one (Stachel 187). As upbeat as the analogy may sound, Stachel's depiction of Opitz, a member of the so-called First Silesian school, as both "modern" *and* "classicistic" here reveals the conceptual error of his Baroque-as-Renaissance claim. As much as Stachel would praise Opitz's ability to initiate a German Renaissance, in other words, it is clear not only that the ancients remain the ultimate measuring stick, but also that the Baroque literature that succeeds this German Renaissance can be only a pale predecessor of what Cysarz will go on to claim is the "true" German Renaissance in eighteenth-century Weimar Classicism (*Klassik*). This is why, even as a "modern," Opitz can never be more than an "imitator poet" (*Nachdichter*) of the ancients (199), to use Stachel's words. The identification of the "first" German poet as a "classicizing" imitator in bondage to the past suggests that precisely the achievements that should integrate the Germans into the "modern" European community of literate Renaissance nations also keep them, in Stachel's rendering, in a permanent state of stylistic nonage. Measured by such logic, the German Baroque tragic drama of the seventeenth century can only appear, in Benjamin's dismissive words, as the ugly stepchild of "Renaissance drama . . . laden down with abundant stylistic incongruities" (G: 1.1: 231; E: 50).[17]

---

17. Claims of stylistic dissonance and generational weakness permeate Stachel's "defense" of the German Baroque in *Seneca und German Renaissance Drama,* a book that Benjamin indicates he had read "for the most part" (*Gesammelte Schriften* 7: 454). Gryphius comes "closer" to Seneca than the earlier Opitz, according to Stachel, but is still Seneca's "heir and descendant" (Stachel 202), for example. Indeed, in spite of Gryphius's famous dismissal of the ancients—"Why inquire after the Greeks? / They must retreat, when the German Muse arrives," which Stachel quotes (206)—his work is superior to Opitz's only in a reversed kind of way, only, that is, because in it one can see more clearly the "living influence of the original" (204).

Stachel goes on to identify the relationship of the later Silesian playwright Gryphius with the literary tradition writ large as "centripetal" (253), with the center occupied by either the ancients (Sophocles, 248) or the non-German "Renaissance" poets on whose work Gryphius depends, such as the Dutch playwright Joost van den Vondel (1587–1679) (238). Lohenstein's achievements are equally dependent on his relationship to either the foreign or the past. Stachel makes the obvious comparisons of Lohenstein's plays with Seneca's, for example, noting the former's use of outrageous scenes of seduction, sacrifices, and ghosts (295–96, 300), and with the plays of Lohenstein's French contemporary Jean de Mairet (1604–86) (293, 297).[18] Such analyses explain why, in the cases of both of these major German Baroque playwrights, whose texts represent two of Benjamin's prime examples of the tragic drama, Stachel more often than not quite logically applies the term "tragedy" (*Tragödie*) to their works. Stachel's closing arguments describe Gryphius's creation of a specifically German "tragic form" (274); Lohenstein's contribution to the tradition is also referred to as his work on the "German tragedy of the seventeenth century" (324). Collapsing the Baroque "tragic drama" into the category of "tragedy" in this way is the very critical narrative in which Benjamin seeks to intervene. His critique of Stachel's work in the "Epistemo-Critical Prologue" can thus be read in two ways: as an interruption of the Baroque-as-Renaissance construction and as a supersessional narrative of its own, which christens the Baroque tragic drama as a new "origin" of what Benjamin calls the "un-Renaissance-like" (*renaissancefremd*) tradition of "modern German drama" (G: 1.1: 240; E: 59).

Herbert Cysarz's engagement with the Baroque foregrounds the national character of this tale more explicitly. Like Stachel, he aims to redeem the period in the face of its earlier detractors, calling Scherer's famously dismissive rendering of the Baroque no more than a "caricature" (Cysarz, "Vom Geist" 243) and "perfidious distortion" (*Deutsche Barockdichtung* 20 n. 3) of the period and its texts. Nevertheless, even though Cysarz is more explicitly committed than Stachel to defining the Baroque as its own period, as an "organic unity" (20) of a German hue, he does so by deploying tropes about the Renaissance similar to the earlier scholar's and thus likewise earns Benjamin's disdain. "The Baroque is our modern literature's first struggle with antiquity," Cysarz writes ("Vom Geist" 245); elsewhere, however, it is "nothing other than an imitation of antiquity" (247), "a systematic imitation of the linguistic art of the Ancients" (*Deutsche Barockdichtung* 40), and a "chain of receptions" (29). Paradoxically, such claims are overtly figural and antiprogressivist at one and the same time. Like all other "Renaissance literatures," German Baroque texts seek only the "imitation and trumping of the forms of antiquity" (95), Cysarz

---

18. Lohenstein's massive annotations to his texts, which often ran to three times the length of the plays, confirm, Stachel explains, the claim that the Baroque playwright was self-consciously the direct heir of the Roman playwright, a "German Seneca" (326). It was conventional, even in the seventeenth century, to call Lohenstein the "German Seneca," and Stachel notes Birken's (281) and Männling's (282–83) praise of Lohenstein to this effect.

argues. Yet, when described in these terms, they can only ever fail to get beyond an "antiquifying" (50, 75, 129, 153, 165) "powerlessness" (296). It would be difficult to characterize this version of a redemption of the German Baroque as anything other than the singularly "negative valorization" of a failed "pseudo-Renaissance" that Cysarz in fact admits his analysis to be (292).

Ironically, it may well have been Cysarz's interest in defining the properties of the Baroque in the "sphere of German linguistic art" (*Deutsche Barockdichtung* 14)—properties that he claims derived from a German "religious, national, and literary foundation" (51) and that Benjamin himself goes on to privilege later in the *Tragic Drama* book—that led Cysarz to introduce into his argument the literary-historical category to which Benjamin takes greatest exception at the end of the "Epistemo-Critical Prologue." According to Benjamin, Cysarz sees the works of the Baroque as no more than the "preliminary stages" (G: 1.1: 233; E: 52) of the developing narrative of a German literary tradition. For Benjamin, Cysarz's attempt to define the role of the Baroque as only "preparatory" (*Deutsche Barockdichtung* 6) and transitional to the true Renaissance of a German tradition in Weimar Classicism reveals that Cysarz's Baroque is no more than a way station on the road from the "humanism" of the historical Italian Renaissance of the fourteenth and fifteenth centuries to the "real" German Renaissance, namely the "idealism" of eighteenth-century German Classicism (35, 235). Such lines of continuity as there were thus passed, according to the Viennese scholar, from a nearly Burckhardtian celebration of the individual in the Italian Renaissance (5 n. 1) directly to the "Germanic individualism" of the Classical era of Schiller and Goethe (35 and 209). As convincing as this argument might be regarding the continuity of the German tradition, its logical result is that the seventeenth-century Baroque cannot in fact be a German Renaissance at all. Rather, it remains only a "proto"- and "pseudo"-form thereof (19, 21, 40, 274), with the final successful "wedding" of the German tradition with antiquity occurring, according to Cysarz, only later, "toward the end of the eighteenth century" (291), in the works of the period that he goes on to call the German "High Renaissance," works that are, moreover, conceptually dependent on Italian forms. Although his Baroque is clearly caught up in the same progressivist logic as the Renaissance proper, Cysarz's version thus cannot really have the genuinely reanimating function with which Benjamin hopes to endow it. Nor is the Baroque, not surprisingly, actually German in spirit at all. Benjamin had commented at length and somewhat condescendingly to Scholem that as useful as he found some parts of the book by Cysarz as a "rising Viennese academic," its confused logic revealed that its author had succumbed to "the vertiginous attraction" of the antithetical period of the Baroque itself (*Briefe* 1: 354). Cysarz's indecisiveness about which "Renaissance" to measure the Baroque against—the historical Italian or the Weimar Classical one—may well be a case in point.

In Cysarz's discussions of the Baroque in 1923–24, the narrative of an all-encompassing "continuity of the German Renaissance movement" (*Deutsche Barock-*

dichtung 292) into which all great epochs, authors, and texts of the German tradition may dip—but only when they are "classical, classicistic, and Renaissance-like" enough (132 and 292)—thus actually effaces any possibility of a distinct or positive "origin" of a German tradition in the Baroque. It is this reading of the period to which Benjamin takes exception. The benchmark of Weimar as the norm produces Cysarz's odd claim that it is only because Baroque poetic theory "is based first and foremost upon a Horatian and Aristotelian foundation" that the period can be said to belong to the "unshaken" German tradition (106) at all. Cysarz's appeal to a tradition of normative German-language poetic theory that reached its high point with Johann Christoph Gottsched suggests the context of Benjamin's famous rejection in the *Tragic Drama* book of any scholarship—and of Cysarz's claims in particular—that considers the tradition of Baroque poetic treatises beholden to Aristotle. When Cysarz and others attempt to "redeem the tragic drama by appealing to Aristotle," Benjamin writes (G: 1.1: 232; E: 52), they mistakenly rely on a tradition of "classicizing poetics" (233; 53) as an essentially foreign-identified and backward-looking critical tool with which to evaluate "modern" drama and thus fail to generate categories for understanding the period out of the texts of the period itself.[19] Here Benjamin seems to identify the texts of the Baroque as themselves nearly synonymous with the ancient "relics" that it had traditionally been the charge of the Renaissance to renew. In his argument, these are the texts that should be received as the sources of a national rebirth.

Cysarz's classicizing logic is Benjamin's explicit target both here in the "Epistemo-Critical Prologue" and in the second chapter of the *Tragic Drama* book, where he dismisses all attempts to redeem the Baroque by apologizing for it as "a necessary transitional stage" (G: 1.1: 240; E: 60). As "contemporary" as his diction may really have been,[20] Cysarz's defense of the Baroque was thus, like Stachel's, both profoundly traditional and fundamentally antitypological. Like Stachel, Cysarz looks only backward, not merely to eighteenth-century Weimar Classicism, but also to disciplinary hierarchies set by the nineteenth-century tradition of what Wilhelm Voßkamp calls positivistic "Classicism-centrism" (*Klassikzentrierung*, 686) that prevented German literature from modernizing at all. In the "Epistemo-Critical Prologue" it is Cysarz's logic of "necessity"—the Baroque must "blossom" and then, grown "tired" (*Deutsche Barockdichtung* 273), "wilt" (274) and fail (265) so that German Classicism, the "authentic" (6) "German High Renaissance" (280,

---

19. The outrage of some early readers of Benjamin's dismissal of the role of Aristotle is surprising, not only because it is clearly polemical in relation to Cysarz, but also because other prominent critics, including Arthur Hübscher, whose important 1922 article on the Baroque I discuss below, also proposed that Aristotle's categories were not central in an understanding of Baroque literary texts. See Hübscher 535 and below.

20. Körner suggests that Cysarz's pronouncements were inspired by the oracular tone of the George Circle, perhaps via Friedrich Gundolf, and thus includes the overly precocious Cysarz among the "Gundolf epigones" (455), whose work was flooding the literary journals at the time.

292), can replace it—that is the object of Benjamin's explicit distrust (G: 1.1: 233; E: 53). Benjamin goes on to write in the second chapter of the *Tragic Drama* book of the need for criticism of the Baroque to "free" itself from approaches that see the period only as a "necessary but inessential transitional phenomenon" (278; 100).[21] Cysarz is clearly still the target here. Hopelessly "entangled" (233; 53), according to Benjamin, in a logic that condemns both the Baroque and innovation of any sort to extinction, Cysarz's argument epitomizes the kind of scholarship Benjamin rejects in favor of an approach that would celebrate the Baroque as capable of giving birth to more modern German literary forms on its own.[22]

Benjamin's discussion of the Baroque tragic drama and its "origin" (*Ursprung*) not as growing out of the past, but rather as indicating a future "development of emergence and fading" (G: 1.1: 226; E: 45) is thus conducted in explicit dialogue with, but also as a deliberate revision of, the terms of Stachel's and Cysarz's "defenses" of the texts of the Baroque as Renaissance clones.[23] Throughout the *Tragic Drama* book, he rejects arguments about the Baroque that assess the genre of the modern tragic drama only as a "distortion" and "clumsy Renaissance . . . of ancient tragedy" (230–31; 50), and repeatedly emphasizes, instead, those "baroque characteristics" of the texts that are specifically "foreign to the Renaissance" (240; 59). "Almost nothing of the German dramatic tradition of the Renaissance survives [in the Baroque]," Benjamin claims (259; 80). Later he explicitly states that the use of

---

21. Although Benjamin also often cites numerous individual details and arguments derived from Cysarz's 1924 study in a positive way, he was not alone in critiquing Cysarz. See, again, the searing review of *German Baroque Poetry* by Körner. Voßkamp takes Körner's review as a signal that a "self-criticism" had already set in within Baroque studies.

22. Benjamin's critique of the terms of "necessity" is also aimed at the work of Julius Petersen, whom he likewise cites and critiques in the *Tragic Drama* book; Petersen's concept of "necessity" in literary-historical analysis is related to but not exactly the same as Cysarz's and speaks more to the "necessity" of the text's relation to what Benjamin calls the "subjective disposition of the author" (G: 1.1: 233; E: 52), and to any particular author's "necessary" containment within the synchronic "total picture" of his times, than to Cysarz's diachronically organized "necessity" of literary history.

23. There were other scholars of the German literary Baroque who, although unnamed in the *Tragic Drama* book, deployed much the same set of tropes about a Baroque that resembled a "classicizing" Renaissance more than itself. One particularly significant voice was that of the young Richard Alewyn, whose *Vorbarocker Klassizismus und griechische Tragödie: Analyse der 'Antigone'-Übersetzung des Martin Opitz* (Pre-Baroque Classicism and Greek Tragedy: An Analysis of Martin Opitz's *Antigone* Translation) (1926) had been accepted as his doctoral dissertation in Heidelberg in the very year, 1925, that Benjamin withdrew his "Baroque book" from consideration at Frankfurt. Benjamin appears to have respected Alewyn's work enough to have been happy to report to Scholem in 1928 that he had heard Alewyn was to review the *Tragic Drama* book (*Gesammelte Schriften* 1.3: 908–9). The review never materialized. Perhaps this was a good thing, because in 1926 Alewyn, like Stachel and Cysarz before him, defines Opitz first and foremost as a "Renaissance poet" (*Vorbarocker Klassizismus* 19), thrusting him into a relation of dependency on the ancients in ways similar to theirs. "The tragic drama of the German Baroque" proper, such as the plays of Lohenstein and Gryphius, constitute, according to Alewyn, no more than a mildly "disruptive" "Intermezzo" between a brace of classicizing periods (53) against which they fail to measure up.

affect by Baroque playwrights, of props on the Baroque stage, and of the highly or-
nate Alexandrine rhyme scheme that so clearly mark the Silesian plays are nothing
at all like these features, as they characterize the texts of either their Renaissance or
ancient predecessors (277, 312, 380–81; 99, 133, 205–6). Even though Baroque poetological handbooks have a "Renaissance-like facade" (239; 59), finally, and thus appear "classicistic," the Baroque tragic drama itself is specifically *not* to be assessed,
Benjamin asserts, via the terminology of "Renaissance tragedy," and certainly not
in terms of imitating the ancients, who could not have had "any less influence" at
the time (240; 60). For Benjamin, the only way to begin to understand the German
Baroque at all is thus to see it *not* as an antiquity-loving Renaissance influenced by
foreign norms, but rather as a period and canon whose "works" are to be assessed
by attention to their own standards, "in the context," as he describes it, "of their
own concise logic" (255; 76).

Benjamin's review and rejection in the "Epistemo-Critical Prologue" of existing
scholarly positions on the German Baroque by Stachel and Cysarz fulfill the traditional function of the German academic introduction, namely to clear the ground
for a new set of claims via indictment of the work of previous scholars. But Benjamin's own position on the Baroque—his crafting of a positive, or productive, argument for an independent "idea" of the Baroque and of the genre of a specifically
German tragic drama—has still to be established. Beatrice Hanssen suggests that
the earlier and less conventional pages of the "Prologue" (which precede Benjamin's dismissal of Stachel and Cysarz and were, again, not included in the thesis
when Benjamin first turned it in for review at Frankfurt) should be read as part
of a dialogue with the theoretical assumptions of historicism and neo-Kantianism,
on the one hand, and the psychologism that was part of contemporary aesthetics and art history, on the other (24, 41). While this is certainly correct, Hanssen
overlooks that these very same additional pages can also be read as providing the
art philosophical logic behind an alternative periodization scheme, one that Benjamin develops to take the place of the approaches to the Baroque, like Stachel's
and Cysarz's, that he critiques. Benjamin's complex discussion of the relationship
between the facticity of individual texts and works of art and the abstractness of
"ideas" in the opening pages of the "Epistemo-Critical Prologue" as it was published in 1928 addresses, I would argue, the very same issues of periodization as the
more conventional "academic" section with which it concludes, offering a defense
of the Baroque that argues for its existence precisely as an independent "idea" of
rebirth. For support of this claim, Benjamin draws on the work of another contemporary scholar, Konrad Burdach.

In the opening pages of the "Epistemo-Critical Prologue" as it appeared in print
in 1928, a tense dialectic emerges between methods that privilege the particular-
ity of single works of art and a set of more or less abstract or idealist methods
that posit a prior category—historical-contextual, period- or genre-specific, or
aesthetic-subjective—as a way of identifying individual works. Given his critique

(in the original "Prologue") of scholarship that posited an "idea" of "Renaissance" tragedy, or of a "classicism" of form that failed to account for the empirical existence of the idiosyncrasies of the tragic dramas of the German Baroque, it makes sense that Benjamin devotes additional attention in the complex pages he added to what has come to be known as his "theory of ideas" (*Ideenlehre*), arguing there against any system of analysis that would "measure" objects against foreign standards or abstract norms even as he also argues for the preservation of a doctrine of independent "ideas" like the Baroque. Thus, as much as the theory-of-ideas section may represent a dialogue with the work of neo-Kantians R. M. Meyer (1901) (G: 1.1: 222; E: 42) and Hermann Cohen (1914) (226; 46), for example, or represent an attempt to push Benedetto Croce even further in his rejection of the "judgment" of individual works of art against a preexisting grid of ideal forms (223–24; 43–45), the notoriously difficult section of the "Prologue" in which these philosophers and art theorists are named may also be read as an integral part of the attempt to develop more apt methods than Stachel's and Cysarz's for dealing with the German Baroque. It is thus not by chance that in this first section of the "Prologue," even before he takes aim at Meyer, Croce, Cohen, et al., Benjamin turns to a text of considerable notoriety at the time, namely Konrad Burdach's *Reformation, Renaissance, Humanismus* (1918), and to Burdach's critique there of any and all period concepts such as "humanism" and "the Renaissance," the "Gothic," and the "Baroque man" (G: 1.1: 220–21; E: 40). In the "theory of ideas" section, it is in fact via several lengthy quotes from Burdach that Benjamin tries to clarify how to respect the realm of the "object," the "phenomenon," and the empirical while *also* preserving the realm of "truth" and of ideas (209–15; 29–35). It is, in other words, Benjamin's adaptation of Burdach's explanation of the epistemology of periodization that allows Benjamin to articulate an "idea" of a German Baroque independent of the "idea" of the Renaissance and thus to distinguish "tragic drama" from ancient tragedy by attending to its peculiar, phenomenal details. Benjamin nevertheless also—and, I would argue, not by chance—uses Burdach's wartime discussion of a much-needed alternative moment of national "rebirth" to perform this task, thereby interpellating the work of a specifically German Renaissance into his definition of the origin of the Baroque appropriate to the times.

Konrad Burdach (1859–1936) was a well-established but exceedingly controversial medievalist, and the editor of numerous Italian and New High German source texts, whose career was at its relative high point in the early 1920s. His essentially anti-Burckhardtian theses about the fundamentally spiritual—rather than political—origins of the Renaissance, and thus its continuities with the "religious upheavals" (Borchardt 427) of the High Middle Ages, on the one hand, and his claims about the impact of the radical movements in Italy on the court culture of Prague and other parts north, on the other, had tested both the disciplinary and geographical, the ideological and chronological limits of what could be said about the secular Italian "origins" of the Renaissance at the time and had caused an immense amount of scholarly debate.[24] Benjamin's discussion of Burdach's claims occurs at what is virtually the center of the most difficult part of the "Epistemo-Critical Prologue," on the pages under the running head "Burdach's Nominalism" (G: 1.1: 220–22). Here he touches less on Burdach's thematic and historical period argument and more on the methodological issue at the center of Burdach's essay "Über den Ursprung des Humanismus" (On the Origin of Humanism), which makes up one chapter of Burdach's 1918 book. In that essay, Burdach discusses the relation of any movement or period label, such as humanism, to the manifold movements, events, and texts it describes. The coincidence of Burdach's problematization of the term "origin" (*Ursprung*) in this essay with Benjamin's famous definition of the term just a few pages later in the *Tragic Drama* book is too obvious to be ignored. The implication in Benjamin's "idea" of the "origin" of the Baroque of Burdach's telic narrative of the fruition of an "other" Renaissance in an epoch-spanning tradition of specifically German humanism is equally hard to miss.

Originally published in the fateful year of 1914, and then reissued in the equally momentous year of 1918, Burdach's "On the Origin of Humanism" has the specific task, as Benjamin's lengthy quote from it reveals (G: 1.1: 220; E: 40), of defeating a tradition of universalizing claims about the secular nature of the Italian Renaissance derived from Burckhardt in order to provide a more inspiring model of spiritual "rebirth" for a wartime and postwar Germany under duress. Burckhardtian claims discard the actual complexity of the period, Burdach argues, with its "endless series of multiple spiritual phenomena and quite different personalities" (Burdach 101), substituting for it (in what Benjamin describes as a "hypostasizing fashion," G: 221; E: 40) an "arbitrary" (Burdach 102) moment of origin and label. The specific position against which Burdach tilts here—identified in the original essay directly following the claims of arbitrariness, but which Benjamin does not cite—is associated with the image of Renaissance man so commonly associated with Burckhardt, namely a "free, genius-like personality, audaciously frivolous in corrupt sinfulness, a type of aesthetic immorality" (Burdach 102). Benjamin confirms that Burdach is correct in this critique (G: 1.1: 221; E: 40). Burdach is also right, Benjamin goes on to note, to reject falsifying abstractions produced by those who would, like the Scholastic realists of the Middle Ages, subordinate the complexity of *realia* to words (cf. Burdach 101). Suggesting that perhaps Burdach was also himself "shy," or wary, about such "constitutive ideas" (G: 1.1: 220; E: 40), Benjamin nevertheless goes on to offer, by way of supplementing the earlier scholar's claims, a defense of the "necessity" of certain kinds of abstractions in any "epistemological theory" that, like Benjamin's own, is concerned with "essences" and "ideas" and their relationship to the "matter" of specific "historical periods" (221; 41). Just as Burdach openly contests the critical hegemony of Burckhardt's claims about the Renaissance, Benjamin's

24. Benjamin was aware of Burdach's anti-Burckhardtian position; see the notes Benjamin made on "Burdach's polemic against Burckhardt" (*Gesammelte Schriften* 1.3: 918).

discussion of the Baroque will provide an alternative to conventional definitions of the period as the poor cousin of a classicizing "Renaissance."

In the essay that Benjamin cites, Burdach undercuts the prevailing "idea" of a ruthless and destructive Burckhardtian Renaissance by advocating instead a picture of the period characterized by a countervailing, yet ultimately equally as abstract "idea" of a religiously inflected and spiritual "rebirth" (107) of "an ideal human-ity" (103) that is, Burdach claims, at the core of the trio of periods indicated in the title of his book: *Reformation, Renaissance, Humanismus*. This rebirth had emerged with particular salience in Germany, he writes.[25] The "constitutive" power of this version of the Renaissance for a demoralized wartime Germany was considerable. Indeed, even as Burdach tries to stay close to the historical "matter" in his sys-tematic review of "multiple spiritual phenomena," his real agenda is to develop the "idea" of a spiritually driven Renaissance out of an elaborate "constellation" of sources from a number of traditions that is capable of moving ever forward in time. The terms are of course Benjamin's (G: 1.1: 214–15; E: 34–35), but they are useful for understanding what he finds significant in Burdach, namely the "parcel[ing] out and redeem[ing]" (215; 34) into a new "representation" of a period of versions of that period that were previously undervalued or ignored because they did not fit the pattern of conventional claims, on the one hand, and then unleashing that period into its own posthistory, on the other.

The Renaissance was a period not of Burckhardtian individualism or the return of antiquity, Burdach argues, but rather one that celebrated the "idea" of the spiri-tual rebirth of mankind. No longer just (although also) an intellectualized "spiritual revolution" (Burdach 10), the actual rebirth that was at the center of the historical Renaissance is best exemplified, he claims, by the contentious career of the Italian visionary Cola di Rienzo (1313–54). According to Burdach, this rebirth was, more-over, not restricted to Italy. It was also at the core of the "German humanism" of the eighteenth century visible in the work of Winckelmann and Goethe (200–202; a trajectory not unlike Cysarz's is reflected here) as well as in the "third flowering of humanism" said to be occurring in the Germany of his own time (202).[26] Given the upbeat tenor of this argument as it was originally developed at the moment war was declared, it is easy to see why Benjamin—in the postwar period of Germany's defeat—might have hesitated to endorse the wisdom of proposing the "idea" of

---

25. Although Burdach's argument about the purely spiritual "origin" of the Renaissance was at odds with the dominant historiographic positions at the time, which argued the greater importance of sociological and political factors in the emergence of the "new" age, it was widely received and debated, especially among German scholars, at the time as a way of linking developments during the Renaissance in Italy with developments in the North, and thus seeing the possibility of a Renaissance in the land of the Reformation. See Fubini; Ferguson.

26. The claim is reiterated in the new "foreword" to Burdach's 1918 book, where he asserts that the ideas he originally developed in the essay, some four years earlier, are "now" (e.g., in 1918) "after the events of the past four years" of even greater relevance for a post–World War I population in desperate need of finding "lofty . . . goals for humanity." On the politically problematic phenomenon of the "third" wave of humanism in pre-1933 Germany, see Malgarini.

such a period and its eternal return, and he deftly sidesteps its overtly patriotic fervor by claiming that such projects are often determined by "contemporary interests and not by historiographic ideas" (G: 1.1: 221; E: 41). Yet Benjamin does go on to attempt to recuperate—in these dense pages of the "Epistemo-Critical Prologue"— Burdach's original discussion of pro- and antinominalist period designations via a close reading of the essay, closing with the claim that although "as far as historical types and epochs in particular are concerned," ideas such as "the Renaissance" and "the Baroque" can never really account for their "subject matter" in full, they are nevertheless necessary to the critic precisely "as ideas" (221; 41). In secret accord with Burdach, then, Benjamin argues that period names are in fact indispensable, even if they do not provide an absolute "methodological guarantee" (221; 41) in the face of the famous "eddy" (226; 45) of historical detail. The "idea" of a Burdachian "rebirth" of the spirit in present-day Germany is thus retained.

Benjamin's concern in the early sections of the "Epistemo-Critical Prologue" with the relationship of the particular to the general, the empirical to the theoretical, thus engages a number of epistemological, philosophical, and historiographic debates about period labels that were being conducted at the time and intervenes in them via his engagement with projects like Stachel's, Cysarz's, and Burdach's. No absolute idealist, Benjamin goes on to critique "polemical discussions" that would propose clean standoffs between "ideas" of distinct opposing sides, as if "the epochs confronted one another openly [*mit offenem Visier*] and in completely above board ways at the great turning points of history" (G: 1.1: 221; E: 41). The "knightly" epochs engaged in "open helm"–combat here are, I would argue, the periods of the Renaissance and the Baroque; at stake is the status of a German rebirth. Burdach had developed a similar critique of the periodization debates in his book, maintaining— in a formulation so close to Benjamin's discussion of origin (*Ursprung*) that it is hard to miss—that because "humanism never existed as a sealed totality" (100–101), it was the job of the historian (Burdach cites Eduard Meyer here) to understand "that which has become as something becoming . . . to place himself in the moment, when what history confronts us with as 'fact' is not yet, but is only in the process of becoming" (97–98). In spite of such qualifications, both Burdach and Benjamin nevertheless ultimately do have recourse to integral period "ideas" in their respective work, since such categories are the only way, as Benjamin states and Burdach's work shows, that "extremes" of evidence can be accommodated as a "synthesis" (G: 1.1: 221; E: 41) of claims.[27] That both Benjamin and Burdach cannot help but

---

27. The genres of tragedy and tragic drama are similarly useful, according to Benjamin, in dealing with manifold dramatic phenomena; "tragic drama . . . is an idea" (G: 1.1: 218; E: 38) that prevents one from dealing with evidence as a matter of mere inventory taking, an approach that is also unacceptably unphilosophical. That his more abstruse formulations in the *Ideenlehre* section of the "Prologue" were always conceived of as a way of expressing his ideas about both period and genre is evident in Benjamin's schematic note (*Gesammelte Schriften* 1.3: 918) to the effect that "the cultural historical period concepts, concepts of style and of genre are ideas."

refer to what are clearly defined as preexisting "ideas," such as humanism and the Baroque, even as they seek to derive their properties only from the "irreducible multiplicity" (223; 43) of their phenomenal "details," may be what Benjamin means when he claims that any scholarship that "protests against the language of its own investigations" is absurd (222; 42). It is as much of an absurdity to write about the Baroque only in the conceptual and critical vocabulary of the Renaissance, in other words, as it is not to assume the existence of an autonomous Baroque, however defined, when turning to its texts. Questions about what exactly the Baroque was that was being assumed to exist, where it resided, and where its "phenomena" could best be observed were at the center of the late nineteenth- and early twentieth-century art historical and art theoretical debates about the Baroque to which I now turn.

Locating Baroque Style

Benjamin claims in a letter to Florens Christian Rang that he wrote as he was working on his *Habilitation* that the issue of "how works of art relate to historical life" was the question that lay at the center of his thinking about the tragic drama (*Briefe* 1: 322). Michael Jennings argues that the overall project Benjamin describes here was designed as a way of "isolat[ing] within individual works those fragments that are inscribed with the structure and proper experience of an epoch, and *only then* to move back from the specific observation to cultural and societal generalizations" ("Walter Benjamin" 78–79). As much of the letter to Rang reads as if it were inserted word for word into the parts of the "Epistemo-Critical Prologue" just discussed, the possibility that it might be necessary to posit the "idea" of the historical Baroque first, and then turn to the works said to embody it, suggests that Jennings's sequence may need to be revisited, if not reversed. Nevertheless, he is correct in his understanding of Benjamin's concerns in the letter, especially if, on the one hand, we understand the "works of art" (*Briefe* 1: 322) to which Benjamin refers to be the actual "phenomenal" texts of the tragic dramas themselves, and, on the other, see the question of their relation to "cultural . . . generalizations" as a matter of "epoch," or period, designations like "the Baroque." In the work of two of the art historians most often associated with the "formalist" method of close readings of works of art and with discussions of how to define the Baroque as an independent period and style, namely Heinrich Wölfflin and Alois Riegl, we see attempts to solve the question of how the relationship between the work of art and the "structure and proper experience" of a new, non-Renaissance Baroque epoch could be both described and explained. Benjamin's discussion of the "origin" of the German tragic drama bears witness to and evolves in conversation with Wölfflin's and Riegl's attempts to define the origins of the Baroque in similar ways, which unlink it from the Renaissance by (re)locating it and its artifacts in a place that is both literally and discursively new.

It is not by chance that Benjamin claims in his *Tragic Drama* book that the only methodologically sound alternative to either the earlier nationalist literary histories that dismissed the Baroque as "un-German," or readings that cast its plays as sterile "Renaissance dramas," lies in what he calls a "serious criticism of style" (G: 1.1: 240; E: 59). He writes that he intends to open a window onto the "form world" (257; 78) of the Baroque tragic drama "far away from the preserve of Hamburg dramaturgy, not to speak of post-classical dramaturgy too" (257; 78). Formal questions have long been claimed to underlie many of the contemporary accounts of what distinguished the style of the historical period of the Baroque from that of the Renaissance, as noted at the outset of this chapter, even as they also provided the terms in which the two periods and their works could be compared. The question of how location, or place, and specific cultural or national traditions, such as the one indicated in Benjamin's reference to Gotthold Ephraim Lessing's *Hamburgische Dramaturgie* (Hamburg Dramaturgy) here, helped define the role of stylistics in periodization theory has received less attention to date.

Discussions of the Baroque were carried on so widely in German-speaking Europe during the early twentieth century that, by 1926, Josef Körner could quip that the issue had already been the talk of the town in "all lanes and squares" (456) for over a decade. The period was nowhere so prominently an object of debate as in the history and theory of art.[28] That the parameters of such discussions were often associated with the work of two of the most visible scholars in these fields, namely Wölfflin and Riegl, emerges in the short review essay "Strenge Kunstwissenschaft" (The Rigorous Study of Art) (1933) that Benjamin began planning in 1931 and finally published five years after the tragic drama study appeared in print. In some ways, the essay can be read as part of Benjamin's apparent preparations for a second edition of the *Tragic Drama* book: a résumé probably dating from the year in which the book originally appeared suggests that Benjamin was interested in making a clearer statement about how to understand a "stylistically" marked work of art also as an "integrated expression, restricted in no area- or discipline-specific way, of the religious, metaphysical, political, and economic trends of an epoch" (*Gesammelte Schriften* 1.3: 886).[29] The terms resonate with those used in the essay. Benjamin's

28. It has long been assumed, at least since Hermand's 1965 *Literaturwissenschaft und Kunstwissenschaft* (Literary Studies and the Study of Art), if not before, that it was the art historical debates that determined the literary-historical and critical ones. See Kiesant (79) and Hans-Harald Müller ("Die Übertragung des Barockbegriffs" 97) for a reconsideration of the "astonishing self-evidence" of the assumption that it was in art history that the Renaissance-Baroque debates found their origin. Alpers also discusses the interpretive problems created by this logic.

29. Benjamin obviously began making notes for a new edition of the *Tragic Drama* book sometime after 1928, as the sheet of paper with the title "Addenda to the Tragic Drama," with its reference to a 1928 number of the *Deutsche Literaturzeitung,* shows (*Gesammelte Schriften* 1.3: 952–54, here 953); that these notes focus primarily on enhancing his understanding of the historical specificity of the phenomenon of the tragic drama as part of early modern political and social history may not have been at odds with his interest in the art theoretical debates he comments on in his essay "The Rigorous Study of Art." I will not be dealing here with the often heated debate about the relationship between the Baroque and the styles and canon of what came to be known as Mannerist art, on which Benjamin's book sheds less light. On the relation of the Baroque and Mannerism, also in terms of discussions about classicism, see Link-Heer.

discussion there of Wölfflin and Riegl shines light on the debates in art history and art theory about the origins of the Baroque as a new and modern alternative to the Renaissance, debates that, like Benjamin's argument in his adaptation of them, offered alternatives to the approaches represented by Stachel's and Cysarz's work.

In "The Rigorous Study of Art," Benjamin claims to see a difference between Wölfflin and Riegl. As Sigrid Weigel, among others, has pointed out (117), Benjamin seems to distance himself from Wölfflin here by claiming that the author of *Kunstgeschichtliche Grundbegriffe* (Principles of Art History) (1915) was both the victim and a continuing perpetrator of the distinction between an "old-fashioned" and "conventional" paradigm of "universal history" and an "academic aesthetics" (*Gesammelte Schriften* 3: 373, 370). Against what he identifies as Wölfflin's "formalist" method of "analysis" (370), Benjamin would thus appear to side with Riegl and with his far more "sober" (372) theory of history, which recaptures the possibility of an apology for even the most unlikely periods of art as well as a combinatory, even interdisciplinary approach to cultural history writ large. Much has been made of Benjamin's allegiance to and even radicalization of Riegl's celebration of so-called decadent periods. His indebtedness to Riegl for methods of determining the relation of the individual works of art to "collectivities" of society and epochs, rather than to the "subjectivities" of individual artists, has also been noted.[30] Nevertheless, the distinctions Benjamin makes between Riegl and Wölfflin in this essay do not undercut what he ultimately announces as their shared commitment to the "overcoming of conventional universal history, with its so-called 'peaks' and periods of decline," or decay (373).[31] What Benjamin perceives as the link between Wölfflin and Riegl is apparent in what Wölfflin's *Principles of Art History,* and, just as importantly, his earlier book *Renaissance und Barock* (Renaissance and Baroque) (1888), do in fact have in common with Riegl's *Die Entstehung der Barockkunst in Rom* (The Emergence of Baroque Art in Rome) (1908), namely the need to develop a narrative of the Baroque that positioned it precisely *not* as the decline of the Renaissance, but, rather, as what Wölfflin in *Principles* calls a "change in style" (*Kunstgeschichtliche Grundbegriffe* 10), a change that emerged out of and in accordance with an integrated "new idea" (*Anschauung*) (131), with its own norms.

Identifying these norms and thus the Renaissance-Baroque relation as a matter of a "change in style" depends in both Wölfflin and Riegl on a logic of comparison between the two periods that was, if not sequential, then at least part of a different

---

30. Jennings claims: "Riegl's method pushes Benjamin toward the idea that the organizing principle of the work of art lies not in the work itself, or even in its individual producer, but in a series of historical principles and attitudes external to the work which are in turn encapsulated in the discrete details of the formal properties of the object" ("Walter Benjamin" 89).

31. Benjamin was not the only one to have seen similarities between Riegl and Wölfflin in this regard. Holly (*Panofsky* 46) cites Dittmann on the "congruency" of Wölfflin's and Riegl's "theories on stylistic change." See also Hauser (158) and Ackerman (319) on their similarities.

narrative of development than the decay thesis.[32] Scholars have suggested that both theorists rejected overly simplistic "materialist" and cognitive causalities (e.g., that stylistic change occurs because of changes in materials and technology, or simply because consumers of art became bored with the Renaissance and needed the stimulation associated with a new style).[33] In the absence of such explanations, Wölfflin and Riegl had to account for what occasioned the difference of the Baroque from the Renaissance in some other way. I argue here that both offered explanations of stylistic difference and change by linking style to the "foundational sensibility" (*Renaissance und Barock* 56) of a period and to "the character of a nation (*Volk*)" (*Kunstgeschichtliche Grundbegriffe* 9), in the case of Wölfflin, and to the famously murky concept of the "artistic will" (*Kunstwollen*) of both places and times, in the case of Riegl (see below). Benjamin's own project to root the independent "artistic feeling" of the German Baroque in a specific national tradition resonates with both sets of ideas.[34] Because a strange division of interpretive labor has made it common to associate Benjamin's work with Riegl, but to exclude the matter of the Baroque, while associating the penetration of art historical debates about the Baroque into literary studies with Wölfflin, but excluding Benjamin's intersection with this process, I deal first with Wölfflin's evaluation of the claim that the Baroque represented "modernity," paying special attention to his struggle to identify the causes of change in either period and national "ethnic" place ("Zeit-" and "Volkscharakter," *Kunstgeschichtliche Grundbegriffe* 9). I then show how these questions find different solutions in Riegl's approach to the Baroque, which identifies it (and by extension, all styles) as the expression of a located, collective "artistic will."

It difficult to avoid Heinrich Wölfflin (1864–1945) in discussions of the Baroque. Indeed, he is—and was, even during his own lifetime—a "classic," as Marshall Brown notes (379), not only because of the reputation indicated by his inheritance in 1893 of his teacher Burckhardt's professorial chair in Basel, but also because he was soon named to positions in art history in Berlin and Munich as well.[35] The Berlin position in particular was a mark of his prominence at the time; his *Principles of Art History* is, moreover, still read as one of the texts, if not as *the* text, that

---

32. Jennings asserts that many of the art historians whose work Benjamin endorsed were moving away from "developmental narratives" in the "history of the arts" to the "study" of the immanent characteristics of "single works" ("Walter Benjamin" 80–83). In "The Rigorous Study of Art," Benjamin nevertheless makes it clear that what he appreciates in the "new" kind of art history that Riegl's work represents is its ability to move "from the individual object" to its larger and somehow historically rooted "spiritual function." See Pächt on Riegl, as cited in Benjamin, *Gesammelte Schriften* 3: 372.

33. See, respectively, Riegl, *Spätrömische Kunstindustrie* 8–9; and Wölfflin, *Renaissance und Barock* 52–54.

34. Benjamin uses the term "artistic feeling" in the "Nachträge zum Trauerspielbuch" (*Gesammelte Schriften* 1.3: 953) in connection with the need to return to the work on post-Reformation art by Helmuth Plessner in preparation for a second edition. Later associated with the Frankfurt School, Plessner became famous for his interdisciplinary philosophical anthropology.

35. On Wölfflin's biography, see Warnke, "On Heinrich Wölfflin," with additional bibliography there.

sets the terms of how to discuss stylistics and the Baroque.[36] The exact details of these discussions and their relation to Wölfflin's earlier *Renaissance and Baroque* may nevertheless need to be reviewed. Benjamin claims in "The Rigorous Study of Art" that Wölfflin's method, predicated primarily on "formal analysis" (*Gesammelte Schriften* 3: 370), was different from Burckhardt's. This is the same "formal analysis" of the five famous elements—linear versus painterly, planar versus recessional, closed versus open forms, unity in diversity versus unity in singularity, and absolute versus relative clarity—that is still often said to define the two different styles of Renaissance and Baroque art. While his reading of Wölfflin is thus not unusual, Benjamin's accusation of formalism here may in fact be a somewhat "glib" reading of what were actually the far more complex ways in which Wölfflin presented his explanation of the "history" of art, ways that were not unlike Riegl's— and also in some respects closer to Benjamin's own.[37]

While Benjamin refers primarily to the *Principles of Art History* in his commentary on Wölfflin, it was in the much earlier *Renaissance and Baroque* that Wölfflin first dismissed the Baroque-as-decay-of-the-Renaissance thesis to which Benjamin also objects. Originally written as his own *Habilitation,* Wölfflin's book has three parts, the first concerned with defining the "essence" of the shift from Renaissance to Baroque, the second with the all-important "reasons" for this shift, and only in the third section with describing the period's "typical" stylistic characteristics as evident in both the sacred and the secular architecture of Italy. This last section is the one that later came to be associated with Wölfflin's signature formalism.[38] Its organization underscores the book's position at a crossroads for both its author and the discipline of art history. Even as the first and last sections are marked by an elaborate call-and-response relationship to existing scholarship, and especially to several of Wölfflin's teacher Burckhardt's books, the rhetorically and methodologically most striking moment of *Renaissance and Baroque* is nevertheless its central section. Entitled "Die Gründe der Stilwandlung" (The Reasons for the Change in Style), this is where Wölfflin issues an impassioned appeal to some of the ideas he had developed in his Munich dissertation of just a few years earlier, "Prolegomena zu einer Psychologie der Architektur" (Prolegomena to a Psychology of Architecture) (1886), as a way of addressing the question of the origin of stylistic change

---

36. *Principles of Art History* went through two printings within three years of publication—and this during the height of World War I. Nevertheless, see Warnke, "On Heinrich Wölfflin" 172–73, on the tempered reaction by more conservative fellow art historians.

37. Holly ("Wölfflin and the Imagining of the Baroque" 350) calls some readings of Wölfflin (although not Benjamin's) "glib." Benjamin's rejection of Wölfflin's approach as still beholden to a "rigidly periodic" "universal history" actually puts Benjamin's reading on a collision course with the more recent approaches to Wölfflin of Holly and Brown, who are interested in a task for the Baroque that differs from Benjamin's.

38. It may be worth noting that Wölfflin also uses the category of "origin" (*Ursprung*) here in not un-Benjaminian ways to address the question of the afterlife of the Renaissance and of what "became" of it in the period of the Baroque (*Renaissance und Barock* 3).

(*Renaissance und Barock* 55 n. 2).[39] The "reasons" he gives here are not entirely satisfactory, however, and he moves to other explanations, including those of national ethnic place, in later work.

In *Renaissance and Baroque,* Wölfflin explains that earlier art historical treatments of the periods had been Vasari-like "lives of artists," which favored implicit hierarchies of achievement and value; these hierarchies had generated many of the sorting categories adopted to organize and display the history of art writ large. His current attempt not merely to describe, but also to explain the "*reasons* for the shift in style" from Renaissance to Baroque in particular as the result of changes in the historical "foundational sensibility" (*Renaissance und Barock* 56) of specific times was in fact a novelty. It also went beyond the kinds of political and social history that Burckhardt had adduced in his book on the Renaissance in Italy as the explanation for period emergence, for example, to holistic arguments about changes in cultural sensibility as they became visible in works of art. Wölfflin's restriction of his discussion in *Renaissance and Baroque* to "Italian art"—"the northern peoples," he claims, "had not yet gone though this phase of development" (1)—calls attention to the fact that here, precisely by avoiding the question of the durability of his period-based claims across national borders, Wölfflin actually fails to address the issue that would have made his explanation a compelling alternative to the decay thesis, namely that the difference was a matter *not* of period change or stylistic "development," but, rather, of place. The elision of comparative material in *Renaissance and Baroque,* to which Wölfflin himself calls attention here, suggests the reasons why he had to return to address these same first-principle questions about the relationship between style, period, and place in the later *Principles of Art History,* where he struggles more openly—and also in a deliberately comparative way—with the categories with which he intends not only to describe differences in style, but also in which he will find the "reasons" (*Gründe*) for them.

Already in the opening chapter, the "introduction" to *Renaissance and Baroque,* Wölfflin rejects an understanding of the Baroque as a period of "decadence," and thus creates the same need to develop an alternative positive explanation for the difference between the Renaissance and the Baroque that Benjamin later confronts. Wölfflin indicates his—and the profession's—more or less antithetical position to the association with the Baroque of terms such as "dissolution" and "decay," as well as to the notion that the period was a "degenerated form" of the Renaissance; he explicitly refers to such dismissals of the Baroque as positions to which "we have become accustomed" (*Renaissance und Barock* 1), but that, along with the associations of the Baroque with the bizarre and the monstrous that abounded "in

---

39. On the dissertation and on Wölfflin's preference for "psychological interpretation" rather than "formal analysis of style," see Brown 389–91. Both Dittmann (64) and Podro (104) correctly see the question of the "reasons" for changes in period style as central for Wölfflin, although both find the issue more compellingly (if not always satisfactorily) addressed in the earlier rather than the later work.

vernacular usage," are not useful, particularly for professionals, who in any case no longer entertain such associations with the period as it is specified under its "art historical name" (11). The need to move away from such stances on the Baroque is important enough to Wölfflin for him to return to it at the opening of the central methodological chapter, where he again cites and reports on, yet also rejects theories of the formal transition between the Renaissance and the Baroque that depend on organicizing metaphors of flowers that necessarily "wilt" and loose their blooms. Such theories, he explains, contribute "little" to an explanation of Baroque style (53). Contra the claim that Wölfflin somehow "subscribed" to "organicist" or "morphological" views that saw the Baroque as emerging with a certain inevitability out of the falling-off of the Renaissance (Hauser 142–43; Brown 381), then, he in fact rejects them here as summarily as he rejected the popular renderings to which he refers earlier on.

The strict oppositions that many scholars have seen in Wölfflin's work between "two distinct styles of art, that of the Renaissance and that of the Baroque," are thus not invoked in *Renaissance and Baroque* to describe the Baroque as a lesser, or failed period.[40] This is not to say that he does not compare and contrast Renaissance and Baroque art in terms of harmonious "Being" versus a more tumultuous "Becoming" (*Renaissance und Barock* 23), for example. The Renaissance is characterized as the age of the famously balanced "golden section" (49) and reveals a certain "graceful ease" (28) and "calm" (41). The Baroque, by contrast, is distinguished by all that is "heavy" (28, 58), massive (34), and "uneasy" (45). These are the adjectives and descriptions of style that, in their association with the two periods in Wölfflin's formulations both here and in the later *Principles of Art History,* rapidly became orthodoxy in stylistic theory; it is thus not surprising that those identified as Baroque resonate with Benjamin's (later) claims about the heaviness of the Baroque prince's "creatureliness," for example, and the "restless" changeability of the Baroque sovereign (G: 1.1: 249–53 and 264; E: 70–72 and 85). Benjamin's use of these Wölfflinian categories to see Baroque traits in the German tragic dramas is nevertheless precisely what allowed him to understand the period and its style in positive terms, since, as often as Wölfflin adopts what Martin Warnke ("Die Entstehung des Barockbegriffs") sees as a negatively inflected rhetoric in association with the Baroque, just as often an even stronger and more celebratory evaluative vocabulary condenses around it as well, particularly insofar as the Baroque is said to represent a new period "spirit" and "way of seeing" that are specifically its own, not evidence of a "belated Renaissance," as Wölfflin explicitly writes, but, rather, of a new epoch and way of seeing and style (*Renaissance und Barock* 60–61). He describes "painterly" elements, such as "layering," for example, that prevent Baroque painting from becoming "boring" (19); its nearly "pathological" (36) and

---

40. See Holly, "Wölfflin and the Imagining of the Baroque" 347.

even "violent" (41) devotion to "movement" is likewise "passionate" and "engaged" (36, 41; 36, 59). According to Wölfflin, it is, finally, the Baroque's signature "movement" that guarantees both "tension" (45) and even a kind of exciting "stimulation" (*Reiz*), both of which are then said to testify to the "resounding and intoxicating richness that is proper to the Baroque" (46). When measured against the excitement of such Baroque "dissonances" and their resolutions (51), which are in any case to be enjoyed by only the sophisticated as opposed to the "untrained eye" (50), the balanced harmonies of the Renaissance begin to appear "trivial" (50), Wölfflin suggests. His "sympathies" would thus indeed appear to lie "with the [B]aroque," as Brown claims (394).[41]

Wölfflin's argument here does not yet offer any fully articulated alternative to the "developmental" thesis about the history of art that Arnold Hauser, for example, already some years ago famously claimed was central to both Wölfflin's and Riegl's "Hegelian" approaches (131, 143, 147–50). Indeed, even though Wölfflin explicitly rejects the thesis that the Baroque either "emerged" out of the failure of the Renaissance or was "in a Hegelian manner . . . a necessary reaction" to it (*Renaissance und Barock* 54 n. 2), he can—in somewhat anti-, or, perhaps better, not-yet-typological fashion—still claim little more than that it is a period best associated with formal impulses that were more or less exclusively and essentially new, both etymologically (as he shows in his discussion of the term "new style," 10) and in the rhetoric of his book. "The Baroque is nevertheless something essentially new that cannot be deduced from that which came before" (54), he writes.[42] The refrain concerning the novelty of the Baroque—specifically in contrast with the Renaissance (22)—is constant; the period exemplifies "the new formal feeling" (4, 42), "the new art" (6, 47), "the new forms" (9), and "the new style" (62).[43] But even this insistence cannot yet accomplish what Wölfflin seems to hope it will, namely "*explain*" (58, emphasis in original) the origin of the formal changes between the

---

41. Brown is nevertheless referring to the later *Principles of Art History* here. Again, see Warnke ("Die Entstehung des Barockbegriffs" 1218–19) for a different reading of Wölfflin's "condemnation" of the Baroque as a critique of the loss of "bourgeois individualism" in the modern (e.g., late nineteenth-century, neo-Absolutist) age in *Renaissance and Baroque*. Warnke also cites Jakob von Falke's celebration of Baroque "individualism" in the latter's *Geschichte des Geschmackes im Mittelalter* (1892) to the effect that, in breaking all the rules of the Renaissance, the "genial artists" of the Baroque were celebrating "the rights of individuality" (qtd. in Warnke, "Die Entstehung des Barockbegriffs" 1222), and claims that the later Wölfflin of *Principles* found his way to a similarly positive evaluation of the period precisely in conjunction with more "modern" developments (1222).

42. Hauser mysteriously argues for reading Wölfflin as representing the position that "every step of development is determined by the one that came before and that is aimed in a clear direction" (134).

43. Wölfflin goes on to argue that the Baroque was the style that first developed "without models" and was "consciously aware" of the need to get beyond "what had been inherited from Antiquity" (*Renaissance und Barock* 10). "Any sense that there is something divine to be adored in even the smallest trace of antiquity is gone" (12). Even at the time, the "epithet" of the "new" was a sign of high praise (10) for a period marked by its "self-confidence" and sense of superiority to things of the past (12). The several freedoms that Wölfflin associates with this unantique Baroque are uncannily similar to Benjamin's regarding the difference between the tragic drama and ancient tragedy.

periods in any compelling way. It is here that he famously admits that defining "architectural style" as an "expression of its time" (55) is as difficult as explaining "which bridge leads from the Jesuits to Baroque style." "Which one is the path that leads from the cell of the Scholastic philosopher to the hut of the architect?" (56), he inquires. The real challenge to confront is thus, as Wölfflin informs us, precisely how to link the newness of Baroque style with the "foundational sensibility of the time" that "produces" the changed historical "products" (56).

In the early *Renaissance and Baroque,* Wölfflin cites his own earlier work on the psychology of art to support his claim that "that which determines" the "formal imagination" of the artist is a "foundational sensibility" (56), which he also describes as the "life-feeling of an era" (57). This "feeling" is in turn captured in and based on the relationship to Baroque architectural forms of Man's "physical being" (56). The explanation is presciently Panofskyian and suggests another origin of the term *habitus.* Architecture is, Wölfflin writes, "the expression of a time to the extent that it [architecture] allows the physical being of Man, the way he carries himself and moves, his manner [*Haltung*] as playfully graceful or as seriously weighted down, his excited or peaceful way of being, to become visible in the relations of the body to monuments" (56–57). The shift from one epochal "manner" of "holding oneself" to another thus explains change; the argument is based on what Michael Podro sees as a flawed "empathy theory" that projects "a sense of the inward feeling of our bodily state onto the inanimate object" (100) but does little to explain how such a feeling is linked "with the surrounding culture" (103) in any way that justifies the claim that style is an "expression of its time." Wölfflin's "rehabilitation" of the Baroque in *Renaissance and Baroque* via claims for its newness may well serve, then, as a demonstration of his famous motto, "Not everything is possible at all times." But it fails to identify the "reasons" for difference that he seeks. It does, however, shed light on why, if he wants to defend the Baroque, Wölfflin must move away from the mere formal description of differing styles most often associated with his work toward an interrogation of other causalities of difference in artistic forms that go beyond the notion of an epochal "sensibility" to arguments from place. This is precisely what Wölfflin does in the better-known *Principles of Art History,* which Benjamin refers to alongside Riegl in "The Rigorous Study of Art." Benjamin's association in the essay of Riegl with the preferred method of looking for the "relationship" between the "historical process" and "the curiosity of the work of art" (*Gesammelte Schriften* 3: 372) notwithstanding, then, there is also a very Wölfflinian set of issues subtending the claim for the autonomy of the historical Baroque and his interest, as Benjamin writes there, in trying to get to the bottom of "the laws and problems of the development of art" (372).

Wölfflin was aware that he had not solved the important questions in his *Renaissance and Baroque.* Indeed, he even corrects his earlier claims at one point in a footnote in the later *Principles of Art History,* calling the 1888 book a piece of "juvenalia" (251 n. 1). Nevertheless, the very continuities between the version of the Baroque he had offered in the earlier study and its subsequent theorization in 1915, which soon became the most cited definition of the period bar none, indicate that many of the same issues were still being addressed. Wölfflin's *Principles of Art History* continues to be firm in its rejection of the decay thesis as a description of Baroque art. Equally as prominent is the ongoing association of "newness" with Baroque style. As in the earlier work, Wölfflin also asserts here, for example, that "the metaphorical analogy, bud—bloom—decay," has played only "a misleading role" in the project of understanding how "periods" relate to one another (*Kunstgeschichtliche Grundbegriffe* 14). Moreover, his claims that the Baroque does not necessarily mean "progress" (31) do not mask his continuing belief in the essentially upbeat novelty of its forms in their "awakening of a new feeling for beauty" (31). The age also displays "a new emotional realm" and "a new ideal of life" (10–11). The Baroque tendency to "unity," which is also evidence of "something that is overall new" (168), in fact conjures up precisely a sense of progress, or, if not progress, then a sense of stimulating excitement; *Reiz* is again the word Wölfflin most often associates with the Baroque here (126–27, 132, 163, 166, 211, 222). Against the liveliness (165) of the Baroque, Renaissance "classicism," in its "obedience" to the "rules" (161), can in turn represent only a kind of stylistic stasis (165) and death (140). Wölfflin states his main point in clear terms: "The Baroque is neither the decline nor the increase of the classical, but rather, in general, an entirely different art" (15).

Wölfflin's refusal to rank the Renaissance over the Baroque is probably the origin of the claim of relativism that critics like Ernst Gombrich have associated with the *Principles of Art History.* But it also explains the elaborate balancing act that is the most prominent feature of Wölfflin's lengthy elaboration of his famous five categories in the book.[44] His detailed exemplification of the categories makes clear why it has been difficult for critics to see anything other than the description of these dyads in *Principles;* Wölfflin's dichotomizing evaluative grids structure the book in its entirety and have thus long been seen as best defining the differences between the art of the Renaissance and that of the Baroque.[45] It may well be that it is the presentational rhetoric of Wölfflin's *Principles of Art History,* in other words,

---

44. Neither the "classical" Renaissance nor the "painterly" Baroque is a superior style or age in these descriptions: "The painterly mode is the later mode and is not imaginable without the first [the linear]. But it is also not the absolutely superior one" (Wölfflin, *Kunstgeschichtliche Grundbegriffe* 20); likewise, "the older [linear] art . . . was able to represent all that it wanted to" and thus did not feel "restricted" by not yet being "painterly" (32). The desire to be what Lepsky calls "value free" (199) may have been what suggested to Wölfflin that he should fill his book with balancing dyads, from the linear "art of being" versus the painterly "art of appearance" (*Kunstgeschichtliche Grundbegriffe* 23) to Dürer versus Rembrandt (25), Sansovino versus Puget (64–65), "Koordination" versus "Subordination" (171), and so on, with facing illustrations always asserting a standoff yet also a truce between the periods and styles.

45. It may well be true, as Holly ("Wölfflin and the Imagining of the Baroque") suggests, that the structure of Wölfflin's book mirrors the Renaissance's "classic" principle of balance and proportionality, but it is difficult to claim that the point of the book is to privilege its art.

and not the substance of his claims, that has had the effect of masking, or at least drawing attention away from, the larger, perhaps even deeper struggle going on in its pages, a struggle not just to describe the two styles, but also to identify the "origins" and "reasons" for their differences. This is a task Wölfflin carried forth with him from the earlier *Renaissance and Baroque,* and which was the conundrum at the heart of both Riegl's and Benjamin's confrontations with the period as well.

In *Principles of Art History,* the identification of the Baroque with the new is no longer part of the more general description of all postancient art, including the Renaissance, as "modern" (*Kunstgeschichtliche Grundbegriffe* 234). Rather, according to Wölfflin, the transition from the Renaissance to the Baroque is explicitly "a perfect example of how a new spirit of the times forces the creation of a new form" (10), a representative case, in other words, of how—telically—modernity is expressed in style.[46] The proposal here that there is a relation between "the spirit of the times" and its expression in form suggests the aspect of Wölfflin's version of the Baroque that, while the object of a sustained critique for its latent Hegelianism, in fact brings it even closer to what Benjamin claims he values in Riegl, namely an increasing methodological commitment to understanding how period style could be seen as an organically integrated expression of a particular located "spirit." Indeed, in this passage from the introduction to *Principles of Art History,* Wölfflin again, as in *Renaissance and Baroque,* makes the argument about the origin of art in "the spirit of the times" and "style of the times" only within the context of a single national tradition; it can be seen "best in Italy," he writes, "where that which persists in the Italian character remains highly visible in [spite of] change" (*Kunstgeschichtliche Grundbegriffe* 10). Introduce another tradition of "national sensibility," however, Wölfflin warns, and one might be "misled" to think the innovation is a matter of the differences between "Teutonic" and "Romance" types rather than of epoch styles (9). In mentioning the possibility, he of course betrays that he has himself already considered precisely this "misleading" thought. Latent in *Renaissance and Baroque,* where any given "system of forms" is said also to be dependent on "race" (*Renaissance und Barock* 57), and the impact of the "heartbeat of the soul of the nation" (57–58) on changes in style has to be weighed, Wölfflin's suggestion in the introduction to *Principles of Art History* is that, even though "the mark of history" and "national style" weigh differently in different artists, the question of a "national psychology of form" is the one that art history needs to address head-on. By 1915, there is thus no doubt that the way in which "historical character

---

46. If we miss the relationship to modernity of the "new" Baroque characteristic of "depth" in a picture by Vermeer, for example, the first question posed in Wölfflin's mind and then to the reader is "What is modern here?" (*Kunstgeschichtliche Grundbegriffe* 90). Wölfflin goes on to explain exactly where "modernity" is in Baroque art, whose "new style" (222) marks it as different from what is here nearly universally referred to as "the classical art of the Renaissance." For Wölfflin, the "modern" is what reminds him of contemporary movements in art, such as Impressionism (24–25), which, echoing his description of the Baroque, he calls an art of "victory of appearances over being" (24).

intersects with national character" is one of the main "reasons" for differences in style (*Kunstgeschichtliche Grundbegriffe* 9).

That Wölfflin entertained such ideas is not surprising, given the context. While Warnke claims that in 1915 Wölfflin "severed all ties binding forms to historical life" as a rejection of the "instrumentalization of the arts" (Warnke, "On Heinrich Wölfflin" 176–77) and the nationalistic slogans of Germany in World War I, he overlooks that the art historian continued all the same to use his "doctrine of the forms of seeing" of periods to lament, for example, that, in "a developmental history of occidental ways of seeing, the differences between the individual and national characters are no longer of great significance" (Wölfflin, *Kunstgeschichtliche Grundbegriffe* 13), on the one hand, and thus to argue for taking into account the possibility that a more powerful national or *ethnos*-based origin of style could account for the differences that set cultures apart, on the other.[47] It has long been assumed that Wölfflin privileged period-related categories in order to make the "developmental" claims that, according to Lorenz Dittmann, became the basis of a theory of the "periodicity" of circularly recurring styles (53).[48] Such readings overlook Wölfflin's repeated reference to place not only in the introduction to *Principles,* where he refers to the intersection of "school, nation, and race" (*Kunstgeschichtliche Grundbegriffe* 6) with period styles, but throughout the book, as when he states near its end: "It is now time that the historical presentation of European architecture no longer be organized merely by period—Gothic, Renaissance, and so on—but, rather, that it carve out national physiognomies" (254). As problematic as we might find their political implications, Wölfflin's claims here show that at the time a thesis that the origin of stylistic change might lie in nation may well have been considered a way not only to escape the problematic proximity to the decay thesis of the argument solely from period, but also to establish the difference between a Renaissance that was predominantly Italianate-Romance and indebted to antiquity, on the one hand, and a new northern—if not also Germanic—Baroque, on the other. In this context, it is interesting to note the contrastive rhetoric that characterizes Benjamin's invocation of Calderón in his discussions of the German tragic drama,

---

47. Warnke's reading supports the interpretation that Wölfflin's assertion of the predominance of period style, which would guarantee a kind of European internationalism, could be understood as a poignant denial of the jingoistic German nationalism around him. Yet the resignation that Dilly says marked Wölfflin in his later years (278) may likewise be linked to his earlier experience of the hysterical patriotism of wartime, which may have already found expression in his depressing recognition in 1915 that "national character" often played an equally important role in determining artistic agendas and style.

48. It should be noted that Wölfflin explicitly refuses the notion that the Renaissance-Baroque pattern merely repeats itself in eternal fashion and does so by introducing the figure of the "spiral" (*Kunstgeschichtliche Grundbegriffe* 253). Nothing ever repeats itself exactly; there is always enough of a difference in what appears to be a repetition that something new emerges. The question is where this difference occurs. It may not be by chance that Wölfflin turns immediately to the force of "national character" here (254).

for example, a dyadic logic that is surely indebted to Wölfflin. Even as he wants to make claims about understanding all drama of the seventeenth century in period terms, "in terms of the era" (G: 1.1: 270; E: 91), he writes, it is clear that for Benjamin, "German theater" tends in one direction in terms of staging, "the Spanish stage" in another (271–72; 93). In turn, what the "ideal courtier of the Spanish author" (e.g., Gracian) could achieve is impossible for "German dramatists" to represent (276–77; 97–98). Like Wölfflin, Benjamin constructs oppositions and then relies on a culturalist-nationalist argument to explain why difference occurs.

In the introduction to *Principles of Art History,* the nation emerges as a crucial factor in the history of style. Wölfflin asserts that, in principle, the "differences in individual and national character" should be subordinated to the homogeneity of a "developmental history" of "types" across all of Europe (*Kunstgeschichtliche Grundbegriffe* 13). However, such a claim for transnational period styles can be made, he admits, only by looking away from the "persistent national differences" that characterize art (194). Later, although the "history" of "linearity" can be said to be "approximately the same in the south and the north," "certain oppositions of national sensibility" (35) cannot be denied; "the linearity of the Latin races seemed somewhat cold for the German sensibility" (61). Indeed, because it is "undeniable that the nations differ from one another from the very beginning" (114), it is not surprising to discover that national and "ethnic" differences are captured in the allegedly permanent formal stylistic properties for which the book is best known. Thus "a painterly essence is lodged in the blood of the German race from the very beginning," Wölfflin writes (73), and "Teutonic art" and an essentialized "North" (159) favor "open form." "In Italy," however, "the most closed of forms" is preferred (157). Wölfflin's strong desire for a kind of transnational stylistic uniformity in any given period as an allegory for European unity may well inform the book that he wrote in the first years of World War I. In the conclusion to the *Principles of Art History,* it is precisely the task of describing a unifying "general path" of ways of seeing (244) that Wölfflin proposes: "As different as national characters may be, the universal-humanistic element that binds them together is stronger than that which separates them" (256). The vision is an appealing one. But as much as Wölfflin may want to argue that "the construction of a national type" is no more than a "rough diagram" for the historian (254) that will and must be superseded, it is clearly a robust enough explanatory principle to ultimately challenge any unifying and universalizing claims the book may want to make about the "development of style" across nations. Wölfflin lets slip often enough that the "newness" of Baroque style in particular may be more permanently anchored in place, or national difference, than the notion of "development" might suggest. "Wherever one goes, one confronts persistent differences in national imaginative forms" (208), he observes.

Most readings of *Principles of Art History* have concerned themselves only with the five interior chapters on the various stylistic pairs. They thus miss the way that Wölfflin's argument about the national character of style, launched in the introduction, careens toward a confusing end in the section ironically entitled "Conclusion"—ironically, because the argument does not really settle the question at all. Wölfflin asserts there that although "the development of modern occidental art" is "unified," "within this unity, we must accept an underlying difference in national type" (*Kunstgeschichtliche Grundbegriffe* 54). His ambivalence about whether or not the argument from nation, or place, might not in fact be more effective than an inter- or transnational developmental logic in accounting for stylistic difference thus seems to run deep. His desire to resist the decay thesis, to not play "epoch against epoch" (255), Renaissance against Baroque, must have in any case made the possibility of keeping them eternally apart via the claim of national styles extremely attractive in spite of its problematic resonances at the time. Or the argument from nation may have been palatable precisely because it accorded with Wölfflin's underlying belief that "every epoch carries its own measuring stick within itself" (77). If this is the case, however, then so too does "every people," every nation, have in its own "history of art" an epoch and style that can be identified as the one that contains "the actual revelation of its own national virtues" (255). "For the Teutonic North," Wölfflin writes, "that era is the Baroque" (256). *Principles* was not the last time that Wölfflin made this argument. The anchoring of a Baroque style in national identity emerges with even greater clarity in his essay "'Kunstgeschichtliche Grundbegriffe': Eine Revision" (Principles of Art History: A Revision), published in *Logos* in 1933. There, Wölfflin explains that some "nations" or "peoples" are simply "more imagistically endowed" than others; the relation of style to "race" is thus "unchangingly determined." His famously controversial "history of seeing" does not insist on an "autonomous and separate process" for the development of form, he insists; rather, since style is "tied to the material," it is "always regulated by the demands of history and race" (216). In an essay published in 1933, the resonances of the terms used are chilling.

By drawing attention to the place of nation and race in Wölfflin's 1933 thought, I am not suggesting a Party-identified position. Rather, the argument suggests that there was room in the debate about the Baroque for an explanation of stylistic difference via reference to "national" ways of seeing. It is not surprising that more explicitly essentializing and celebratory claims about the relation of styles to what Wölfflin in *Principles of Art History* calls "the foundations of the entire world view of a nation (*Volk*)" (256) emerge in future elaborations on this same argument by others, including Benjamin, about specifically German Baroque forms. One of Wölfflin's most famous "imitators," the Germanist Fritz Strich, wrote an essay in 1916 on the "lyric style" of the Baroque, for example, in which he uses Wölfflin's vocabulary to identify this style not only as the epoch-specific expression of an explicitly German spirit, but also as one in a spiral-like series of such epochs, which, taken together, constitute the German tradition writ large. Benjamin knew Strich and cites this ground-breaking essay, as well as a 1922 essay by Arthur Hübscher that makes much the same argument, multiple times in the *Tragic Drama* book. Before turning to Strich and Hübscher, however, I address another set of arguments used to explain the difference that was the Baroque in the work of Alois Riegl (1858–1905). While most scholars focus on Benjamin's rather more loosely formulated references to Riegl's theory of "decadent periods" (G: 1.1: 235; E: 55) and the "artistic will" of epigonal art in association with his *Spätrömische Kunstindustrie* (Late Roman Art Industry) (1901), it is not this book, but, rather, Riegl's own "Baroque book," *Die Entstehung der Barockkunst in Rom* (The Emergence of Baroque Art in Rome) (1908) that Benjamin explicitly cites in the first part of the second chapter of the *Tragic Drama* book (G: 1.1: 239, 277; E: 59, 99).[49] The contexts in which Benjamin cites Riegl, namely as part of an argument about how to read the poetological treatises of the Baroque as sources rather than as normative statements about the period's style, on the one hand, and as a way of understanding the distinction between Renaissance and Baroque theories of affect, on the other, draw attention to the methodological points he inherits from Riegl, points the Viennese art historian and theorist made in *The Emergence of Baroque Art*. While different from Wölfflin's, Riegl's theses served the same urgent project to locate the "reasons" for the emergence of an autonomous period style in a particular time and place.

The messy questions about the relation between period and nation as guarantors of Baroque style that Wölfflin's work raises, but does not answer in any unambiguous way receive a preliminary solution in Riegl's book on Baroque art, originally published posthumously in 1908. Riegl's influence on the "democratization" of art history in terms of the media it considers has been referred to time and again by Lorenz Dittmann, Henri Zerner, and Michael Podro; his influence on Benjamin's thought about "marginal" epochs and genres has been explored by Burkhardt Lindner (*"Links hatte noch alles sich zu enträtseln"*) and Michael Jennings ("Walter Benjamin"). As a specialist on textiles and professionally interested in the history of the decorative arts, Riegl did in fact focus in some of his work on artifacts and genres traditionally considered marginal to what he labels "so-called higher art" (*Stilfragen* v). Yet he was also a dedicated historian of "high" Baroque culture and lectured on the subject over the course of the final decade of the nineteenth century in Vienna; these were the lectures that became *Die Entstehung der Barockkunst in Rom* (The Emergence of Baroque Art in Rome), the book that Benjamin cites in its second edition of 1923. Adamantly opposed to designating any periods or genres as "decadent" (cf. Zerner 178), Riegl, like Wölfflin, assesses the Baroque not as marginal, but rather as a privileged period and set of artifacts, as part of a project to defeat the negative judgments, based on Renaissance standards, of "the reprehensibility of Baroque style" (*Die Entstehung der Barockkunst* 9). Throughout *The Emergence of Baroque Art* Riegl in fact sounds very much like Wölfflin in this

---

49. Benjamin famously included the 1901 book in his list of "Bücher, die lebendig geblieben sind," in his 1929 review of the same title. See *Gesammelte Schriften* 3: 169–71.

respect, not only when he states that it is "now" considered "dilettantish" to see in the Baroque nothing but the "decay" of the Renaissance (11), but also in terms of his assumptions that there is an "Italian" versus a "Teutonic" art, if not also a "northern" and "Teutonic artistic will" (1–4). It is no wonder that Benjamin thought to discuss the work of the two men together in "The Rigorous Study of Art."

Nevertheless, even though in *The Emergence of Baroque Art,* Riegl praises the recent turn to the period on the part of professional art historians, including Wölfflin in his *Renaissance and Baroque,* which Riegl calls "the best" that has been written "about the Baroque style of the Italians" (14), he also critiques Wölfflin (accurately, as it turns out) for not addressing adequately "why it had to be this way" (14), that is, why the "new" art of the Baroque emerged not only when but also where it did. It could have been via such commentary that Benjamin became familiar with the arguments of Wölfflin's earlier book to begin with. It is Riegl's deployment in *The Emergence of Baroque Art* of his (in)famous concept of "artistic will" (*Kunstwollen*) as that which "explains" the integrity and autonomy of any given style that in fact attempts to solve the conundrum that characterizes both of Wölfflin's books. It does so by offering not only a theoretical defense of, but also a concrete method for, the evaluation of the factors that produced the newness of a situated Baroque in integrative ways. It is thus Riegl's *method*, in addition to his thematic claims about the period of the Baroque, that Benjamin so appreciates in "The Rigorous Study of Art" and imitates in his own "Baroque book" of 1928.

The exact meaning and significance of Riegl's concept of "artistic will" has long been discussed—most famously by Erwin Panofsky—independently of the ambiguous way in which it appears in Benjamin's *Tragic Drama* book.[50] One attempt to establish the exact meaning of Riegl's term by his student Hans Sedlmayr has been especially influential in the term's reception. In his "Quintessenz der Lehren Riegls" (Quintessence of Riegl's Theories) (1927), which appeared as the introduction to Riegl's *Gesammelte Aufsätze* (Collected Essays) (1929), Sedlmayr defines "artistic will" as that "behind which" "empirical art history" cannot go in its search for the cause, or "reason," for changes in style (xvii). Neither the "will," or intention, of the individual artist nor the "meaning" of any individual work of art, nor, finally, even the "abstraction" of a claim about style based on the analysis of many individual works, the "artistic will" resides both elsewhere and, following Sedlmayr, everywhere, emerging from all art that is produced at a given time and place. The definition seems an almost direct solution to Wölfflin's double claims about the impact of both "history" and "nation" on style.

Sedlmayr asserts that race is not, however, the final anchor for Riegl's concept of "artistic will." The "representatives of the artistic will" are not to be understood "in a racially identified way," but rather as "a specific group of individuals" whose

50. In addition to Panofsky, see Sedlmayr xxxiii; Holly, *Panofsky*.

"will" is "of a more-than-individual sort" (xviii-xix). Sedlmayr's definitions might seem more properly associated with Wölfflin than Riegl, for he neglects—and perhaps even seeks to distract readers from—the assumptions that Riegl does in fact make about the identifiability of the collective traits that he associates with what he calls the "artistic nations" in *The Emergence of Baroque Art* (5). Riegl also attributes explicit racial or ethnic identities to various "consumers" of Baroque art, claiming, for example, that "viewers of the Teutonic race" and "the northern viewer" (153) prefer the "Baroque" Michelangelo to other artists.[51] Riegl's descriptions here of models for how to observe the relation of "groups" and their "will" to what he early on in the lectures calls the "artistic tendency" of a specific and "determinative time and place" (17) could have provided Sedlmayr and subsequent scholars with additional evidence for glosses on the "artistic will" as a national trait.

In Riegl's "Baroque book" itself, the "artistic will" is nevertheless a moving target. He celebrates the Baroque not at all as a "marginal field," but rather as a moment when the greatness of major artists, particularly Michelangelo, emerged. Here, for Riegl, it is the "Baroque artistic will" (*Die Entstehung der Barockkunst* 43) of the individual master artist ("his specific artistic will," 32, 46, 123) that is a category of concern.[52] Riegl tracks the "emergence of Baroque style" (31–78) in Italy by following a number of specific artists, including Correggio (46–54) and Bramante (58, 63–66), whose "artistic will" can be seen in various monuments in St. Peter's (64). Not only individual artists, but also individual Renaissance popes, such as Sixtus V, also have a defining "artistic will" (98). Riegl's is thus clearly not an "art history without names," in Wölfflin's famous phrase. Counterbalancing his readings of architectural monuments, sculpture, and painting organized either explicitly or implicitly by "auteur," he nevertheless also goes beyond cases of "artistic will" visible in individual artists or works to posit a version of this "will" that seems to preexist and precede them. Even the greatest artist does no more than capture the preexisting "artistic will" "of his entire time" (43), Riegl explains; thus, in the case of Michelangelo, who is famously identified as the "father of Baroque style" (30), the "artistic will" of the epoch is something of which even he (Michelangelo) must

---

51. In his earlier *Stilfragen* (1893), Riegl argues against the "enthusiasm for the spontaneous-autochthonous beginnings of the various national arts" (xvi). Some of his assumptions in *The Emergence of Baroque Art* nevertheless contradict this position. For example, in his description of the "movement" (*Die Entstehung der Barockkunst* 35) and unity (33) of the Medici graves (32–39) in terms that could be Wölfflin's, Riegl identifies a style that is contrary to "the satisfied being" of Renaissance sculpture, a tumultuous "sensibility" that he claims is not only "new" vis-à-vis both antiquity and the Renaissance (36), but also somehow typical of how "the Italians" show the intersection of "sensibility" and "will" in their Baroque sculpture; for Riegl, "the Dutch," by contrast, show only "sensibility" (39). Correggio likewise shows his difference from the "Northerners" in allowing "sensibility" (46), an intersection that, again, the "Northerners" ban from their art (51). At stake here is always whether or not the Italian artists have adopted a style that is "attractive to the Northerners" (47, 49).

52. It may be worth noting that Benjamin too focuses on individual "masters," and in particular on Shakespeare and Calderón, as the bearers of the *Kunstwollen* of their own periods, nations, and ideological-theological moments.

first become "aware" (31) and then express in his art. Given the plethora of ways in which the term is used, the questions that Sedlmayr asks in general of Riegl can thus also easily be asked of *The Emergence of Baroque Art* book itself, namely "What is that thing called the 'artistic will'?" (xvii). Is it in people or objects or somewhere else? Moreover, what help does the term provide in answering the question of the origin of style? "How does this concept emerge?" (xiv).

How Riegl construes the concept of the "artistic will" of a period can be seen in part in the way *The Emergence of Baroque Art* refuses the methodological label that Dittmann, for example, applies to Riegl's work in general, namely that it is "transhistorical" (Dittmann 35) and "unhistorical" (41) because it is too concerned with assessing the more or less strictly cognitive impact of works of art on the individual observer. Indeed, before Riegl actually begins to discuss either artists or monuments and works of art and how they are perceived, he reviews not just earlier scholarship on the material (in the section entitled "Literatur," *Die Entstehung der Barockkunst* 9–16; it is here that he mentions Wölfflin's work), but also the additional "sources" (17–30), which, under-"exploited" to date, are actually where the "artistic tendency of the period [of the Baroque]" and its "determination by place and time" can be observed (17). What he is referring to here, Riegl explains, are both print and manuscript sources, books as well as the hugely rich resources of the "Roman archives of families related to and favored by the popes." Other sources include Vasari's *Lives,* the biographical works of Giovanni Baglione (1644), and the *Vite* of Giovanni Pietro Bellori (1672). Riegl describes each of these texts in great detail; what he finds in them is the kind of material that gives access to the "artistic sensibility" of the period (*Die Entstehung der Barockkunst* 22), including information about the relation of the trends in architecture and art to papal history (19) and curia rivalries (28), documentation of the place of philosophical debates about the role of the (neo)Platonic "idea" (24), and contemporary discussions of the concept of style itself (25). These kinds of sources allow the art historian or critic to "locate himself" in the highly overdetermined context of the specific period of art being observed (28); they thus function as a kind of model for how to undertake an "authentically modern art historical task" (29) of the kind that he himself practices in *The Emergence of Baroque Art* and that Benjamin valued as well.[53] In such materials and in a calibration of their intersection not only with other "local" (29) sources and knowledges, but also and crucially, with what he observes in the monuments and artifacts themselves, the collective "artistic will" of the Roman Baroque—indeed, of any period and place—can be observed.

In Riegl's *The Emergence of Baroque Art,* the actual relation of such sources to the artworks themselves, and thus the status and location of the conduits along which the "artistic will" must travel between the two, is nevertheless left somewhat

---

53. See Benjamin, "Rigorous Study of Art" 372, on Riegl as the "progenitor" of a "new kind . . . of science of studying art."

imprecise. "Artworks" are described somewhat vaguely as "representatives of the spirit of the Counter Reformation" (*Die Entstehung der Barockkunst* 119), for example. That there is a "relationship between the Counter Reformation and Baroque art" and that both are "determined by some third higher force" (93) is, again, somewhat loosely declared. Riegl admits that exactly how both "the ethical and the aesthetic" are the "expression of a common third higher force" cannot be "determined" quite yet (93). Such hesitations aside, it is nevertheless this "higher" third moment that is the place of the local, epochal "will," which then finds universal "expression" in papal preferences and the internal politics of monastic orders, in the stylistic details of churches and suburban villas, and in decorative fountains in these and urban settings alike. Riegl famously claims at the end of his *Art Industry* book that "at any one time" there is "in general only one direction of the artistic will," and it is visible in "religion, philosophy, economics, and in the state and the law," as well as in the style of the "fine arts" (*Spätrömische Kunstindustrie* 400). All realms of expression are bound together by an otherwise unspecified "internal coherence" (401).[54] Riegl's *Art Industry* book was first published in 1901. What we can observe in his lectures on the Baroque are thus the results of a decade-long attempt to model for his students exactly how this "relationship" was to be understood. In *The Emergence of Baroque Art,* Riegl provides what we might now call an interdisciplinary approach to the period, whereby the Baroque is "redeemed" not by attention just to style or to the cognitive operations involved in observing period artifacts, but rather by means of an emphasis on their complex historical embeddedness in time and place. It is thus no wonder that, when Benjamin writes in a résumé probably penned in the same year that the *Tragic Drama* book appeared that his project there was to see the work of art as an "integral expression, not restricted in terms of field or discipline, of the religious, metaphysical, political, and economic tendencies of an era" (*Gesammelte Schriften* 1.3: 886), it is Riegl's work that he cites.

Benjamin's interest in Riegl's concept of *Kunstwollen* did not remain at the level of mere citation, however. Indeed, Benjamin's injunction, in the third chapter of the *Tragic Drama* book, to readers and scholars to "engage with the source documents in an open way" (G: 1.1: 376; E: 201) would appear to echo Riegl's methodology in his "Baroque book" quite closely and thus goes far beyond relying only on Riegl's nearly "formalist" approach as an "interpreter of cultural objects" (Jennings, "Walter Benjamin" 86). Benjamin's indebtedness to Riegl's interdisciplinary approach is particularly visible in the first section of Benjamin's second chapter, "Trauerspiel und Tragödie" (Tragic Drama and Tragedy) (238–78; 57–100), where, at the beginning of the section in which he first cites Riegl, Benjamin turns to the very same kinds of sources to which Riegl refers in *The Emergence of Baroque Art,*

---

54. Kemp, following Endre Kiss in a reading of *Art Industry,* finds that Riegl does not go far enough here in the direction of what he (Kemp) calls the implicit "history of structures" for which such a method calls (Nachwort 10–11).

that is, to the "poetological treatises and handbooks" of the Baroque as "indispensable sources for analysis" (239; 58). He also reads deeply in other "historical sources" (244; 64), including those analyzed by Bernhard Erdmannsdörffer in his *Deutsche Geschichte vom Westfälischen Frieden bis zum Regierungsantritt Friedrich's des Großen, 1648–1740* (German History from the Peace of Westphalia up through the Beginning of the Reign of Friedrich the Great, 1648–1740) (1892), as well as texts by legal theorists and historians, such as Carl Schmitt's *Politische Theologie* (Political Theology) (1922), Hans George Schmidt's *Die Lehre vom Tyrannenmord: Ein Kapitel aus der Rechtsphilosophie* (The Doctrine of Tyrannicide: A Chapter in the Philosophy of Law) (1901), and the fifth edition of August Koberstein's *Geschichte der deutschen Nationalliteratur vom Anfang des siebzehnten bis zum zweiten Viertel des achtzehnten Jahrhunderts* (History of German National Literature from the Beginning through the Second Quarter of the Eighteenth Century) (1872), all of which give Benjamin the terms with which to characterize the Baroque (G: 1.1: 245–48; E: 65–68).[55] Following Riegl's logic that all layers of culture at a specific time will reflect the common concerns of the period, Benjamin's references to these texts and to the complex array of historical, institutional, and ideological contexts they describe thus join his argument about the visibility of an epoch's "artistic will" in its painting and sculpture via citations of the equally synthetic art historian and journalist Wilhelm Hausenstein's immensely popular *Vom Geist des Barock* (On the Spirit of the Baroque) (1919).[56] Benjamin cites Hausenstein on El Greco (250–51; 71) and comments on Baroque mathematical theory (271; 92) and conceptions of time (275; 97); in so doing, he follows Riegl in interrogating a cross-section of a period's sources as a way of locating its integrated "artistic will."

In the section of the *Tragic Drama* book in which Benjamin cites Riegl, his argument about a common period "spirit" is tempered by a series of claims to the effect that the texts of the Baroque with which he is concerned were not yet as accomplished as what Benjamin calls "the Romantic drama from Calderon up through Tieck" (G: 1.1: 262; E: 83). Yet they were "specifically German" (260; 81) and, written by "German Protestants," specifically Lutheran as well (263, 267, 276; 84, 88, 98). This cascade of claims about the German-Protestant identity of his data is striking, given that many theorizations of the Baroque, including Wölfflin's and Riegl's, occurred in tandem with an examination of a specifically Catholic and often Counter-Reformation and Romance world. It is perhaps not by chance, then, that

55. Benjamin famously cites Carl Schmitt alongside Riegl in the 1928 curriculum vitae as an influence on his (Benjamin's) attempts to argue for a method that relies on the "integration of multiple phenomena" (*Gesammelte Schriften* 1.3: 886). See Garber (*Rezeption und Rettung* 91–96) on Benjamin's use of Schmitt as a historical source.

56. Hausenstein's book was enormously popular, and Benjamin cites it often. In a review in 1922, Hermann Bahr underscores that Hausenstein's book demonstrates that "the Baroque is indeed our problem . . . just as the Renaissance was the problem of Burckhardt's and Nietzsche's time" (qtd. in Migge 64).

here Benjamin mentions the Spanish example and Calderón in particular (260–67; 81–88) in clear contrast to what "German drama" and "the German playwrights" do not and "could not dare do" (261, 263, 277; 83, 84, 98). The combined effect is to place additional emphasis precisely on the "seriousness of the German tragic drama as nationally determined" (265; 86).[57] The rhetorical choreography of these pages is not coincidentally reminiscent of Wölfflin's elaborate balancing act of Renaissance versus Baroque, as noted above, as well as, and just as important, of northern "Germanic" versus southern "Romance" styles. Benjamin claims, for example, that "Spanish drama discovered in the essence of honor a creaturely spirituality adequate to its creaturely embodiment and, in so doing, found a profane realm that remained off limits not only to the German poets of the Baroque, but even to later theorists as well" (266; 87). Later, he continues to emphasize differences between "German theater" and "the Spanish stage" by returning to his claims about the differences between a "Protestant" theater and the theater of Catholic Spain (276; 98). My point here is this: interdisciplinary Rieglian concerns to embed the "artistic will" of the Baroque in a thickly described location intersect in the *Tragic Drama* book with Wölfflinian ways of displaying different "national"—and confessionally identified—styles in dyadic ways. While the result is something of a methodological hybrid, the presence of the mix is not all that strange, given that it was a combination of Riegl's and Wölfflin's ideas that had set the terms of debates about the Baroque in the first place. The penetration of their art historical approaches into literary-critical studies of the Baroque more generally at the time was quite common and is visible in work by scholars like Fritz Strich and Arthur Hübscher, on whose ideas from the 1910s and early 1920s Benjamin also draws heavily in the *Tragic Drama* book.

Origin and the "Heroic" Age of the German Literary Baroque

Benjamin refers repeatedly in the *Tragic Drama* book to a number of literary-historical treatments of the Baroque that are heavily indebted to a mix of Wölfflinian and Rieglian paradigms. In addition to introducing the art theoretical debates into a new disciplinary home, this work, by scholars Fritz Strich and Arthur Hübscher, had the uncanny effect of collaborating with the methodologically distinct, but ideologically consistent celebratory narratives of German cultural and literary history by the well-known scholars Karl Lamprecht (1856–1915) and Josef Nadler (1884–1963), both of whom Benjamin also cites. Lamprecht's and Nadler's work laid both the literal and the conceptual groundwork for the "heroic" age

---

57. It is clear that Benjamin values Calderón and the Spanish over the Germans; "Germany has nothing that can compete with" the "tragic drama of the Spaniard" (G: 1.1: 263; E: 84). My point here, however, is that Benjamin must nevertheless set the two kinds of drama and nations side by side to illuminate the "typical," situated characteristics of each.

of the study of Baroque literature in general and of the plays of the Second Silesian school in particular, by including it and them in the canon of German literature from which both had been emphatically excluded by earlier theorists such as Gottsched. Lamprecht's controversial cultural history and Nadler's monumental linguistic geographies were based on a kind of encyclopedic inclusionism that permitted, even demanded, that all epochs and linguistic monuments, regardless of style, find a place in the grand narrative of national culture.[58] The specifically German stylistic elements of Baroque texts and the correspondingly all-inclusive German "spirit" of the Baroque identified by Strich in his famous article "Der lyrische Stil des siebzehnten Jahrhunderts" (The Lyric Style of the Seventeenth Century) (1916) and by Hübscher in his "Barock als Gestaltung antithetischen Lebensgefühls" (Baroque as the Formation of an Antithetical Sense of Life) (1922) made the Baroque eligible for a place at the German literary- and cultural-historical table as it was defined in such texts. Strich's and Hübscher's celebrations of the period and its style were indebted both indirectly and explicitly to the defenses of the Baroque mounted by the art historian-theorists discussed above, defenses whose logic they embraced as a way of offering alternatives to approaches like Stachel's and Cysarz's, to which Strich, for example, like Benjamin, refers when he complains about the "misleading" designation of the seventeenth century as related to the Renaissance in any essential way ("Der lyrische Stil" 21).[59]

The famous 1916 "Lyric Style" article by Fritz Strich (1882–1963) is often identified as one of the earliest, if not also the most important, translation of Wölfflinian art-historical stylistic analysis into the specific domain of literary studies.[60] Strich's essay plays this inaugural role in Benjamin's *Tragic Drama* book too, where it is cited for the first time as part of the "Epistemo-Critical Prologue"'s argument for an art philosophical logic with which to defend the use of the category and term *Baroque*. For Benjamin, Strich's work—here, his "idea" of "the literary Baroque" (G: 1.1: 221; E: 41)—provides an example of a position within the period-style debate that is positively invested in the legitimacy of developing an autonomous period "idea."

---

58. Benjamin cites Lamprecht in G: 1.1: 231; E: 51 (albeit critically) and 240; 59, and Nadler at 379; 204. Nadler's work is particularly interesting in connection with Benjamin, not only for its specific focus on the issue of language, so important to Benjamin, but also because of Nadler's tremendous influence on Hugo von Hofmannsthal, whom Nadler saw as recreating a "southern" German/Viennese Baroque in the here and now. On Nadler, Hofmannsthal, and Benjamin, see Schoolfield; König.

59. Voßkamp (691–92), relying on Hans-Harald Müller (*Barockforschung*), also argues for the importance of the art historians Wilhelm Worringer and Georg Dehio for Strich in particular. Worringer famously wrote of "the northern Baroque" in his 1911 *Formprobleme der Gotik* (Formal Problems of the Gothic) (qtd. in Voßkamp 692). On Worringer's importance for Benjamin, see the conclusion.

60. Strich may himself have helped encourage this understanding of his foundational role; some forty years after the publication of the original article, he claims that it was he who was responsible for the "translation" of the concept of the Baroque from the arts to literature (see Strich, "Die Übertragung des Barockbegriffs" 307). Hans-Harald Müller (*Barockforschung* 118–33) notes that a number of contemporaries dismissed Strich's collapsing of the Baroque into "Teutonicism," while also admitting that his theses in the article had become somewhat of an orthodoxy.

In his discussion of Burdach, Benjamin dismisses, we may remember, the "uncritically inductive" methods of a literary history that would look at masses of "heterogeneous sources" without the aid of "concepts," such as genre (tragic drama) and period (Baroque). According to Benjamin, Strich offers instead "synthetic" claims about the consistency and integrity of the "formative principles" of the seventeenth century, claims that Benjamin then goes on to associate with Rieglian "views of a higher type" (221–22; 41), which must be assumed before turning to the works themselves. Strich was also the first to give Baroque literary studies "an orientation within stylistic history" (231; 50) of the Wölfflinian sort, which understood the period explicitly as non- or other-than-the-Renaissance, according to Benjamin; the possibility of turning away from a tradition of work such as Stachel's could thus in fact be said to have had its origins for Benjamin in Strich's importation of art historical categories into the literary-historical and critical world.

In his essay, Strich's celebration of the "idea" of the Baroque tout court relies on claims about the stylistics of *German* Baroque poetry in particular. Published two years into World War I, the piece renders Wölfflin's emerging thesis about the national "origins" of the coherence of style even more visible. The argument for the integrity of period style is based on what Strich later identifies as Wölfflin's greatest achievement, which was to have assembled "the individual cases [of works of art] into styles of a period and a nation" ("Der lyrische Stil" 43).[61] The grammatical collapsing of "period" and "nation" into a single category here is Strich's addition, or, perhaps better, his completion of the argument that Wölfflin had not yet made explicit in 1915.[62] The plural ("styles") suggests, moreover, the concept of periodicity, the recurrence of Baroque moments throughout history, proposed by Wölfflin; it is this kind of periodicity that goes on to become a central part of an argument from nation by Strich. Rather than arguing in favor of deracinated typological thinking,

---

61. Indeed, Dilly (278) cites a 1924 letter from Wölfflin to Strich, thanking him for the copy of one of his books he had sent to the man Strich elsewhere calls "my sole teacher" (Strich, "Zu Heinrich Wölfflins Gedächtnis" 222), in which Wölfflin indicates that he is himself now becoming more convinced of the "decisive power of national character." Dilly's claim about the apparent standoffishness of the senior scholar vis-à-vis Strich notwithstanding, then, there may also have also been influence in the other direction, with Wölfflin learning from Strich's work. Hans-Harald Müller ("Die Übertragung des Barockbegriffs" 102) claims, however, that there are only "marginal similarities" between Wölfflin and Strich.

62. Strich was of course neither the first nor the only one to invoke the (German) "nation" as a culturally unifying category at the time, and it is important to note the similarity between his arguments and those of Oskar Walzel, for example, whose work Benjamin knew but does not cite in the *Tragic Drama* book. Also important was Worringer, whom Jennings claims Benjamin has to thank for his "complex theory of culture" ("Walter Benjamin" 90). Hans-Harald Müller ("Die Übertragung des Barockbegriffs" 107–9) in fact argues that most of Strich's ideas came directly from Worringer's *Formprobleme der Gotik* (Formal Problems of the Gothic) (1911). In a more pointed way than Walzel and Worringer (who was the former's student), although in much the same terms, Strich celebrates in the Baroque the integrity of German tradition and culture based on the expression of "the Teutonic spirit" in lyric forms ("Der lyrische Stil" 37). On Walzel's and Strich's common endorsement of a kind of "Teutonic artistic will," both throughout German literary history and in the Baroque in particular, see H.-H. Müller, "Die Übertragung des Barockbegriffs" 96 and passim.

his claims for the regular reemergence of a Baroque style in the German literary tradition become, rather, part of a defense of the cultural integrity and autonomy of a no-longer-belated German spirit also no longer indebted to external norms. In the 1916 article that Benjamin cites, Strich characterizes "the new style" of the Baroque as "more national" than commonly assumed ("Der lyrische Stil" 22); it makes sense that the terms in which he makes this argument resurface in Benjamin's logic about a specifically German tradition of tragic drama as well.

In his 1916 article, Strich calls attention, first, to the "natural" attributes—rhythms, rhymes, and tonal emphases—of "the German language" that enable the innovations of German Baroque lyric (21), especially vis-à-vis ancient and foreign models, which for Strich, as for Wölfflin, were of a completely "different kind" (50). The characteristic move in German translations, for example, was to take "ancient" (i.e., classical) simplicity and "complicate," "expand," and "heighten" it (24), thus creating the "new style" (25). For Strich, as for Wölfflin, it was "Germanness," here the German language in particular, that endowed Baroque lyric with the novelty of a "greater freedom" (24) of both form and content, a freedom that did not allow itself to be "bound" (25). That the poetry of the period had "a character of becoming rather than being" (33) and was "painterly" rather than linear (42), on the one hand, and consistently revealed a "stimulus of movement" (26), on the other, confirms that it was Wölfflin's principles of the Baroque that Strich was seeing in the literary texts he treats. Indeed, he sometimes even proves the superiority of the anti-Renaissance innovations of the Baroque vis-à-vis ancient and foreign traditions by means of Wölfflinian pairings of older and "classical" texts with Baroque ones, side by side on the page (22–23, 24, 27, 43). Yet Strich's main point is not to remain at the level of description or exemplification, but rather to pursue the Wölfflinian question of the "origins" of the specificity of the new style. He answers this question in a far less conflicted way than his master by collapsing into a single claim two of Wölfflin's suggestions about the recurrence of style as part of an argument from place.

The attribution to Baroque style of a specifically German "origin" that is eternally present in its periodic recurrence in the national tradition (Benjamin signals this periodicity in his discussion of the concept of "origin" in the terms of its "pre- and post-history," G: 1.1: 226; E: 46) occurs in Strich's essay, first, in the assertion that there are already preforms of the Baroque to be discerned in earlier German literature. Unfortunately, but symptomatically in 1916, he simply declares rather than describes these prehistories in his essay. For example, the more animated, interiorized, and characterized by the "piling up" of words Baroque lyric becomes, the more it begins to resemble, Strich announces, the "character of old Teutonic poetry" ("Der lyrische Stil" 29) and the "primal German usage" (39) of a "primal German poetry" (45), which are in turn taken to be expressions of some equally as primal "Teutonic spirit" (37). Baroque attention to rhyme, specifically described as antithetical to "ancient rhythms" (48), is likewise identified as an "expression of the

German spirit" (48), which is then "reborn" in the Baroque via poets who attended to the natural properties of the German tongue. Strich's relatively imprecise argument about how Baroque lyric occasions a Renaissance (*Wiedergeburt,* 21) of an ancient and primal (Ur) German spirit here nevertheless provides a clear alternative to Stachel's by finding the "restoration" (*Restauration*—Benjamin's term, G: 1.1: 226; E: 45) of this early "primal law of all Teutonic poetry" ("Der lyrische Stil" 21) in the Baroque.[63] Much more specifically and in clear counterpoint to an argument such as the one made by Cysarz, moreover, who claims that only classicizing styles could guarantee the rebirth of the German tradition, Strich argues—with a nod in the direction of Wölfflin's claims about the periodic return of a national style—that the "new rhythm" of Baroque lyric extended this "primal" German poetic practice well beyond its own time into the rhythms of later German poetry, including Classicism and Storm and Stress, but most prominently, into Romantic lyric (25, 29, 43) as well. The Baroque tendency to mix genres and forms (prose and lyric, music and text), to mutually reinforce combinations of rhythm and rhyme, and to create antithetical combinations of spiritualism and sensualism (30) recalls poetic practice in "Romantic times" (45) in general, he argues. "Romanticism," with whose lyric the Baroque has "an extensive similarity" (39), specifically possesses "a spirit linked to the Baroque" (53).

Against the background of his reliance on a Wölfflinian logic of periodicity in the German tradition, it is not surprising that Strich uses the art historian's model of pairing to reveal differences between the Baroque and "classical" forms in a Wölfflinian manner and to show the afterlives of Baroque in German Romantic poetry ("Der lyrische Stil" 46–48); a seventeenth-century Nuremberg poem is juxtaposed with poems by Clemens Brentano, Ewald von Kleist, and Ludwig Tieck, for example, all of which are characterized by rhythmic patterns that likewise "oppose" "ancient" and foreign forms (48). The Baroque recalls poetic practice not visible since the "days of primal Teutonic poetry," on the one hand, and anticipatory of "Romanticism" (48–49), on the other. As much as Strich would claim that the "animated" lyric style of the Baroque was unique to its time (it had a "movement that existed neither before nor since," 33), then, his actual practice in the article is to collapse his descriptions of historical Baroque texts into a typological claim about the expression of a single style that begins in a pre-Baroque "primal German" moment and moves ever forward into its post-Baroque fulfillment in the Romantic Age. Wölfflin's uncertainty about what can be identified as the "reasons," or "causes,"

---

63. That Strich feels no need to document the permanent quality of such recurring German poetic traits suggests that Voßkamp's claim (692) about Strich's unacknowledged sources in Worringer is correct. Hans-Harald Müller ("Die Übertragung des Barockbegriffs" 106) cites from Strich's introduction to his 1921 collection of Baroque lyric to the effect that the most recent "Renaissance" (*Wiedergeburt*) of the German Baroque spirit was to occur in the poetry of his own early twentieth century, thus confirming his belief in the permanence of a Germanic *Kunstwollen*, indeed, its culmination in "modern" Germany.

of the change from a Renaissance to a Baroque style thus dissipates almost entirely in Strich's "Teutonifying understanding of the Baroque" (Kiesant 84), in which a national "spirit" emerges as the "origin" of both a past and a future of specifically German poetic forms.

Strich's argument found echoes in contemporary literary-historical and critical circles and in the work of Arthur Hübscher (1897–1985) in particular, whose 1922 article, "Barock als Gestaltung antithetischen Lebensgefühls" (Baroque as the Formation of an Antithetical Sense of Life) is often cited alongside Strich's as exemplary of "heroic age" Baroque studies.[64] As much as Hübscher claims in his lengthy two-part article, which appeared in the by-then establishment journal, *Euphorion,* that he would nuance Strich, indeed, as far reaching as his article is, Hübscher creates a Baroque that for all intents and purposes is quite similar to Strich's in its identity, which is informed by a specifically German "sense of life" with the power to bequeath its forms to the future.[65] Benjamin cites Hübscher's essay repeatedly in the *Tragic Drama* book, and not surprisingly. Published more recently than Strich's, Hübscher's article is designed to combat the "incorrect extension of the designation, Renaissance, to include the seventeenth century" (518). While Stachel is not named as the prime culprit here, he certainly could have been. Hübscher also targets for critique assessments of the Baroque that dismiss it as no more than a "preparatory era" (518). Cysarz's 1924 book, in which precisely this argument appears, had of course not yet appeared, and it is actually another member of the George Circle, the maverick Friedrich Gundolf, whose arguments are singled out by Hübscher as the culprits here. Contra such tendencies, Hübscher's main project is to identify what is "proper" to, and thus the property of, the Baroque as a "sense of life" (519). Baroque poetry is associated with a nearly Burckhardtian "modern essence" (527) and "new energies" (546) as well. To this end, he repeatedly notes in now familiar ways how Renaissance concerns and styles, indeed, the "spirit of the Renaissance" (550) writ large, differ from that which is specifically Baroque, that is, from its "antithetical sense of life" (535, 546, 777).[66] Hübscher dips not only into Strich's, but also into Wölfflin's and Riegl's rhetorical and methodological arsenals as he explains what it

---

64. Unlike Strich, who became known for his work on canonical literary figures and periods in the German tradition, such as Goethe and Weimar Classicism, Hübscher went on to work in more journalistic venues. This may be why the work of the former is sometimes given more weight in discussions of early twentieth-century Baroque studies.

65. Hübscher's need to both praise and "correct" Strich (519–27), particularly in terms of his "cyclical idea" in light of its similarity to Spenglerian concepts, is curious, yet ultimately Rieglian. That is, for Hübscher, the most important point in these opening polemical pages is to assert that, while there may be recurring styles, "peculiarities" always characterize individual periods (522). Nevertheless, all "antithetical" oppositions in a period should ultimately be capable of "harmonized" synthesis (522). As I note below, Hübscher relies heavily on Strich's Wölfflinian categories throughout, making clear the benchmark nature of Strich's essay.

66. Cf., however, Hübscher 761, where in the context of discussing the (self-) underestimation of Baroque poets, Hübscher claims they thought of themselves as extensions of the Renaissance.

is that he is designating as this Baroque "sense."[67] Early on in the article he includes a complex chart of clearly distinct and opposing principles, for example, such as coordinating versus subordinating patterns, and a "tendency toward rest" versus a "tendency toward expression" (526); here we are clearly reminded of Wölfflin, whose linear and painterly principles are also explicitly invoked (770–71). Elsewhere, a nearly Rieglian "will to form" emerges out of the mass of "antithetical" texts and artifacts, contextual events and belief systems of the period he describes (540), explaining Hübscher's appeal to a "synthetic science" that will show "the picture of a man of [the] era" in all of the "individual fields of human culture" (527).

While Hübscher claims repeatedly in the introductory pages of his article that it is a specifically Pan-European "occidental" and "epochal" rather than a narrowly national, or merely "German," antithetical "sense of the world" of the Baroque in which he is interested (527), in the course of this sprawling article, it is nevertheless clear that it is Germany that emerges as the model for this allegedly universal "antithetical sense of life." The "artistic will" Hübscher describes is, for example, visible in a literary world that is de facto exclusively German. At the level of thematics, he notes the topos of "transitoriness" only in the texts of individual German Baroque poets (Opitz, Gryphius, and Theobald Hock, 527–29). Additional expressive forms, paintings and sculpture, from the period are then adduced.[68] Staging techniques associated with a specifically German dramatic tradition, such as the "transformative stage" (*Verwandlungsbühne*, 529), which also fascinate Benjamin in the *Tragic Drama* book, are likewise discussed as the primary indication of the universal ironic tensions between the antithetical principles of flesh and spirit, life and death. As the argument develops, evidence of the antithetical "sense of life" that marked the German seventeenth century in particular begins to dominate. The Baroque was an age of both reason and superstition (532), of the celebration of the individual combined with a tendency to form groups (548–49), of an ironic tendency toward cosmopolitanism and loyalty to "national" causes and duties (551–52), and of an awareness of pressing historical concerns versus a flight into dreamlike, utopian states (553–54). Accompanying such period trends were—in a return to specifically literary texts—a celebration of both reliance on foreign literary models and the cultivation of the "national" vernacular (533, 537), the combination of the "sensual" and the "immaterial" in Baroque metaphors (556), the antithetical relation of the main action of the plays in the "real world" and their "ideal" allegorical choral interludes (557), and the like. Hübscher absorbs so many aspects of German Baroque history and textuality into his claim about the period's omnivorous,

---

67. Hübscher cites both Wölfflin's *Renaissance und Barock* and Strich's 1916 essay at the outset of his article, suggesting that Benjamin could also have discovered them there (518–19).

68. The examples here are clearly borrowed from Riegl and Wölfflin, and include Michelangelo's Medici tomb and the "ruins" of Ruisdael's paintings (Hübscher 528); although not German, these artifacts appear to count as expressions of a German "Baroque sense of life" (531), perhaps because they were originally found in German-language art theoretical and art historical texts.

antithetical "will to form" that it may well have functioned as a model for "origin" when understood in the Benjaminian sense. Benjamin writes: "Origin is an eddy in the stream of becoming, and in its current it swallows the material involved in the process of genesis" (G: 1.1: 226; E: 45). Benjamin not only helps himself to many of Hübscher's examples in his own examination of the "antitheses" (250; 70) of the period, then. He also adopts Hübscher's whirlpool-like method of absorbing a whole host of period artifacts into his definition of the Baroque.

What allows Hübscher's argument to resemble Strich's perhaps even more than the former might have been ready to admit is that Hübscher goes on to insist on the common characteristics and parallel concerns of the historical Baroque with other specifically German "antithetical periods." Although "the specific tendencies emerge with different emphasis in the various periods to be considered" (541), he explains, "all antithetical periods display an especially strong expression of the autobiographical moment" (546). Hübscher goes on—almost relentlessly—to find other analogies to the Baroque in the German movements and periods of Storm and Stress, Romanticism, and contemporary Expressionism. Sometimes these parallels reveal the "non-developed nature" of the Baroque in terms of real equality for women (544) or patriotic "political action" (552). But more often, they show persistent and common interests (531 on scenes of infanticide and 554–55 on pastoral poetry) and parallelisms (the term "correspondences" is also used, 787) between the seventeenth century and other high points in the German tradition. As an example, Hübscher points to the common interests in dialect poetry (538) and to the similarities between the collectivities of the seventeenth-century language societies (*Sprachgesellschaften*), on the one hand, and the Romantic groups and the so-called George Circle of the present day (549), on the other. Given this kind of evolutionary logic, it is not surprising that Hübscher takes particular interest in the parallel devotion during the different periods of the German "baroque spirit" to "an elevated national challenge" (537) and to all that was "ancient" about the German tradition: Albrecht Dürer, mysticism, Germanness (*Deutschtum*), and national folk tradition (*Volkstum*), all in one. The argument makes sense in the context of a deep commitment to the concept of a "national" spirit that becomes for Hübscher the basis for his invention of a new kind of literary history of "antithetical" periods and an "antithetical" canon. His celebration of German poets and writers who are indebted (rather than superior) to their Baroque masters offers a direct counterpoint to Cysarz; Johann George Hamann and the Romantics thus join (rather than replace) Jakob Böhme (538) in their belief in the power of the vernacular. Even today's "study of German language and literature" (538) finds an ancestor in Opitz. What Hübscher depicts here is something very much like a Benjaminian "origin" for a Baroque "antithetical sense of life," originally visible in the seventeenth century, on the one hand, and endlessly capable of infinite afterlives, on the other.

Benjamin's arguments about the German Baroque in the *Tragic Drama* book are everywhere indebted to Strich and Hübscher in both substance and arrangement.

His initial citations of Strich's article occur in the context of his epistemological reflections in the "Prologue" on the necessity of assuming the "idea" of the Baroque as distinct from the Renaissance (G: 1.1: 221, 231; E: 41, 50); the quotes occur in both the challenging "theory of ideas" section and in the later, more conventional pages, suggesting the relevance of Strich's argument to both the more arcane and the more profane versions of Benjamin's theorization of a method for "redeeming" the period after its prior false assessment via Renaissance-bound categories and norms. Benjamin also praises Hübscher in the "Epistemo-Critical Prologue" as one of the few contemporary critics whose work shows an authentic "revaluation" of the Baroque in terms of its own standards and works (234; 54). Hübscher's rejection of the relevance of a Renaissance-like adherence to Aristotelian norms is noted in this same spirit later on (278; 100). Both critics had argued for their more abstract notions of the national origins of style and form based on the evidence of the historical texts of the period, and then offered exemplary close readings of how to find evidence of Baroque style and "will to form" and "artistic will" in the literary documents of the period with which Benjamin was concerned. As often as not, Benjamin borrows both the actual texts and Strich's and Hübscher's readings of them and inserts them nearly verbatim into the *Tragic Drama* book, also in the later sections on Baroque emblematics, where he undertakes the construction of an alternative lineage for Baroque allegory as distinct from the more classical notion of the symbol. The intricate choreography that knits the "Epistemo-Critical Prologue" and the section on allegory together is thus another example of Benjamin's earlier narrative about the afterlives of the Baroque tragic dramas in the later German Romantic drama, and he mines Strich's and Hübscher's work for specific arguments and examples to buttress his reading of the specifically allegorical nature not only of German Baroque poetry and poetic forms (358–59, 369, 389; 183, 193, 215), but of the German language itself (380; 205). Their models have shown him how to arrange the historical evidence on which to base his claims about the afterlives of a national Baroque.[69]

Benjamin's citations of Strich's and Hübscher's work in the context of his discussion of allegory in the first and second parts of chapter 3 of the *Tragic Drama* book are especially significant in terms of the ways in which they reveal the pressure that arguments like theirs, indebted to Wölfflin and Riegl, placed on constructing a longer-term presence, or afterlife, of specifically German Baroque forms. The overall shape and direction of the argument are initially clear when Benjamin argues—in terms for which he ironically thanks Cysarz (G: 1.1: 339; E: 163)—that the allegorical imperative in the Baroque is the "speculative opposite" of, or a response to, the classical concept of the symbol (337; 161). In a completely different tone from that of the Viennese scholar, however, Benjamin sees in the Baroque's allegorical use

---

69. Benjamin's understanding of allegory is intimately involved with contemporary discussions about emblems. I discuss these alliances in greater detail in chapter 3.

of language an example of how "the Baroque" is a "sovereign opposite of Classicism" rather than a transitional form thereof. The Baroque is, in Benjamin's words, the "correction of Classicism," indeed, of "art itself," that scholars had recognized only "in Romanticism" before (352; 176). The arc from theories of allegory in the Baroque to those in German Romanticism, with which the Baroque has an "elective affinity" (387–88; 213), bypasses Classicism, according to Benjamin, and reveals the "constants" (352; 176) between the two. The claim is supported through reference especially to the work of Friedrich Creuzer (1771–1858) (340–44; 163–67) and Franz von Baader (1765–1841) (360–61; 184). Both theorists were identified with German Romanticism; extracts from and citations of their work appear cheek by jowl with references to Strich and Hübscher, whose arguments about the afterlives of Baroque principles in the period of German literary Romanticism are confirmed by Benjamin's invocation of their work.

Benjamin's complex commentary on Baroque allegory in these sections is consistently interrupted, moreover, by sustained asides to and extended discussions of other Romantic figures, such as Johann Joseph von Görres (1776–1848) (G: 1.1: 342, 362; E: 165, 186–87), E. T. A. Hoffmann (1776–1822) (347–48; 171), Novalis (1772–1801) (363, 367; 188, 191), and Jean Paul (364; 188), giving the appearance that German Romanticism and the authors and texts Benjamin had dealt with in his dissertation might nearly edge out the Baroque as his main object of concern in the *Habilitation*. Yet the parallels between Benjamin's, Strich's, and Hübscher's arguments, which emerge in Benjamin's claim that Creuzer's understanding of myth and allegory can and should be understood as a more or less "modern" version of Baroque thoughts (343; 166), for example, and in his assertion that Novalis's understanding of allegory was also based on a "Baroque practice" (363; 188), suggest that Benjamin's method in these pages is not at all unlike theirs, namely the invention (in Wölfflinian-Strichian fashion) of an afterlife for the Baroque in the other epoch of the German tradition, namely Romanticism, that he knew well. The cited texts merely make visible, in other words, that the former period is a "pre-history" that bears fruit in a later one; "the genius of Romanticism dialogues with the Baroque spirit precisely in the space of the allegorical" (363; 187), Benjamin claims. The Rieglian density of citation here, not only from eighteenth-century texts, but from the original "source texts" of the seventeenth century as well, is nearly unparalleled in the rest of the *Tragic Drama* book. It nevertheless yields in the pages that follow to a host of citations from the work of physicist and theorist Johann Wilhelm Ritter (1776–1810), whose work was so influential for the German Romantics. Benjamin describes Ritter's ideas as "an unmistakable tribute to the connection between the Baroque and Romanticism" (387–89, here 388; 213–15, here 214); citations from Ritter's 1810 *Fragmente aus dem Nachlasse eines jungen Physikers* (Fragments from the Estate of a Young Physicist) complete the creation of an originary "eddy" (226; 45) of German allegorical thinking into which both the Baroque and Romanticism can be absorbed.

The "redemption" of Baroque allegory lies in its survival into German Romanticism, then. Benjamin had already made a similar argument earlier, in the second chapter of his book, about the Baroque form of the tragic drama itself, which as a generic "idea" emerges periodically in history, creating an alternative "lineage" (*Sippe*) for a specifically "German literary history" (G: 1.1: 307; E: 128). That chapter is of course choreographed to define this lineage in counterpoint to ancient and Renaissance tragedy, with the majority of the first part of the chapter devoted to a discussion of the properties specific to seventeenth-century German plays of the Silesians, with their devotion to history, to the sovereign as tyrant and martyr, to intrigue and the court, and to a complex, perhaps even incomplete process of secularization (242–78; 62–100; see Weidner). It is here that a recourse to historical sources roots the tragic drama in an "epochal feeling" (251; 72) all its own; Riegl can thus be cited (277; 99), as is Hübscher (278; 100) in turn. The second part of the chapter juxtaposes these very distinct forms of the tragic drama to those of ancient tragedy (279–99; 101–38), which, as if to confirm the historical specificity of the seventeenth-century dramas just presented, must be explained as equally rooted in its own age. Classicists Ulrich von Wilamowitz-Moellendorff (282, 284–85, 292; 104, 106, 113) and Kurt Latte (295; 116) are cited to ratify a reading that also sees tragedy as a "historical fact" (282; 103) rooted in a different place and time, with its preference for the matter of legend, for example, and related to ancient judicial procedure. Tragedy is thus precisely not the transhistorical witness that Johannes Volkelt's *Ästhetik des Tragischen* (Aesthetics of the Tragic) had defined it to be, not the articulation of transcendent ethical norms "with no relation to historical subject matter" (279; 101). Rather, in Wölfflinian fashion, Benjamin presses the Baroque tragic drama up against ancient tragedy in this way in order to show the specificity of each.

Benjamin's return, at the end of the second section of the second chapter of the *Tragic Drama* book, to the "idea" of Baroque tragic drama as it emerges in subsequent periods of German literature, most prominently, Storm and Stress and Romanticism, thus allows a narrative of national fulfillment to be written. "The effect of the Baroque world of forms" (G: 1.1: 300; E: 121) can be observed in the plays of Zacharias Werner (1768–1823) and Heinrich Wilhelm von Gerstenberg (1737–1823), for example, as well as in the distorted form of "the apocryphal afterlife of the tragic drama . . . in the classicizing attempts at historical drama" (301; 122) by Friedrich Schiller (1759–1805). The claim reminds us that earlier, Goethe's play *Die natürliche Tochter* (The Natural Daughter) (1804) had emerged, if somewhat apologetically, as a tragic drama for Benjamin (268; 89), as had Friedrich Schlegel's *Alarcos* (1802) as well (314; 136). It is probably not by chance that in addition to the playwrights of the clearly "anticlassical" periods of German literature, such as Storm and Stress and Romanticism, it is the great figures of Weimar Classicism, Goethe and Schiller, whose works must be "reinterpreted" here, not as a self-fulfilling Renaissance moment, however, but rather as the most potent proof of the afterlife of a specifically German Baroque. The "drama of fate," unancient and untragic, and yet nearly Renaissance-like as a "blossoming space of drama" (307; 128), proves, finally, the periodicity of the Baroque best. "The tragedy of fate is [already] anticipated in the tragic drama" (312; 133), Benjamin writes. The plays adduced here as evidence of the afterlife of the German Baroque are primarily those of Calderón and Shakespeare; that these non-German playwrights provide proof positive of the survival of the Baroque in the German Romantic tradition is explained when we look to the names of their translators, Johann Diederich Gries, Wilhelm Schlegel, and Ludwig Tieck, in whose editions Benjamin read their now German Baroque plays.[70]

In addition to references to dramatic texts by post-Baroque and especially Romantic authors, Benjamin offers in these pages an even more prominent reprise of Strich's and Hübscher's theses about the German Baroque in his analyses of the peculiarly German dramatic genre of the "Haupt- und Staatsaktionen"—loosely translated, plays about "affairs of state"—based on the work of Romantic literary historian Franz Christoph Horn (1781–1837), in his *Poesie und Beredsamkeit der Deutschen* (German Poetry and Rhetoric) (1822–23). Horn's volume and its importance for Benjamin's access to a "Baroque" tradition are the subject of a more detailed discussion in chapter 2. Here it is interesting to note that it is not by chance that Benjamin quotes Horn in his assessment of these plays as "authentically German [in] origin and entirely appropriate for the character of the Germans" (G: 1.1: 302; E: 123). Throughout this section (299–307; 120–28), Benjamin places his own citations of Silesian dramas by Gryphius and Lohenstein alongside references to Horn's commentary on the plays of Josef Anton Stranitzky (c. 1676–1726), for example, from the volume that Horn calls his "cultural history of the fatherland" (2–3), as well as alongside other less well-known dramatic texts collected in Franz Josef Mone's *Schauspiele des Mittelalters* (Medieval Plays) (1846) and Karl Weiß's *Die Wiener Haupt- und Staatsactionen* (Viennese Plays about Affairs of State) (1854). I also discuss Mone and Weiß in more detail below. Alongside Horn's collection, these anthologies belonged to a tradition of celebrating the cultural patrimony of the nation. In marshalling the evidence he finds in texts such as these as proof of a continuous German dramatic tradition, Benjamin follows Strich's and Hübscher's commitment to defining the longer history of German literature as the fruit of the Baroque. Benjamin had already alluded earlier in his study to the "pre-history" of the Baroque tragic drama in the "relation" of Baroque drama to "medieval religious" dramatic forms, such as the "Passion play" (254–55; 75–76) and medieval mystery plays, both of which display, he writes, "the world of forms of the Baroque

---

70. Benjamin was not the only one to argue that Calderón's plays had an important afterlife in German Romanticism; see Berens's 1926 article, "Calderons Schicksalstragödien," 11 and 58, 60, 65–66, for example. Most of Benjamin's arguments about the importance of stage props (e.g., G: 1.1: 311–12; E: 132–33) are derived from Berens.

tragic drama" (257; 78). Both these relatively indistinct prehistories (one is reminded of Strich's "primal German poetry") and their afterlives up through the eighteenth and nineteenth centuries demonstrate the robustness of a specifically German "lineage of the German tragic drama," as noted above (307; 128). Nontragic, and thus neither "classical" nor imitative in a Renaissance mode, as Stachel or Cysarz might have had it, this lineage testifies to the origin of a continuous and nationally rooted German dramatic tradition out of the spirit and style of the period of the Baroque.

The story of debates about the Baroque indicated in this chapter demonstrates that, while certainly not unanimous, most of the scholars engaged in defending the period and its forms did so by pressing the Baroque into the service of a narrative about the power of a new kind of style to express an often complexly overdetermined, yet durable national-cultural sensibility. To anchor the (re)birth of a collective German modernity in a Baroque "will to art" and "feeling of life" appears to have done work not unlike the work done by related, Renaissance-based arguments about the (re)awakening of a nation's vitality. Unlike those arguments, however, the case being made for the Baroque adduced indigenous rather than foreign cultural capital and texts as the origin of a national tradition gradually reaching its fulfillment. While it may seem odd to insert Benjamin's argument about the Baroque into this critical tradition, given his rejection in the "Prologue" of a "nationalist philology" that had underestimated the achievements of the Baroque, it is clear that he was wrestling with exactly the same issues as the art and literary theorists and critics he cites when he addressed the question of the "origin" of a specifically German tragic drama in their terms. Like Wölfflin and Riegl, Strich and Hübscher, then, Benjamin saw the Baroque as a kind of canvas on which to image forth theories about a period and its cultural integrity as they emerged out of a close reading of the "phenomenal" details of works of art and texts. But his and their literary-critical and art theoretical texts were not the only ones to address the way that the "idea" of the Baroque "encounters the historical world again and again" (G: 1.1: 226; E: 45). The significantly more literal question of where to locate and how to find material versions of these many historical formations of the Baroque tragic drama—which, taken together in their "totality," constitute the "origin of the German tragic drama" (226–27; 45–46)—was posed in and answered by the production of a variety of critical editions, anthologies of texts, and translations of "Baroque" dramas to which I now turn.

2

THE PLAYS ARE THE THING

Textual Politics and the German Drama

In addition to being the subject of important art theoretical and literary-historical debates during the late nineteenth and early twentieth centuries, Baroque texts were crucial as material objects to the enterprise undertaken during these same years to define and celebrate the period as something other than a foreign Renaissance's poor cousin. It is to these print objects, and to the multiple editorial ideologies, anthologization practices, and translation projects that constructed the Baroque as an object of the national imagination in the late nineteenth and early twentieth centuries, that I now turn. It is well known that Benjamin was himself a book collector and bibliophile; the claims he makes about the ways that history can be captured in print in his famous essay "Ich packe meine Bibliothek aus" (Unpacking My Library) of 1931 are examined below.[1] Less well illuminated is the relation of his lively interest in the physical book to the question of how he was able to identify any specific volume he held in his hands as part of a specifically German "Baroque." The question is not an abstract one. In his review of Gabriele Ecke-hard's *Das deutsche Buch im Zeitalter des Barock* (The German Book in the Age of

---

1. On Benjamin as a collector, see Köhn, who argues that a new, nearly affective relation to collect-ing began in the late nineteenth century in Germany (697). Benjamin's book collecting and selling be-longed to this trend, although it was also often pragmatic—that is, an investment practice and a mode of survival.

the Baroque) (1930), which appeared in the well-known periodical *Die literarische Welt* (The Literary World) that same year, he wrote, for example: "For the true collector of books, there are few objects that speak to him as aptly as the books of the era of the German Baroque" (*Gesammelte Schriften* 3: 237). Benjamin would have known, as he was himself a collector of Baroque books.

Benjamin had owned a volume of Baroque tragic dramas since 1917, when, as he remarks to Ernst Schoen in July of that year, he received a copy of the plays of the Silesian playwright Andreas Gryphius in a "beautiful old edition" for his birthday (*Briefe* 1: 140). The description is somewhat misleading, since both the inventory of books that Benjamin read and the notes to the *Tragic Drama* book indicate that it was not a "Baroque" (i.e., seventeenth-century) book that he received as a gift, but rather the Hermann Palm edition of Gryphius's plays, published in 1882. Clearly not as "old" as the seventeenth- and eighteenth-century editions in which Benjamin read the plays of the other members of the Second Silesian school, Hallmann and Lohenstein (*Gesammelte Schriften* 7: 438 and 452–54), for example, the scholarly, yet also exceedingly nationalist Palm Gryphius may nevertheless have been somewhat "older" than the other "old edition of the works" of a different Baroque writer, Hofmann von Hofmannswaldau (1616–79), that Benjamin indicates he purchased as something of an extravagance at an auction in January 1924, when he was in the middle of work on his thesis (*Briefe* 1: 328). Two texts by Hofmannswaldau are cited in the *Tragic Drama* book: one, a 1680 edition of Hofmannswaldau's *Helden-Briefe* (Heroic Letters) (G: 1.1: 247; E: 66); the other, the anti- or at least non-academic selection of Hofmannswaldau poems put together by Felix Paul Greve in 1907 (234; 54). The former would indeed have been an extravagance; three years later, it sold for seventy-five marks at a famous auction of Baroque books. The volatile currency markets in 1924, together with the precariousness of Benjamin's financial situation at the time, make it difficult to believe this was the volume he bought. The slim Greve volume would have been more affordable. In addition to these books, Benjamin appears, finally, to have owned some very special and genuinely "old" texts, namely two collections of Baroque emblems that he mentions in a letter to Gershom Scholem (*Briefe* 1: 340). This selection of volumes makes it clear that the Baroque was available in as many different editorial "generations" and material versions of itself as there were consuming publics for it at the time. Of "origin" (*Ursprung*), Benjamin writes: "The category of origin is thus not, as Cohen asserts, a purely logical one, but, rather, historical." Taken in their historical "totality," these books testified to the "origin" of the German Baroque as the sum of its "pre- and post-histories" in material form (G: 1.1: 226; E: 45–46).[2]

---

2. Benjamin continued to be fascinated with collecting the Baroque even after he withdrew his *Habilitation* from consideration at Frankfurt. Indeed, his work on his thesis appears to have increased his taste for its books. He writes to Scholem in September 1926: "If I come to Berlin, one of the first things I plan to do is to undertake a general inspection and sorting out of my library . . . I want to throw out a

Benjamin was not alone in expressing his interest in the Baroque by collecting it during the early twentieth century. Victor Manheimer, a close friend of Hugo von Hofmannsthal and Walter Brecht, owned the most famous private collection of Baroque literature in Germany at the time. It is Manheimer's earlier "positive," although "sentimental" relationship to the Baroque in his 1904 dissertation on Gryphius that was the premonition of "the artistic sensibility of today" to which Benjamin is referring when he writes of contemporary interest in the Baroque in the "Epistemo-Critical Prologue" (G: 1.1: 235; E: 54). Sold off at an auction in 1927, Manheimer's library, like Benjamin's, contained both the Palm Gryphius and a large number of contemporary anthologies, including Greve's (Wolfskehl 89, 90, and 86–96). The main strength of Manheimer's much more extensive collection lay in its inclusion of the crème de la crème of historical—that is, seventeenth-century—texts. The descriptions of these volumes given in the catalog for the auction indicate just how rare many of these genuinely old books were. Moreover, the list of prices paid for parts of the Manheimer collection indicates some very high sums for volumes like the 1680 Hofmannswaldau and suggests that Benjamin may indeed have been as restricted by his limited finances in his acquisitions as the 1926 letter to Scholem suggests.[3] Curt Faber du Faur, born in 1890, collected German Baroque books on the same grand scale as Manheimer in Germany throughout the 1920s; he began to form his own library while he was a book dealer, and took it with him when he left Germany for the United States in 1939, settling first in Cambridge, Massachusetts, but soon moving to New Haven, Connecticut, where he lived and worked until his death in 1966. Yale University now owns his collection.

While Benjamin does not appear to have known of Faber du Faur or to have enjoyed either his or Manheimer's means, the parallels between the ways all three men understood their collections are striking. In an article written in 1958, for example, Faber du Faur comments that book collecting occurs both "in the service of the past" and as a way to the future; in a university context, the collector collects in order to prepare a "new generation [of students] for the future" by opening up the past to them in the form of texts ("Eine Sammlung deutscher Literatur" 8). Manheimer's friend Karl Wolfskehl claims in 1927 that Manheimer understood "the magical and radiating power" of the volumes in his "Baroque library" (1) in

---

great deal, and restrict myself primarily to German literature (recently, with a certain privileging of the Baroque, which my finances nevertheless make very difficult), French literature, the study of religion, fairy tales and children's books" (*Briefe* 1: 434).

3. See *Jahrbuch der Bücherpreise* (Yearbook of Book Prices) (1927), in which two of the texts Benjamin cites in the *Tragic Drama* book, a 1663 edition of Gryphius (*Trauerspiele auch Oden und Sonnette*) and a 1680 collection of Lohenstein's plays, are priced at 120 and 205 marks respectively (104 and 136). For comparison's sake: Benjamin laments to Scholem in 1925 that even if his *Habilitation* is accepted, he can expect no more than 180 marks a month in support (*Briefe* 1: 379). The compiler of the price list, Gertrud Hebbeler, mentions that the "interest for the art of the Baroque" that had emerged in the preceding two decades is "visible in the prices" (Vorwort, v–vi).

ways not unlike Faber du Faur. In 1930, finally, Benjamin writes that he considers Wolfskehl one of the best "collectors" of whom he knows, and finds it not at all curious that Wolfskehl was also an "enthusiast of the Baroque" (*Gesammelte Schriften* 3: 237). Benjamin's thoughts about collecting the Baroque were thus in line with those of these premier collectors of his day. That he nevertheless needed to rethink his own collecting habits in 1926 was the result of number of financial factors, not the least of which was the debacle of the *Habilitation*. Moreover, he had changed addresses repeatedly during the years just before beginning his thesis, as he was to continue to do throughout his life. As a result, he had to endure both temporary and permanent losses of his collection at various times. The situation had become acute by 1920, when much of his personal library lay packed away in "crates," as he writes to Scholem, and distributed among family and friends (*Briefe* 1: 240). Although in the winter and spring of 1920–21, he and Dora Benjamin finally had their own apartment in Berlin, and he was able to celebrate the "reunification" of his "libraries" there (*Briefe* 1: 254, 262), by 1923, he was to his own chagrin living again with his parents (*Briefe* 1: 297) and having to barter and sell books to support himself (307). After the withdrawal of his thesis from Frankfurt, questions about where to live, how to survive, and what to do with the books he could afford to purchase and keep became only more pressing.[4]

The combination of the high cost of historical Baroque books and the great interest on the part of more well-endowed contemporaries in collecting them, on the one hand, and the actual unavailability of his personal library, with its various Baroque volumes, on the other, poses the question of how else Benjamin might have had access during the years he was working on the tragic drama study to any of the myriad primary texts he quotes there. Benjamin indicates one important answer to this question in a letter to Florens Christian Rang on 24 October 1923, when he writes: "By the way, my study of the Baroque is allowing me to become acquainted almost daily with bibliographic curiosities" (*Briefe* 1: 307). The bibliographic novelties to which he refers could have been ones he discovered in auction catalogs like that for the Manheimer collection or in Berlin's famously abundant secondhand bookstores. But it is just as likely that here Benjamin is referring to the books he had begun to come across while working in the main reading room of the Prussian State Library on Unter den Linden in Berlin, where he did much of the preliminary research for his thesis during the fall and winter of 1923–24. There he would have been confronted with a considerably more extensive collection of Baroque texts than those he himself and even any other of the private collectors owned—and one that

---

4. Benjamin's interest in books was neither fetishistic nor antiquarian. Rather, in the years just before his work on the *Tragic Drama* book, he was being exceedingly pragmatic. He writes of the purchase of books as investments (*Briefe* 1: 270, in 1921; 290, in 1922), and contemplates with great seriousness and strategic foresight the opening of a secondhand bookstore (*Antiquariat*) as a solution to his financial woes (*Briefe* 1: 292–93, in 1922).

also included both Palm and Greve.[5] The depth and breadth of the State Library holdings, on which Benjamin based what he refers to in a letter to Scholem as his "study of the literature" of the Baroque (*Briefe* 1: 319), are testified to in the footnotes to the *Tragic Drama* book. It may well be the State Library's Baroque collection to which Benjamin is referring at the end of the "Epistemo-Critical Prologue" when he writes of the "feeling of dizziness" that accompanies the reader when he confronts what, citing Arthur Hübscher, he calls the vast "panorama" of the period's most "antithetical" texts (G: 1.1: 237; E: 56). Only by adopting what Benjamin calls an "ascetic attitude," which refuses "to plunge from the heights of understanding into the monstrous depths of the Baroque mind," can the scholar "steady himself" when confronted with such an abundance of texts. The State Library collection provided evidence of just such an abundant and variegated Baroque, a Baroque that was the result of what Benjamin elsewhere calls the "metamorphoses of poetry" that become visible in the physical embodiment of texts over time (*Gesammelte Schriften* 2.2: 649).

It was the diverse books in these "libraries," understood as both Benjamin's private collection and the holdings of the State Library, that constituted the archive that defined the Baroque for him at the time he wrote the *Tragic Drama* book. As abstract as something like the Rieglian "artistic will" of the period may have been, the "monstrous depths" and dangerous vortex of the Baroque of which Benjamin writes were thus not merely the property of an intangible "Baroque mind." Rather, the period's "will" came alive in the literal matter of the books that he read. In his famous essay on "the collector" Eduard Fuchs, published in 1937 in the *Zeitschrift für Sozialforschung* (Journal for Social Research), Benjamin provides useful terms for describing how books, usually understood as static objects, can also be understood as being in motion, when he writes, with reference to a letter from Engels to Mehring: "For [the reader] committed to a historical-dialectical approach, these works contain both their pre- and post-history, by virtue of which their pre-history becomes visible as implicated in an ongoing process of change" (2.2: 467). A decade earlier, he had used these same terms to define the "natural history" (1.1: 227) of the works he analyzes in the *Tragic Drama* book. What is meant by the claim that a book has a "natural history" emerges with greatest clarity in Benjamin's short essay of 1931, "Unpacking My Library." There, he writes of the "dialectical conditions" of both book collecting and the collected volumes themselves. The work of the "collector" takes place, Benjamin writes, between the poles of "disorder" and "order" (*Gesammelte Schriften* 4.1: 389). On the shelf, books exist in a kind of precarious "balancing act" over the abyss of chaos from which they derive and which, in their very material survival and presence, they also represent. For the

---

5. The Greve volume was sent directly to the State Library by the Insel publishing house in 1914. My thanks go to Robert Giel and especially Eva Rothkirch of the Abteilung Historische Drücke at the Prussian State Library for helping me with questions concerning the dating of library acquisitions.

"true collector," the book, now his "property," represents a kind of "magical encyclopedia" that contains all that has contributed to its "fate." Benjamin is not referring here to books in the abstract, but rather to individual "copies" (389). It is the
purchase, procuring, even physical holding of a particular volume in one's hands
that enables a kind of "rebirth" (*Wiedergeburt*), a Renaissance, he writes, of the object as Benjamin's famous "angel of history" has swept it forward in time. Feeling
the "depths" of a Baroque book every time he picked it up could have created the
sense of dizziness of which Benjamin writes in the "Prologue."

In this chapter, I discuss a selection of the books in Benjamin's libraries in terms
of their "fate" at the hands of the editors, textual critics, anthologizers, translators,
and literary historians, each of whom was responsible for a different Renaissance-
like "restoration" (G: 1.1: 226; E: 45) of the Baroque contained in the books Benjamin cites.[6] Burkhardt Lindner's claim that Benjamin's thesis was much more than
just a "monograph about Baroque drama" ("Habilitationsakte Benjamin" 163)
notwithstanding, it was the plays of the Second Silesian school in particular that
were one of his central concerns there. My focus here is thus on the versions of
these and other German plays (rather than the lyric, for example) that Benjamin
cites. I begin in the first section below with the late nineteenth-century collection
of Andreas Gryphius's plays edited by Hermann Palm, a volume that Benjamin
owned, as noted above, but that was also present in the Prussian State Library in
Berlin. While the Palm Gryphius was in fact *not* "Baroque"—that is, not one of the
seventeenth-century editions of Gryphius that the library owned at the time (and
thus also not one of the seventeenth- and eighteenth-century editions of the dramas of the other Silesian playwrights, Hallmann and Lohenstein respectively, that
Benjamin cites)—it does capture one highly overdetermined version of the period
in the historically specific orthographic and text-editorial practices that contributed
to its identity as an icon of the modern German nation-state. The 1882 Gryphius
was no unicum in this respect, but rather the natural extension of developments
in the study of the history of German-language literature, and especially drama,
discussed in chapter 1.

These developments found additional material expression in the collections and
editions of German-language dramatic texts prepared in the mid-nineteenth century by the archivists and librarians Karl Weiß and Franz Josef Mone. Weiß's work,
in turn, found its own critical and textual afterlife in Rudolf Payer von Thurn's
1908–10 edition of the plays of the Viennese actor and impresario Josef Anton
Stranitzky. Benjamin knew and cites extensively from these texts, which are the

---

6. On "restoration" as part of "origin," see Benjamin (G: 1.1: 226; E: 45). The set of texts I deal with
here is of necessity selective. Glaringly absent, for example, are the plays of Calderón, which Benjamin
claims in a letter are the "virtual object" of his thesis (*Briefe* 1: 366). As important as Calderón's oeuvre is
for Benjamin, the translations of the great Spanish Golden Age playwright that he read, by Johann Diederich Gries, belong to the same tradition as the Ulrici Shakespeare I discuss in detail below.

focus of the second section below. In curiously anachronistic fashion, he "collects" the "Baroque tragic drama" out of these several nineteenth- and early twentieth-century anthologies, thereby fulfilling the charge of the German Romantic literary historian Franz Horn to produce a "cultural history of the fatherland" (Horn 1: 3), a task Horn describes in the first volume of his *Die Poesie und Beredsamkeit der Deutschen, von Luthers Zeit bis zur Gegenwart* (German Poetry and Rhetoric from the Time of Luther to the Present) (1822–29), a book that Benjamin knew. The edition of Shakespeare that Benjamin cites is, finally, curiously equal in weight to this tradition of German plays, and I turn to a discussion of it in the third and final section of this chapter. Precisely because Benjamin did not read the Bard in a sixteenth-century English original—and the question of what an "original" Shakespeare text would have been for either British scholars of Shakespeare at the time or the German Shakespeareans who relied on them looms large—but rather in a heavily annotated nineteenth-century German-language translation, he was able to see the author of *Hamlet* as contributing to the creation of the tradition of the *German* tragic drama. That Shakespeare could not only be German for Benjamin, but could also be identified as "Baroque" fits easily with the way this edition was conceived and read at the time, for a Baroque Shakespeare had already become part of Germany's national patrimony during World War I. The literal and figurative translation of Shakespeare into a German Bard occurred in articles and books by the well-known scholars Friedrich Gundolf and Oskar Walzel. Benjamin was familiar with both men's work, as I show.

The Origin of the Silesian School: Nationalism and the Baroque Tragic Drama

The plays of three major Silesian scholar-statesmen and playwrights—Daniel Casper von Lohenstein (1635–83), Andreas Gryphius (1616–64), and Johann Christian Hallmann (c. 1640–1704)—are some of the most bizarre literary artifacts of the German Baroque era. They figure importantly in Benjamin's thesis on the German tragic drama. Little known to most Benjamin scholars, these plays' literal beginnings, the contexts in which they were originally written and produced, are worth examining briefly before turning to the editions in which Benjamin read them as he prepared to write the *Habilitation*.

The plays of the Second Silesian school are extravagant, scandalous, and in many cases downright offensive. They are also monuments to the imbrication of a highly conventional and learned school culture in a broad array of contemporary political and social institutions in seventeenth-century central Europe. Designed for production by adolescent schoolboy actors, who were students at the Protestant schools (*gymnasia*) of the major Silesian city of Breslau (now Wroclaw, Poland), where their authors also held important political positions, as Benjamin knew (G: 1.1: 236; E: 56), the plays often featured boys cross-dressed as female characters, who, in the plays, often cross-dressed as men. The plots of the plays frequently called for the young actors to stage exotic and often lascivious scenes of political intrigue, seduction, human sacrifice, torture, execution, and murder derived from contemporary and ancient accounts of events at the courts of seventeenth-century England, medieval Byzantium, the Ottoman Empire, and ancient Rome. The political and erotic powers of female protagonists, including Cleopatra, Agrippina, Catharina of Georgia, and Sophonisbe, are often the focus of the plays; the historical anomaly of a long-standing tradition of female leaders in the small principalities of Silesia during these years may help explain the frequency of the playwrights' choices in this respect.[7] Given that issues of rulership and power were the plays' major concerns, it is no wonder that Benjamin was fascinated in his book by the topic of sovereignty—"the putting to the test of princely virtues, the representation of princely vices, insight into the workings of diplomacy, and the handling of all political machinations" (G: 1.1: 243; E: 62)—as well as by the intricacies of tyranny and martyrdom, state stability, and courtly display. These and related topics belong to the thematic center of most of the Silesian plays, out of which, as Benjamin quite correctly intuits, "theatricality" speaks "with special force" (231; 51).[8]

While part of a performance tradition in early modern central Europe known as school drama (*Schuldrama*), the Silesian plays were also published, usually in the year following their production, in elaborately annotated editions, with a textual apparatus of notes (*Anmerkungen*), as Benjamin points out (244; 63), that teemed with references to both ancient and contemporary sources in political theory, geographical and protoscientific description, and collections of arcane monuments and artifacts.[9] As closely as the notes indicate that the plays were bound to the book culture that Benjamin accurately describes as an un-Renaissance-like world of "learnedness" (270; 91; "The Renaissance takes the universe as its object of study, the Baroque takes the libraries," he later writes, 319; 140), they also reveal that the tragic dramas were part of the professional preparation and ideological training of the young schoolboys who performed them. Their education was designed to shape them as male civil subjects destined for positions in the early modern administrative bureaucracies of the Holy Roman Empire, the cities, and the smaller principalities of eastern central Europe. That the plays were often produced not in the schools, but rather in the homes and courtly residences of the local Silesian political elite between about 1665 and 1679, an elite whose Piastian Protestant leanings often

7. On the female leaders of the Piastian houses of Silesia in the seventeenth century, see Newman, *Intervention of Philology*.
8. Here Benjamin is disputing the common assumption that these learned plays were "not stage friendly," or unperformable, and accurately notes that their "violent events" would have been very appealing to audiences.
9. Lohenstein's notes in particular compete with the main texts and plots of the plays for the reader's attention. The annotations often run to thirty or forty closely printed pages for plays just some hundred pages in length.

put it at odds with the Catholic Holy Roman Empire of the time, drives this point home. When Sophonisbe, the famous Numidian queen of the Second Punic War, for example, was seen resisting Rome in the homes of local Silesian leaders, it is entirely possible to conjecture that the young actors were being trained for similarly subversive political roles offstage. Or, if that is too strong, then they were at least being taught to understand the mechanics of this kind of subversion as well as the actions of the imperial authorities in Vienna, who were still trying to exert control over the volatile body politic of central Europe in the post–Treaty of Westphalia years. Benjamin writes of the plays of the Second Silesian school that they were concerned with "fratricide," "incest," "infidelity," and "spousal murder"—and were also performed (249–50; 70; and 231; 51).[10] The list of issues he enumerates as central to this peculiar early modern stage tradition is entirely accurate and makes clear that he read enough of these dramas to get the description right.

While Benjamin appears to have owned the single-volume late nineteenth-century edition of Gryphius's plays edited by Palm, as noted above, a huge selection of both Gryphius's and the other Silesian playwrights' dramatic texts was also available to him in the Prussian State Library on Unter den Linden in Berlin in a series of historical editions. The vast holdings of the library in this field—Benjamin insists in a letter to Rang in 1924 that he has read only a small selection of the available plays, "by no stretch all that come in question" (*Briefe* 1: 326–27)—would have been apparent to him already in the catalog volumes (*Bandkataloge*) of the Old Subject Catalog (*Alter Realkatalog*) there. These large, folio-size tomes, three to six inches wide, were used by readers to locate both primary and secondary works in the library's noncirculating collection. Although the State Library had begun to be formed already in the 1660s (it was then the Kurfürstliche Bibliothek, or Electoral Library), cataloging did not begin until the early nineteenth century. Work began on the Old Subject Catalog after 1842 under the leadership of Julius Schrader (1808–98) and was completed by 1881.[11] The volumes as they were available in the early part of the twentieth century, when Benjamin worked in the State Library, are visible in pictures taken of the catalog room at the time.[12] Having decided on the plays of the Second Silesian school as his topic, Benjamin, like any reader, would probably have turned to—or been assisted by a librarian in the consultation of—specific volumes of the Old Subject Catalog, each of which is identified

10. Benjamin is also interested in the poetological treatises and the lyric of the Nuremberg poets, Harsdörffer, Birken, and Klaj, all of whom were members of the Order of Flowers on the Pegnitz (Pegnesischer Blumenorden), one of the so-called German-language societies (*Sprachgesellschaften*). On the Blumenorden, see Newman, *Pastoral Conventions*. There has been virtually no work to date on Benjamin's understanding of the Nuremberg texts, citations from which are as frequent in the *Tragic Drama* book as citations from the Silesian plays.

11. On the history of the Old Subject Catalog, see Kittel; Roloff.

12. Photographs of the catalog volumes from c. 1905 and 1920 appear in Roloff 156 and 157. These volumes are still used by librarians today.

by national tradition, genre, and date on the spine and title page. Inside, the genre volumes are further subdivided by author, text, and the sequential editions that the library owned. Each main entry thus displays the "totality of history" of each text or edition as it had existed to be acquired by the library. Benjamin's definition of "origin" in precisely these terms in the *Tragic Drama* book (G: 1: 226; E: 45) comes uncannily close, in other words, to being a description of what he would have seen on the pages of the Old Subject Catalog when he consulted it there.

The sheer abundance in the State Library holdings of texts by the Silesian playwrights in whom Benjamin was interested is documented in volume Y24 of the Old Subject Catalog, identified as "German Literature, VII-B: Drama, 1601–1772" on the spine. The continuity of editorial interest in the Baroque plays would have been immediately obvious as soon as he opened the book. All of the library holdings of works in this category are inventoried alphabetically by author, and, most importantly, within the author category, chronologically by edition. In volume Y24, for example, on the right-hand pages, earlier acquisitions are indicated in a light and regular "German script," with later acquisitions added at the appropriate place in the chronological sequence either in a different and darker hand or typed and pasted in. Call numbers are listed on the right. A small superscript and underlined *a* after some call numbers indicates a second copy; a capital *R* accompanying others designates *rara,* or rare, texts.[13] In addition to the primary texts available in the collection, both historical and contemporary critical work held by the library on the individual playwrights is often documented in these volumes; the facing, left-hand pages appear to have been left blank for entries of relevant secondary studies and other bibliographic notes. Thus, even though he complained bitterly of a lack of time for his research, it is in some cases easy to see both from the layout of the catalog volumes and from the various entries on the left-hand sides of their pages how Benjamin could have used these volumes as a kind of bibliographic shortcut, with the titles of various relevant studies of the individual Baroque authors conveniently located directly across from the chronological listing by edition of the library's holdings of their primary works.[14]

---

13. The superscript *a* in most cases indicates a replacement copy; a huge number of State Library books—and 218 volumes of the Old Subject Catalog itself—were either lost or destroyed as a result of the removal of library holdings to locations other than Berlin after the city began to be bombed during World War II; after 1945, a systematic shelf read was done to confirm which of the some three million books from the prewar collection were missing, and efforts were made to replace them. The missing catalog volumes could of course not be replaced; the so-called "gap files" (*Lückenkarteien*), now available on microfiche, represent efforts to replace them. The *Lückenkarteien* nevertheless contain only the titles that could be determined to have been returned to the library after the war.

14. Some of the entries seem to shadow Benjamin's own scholarly notes (or, perhaps, vice versa). See, for example, the references to Kerckhoff's book on Lohenstein's plays on 502 of volume Y24 across from the listings of Lohenstein's dramatic work on 503. Benjamin cites Kerckhoff at G: 1.1: 370; E: 193 of the *Tragic Drama* book.

The pages of the Old Subject Catalog in volume Y24 reveal that the holdings of the Prussian State Library in the area of Second Silesian school drama were extensive at the time Benjamin worked there. The plays of Lohenstein, for example, listed in this volume were available in numerous individual and collected editions, from the very earliest (1659) through sequential printings during Lohenstein's lifetime (1661, 1665, 1680), as well as in the early posthumous edition of the complete plays in 1685 and in later, early eighteenth-century editions (1701, 1708, 1709, and 1724) (Old Subject Catalog, vol. Y24, 503–9). The plays of Gryphius were similarly well represented, in editions dating from the mid- to late seventeenth century (1650, 1652, 1658, 1659, 1663, and 1681) as well as in the later, nineteenth-century edition of 1882 by Palm (Y24, 489–95). Perhaps appropriate for his somewhat lesser status and degree of renown, the plays of Hallmann were also adequately, if less extensively, represented in seventeenth-century editions. The Old Subject Catalog indicates holdings from the 1660s and 1670s (Y24, 533–35), and Benjamin's notes indicate that he read the plays of Hallmann in these editions. He cites Lohenstein *not* in the early editions from the 1650s through 1680s that the State Library owned, however, but rather in subsequent versions printed in the early eighteenth century (1708 and 1724, respectively). Finally, the plays of Gryphius are cited in the even more recent, late nineteenth-century edition (1882) by Palm.[15] The notes in the *Tragic Drama* book to these volumes of Baroque plays thus reveal to contemporary scholars as they would have to Benjamin too that the school drama of the Baroque, although originally part of the complex cultural milieu of the seventeenth century discussed above, was—in the holdings of the State Library—visibly *not* bound to what he might have referred to as its "genetic" moment of *Entstehung* (cf. G: 1.1: 226; E: 45). Rather, the diverse editions of the German-language plays as they would have lain, "torso"-like, before Benjamin on the tables of the main reading room, would have made it clear that the Baroque had taken on various editorial guises in the very "metamorphoses of poetry" referred to above, its various layers open to "excavation" in both a literal and a metaphorical sense.[16] In the Palm Gryphius edition in particular, the historical guise in which the Baroque appeared is a particularly "mythological" one, whose material form confirms just how much part of the "modern" German nation the Baroque had become.[17]

---

15. Most of the primary texts that Benjamin cites in the notes to the *Tragic Drama* book can still be located in this and other volumes of the Old Subject Catalog, which indicate the range of editions to which he would have had access. The State Library holdings of the plays of Calderón, for example, can be found in volume X17, and those of Shakespeare in volume Z6b.

16. Benjamin discusses memory as an archeological site in terms similar to Freud's in a fragment entitled "Excavation and Memory" (*Gesammelte Schriften* 4: 400–401) from about 1932. It is in this fragment that he refers to the "torsos" of the past that stand "broken free of all earlier contexts" (400) in the present.

17. Benjamin critiques the mythologizing work of historicism that celebrates only the victors. The Palm edition makes clear that claiming such mythic status for the Baroque plays took considerable work. On Benjamin's critique of historicism, see Raulet; Kittsteiner.

The 1882 Palm edition after which Benjamin cites Gryphius was considered a professional critical product at the time. It was published under the auspices of the venerable series Bibliothek des Litterarischen Vereins in Stuttgart (Library of the Literary Society in Stuttgart), in which it was volume 162. The Literary Society was first established in 1839; the series was designed to make available in modern editions the textual monuments of the German literary tradition from the nation's medieval and early modern past. In this edition, Palm provides an overview of the textual history of each of Gryphius's plays in the respective forewords; the complex provenance of the plays is indicated in the detailed bibliographic apparatus at the bottom of each page, where the variants of several editions of the plays are compared.[18] The relatively confusing textual history of Gryphius's plays—individual plays published in numerous editions both before and after the author's death in 1664—would already have been apparent to Benjamin in volume Y24 of the Old Subject Catalog (489–95); it could have been this very complexity, along with the more pragmatic factor that ordering numerous plays in their various editions would have cluttered his place at the reading-room table, that encouraged Benjamin to use the later and far more convenient single-volume Palm edition, which he also owned. Moreover, the Palm volume is provocatively entitled simply *Trauerspiele* (Tragic Dramas) on the front page—and thus captured Benjamin's topic in concise form.[19] Perhaps most importantly, however, the Palm Gryphius distinguishes itself from both the other available copies of his works and from the seventeenth-century Hallmann and eighteenth-century Lohenstein editions Benjamin consulted, by its systematic use of a practice at the center of an ideologically explosive orthographic controversy raging in the nineteenth and early twentieth centuries (and still under discussion in some quarters today), namely that of the noncapitalization, or *Klein-schreibung,* of German nouns.

The decapitalization practices at the heart of this debate are intricately encoded in the *Tragic Drama* book. In the discussion of the theory of sovereignty, for example, where Gryphius's plays feature prominently in the evidentiary logic undergirding Benjamin's claims, he cites the famous speech of the title character of Gryphius's *Leo Arminius* on the indivisibility of sovereign power.[20] At stake is what Benjamin calls the "cosmological" logic of the Baroque, which equated the ruler

---

18. See, for example, Gryphius's *Leo Arminius* (a play Benjamin cites often), in which editions A (1650), B (1657), C (1663), and D (1698) are compared to one another in the apparatus; see also Gryphius's *Papinianus* (cited equally as frequently by Benjamin), in which editions A (1659) and B (1698) are compared.

19. For the textual history of Gryphius's plays up to and including the "modern" Szyrocki and Powell edition of the 1960s through the 1980s, see Mannack 26–30.

20. Scholarship has confirmed that the issue of monarchical legitimacy, its strengths and, above all, its weaknesses, was of central concern to the Silesian playwright's entire dramatic oeuvre and, indeed, to his career. See Wiedemann's excellent discussion of Gryphius. On Gryphius's own involvement with the Piastian princes of Silesia, his "local" version of the monarch or sovereign, see Pietrzak. On Gryphius's *Catharina von Georgien,* a play about a woman ruler, see below, chapter 3.

not only with God, but also with Nature's sovereign instance, the sun. Benjamin cites Palm's 1882 edition as the source of the quote. The citation of the play in the first print edition of the *Tragic Drama* book (1928) reads: "Whosoever might set another at his side on the throne is worth [only] having his robes and crown taken away. There is only one prince and one sun in the world and kingdom." In German, the text reads: "Wer jemand auff den Thron / An seine Seiten setz't; ist würdig daß man Kron / Und Purpur ihm entzih. Ein fürst und eine sonnen / Sind vor die welt und reich" (Benjamin, *Ursprung des deutschen Trauerspiels* [1928] 57; cf. G: 1.1: 247; E: 67). While not changing the sense of the passage, Benjamin has altered the rendering of it as it appears in the 1882 Palm Gryphius in a decidedly different orthographic form:

> Wer *iemand* auf den *thron*
> An seine *seiten setzt,* ist würdig, *dass* man *cron*
> Und *purpur* ihm entzieh. Ein fürst und eine sonnen
> Sind vor die welt und reich. (Gryphius, *Trauerspiele* 61, emphasis added)

While the changes that Benjamin has undertaken in his citation of the Palm edition are neither uniform nor systematic, they do intervene in the nineteenth-century editor's resolute decapitalization of most of the nouns throughout Gryphius's plays; *thron* has been capitalized in Benjamin's 1928 version, for example, as have *seiten* and *purpur.* Benjamin also replaces some of Palm's spellings, which appear archaic to a modern German-speaker and reader, with more "modern" spellings—*iemand* to *jemand, setz't* to *setzt, dass* to *daß, cron* to *Kron*—more closely aligned with orthographic practice in New High German, both in the 1920s and today. Benjamin's updating of the language of Palm's 1882 edition in 1928 draws attention to the ideological rootedness of Palm's orthography—and thus of his presentation of the Baroque—as an artifact of modernity at the time he was working.[21] Benjamin's Baroque represents a further "modernization" of Palm's Baroque in turn.

Palm's late nineteenth-century version of the Baroque was designed to serve the modern German nation in several ways, first and foremost, as a material print artifact with an ideologically inflected orthography most clearly visible in its decapitalization of nouns. The procedure belonged to a well-known project of cultural

---

21. The editors of the Frankfurt edition follow the Palm version in their rendering of this quote (G: 1.1: 247), rather than Benjamin's "original" updating of the Palm orthography in 1928. Benjamin nevertheless does follow Palm's editorial principles in some places. Palm had edited Gryphius's 1659 *Papinianus,* for example, in such a way as to reflect the more "modern" nineteenth-century spellings of *umsonst,* for example, for *umbsonst* and *so viel* for *so vil* (Gryphius, *Trauerspiele* 635; *Großmüttiger Rechts-Gelehrter* n.p. after H v); Benjamin follows Palm in his citation of these lines (*Ursprung des deutschen Trauerspiels* [1928] 53) and in Palm's decapitalized *purpur* (Gryphius, *Trauerspiele* 212), an updating of the synecdochic *Purpur* from the 1663 *Leo Arminius* in *Freuden und Trauer-Spiele* (147). There are some fifteen citations from Gryphius plays in the text of Benjamin's *Tragic Drama* book.

nationalism developed after the creation of the German nation-state in 1871. Benjamin was no stranger to this program, as it was still part of the controversial politics of education during and after the time he was a schoolboy in Berlin. The history of the debate about *Groß-* and *Kleinschreibung,* or the capitalization and decapitalization of nouns, or substantives, in German, dates back to the fifteenth and sixteenth centuries and the earliest days of mass production of vernacular texts, on the one hand, and the resulting movements to standardize the enormously heterogeneous regional dialects of the north, northeastern, central, central-eastern, and southern German-speaking territories, on the other. Efforts reached a high point in the very periods in which both Palm and Benjamin were interested, namely the sixteenth and seventeenth centuries, as the desire for politico-confessional religious orthodoxies of several sorts emerged at the same time as projects were being initiated to create a standardized German literary tongue.[22] The use of capital letters at the beginning of sentences began as a way of clarifying syntax and allowing for greater ease in oral reading. The more complicated status of the use of capitals in the "interior of a sentence," which became widespread in the early sixteenth century, seems, in spite of the relatively unsystematic application of the rule by printers, for example, to have become a generally accepted principle by the end of the seventeenth century. Benjamin would have been able to observe the orthographic precipitate of this particular historical (i.e., seventeenth-century) orthodoxy in the edition of Hallmann that he used; he comments on the "naturalization" of "the capital letter" in "normative spelling in German" during the Baroque period in the *Tragic Drama* book (G: 1.1: 382; E: 208).

Early reasons given for nearly universal capitalization of nouns in German included the importance of signaling graphically the centrality of what at the time were called *Hauptwörter* ("main words," thus "nouns") by capitalizing them. Subsequently arguments were derived from extending this privilege to other important words, such as proper names, the virtues and vices, and the days of the week. The development of contemporary philosophical doctrines, such as Spinoza's "philosophy of substance" (*Substanzphilosophie*), is also sometimes invoked as an explanation for this trend. Benjamin's comments about the ways that capitalization revealed a new status for language during the Baroque period because of its ability to work allegorically (G: 1.1: 382; E: 208) recognize this tradition of claims. The practice was then rendered a near orthodoxy by Johann Christoph Adelung in his *Vollständige Anweisung zur deutschen Orthographie* (Complete Instructions for German Orthography) (1788), which soon became the Enlightenment Bible of German orthography. It is significant that Adelung famously claimed that the authority of

22. The history of normative spelling in German (*Rechtschreibung*) is hugely complex. The following is based on a series of studies of the subdiscipline of the capitalization of substantives by Ewald and Nerius, Nerius and Scharnhorst, Mentrup, Mentrup et al., and Nerius.

his stabilization of both orthographic and grammatical norms was based on nor-mative "popular" usage: "Write German and what is considered German with the conventional written signs as you speak it, in accordance with the pronuncia-tion that is generally considered the best, following the closest possible and proven derivation, and, when all else fails, according to general usage" (qtd. in Nerius and Scharnhorst 6). The eighteenth-century Lohenstein editions that Benjamin used were based on Adelung's norms.

Obscured by these efforts at standardization and, indeed, by the widespread adoption of and support for Adelung's rules by the greats of German literature in the eighteenth century, such as Wieland and Goethe, was the fact that, like many of the standards set in the encyclopedic tomes issued during the seventeenth and eigh-teenth centuries (many of which included dictionary-like lists and inventories of German words), these rules may well have been derived from "common" *usus,* but from a far from universal usage, indeed, from a highly homogeneous, limited, and elite one. Already in the sixteenth century, for example, it was the "Meißen" Ger-man of Upper Saxony that dominated the linguistic landscape of both the north and the south by virtue of the concentration there of political-confessional and printing power associated with the spread of the Reformation and its mechanically repro-duced Word (Nerius and Scharnhorst 1). In the seventeenth century, the founding in these same areas of the so-called language societies (*Sprachgesellschaften*) helped elevate this particular dialect and the way it was written by language-society mem-bers and sponsors, namely the noble and upper classes, to the status of orthographic orthodoxy and law.[23] In the mid-eighteenth century, Johann Christoph Gottsched's imperious declamations about the German language—which were resented, but nevertheless continued to be widely influential "abroad" precisely because they provided standardized norms—were likewise based on Upper Saxon usage. Ade-lung merely extended in more systematic fashion and in more detail what he called "Gottschedian orthography" (Mentrup et al. 255); the project of working toward a uniform "national" linguistic practice thus had something of a hegemonic feeling to it from the very start. The printing and dissemination in the seventeenth and eighteenth centuries of a huge number of texts devoted to cataloging the details of German normative spelling from an Upper Saxon perspective—and to proclaim-ing the natural reasonableness of one of those details, namely capitalization—may explain why later theorists and practitioners were gradually able to (re)write the history of the practice as a narrative about an "ancient custom" specific to a Ger-man language that always already allowed the "natural shape, beauty, and reason" of its nouns to emerge precisely by capitalizing them.[24] Matters of orthographic

---

23. See Newman, *Pastoral Conventions* 69–131. Benjamin remarks on the language-society reforms at G: 1.1: 379; E: 204.

24. This according to one of the first representatives of this school, Johann Balthasar Antesperg, in his *Kayserliche deutsche Grammatik* (Imperial German Grammar) of 1747 (qtd. in Mentrup 254).

standardization were, in other words, matters of regional and class hegemony masked as national, or perhaps better (because less anachronistic), regional unity and pride.

Effaced along with, yet also ironically preserved within, these "organic" origins of High German (*Hochsprache*) in political, confessional, and linguistic localisms of several kinds was nevertheless also a tradition of resistance to the exceptionalist narrative about the Upper Saxon dialect, even among contemporary scholars, some of whom championed other local dialects, but all of whom resented the homogenization and reduction of German to just one form of itself. This is where the story of Palm's Gryphius begins. The most complex and prolonged of the historical battles over which dialect should function as the basis of a "universal" and normative High German was in fact the one between the much-praised "Meißen" German of Upper Saxony and none other than the dialect of Silesia, made famous by Martin Opitz, the "father of German poetry," author of both the first defense of vernacular usage in Germany (*Aristarchus,* 1617) and the first defense of German poetry (*Buch von der teutschen Poeterey,* Book of German Poetics, 1624), and a leader of the so-called First Silesian school.[25] The widespread availability of printed texts by the second generation of Silesian poets, the playwrights, including Gryphius, about whom Benjamin wrote and to which the holdings of the State Library attest, made it possible for the mid- to late nineteenth century to take over wholesale the German language that the *Silesians* wrote—with its localisms, archaisms, and idiosyncracies intact—as a countermodel to "Upper Saxon" for the "standard" German that the newly unified, "modern" German nation would need. A veritable industry of work on the Silesian dialect and its presence in the works of the Silesian Baroque poets, among them, again, Opitz and Gryphius, thus arose at the very same time that the standardization debates about German orthography reached their peak in the mid- to late nineteenth century. From Joseph Kehrein (1844) to Ernst Heilborn (1890), scholars saw in the Silesian dialect the embodiment of the forces that would lead to a Renaissance-like "rejuvenation of the German language" and in turn—but ironically, given the dialect's competition with the equally as local Upper Saxon—to the (re)birth of a unified German nation-state.[26] That Benjamin found in the plays of the Silesian Baroque proof of a "more-than-Renaissance" rebirth is thus not at all strange.

Given the ways in which the struggle over uniform orthography was cast as part of larger political and ideological debates, it should come as no surprise that a

---

25. Even though Opitz himself declared that local dialects (*Mundarten*) ought not to function as the basis of a standardized German language, "Silesian localisms" in fact crept into his writing; contemporaries were aware of this fact and were critical (Andreas Tscherning) and laudatory (Friedrich Logau) in turn. It was Logau's linguistic practice, moreover, that overtly sponsored and utilized the Silesian dialect in matters of orthography, pronunciation, and rhyme, which both Leibniz and Lessing later saw as exemplary. See Henne.

26. Kehrein and Heilborn are cited in Henne 4.

scholar famous for his devotion to creating a standardized and, most importantly, a simplified and universally available German language, namely the famous linguist Jacob Grimm, who was, with his brother, Wilhelm, the collector of German fairy tales and author of the massive *Grimmsches Wörterbuch* (Grimm Dictionary) (1854–), declared himself a foe of the by-then nearly orthodox practice of capitalization. He did so by using a curiously parallel logic of nostalgia that converted historical norms into naturalized standards that would guide the rejuvenation of the national tongue by devising a way to capture these standards in decapitalized form (*Kleinschreibung*).[27] Based on his earlier text critical and philological work on Old and Middle High German texts, in which he championed the production of editions that reproduced the dialectological specificity and individuality of the texts, Grimm's decision in favor of *decapitalization* developed out of a comparative historical approach to the systematic study of various "ancient" Germanic languages. Ultimately he came to advocate a new normative orthography for New High (i.e., modern) German based on its proximity to "organic" Middle High German usage as the purest form of the vernacular; historical sources for this modern "national" language were available in manuscript collections of primarily unpunctuated and decapitalized texts. In his German dictionary after 1850, the legitimacy and organicity of the words derived from such sources were to be signaled graphically by the systematic decapitalization (*Kleinschreibung*) of all nouns to indicate their "origin" in "ancient" texts and in "patriotic" Middle High German linguistic forms.

Acolytes of Grimm's, including Karl Weinhold, who became the rector of the Königliche Friedrich Wilhelm Universität (King Frederick William University) in Berlin in 1893, lauded "the idiomatic" and "the national" in the German language as it was cataloged in the massive tomes of the Grimm *Dictionary* after 1854, not as so much "deaf rubble and discarded stone" of an archaic past, but rather as modern "witnesses" to "the history of the spiritual and moral life of our nation" (Weinhold 10–12). Soon, as Wilhelm Scherer describes in his biography of Grimm (1885), many scholars, following the now institutionally accepted and materially available practice, began equating Grimm's "scientific" approach to spelling with a kind of unifying and "patriotic" learnedness tout court, and began to have their own texts printed in entirely "decapitalized" form (Nerius and Scharnhorst 9–11). By 1903, in spite of the orthographic controversies between 1876 and the beginning of the new century, the imperial interior minister of Prussia issued guidelines for the normative spelling of German in the schools of the realm, including the recommendation that, "in cases of doubt about capitalization, decapitalization is preferred" (qtd. in Nerius 266). Hermann Palm's 1882 edition of Gryphius's plays collapsed these two

---

27. Scharnhorst has argued that Grimm's critique of Adelung's normative orthography—with its endorsement of normative capitalization—began in his "historical grammatical" period, a time in which his work centered on the *Deutsche Grammatik* (German Grammar) (1819–1840 in three editions).

historically specific and ideologically informed dialectological and orthographic agendas into a single textual moment by celebrating the modern unity of Germany via a celebration of the glories of Silesian literature in the preferred decapitalized mode.

Palm's investment in the literature of Silesia was not merely professional. Born in 1816 in Silesian Grunau bei Hirschberg, he studied in Breslau, held various positions in the schools there in the 1840s though the 1860s, and in 1881 became the pro-rector of the city's two Protestant *gymnasia,* the very schools that had originally sponsored the Baroque tragic dramas about which Benjamin writes. Palm's scholarly devotion to the textual monuments of what he considered a Renaissance-like "ancient efflorescence of German poetry" (*Beitraege* 1) in the Silesian seventeenth century was thus partly a matter of local pride. There is nevertheless also consistent evidence of his commitment to fitting this localism into a larger national frame. In his essays and books on the Silesians Martin Opitz and Christian Weise, for example, as well as in his work on Gryphius, Palm never fails to highlight the centrality of their texts to the "birth"—or at least prehistory—of a new "national" literary culture. In a short monograph in 1862, for example, Palm praises both Opitz and Gryphius as Silesians who contributed to the "greatness and beauty of our German national literature" (*Martin Opitz von Boberfeld* iv). Later, in his 1877 *Beitraege zur Geschichte der deutschen Literatur des XVI. und XVII. Jahrhunderts* (Essays on the History of German Literature in the Sixteenth and Seventeenth Centuries), Palm remarks that even though there was no significant dramatic tradition in Silesia before the "special efflorescence" of the seventeenth century (113), the dedication of the ruling Piastian princes there to "the German essence" (113), and their "always enthusiastic ties to the rest of Germany" (114), meant that their commitment to sponsoring local culture rapidly acquired a proto-"national" profile as well. "Even if one is used to considering this province |Silesia| as too far away from the center of Germany," Palm writes (113), his research shows "that in the German east too the understanding of art took a major hold on German culture" early on (113). Oddly, yet logically, then, given the promotion of the Silesian dialect to the status of one possible measure of Pan-German linguistic orthodoxy at approximately the same time, the Silesian drama of the seventeenth century can be said to be the "early proof of an autonomous national spirit" that paved the way for "German drama" well before its founding by Lessing later in the eighteenth century, the historical moment more conventionally given in narratives of the origins of a German national theater (*Beitraege* 2).

In light of Palm's mid- to late nineteenth-century investment in constructing a narrative about the importance of the seventeenth-century Silesian tradition to the future development of a "modern" national literature, it is at first difficult to understand his harsh assessments of the very tragic dramas by Gryphius that he edits for the Stuttgart Literary Society in 1882. In the forewords to the plays in this volume (that, again, Benjamin appears to have owned), Palm points to "the weaknesses of the structure of the play" and "imbalance of the acts in relation to one another" (Gryphius, *Trauerspiele* 10) in the case of *Leo Arminius,* for example, and remarks that Gryphius's historical drama, *Ermordete Majestät oder Carolus Stuardus* (Sovereignty Slain, or Charles Stuart), suffers from "all the crimes that the plays of our poet suffer in general, among them the thoroughly rhetorical character, the dominance of the ugly, that culminates in bloody scenes, the entirely guiltless hero, the absence of an inner coherence in the action, all of which are constitutive parts of a drama that Gryphius considered necessary and permissible" (351). Gryphius's other tragedies fare little better. Palm's criticisms here of the failings of the German Baroque were of course common in contemporary literary histories of the kind that Benjamin dismisses in the prologue to the *Tragic Drama* book.

Nevertheless, Palm's overall logic in preparing an edition of plays of which he seems to so disapprove does manage to peek out in the "Vorwort des Herausgebers" (Editorial Foreword) to the tragicomedy *Cardenio und Celinde* (Gryphius, *Trauerspiele* 259–62). As a form of "bourgeois tragic drama," with characters from the middling rather than from "upper classes" (259), this particular play by Gryphius is "pioneering," according to Palm, precisely in its choice of genre, personnel, and tone, choices that Lessing was to join Gryphius in celebrating more than a century later (260). Palm had already highlighted the relationship between Gryphius and Lessing in his earlier, 1877 essay on Christian Weise via a differentiated assessment of Gryphius's various dramatic efforts, all of which prepared the way for Palm's praise of *Cardenio und Celinde:* "It is obvious that A. Gryphius' tragic plays, with their bombast, could not grip the healthy mind of the people; the brutal tastelessness of a Lohenstein and his epigones even less. Weise confronted this unnaturalness, as he confronted everything before, with fortitude and led [drama] back to the natural and the national" (*Beitraege* 41). In true nineteenth-century style, Palm explains the problem in the following way, namely as a result of the fact that the tragic dramas of the seventeenth century had moved too far away from the "popular theater" of the sixteenth century, "without replacing for the people that which had been taken away from them" (40–41). It took until Lessing's rediscovery of what Palm earlier calls Weise's dedication "to the popular" (*volkstümlich,* 9) for this aspect of the Baroque to be recognized (41, also 71).

Palm explains that Gryphius had nevertheless already shown an understanding of the needs of the people (*Volk*) in his "comedies," which had served as models for Weise (*Beitraege* 41).[28] Precisely as a "new genre of theater," then, and although the play "did not deserve the name tragic drama [even] for the sake of its conciliatory end," as Palm writes in the foreword (Gryphius, *Trauerspiele* 259) to the 1882 edition of the play, *Cardenio und Celinde* was in fact the closest of the tragic dramas to

---

28. Palm had edited Gryphius's comedies (*Lustspiele*) for the Literary Society several years earlier, in 1878 (vol. 138).

this new and prescient category of a national German theater. Palm had already explained in 1877 that the tragic dramas themselves, although characterized by "far more mistakes and artificial efforts" than by "healthy or natural" character- istics, were the early signs "of the spiritual life" of the nation, of interest not in and of themselves, but only in their "relation to the present, to the emergence and growth of that which now is, in a word, to the historical element," and thus a pre- monition of the glories of German literature to come (*Beitraege* 1–2). Publishing an edition of *all* of Gryphius's works—tragic dramas (*Trauerspiele*) and comedies (*Lustspiele*) alike—just five years later was thus the equivalent of preserving these important first steps in the development of the modern inheritance of the German *Kulturnation*.[29]

Palm's insertion of the plays of the Silesian Baroque into the ranks of texts that supported the task of a greater German cultural revival represents an only mildly idiosyncratic and innovative solution to the conundrum of how to make a place for the Baroque in the nationalist literary histories of the nineteenth century to which Benjamin alludes in the "Epistemo-Critical Prologue" of the *Tragic Drama* book. Unlike presentations of the period for nonprofessional target groups, such as can be found in Edmund Hoefer's *Deutsche Literaturgeschichte für Frauen und Jungfrauen* (The History of German Literature for Women and Young Ladies) (1876), for ex- ample, in which the Silesian dramatists were especially targeted for the low moral and ethical niveau of their work, scholarly studies, such as Carl Lemcke's much- cited *Geschichte der deutschen Dichtung neuerer Zeit* (History of Modern German Poetry) (1871) and others, had seen the period as problematic because of its suscepti- bility to "foreign" influences and thus its too great distance from the concerns of the "people."[30] Palm's critiques of Gryphius's tragic dramas echo this argument. In the most well-known of these literary histories, however, Wilhelm Scherer's *Geschichte der deutschen Literatur* (History of German Literature) (1880–83), the "anti"- or non-national and socially elitist Baroque is somewhat counterintuitively acknowl- edged as crucial to the gradual rise in the fortunes of a "national" literature insofar as its reliance on foreign models is said to have actually led to *increased* attention to the noble vernacular. "A patriotic attitude accorded quite well with the foreign bombastic style," Scherer writes, "since all imitation was of course competition,

---

29. Palm was no stranger to conceiving of editorial work as embedded in a larger political agenda. He had spent the better part of the ten years from 1865 to 1875 collecting and publishing volumes con- taining the *acta publica*, or public documents (e.g., treaties, proclamations, and correspondence), of the Silesian princes and city officials, issued during the important years of 1618–21, at the outset of the Thirty Years' War, when events in Silesia often allowed it to emerge and play a role on the world histor- ical stage. Palm understood this project as a "patriotic enterprise" that would earn the gratitude of "all friends of the history of our fatherland" (*Acta publica* 1: vi) precisely because it linked Silesia to events of great consequence for the future of the German state. All the documents are printed without capitals.

30. See Fohrmann, "Das Bild des 17. Jahrhunderts" 582, on Hoefer, and 585, on Lemcke. On the lack of attention to the "people" in Wackernagel's *Geschichte der deutschen Litteratur: Ein Handbuch* (History of German Literature: A Handbook) (1848), see Fohrmann 586.

merely an attempt to oppose something of equal value and worth to the foreign."[31] Jürgen Fohrmann has argued that even the far more common and less generous condemnations by a figure like Lemcke of seventeenth-century literature as too far from the interests of the "people" also saw an important and necessary role for the Baroque as a kind of warning to his own nineteenth-century contemporaries about which elitist pitfalls to avoid as they invested in promoting the "cultural blossoming" of "German poetry" in a post-1871 world (Fohrmann, "Das Bild des 17. Jahrhunderts" 587). The deployment here of what Wolfgang Höppner calls a strategy of historical analogy, whereby the literary-historical products of the seventeenth century could function as prototypes, or, if that is too strong, as indicators of the general direction in which contemporary literary history should move, may have provided the template for something like Palm's assessment of the relationship of Silesian drama to the subsequent birth of a national theater under Lessing and then Goethe ("Die Mode des Barock" 597)—as well as for Benjamin's subsequent "discovery" of analogies between the Baroque tragic dramas and Storm and Stress and Romantic plays. Palm's edition of Gryphius participates in this kind of analogistic logic when it orthographically "updates" and absorbs seventeenth-century texts into a nineteenth-century narrative of a national language and literature on the cusp of being "reborn" into "modern" excellence, while also investing them with an already achieved foundational profile and function via their publication in the Bibliothek des Litterarischen Vereins series. The universal decapitalization of nouns in the texts testifies to the tradition's venerable antiquity in turn.

Again, Benjamin was not unaware of the vexed history of the capitalization and decapitalization practices in the Baroque. As noted above, the different historical afterlives of the several Silesian authors he cites would have been obvious to him in the competing orthographies of the volumes that lay spread out on the tables at the Prussian State Library before him, a seventeenth-century Hallmann next to an eighteenth-century Lohenstein next to the nineteenth-century Palm Gryphius. All nevertheless provided evidence of the Baroque as it had been unleashed into history in textual form. Benjamin's own "modernization"—not only of Palm's already "modernized" Gryphius, but of the Hallmann and Lohenstein volumes he cites too—simply added to the afterlives of the Baroque and moved in the direction of a contemporary inventory of the genre's "totality." The "updating" of these other Baroques in Benjamin's citations in the 1928 edition of the *Tragic Drama* book is fairly consistent with his rendering of Palm. Hallmann's seventeenth-century "Tantz" (dance) (Hallmann, *Trauer- Freuden- und Schäffer-Spiele* 36) becomes the more modern "Tanz" (Benjamin, *Ursprung des deutschen Trauerspiels* [1928] 114), for example,

---

31. Scherer, *Geschichte der deutschen Literatur* (History of German Literature), qtd. in Höppner, "Die Mode des Barock" 602. On this argument in Scherer, see also Fohrmann, "Das Bild des 17. Jahrhunderts" 588–89.

and the early "Aegyptens Nacht" (Egyptian night) (Hallmann 90) becomes "Ägyptens Nacht" (Benjamin 179), with the umlaut replacing the diphthong, as is still conventional today; Benjamin also separates out into three words, "höchst trauriges Ballet" (highly tragic ballet) (179), the seventeenth-century "höchsttrauriges Ballet" (Hallmann 69), in which the adverb and adjective are combined, signaling his as the more "modern" version. When quoting from another Hallmann text, the *Leich-Reden: Todten-Gedichte und Aus dem Italiänischen übersetzte Grab-Schrifften* (Funeral Orations, Funeral Poems, and Funerary Inscriptions Translated from the Italian) (1682), also available in the State Library, Benjamin likewise updates Hallmann's "privilegirte Personen" (Hallmann, *Leich-Reden* 88) to "privilegierte Personen" (Benjamin, *Ursprung des deutschen Trauerspiels* [1928] 76), with the modern German *ie* replacing the archaic *i*. When he quotes from the eighteenth-century edition of Lohenstein's *Sophonisbe* play, finally, the modernizing pattern replays itself again and again: the 1724 "Scepter" (*Sophonisbe, Trauer = Spiel* 11, already changed from the "Baroque" "Zepter" in 1680, *Sophonisbe: Trauerspiel* 11) becomes the updated "Szepter" in 1928 (Benjamin, *Ursprung des deutschen Trauerspiels* [1928] 119), just as the eighteenth-century "Liljen" (lilies) (*Sophonisbe, Trauer = Spiel* 76) becomes the more modern "Lilien" in 1928 (*Ursprung des deutschen Trauerspiels* [1928] 190).

Benjamin's modernizing adjustments in the 1928 *Tragic Drama* book of the orthography of the Baroque texts he read are thus abundant and integrate the plays of Hallmann, Lohenstein, and Gryphius, in their respective seventeenth-, eighteenth-, and nineteenth-century formations, into what Benjamin elsewhere calls (with reference to translation) the continual "afterlife" of "the original."[32] The altered citations thus contribute to the production of an ongoing and nonstatic "origin" for the tragic dramas of the German Baroque in the way he describes at a more theoretical level as well. Already signaled in the tidy sequence of historical periods in the volumes of the Old Subject Catalog as he consulted them, and nearly palpable in any given copy of a "Baroque" text that he or others would have held in their hands, the Baroque that was on the move between the covers of Benjamin's own "Baroque book" in that text's idiosyncratic orthography is merely its next iteration, a sign of the "incomplete" and "unfinished" side of the modern "restoration" (G: 1.1: 226; E: 45) of a "national" Silesian Baroque.

Collecting the Baroque: Editing the German Dramatic Tradition

At the beginning of the second chapter of the *Tragic Drama* book, Benjamin gives two reasons for looking at "extremes" in order to come to an adequately

---

32. On translation, see Benjamin, "Die Aufgabe des Übersetzers" (The Task of the Translator) (*Gesammelte Schriften* 4.1: 9–21, here 11).

"philosophical" concept; his specific example here is the "development of the concept" of the "origin of the German Baroque tragic drama" (G: 1.1: 238; E: 57). It is the first of these reasons that is of interest in the context of the versions of the Baroque available in the early twentieth century to Benjamin in book form, namely his claim that the examination of the "extreme" guarantees that a "wide material spectrum" will be considered in the construction of the "concept" of the tragic drama; only out of the "elements" of as many examples as possible, he explains— examples that will of course initially appear "diffuse and disparate"—can the "concept" be created as the "synthesis" in which the genre's "form" can be observed. The best way to find such a multitude of extremes is to consider the dramatic production of both the "greater" and the "lesser," even "weaker poets," he writes, all of whose plays are the witnesses according to whose testimony this "form" can be deduced (238; 58).

Although the evaluative vocabulary of the "lesser" and "weaker" poets that Benjamin uses here reminds us of his claim at the end of the "Epistemo-Critical Prologue" that the "artistic will" of a period will be best found in the work of "epigones" (G: 1.1: 235; E: 55), it is more significant that Benjamin takes the opportunity here *not* to create a hierarchy of "good" and "bad" tragic dramas in and among just the small selection of Silesian playwrights, namely Gryphius, Lohenstein, and Hallmann, to whom he devotes most of his book on the Second Silesian school. Rather, he turns to a number of other authors and texts even *less* well known than the Silesians today, and does so precisely because they can serve as even better "witnesses" to the genre of the tragic drama writ large. It may be significant that the volumes of the Old Subject Catalog in which these other texts were listed were *not* the same as those that contained the lists of texts by the Silesian playwrights; rather, they are volumes A21a and Y22a, entitled "Miscellany and Academic Publications" and "German Literature, VIIa2, Individual Theaters/Stages," respectively. In these volumes, and especially in volume Y22a, Benjamin found collected the "extremes" of what he goes on to identify as the tragic drama of the Baroque.[33]

---

33. It is unfortunate that precisely these volumes of the Old Subject Catalog—A21a and Y22a—did not survive the war, although the volumes of dramatic texts and plays themselves did. Their destruction makes it impossible for us to see what else Benjamin might have observed on the catalog pages on which the books he did read were listed, or, indeed, how he might have come upon just these books in the first place. For a variety of reasons, I would argue that he probably discovered or was referred to volume Y22a, with its greater coverage of the dramatic tradition, first, found the Weiß volume listed there, and quoted from it as part of his argument for "wide material spectrum." Weiß refers in his book to Mone and to Horn; Benjamin may thus have encountered the titles of their texts there. The location in volume A21a of the von Thurn text—with a title that was identical to the title of Weiß's book—may have been indicated in a cross-reference in volume Y22a in association with Weiß. In any case, it seems unlikely that Benjamin would have turned to volume A21a first, as it carried an unpromising "title" on its spine—merely "miscellaneous" "academic" works—which, in this case, probably referred to the series, the Schriften des Literarischen Vereins in Wien (Texts of the Literary Society in Vienna), in which the von Thurn volume appeared. See below.

What is striking about these additional books from which Benjamin quotes is, first of all, that they include editions and collections of plays from periods not only both before and after those traditionally identified as the Baroque, but that they are also associated with locations quite distant from "German" Silesia. Prominent among these locations was Vienna. The geographical breadth is not surprising from a contemporary political perspective. Beginning with the early to mid-nineteenth century's enthusiastic interest in what Fohrmann calls the "fostering of national poetry" (*Das Projekt* 185), there had in fact been a preoccupation with the cultural heritage of not just specific or individual locations, but also the greater German *Kulturnation*, including—with a hint of hegemonic desire—the Austro-Hungarian territories too. The concept had become a fashionable one to cultivate—both intellectually and politically—ever since the Napoleonic incursions. In the tradition of Achim von Arnim's and Clemens Brentano's collection of traditional folk songs in *Des Knaben Wunderhorn* (The Boy's Magic Horn) (1805–8) and the Grimm brothers' *Kinder- und Haus Märchen* (Fairy Tales) (1812–15), for example, the anthologies of German-language dramatic texts from the medieval period through the early eighteenth century from which Benjamin cites contained the "elements" of a national dramatic tradition that, precisely because it included neither ancient tragedy nor the "high" texts of an imitative Renaissance, could be identified as a specifically anticlassical, and specifically anti-French, German Baroque. Although not well known in either Benjamin or Baroque studies today, it is thus no surprise that these collections, edited by Mone, Weiß, and von Thurn, were produced when they were, or that the State Library owned copies of these books. Archivists and librarians all, these men's primary interest as editors was in the cultural-political program of making accessible to as broad a public as possible a legacy of specifically German-language texts, documents that, before the publication of the books, had been available only in manuscript form.[34] As abstract as the argument for the "development of the concept" of an "origin" for the Baroque tragic drama may appear, then, in the context of the *Tragic Drama* book, the quite literal "wide material spectrum" (G: 1.1: 238; E: 57) of plays available in this series of volumes contributed to Benjamin's ability to "discover" and "invent" a much more textually embodied "lineage of the Baroque tragic drama" (307; 128) than had previously been seen. In these editions and collections, the greater "law of the tragic drama" (315; 136) that he sought could be discerned.

Franz Josef Mone (1796–1871) was originally a historian. In 1825, he became the director of the university library at the University of Heidelberg; ten years later, he took over as the main archivist and director of the State Archive of Baden, where

---

34. See Fohrmann, *Das Projekt* 184–210, on the upsurge at midcentury of literary and historical *Vereine* (societies), public lecture series, publishing initiatives, and public poetry festivals designed to appeal to as broad a segment of the population as possible, in both class-specific and mixed groups, to the end of creating an "educated" German nation.

he worked until his retirement in 1868. An enthusiast of Celtic lore and texts, he was also involved in publishing projects concerning one of the oldest German epics, the *Nibelungenlied* (Song of the Nibelungen) (1818), as well as *Quellen und Forschungen zur teutschen Litteratur und Sprache* (Documents and Research on German Literature and Language) (1830). Mone's participation in the editing of a vast array of texts about the "ancient" history of his home state of Baden also suggests the kinds of genealogies of the present with which he was concerned. His two-volume collection of medieval plays, *Schauspiele des Mittelalters* (Plays of the Middle Ages) (1846), the first volume of which is the book that Benjamin cites, was designed, as Mone writes in the "Preface," to fill the "significant gap" in the "history of our literature" and, in particular, in "the history of German dramatic poetry" (vii). His production of a book of manuscript transcriptions was thus not merely an archivist's task. Rather, it was part of the mission sweeping the learned classes at the time to support the "promotion of national literature" (viii), as he writes. Mone was also an active participant in the patriotic gathering of the first professional organization of Germanists in 1846, the year his volume appeared (Meves). While the thought of a literal German "nation" was of course premature in that year, the sentiment was in keeping with the upsurge of patriotic idealism and celebration of the *Kulturnation* that had begun at the time of German Romanticism. Benjamin's citation of Mone in close proximity to his reference to the arguments by the Romantic Franz Horn (G: 1.1: 302–5; E: 123–26) thus makes a great deal of sense. It is clear, finally, from the descriptions of the various manuscripts that Mone had found in monastery libraries and private collections across Germany that it was the documentation of a coherent and continuous German dramatic tradition with which he was concerned. Brought together between the covers of a single book, the diverse texts joined one another to produce a kind of "national" textual unity explicitly designed to rival similar products that the French had already created to celebrate "the ancient drama of their nation" (Mone xi).[35]

Mone clearly did not intend to create a continuous German-language dramatic tradition on his own. The cultural work still to be done would involve support by what he describes as a national collective of archivists and editors, who, in solidarity with him, would produce a "coherent" history with no gaps (Mone vii). The notion that it was in the nature of the German "character" to form such collectives of citizen-scholars dedicated to the cultivation of the national past had in fact been the topic of an essay entitled "Ueber das deutsche Vereinswesen" (On the Essence of German Societies) that Mone published in the *Deutsche Vierteljahrs Schrift* (German Quarterly) three years before (see Fohrmann, *Das Projekt* 185–86). The book from which Benjamin cites some of the texts that Mone had collected participates in

---

35. On Mone's exceptionalist argument about the German character and its autonomy, see Fohrmann, *Das Projekt* 185–86.

this project in material form in its transcriptions of the manuscripts, which, in the case of "Die sieben Todsünden" (The Seven Deadly Sins), from which Benjamin quotes, is printed entirely in "national" decapitalized form and also in the archaizing typeface of a Gothic *Fraktur*. For an early twentieth-century reader like Benjamin, the typeface would have signaled an even more "authentic" version of these ancient "national" texts. Benjamin famously himself chose the *Fraktur* typeface in which his *Tragic Drama* book was printed in 1928.

The seamless history of the early dramatic legacy that Mone offers in his 1846 collection is visible first and foremost in the sequencing of texts there, with a series of early sung pieces for Easter and "the very oldest German play," a "Lament for the Virgin Mary" (27–37) from "the end of the thirteenth century" (27), at the beginning, up to the confessional "Seven Deadly Sins" (324–36), also thirteenth century, at the end. Mone points out that he has deliberately arranged the texts "chronologically" (vii–viii) in order to create a continuous narrative of the history of German dramatic forms. Crucial to the project—as well as potentially of importance in Benjamin's mind—was Mone's correction of the standard dating to the fifteenth century of the "origin of drama" (x). Contra Georg Gottfried Gervinus and Karl August Koberstein, whom he, like Benjamin, cites, Mone would push such origins back into the thirteenth and even the twelfth century (1). His attention in the "Introduction" to the relationship between theater and history, theater and the church, and theater and its performance on certain feast days (1–4) embeds the "dramatic" texts that follow in the clearly medieval—and thus also non-Renaissance—context out of which they emerged. Organized as a series of eleven genres of textual "monuments," such as seven examples of texts celebrating "The Childhood of Christ" and six examples of "Last Judgment" texts (to which the "Seven Deadly Sin" text belongs), Mone's book also includes information about the location of the manuscripts, and descriptions of their appearance. Along with the transcriptions themselves, the book would have offered Benjamin a conveniently packaged anthology proving the "ancient" lineage of a "national" German dramatic form.

The availability of early dramatic texts such as those in Mone's collection was crucial to the argument that Benjamin sought to develop about the non-Renaissance nature of the Baroque discussed above, in chapter 1. Moreover, the texts Mone reproduces would have endowed Strich's grand, but imprecise claims about the Baroque's affiliation with "old Teutonic" and "primal German poetry" ("Der lyrische Stil" 29 and 45) with much more heft. The "Deadly Sins" text (Mone 324–36), as reproduced in Mone's collection, probably did resemble the format and hand of the thirteenth-century manuscript as Mone had originally read it in a private collection in Karlsruhe some years before; the 1846 print edition retains the archaic spellings of the manuscript text and notes, as well as the original punctuation. Mone remarks that the "punctuation" of the original was so "curious," or strange, that he has chosen to mimic it exactly in his edition (324) in order to give the reader a sense of the original. The archaizing message of the "Seven Deadly Sins" text would thus have resembled that of the decapitalized Palm Gryphius discussed above. Benjamin nevertheless modernizes the orthography of the "Deadly Sins" text as transcribed by Mone in his quote from it in the 1928 edition of the *Tragic Drama* book, just as he modernizes Palm, changing the archaic spelling of the adjective "erbeitsamen" (industrious) to the modern "arbeitsamen," and the old German "unt" to the modern "und" (Mone 329; Benjamin, *Ursprung des deutschen Trauerspiels* [1928] 151), for example. He may have been trying to make these "ancient" words more comprehensible to the "modern" reader. But he simultaneously retains in his quotes the decapitalized nouns from Mone's "original" pre- and non-Renaissance texts, even inserting an additional archaizing diacritical mark (the famous "virgula suspensiva," or oblique slash[36]) at one point where it does not appear in Mone's 1846 text. The pre-Renaissance origins of German drama in the medieval period that were typographically visible in Mone's book thus find an equally robust afterlife in Benjamin's *Tragic Drama* book.

The creation of the link between Baroque plays and their medieval antecedents is central to Benjamin's argument about the specifically German lineage of the tragic drama. In either deliberate or inadvertent solidarity with Mone, Benjamin writes just before his first citation of Mone of the need to invest further in an "account of the medieval elements of the drama of the Baroque"; his own brief reflections should serve merely as a "prolegomenon to further comparative discussions of the medieval and the Baroque spiritual worlds" (G: 1.1: 256; E: 76). It is in specific reference to the necessity of seeing the medieval "Passion play character" of the Baroque (255; 75) that Benjamin cites Mone; the nineteenth-century editor's claims about the medieval tendency to see the history of the world as itself "one big tragic drama" accord perfectly, according to Benjamin (256; 77), with statements made about the interpenetrability of the world and the stage during the later period. "The word 'tragic drama' referred in the seventeenth century to the theatrical and the world stage in the same way," Benjamin writes (244; 63). The prehistory of "the formal world of the Baroque tragic drama" in the dramatic products of "the Middle Ages" (257; 78) can thus be seen in the transcriptions of the texts that fill Mone's book. Via citation of it, Benjamin allows the Baroque to rebirth the medieval German tradition in a more-than-Renaissance way.

The impact of the Mone collection on Benjamin's ability to create an extended German dramatic tradition is clearest in Benjamin's second reference to Mone. Although Mone is not named directly, when Benjamin quotes from an otherwise unidentified "manuscript from the thirteenth century" (G: 1.1: 332; E: 155) in the last section of the second chapter of the *Tragic Drama* book, as part of his narrative about the genealogy of the long-standing German fascination with melancholy, or

---

36. The "virgula suspensiva" was developed, according to M. B. Parkes, to indicate the briefest pause or hesitation in a text. It was in common use from the thirteenth to the seventeenth century.

"Acedia," as a "theological" concept, it is the Mone collection that is his source. Immediately following the citation, which is from the beginning of "On Lethargy," part of the thirteenth-century "Seven Deadly Sins" text in the Mone volume, Benjamin goes on to cite a lengthy passage from Aegidius Albertinus's more properly "Baroque," that is, seventeenth-century, text, *Lucifers Königreich und Seelengejaidt: Oder Narrenhatz* (Lucifer's Kingdom and Hunt for Souls; or, The Hounding of Fools), published in 1617, entitled "Accidia," or "Lethargy" (333; 156), which repeats and elaborates on the earlier "Seven Deadly Sins" text. I return to Albertinus's text and its relation to Benjamin's understanding of the "Lutheran" Baroque in chapter 3. Here it is more important to note that Benjamin's serial quotations from the thirteenth- and seventeenth-century texts at this point in his argument quite literally create a visual link on the page between the medieval and the later Baroque period. They also confirm and extend Mone's own claim about the continuity of the German tradition by producing an even longer "history of German dramatic poetry," a history that matches and outdoes the one available in the nineteenth-century archivist's book. Benjamin's ability to absorb and extend Mone's earlier assertions about specifically German traditions into the seventeenth century is central to his argument about Baroque melancholy in particular, and he relies heavily in these pages on a strategy that piggybacks on arguments already made about the afterlives of medieval thought in the Reformation by art historians Karl Giehlow, Aby Warburg, Fritz Saxl, and Erwin Panofsky, also extending what, in their work, is a specifically Lutheran tradition into the seventeenth century of his sample. Benjamin's juxtaposition here of the citations from Mone with his citations from Albertinus calls attention to this move.

As crucial as Mone's little book was in providing Benjamin with medieval textual antecedents for the tradition of the Baroque tragic drama, it was in the work of Karl Weiß (1826–95) that the specific connection between collections of texts such as Mone's and the canon of authors and texts more conventionally understood as the dramatic tradition of the Baroque proper, including the Silesians, was made. Weiß's *Die Wiener Haupt- und Staatsactionen: Ein Beitrag zur Geschichte des deutschen Theaters* (Viennese Plays about Affairs of State: A Contribution to the History of the German Theater) (1854) was less an anthology, or collection, than a literary-historical brief on behalf of the Viennese dramatic tradition in general and about the holdings of the Kaiserliche Hofbibliothek (Imperial Court Library) in particular. It includes transcriptions of some fifteen manuscripts of popular "political" plays from the early eighteenth century associated with the Viennese playwright and impresario Josef Anton Stranitzky (c. 1676–1726). Fourteen of the manuscripts are described in detail; their library call numbers are included for easy referencing (Weiß 58), the plots summarized, characters listed, and the stage sets described. One especially accomplished play ("the inimitable and most valuable," 58), *Die Glorreiche Marter Joannes von Nepomuck* (The Glorious Martyr John Nepomuck) is reproduced in its entirety in an appendix (113–92). This is the play from which Benjamin quotes numerous times in his discussion of such plays as "extremes," as some of the "most radical" and thus "most unartistic" examples of the dramatic genre of the plays about rulers and affairs of state that exist (G: 1.1: 302; E: 123). The thematic, plot, and production parallels between this "lower" genre of theater and the "high" learned Silesian tragic dramas—with their own political and erotic intrigue in courtly circles and extravagant staging of horrific scenes—confirm the external logic of the juxtaposition.

Weiß's attention to these plays about "affairs of state" and to Stranitzky as a native son was understandable.[37] Weiß was a devout citizen of Vienna. Even though the actual text collections, including presumably the manuscripts on which his book was based, had initially been owned by the city, they had been absorbed into the imperial library already in 1780. Weiß was instrumental in wrenching them back into civic hands when he established a city library in 1855. From this time on, the play texts as well as numerous other historical documents and artifacts were held there. He also helped found a city historical museum in 1888. The decision to continue the celebration of local cultural heritage by collecting its dramatic traditions in book form is thus not surprising. Weiß's project represents, moreover, the articulation of a "patriotic" task of excavating the German-language literary heritage not unlike the one in which his near contemporary Mone was engaged. That it was at a different location, Catholic Vienna, rather than predominantly Protestant Silesia, that Stranitzky flourished is additionally suggestive of the role that Weiß's book played, also for Benjamin, in capturing a Pan-German dramatic tradition in print. Aware of but not bothered by distinctions between these discrete geopolitical and confessionally distinct states, Weiß clearly considered—or, in a politically vexed time, would like to have seen—the northern and southern branches of the German *Kulturnation* as one. The notion of a reorganization of the two great Germanic powers—Prussia and the Austrian territories—under a common banner, with the latter even in the lead, had been a popular one, particularly among Catholics of course, since the beginning of the century. Although not in direct proximity to the Weiß quotes, even Benjamin endorses the claim that the "Protestants of the Silesian school" and the Catholic "Jesuit" tradition (as well as Calderón) should be considered together (G: 1.1: 258; E: 79).[38] In his lengthy background chapters, Weiß endorses this vision as he embeds the Viennese story of Stranitzky and his plays in a kind of apologetic and melancholy narrative of a unified "national poetry" and cultural heritage that had been put asunder during the confessional chaos of the Thirty Years' War (1–2), but that it was now time to redeem.

---

37. See the entry on Weiß in the *Allgemeine Deutsche Biographie* 41: 577–79.

38. The role of Catholic Vienna in the literary-historical developments of the nineteenth century in Germany and particularly among the German Romantics, including the Schlegels, for example, is (and was, also for Benjamin) well known. Many of the originally Protestant Romantic writers converted to Catholicism.

In a backhanded argument, Weiß claims, moreover, that the drama of the seventeenth century represented the beginnings of a "modern" kind of literature with the "artistic character of the new poetry" (2). The "modernity" alluded to here may not have been an exclusively enviable one, however, precisely because it mirrored the divisiveness of the "nation" between 1618 and 1648. The story Weiß tells is thus in fact one of the *failure* of the two dominant strains of drama in the seventeenth century, the "high" "learned drama" of the Silesians, on the one hand, and the often farcical "folk play" genre to which Stranitzky was indebted, on the other, to form the unity he desires. His project consists in trying to bring the two strains together in the "regeneration of German drama" (26) writ large. In the present absence of such a joining and because they appealed to different classes and segments of society, the continuing separation of these genres cannot help but produce a "complete splitting of the artistic powers" that sadly mirrors the fraught "modern life of the nations" (35) of his own time. Even though such cultural class stratification was not known by either the Greeks or the Romans (35), according to Weiß, the non- or anti-Renaissance pattern he discerns can thus only serve not as an uplifting distinction of the moderns from the ancients, but rather as a downbeat allegory of the entire "process of modern society" (3) that threatened to engulf the entire German heartland at the time. Given this dark picture of the legacy of the seventeenth century for the mid-nineteenth century, it is not surprising that Weiß claims that it is his goal to restore a forward-looking potential to this "awakening of a new taste" (3). The rhetoric of a rebirth of the modern is audible here.

Weiß begins his own restoration of the unity of the German dramatic tradition by knitting the two kinds of drama together in a wide-ranging literary-historical narrative about the popular theater of pre-Enlightenment Germany, claiming, for example, that a "naturalized" form of the plays of the so-called English comedians of the sixteenth-century traveling theater troupes intersected in the late sixteenth century with local German dramatic traditions. This mixing provided the textual antecedents of a hybridized high "learned drama" (Weiß 14) in turn. It is of particular importance to Weiß that both the "people" and courtly audiences were entertained by these popular plays (17), and that the great German playwrights of this period, Johann Ayrer (1543–1605) and Herzog Julius von Braunschweig (1554–1613), were able to create an authentically mixed German theater (22–23) out of this legacy, a dramatic tradition that could heal the wounds of cultural division that were so prominent both then and in his own time. Weiß introduces the plays of the Silesians, especially those by Gryphius, but also by Lohenstein and Hallmann, at this point in his narrative as additional important links between the "popular theater" and Stranitzky's later "affairs of state" plays (22–25), even claiming (as it turns out, incorrectly, but this is of little import to his argument) that Gryphius represented the best in the earlier national German tradition, as he was "opposed to all translations and imitative texts" (25). Had the learned Silesian playwrights continued in this direction, Weiß argues, and attended to the synthesis of popular tradition with their own work, the much longed-for "regeneration of German drama" (26) would have occurred. Instead, they and their courtly sponsors tried to ingratiate themselves with the dreaded French ("via cuddling up with France"), thus losing their native "feeling for national greatness" (26). Although displaced back into the context of a literary history of the seventeenth century, an anti-French and also anti-Prussian sentiment appropriate to the mid-nineteenth century is clearly in evidence here. The celebration of an authentically "German" dramatic sensibility is the only antidote Weiß can recommend.

Weiß concludes his pre-Stranitzky literary history of German popular drama with a discussion of the efforts of Johannes Velten (1640–93?), whose translations of ancient Greek and contemporary Spanish and French plays, on the one hand, and disciplinization of stage productions, on the other, began the work of creating a more respectable and, above all, more unified "branch of German literature" (28–30, here 28). The firmly indigenous, or native, commitment of this tradition was guaranteed by the presence of the traditional folk figure Weiß refers to as "Hannswurst," the Falstaff-like clown figure, in his productions (29). Moreover, Velten's improvisations, which Benjamin apparently knew about via Horn (G: 1.1: 302; E: 123), guaranteed their popularity "in all of Germany" (31), according to Weiß, and thus also worked to counter the earlier split. The introduction of the figure now known as Hans Wurst, a character out of a Punch and Judy–like popular tradition, is key to what turns out to be Weiß's patriotic story of the connection between *all* of these dramatic traditions and the "popular stage" of Vienna, to which he turns in the pages that follow (45–49). Seen as a follower of the Veltenian tradition, Stranitzky—whose plays are the center of Benjamin's discussion of this brand of tragic drama—was in fact best known precisely for his signature performances as the burlesque Hans Wurst in the "affairs of state" plays. Nevertheless, even as he embeds an account of the Stranitzky plays and their "author" and main actor in a general social, political, and even architectural history of Viennese culture (32–50), Weiß's emphasis is on Stranitzky's move away from mere improvisation in his acting of the Hans Wurst role toward an integration of the clownish figure into a scripted position within the main plot (rather than as an interlude entertainment, for example), specifically as an instigator of the all-important political and erotic "intrigue" (48) that was the motor of these plays.

It should not be surprising that Weiß quotes Mone at this point in his argument about the medieval "clown" figure functioning as a precursor to Hans Wurst in order to underscore that such a figure was not a foreign "import" from texts "from other countries" (Weiß 48). Rather, Hans Wurst was part of the preexisting and indigenous "German" tradition that the Vienna plays both embodied and defended into the eighteenth century and beyond. Benjamin, citing Weiß, also juxtaposes the comic figure of "Hanswurst" with the medieval "clown" as described, according to Benjamin, by Mone (see G: 1.1: 304–5; E: 126). Following Weiß, Benjamin also associates Stranitzky with the melding together of the two strains of German theater, the popular and the high, the comic and the serious, the south and the north, into a "unity" of native "dramatic forms" (304; 126–27). Weiß argues—contra an earlier scholarship that apparently saw in this tradition a "Protestant bias" (51)—that it was Stranitzky and the Viennese popular theater, which was decidedly Catholic, that began to achieve independence, indeed, began to be the source of a future (i.e., later eighteenth-century) German popular theater (44). Its "thoroughly" "independent" (i.e., not imitative) "works" (52) had a clear appeal, moreover, to the "lower classes," which, according to Weiß, had always remained loyal to "national poetry" (53). The pressures of the times, on the one hand, and an Austrian, but also Pan-German, "patriotic" charge to protect the folk tradition, on the other, thus condense in Weiß's celebration of the actor, Stranitzky, and his plays. Benjamin's insistent deployment of Stranitzky texts in the *Tragic Drama* book adopts many of the same arguments about a unified German tradition of tragic dramas.

As complex as Weiß's literary-historical and formal arguments about the merging of "national" high and low dramatic forms achieved by Stranitzky are in the descriptive section of his book, it is in the transcription of the entire *Nepomuck* play, from which the majority of Benjamin's quotes from Weiß derive, that the unifying and thus tradition-guaranteeing link between the "popular plays" and the high "learned drama" of the Silesians is best achieved. The text of the play runs some seventy-five pages in Weiß's edition; in its orthographic irregularity, archaic spellings, and erratic punctuation, it appears to mimic the manuscript on which it was based. Written in the same "careless" (112) hand as the other fourteen plays, according to editor Weiß, the original *Nepomuck* text was characterized by numerous repetitions, which his transcription retains in the interest of authenticity. The typographical appearance of the play in the Weiß volume, and the short introduction's emphasis on the presence of a Hans Wurst character in the play (112), work to root it in the historical Viennese context and tradition of popular theater. In an interesting move, Weiß also devotes considerable attention to pointing out that precisely this text, again, the "most valuable" of all of the manuscripts (54), was in all likelihood not by the same author as the other fourteen (it "was probably penned by another hand," 55), even though the copyist's version resembles the hand there. Both its unity of plot and seriousness of theme, including the foregrounding of both the piety of Queen Augusta and the loyalty of her confessor, Nepomuck, in the face of threats by her jealous husband, King Wenzeslaus, and the liberal sprinkling of Latin sayings and the grace of the "poetic forms" throughout the text, suggest, Weiß writes, that the play was written, rather, by a "learned author" (111–12) and simply adapted to make it more appropriate for the popular stage. Additional exaggerated stage effects and occasional obscene gestures (112) call attention, for example, to the need to sell the more serious play to a Viennese audience expecting to be entertained. The *Nepomuck* play—in both the original early eighteenth-century Viennese manuscript and in the mid-nineteenth century transcription in the volume from which Benjamin cites—thus unites in itself the high and low strains of the German dramatic tradition, whose distance from each other had been the cause of such concern to the patriotic Weiß.

Given the synthesizing work that the *Nepomuck* text does in Weiß's book, it is not surprising that even though Benjamin finds the play (which he appears to have actually read) otherwise "uninteresting" (G: 1.1: 383; E: 209), he explicitly identifies it as belonging to the genre of "Viennese plays about affairs of state," on the one hand, and as an exemplification of the language theory of a more generalized Baroque, on the other. Benjamin had cited the Weiß *Nepomuck* play earlier in more generous terms, as the "not inglorious end" of the Baroque tragic drama and in connection with the "end in Vienna of the tradition that parodied" the "affairs of state" genre. As part of the "southern" tradition, it paralleled, Benjamin suggests, the "northern" end of the genre in opera in turn (G: 1.1: 248–49; E: 68–69). This north-south alignment is clearly derived from Weiß's narrative of the two-strains theory of German drama. In its claims for their parallel development, Benjamin's juxtaposition thus reproduces his source's dedication to the creation of a unified dramatic tradition. Finally, while Benjamin does modernize the quotes from Weiß's transcriptions of the *Nepomuck* play in modest fashion when he quotes them, his interventions in the orthography of the play are minor and thus allow the early eighteenth-century Viennese plays to join the ranks of the medieval dramatic forms cited after Mone. "Originally," he writes, "the two were very close to one another" (305; 127). The updating of the Weiß Stranitzky text in the *Tragic Drama* book is in any case not nearly as extreme as that which characterizes the new edition of the texts of the Stranitzky plays prepared by Rudolf Payer von Thurn a half century later. Von Thurn's version of the Viennese legacy, which Benjamin also cites, serves the project of creating the German national tradition in different ways than Mone's and Weiß's. Von Thurn's devotion to the same cause would nevertheless have been obvious to the young scholar, Benjamin, as he held von Thurn's books in his hand.

Rudolf Payer von Thurn's (1867–1932) book, *Wiener Haupt- und Staatsaktionen* (Viennese Plays about Affairs of State) (two volumes, 1908–10), carries the same title as Weiß's. Both von Thurn and his book of course belonged to a different generation (see Adel). His version of the German dramatic legacy as captured in Stranitzky's Viennese oeuvre likewise took a somewhat different form. It nevertheless offered equally compelling material proof of Stranitzky's plays as part of the literary-historical narrative on which Benjamin relied. Von Thurn studied in Vienna with the famous Germanist Jakob Minor, whose work on the "tragedy of fate" was so central to Benjamin's understanding of that genre, and became an archivist and librarian in state service, first in the Ministry of Culture and Education in Vienna, and later at court. Von Thurn's many publications were the result of his access to materials in his archival positions; he wrote a history of the Order of the Golden Fleece, for example, while he was in charge of the Order's archive. His interest in the manuscripts of the folk plays in the imperial library in Vienna is thus not surprising. Von Thurn used his edition of the plays of Stranitzky as part of his own application for the *Habilitation* in Vienna in 1921, after which he taught at the university until 1932. Finally, in addition to being an archivist and a scholar, von Thurn was a public promoter of the celebration of both local and Pan-German literary culture in Vienna. He wrote frequently on Franz Grillparzer, founded the Vienna Goethe Society and edited its journal, and in 1932 was the organizer of the Goethe exhibit there on the centenary anniversary of the great literary icon's death. Von Thurn's efforts were thus not unlike those of Mone and Weiß, as he used his professional and academic expertise to cultivate familiarity with the German literary tradition and to make it central to a kind of unified linguistic and ethnic culture. Benjamin's use of von Thurn's texts was likewise designed to publicize the "lineage" of a specifically German tragic drama in turn.

Given his professional and scholarly profile, it makes sense that the volume of Stranitzky plays that von Thurn edited was published in a series, the Schriften des Literarischen Vereins in Wien (Texts of the Literary Society in Vienna), which resembled the Bibliothek des Litterarischen Vereins in Stuttgart (Library of the Literary Society in Stuttgart) in which the Palm Gryphius had appeared. Von Thurn's edition differed from Weiß's in that it included transcriptions of all fourteen Stranitzky plays that had not been published before, seven plays in each volume (Benjamin cites only from volume 1, 1908). The result is something like a critical edition of Stranitzky's oeuvre, which thus creates the image of the playwright as something of a legitimate auteur.[39] Published in twenty-four volumes between 1904 and 1919, the mission of the Texts of the Literary Society in Vienna series was to make available, in more or less "modern" format, documents (diaries, letters, biographies, and literary texts) from the literary life of Vienna in the eighteenth and nineteenth centuries as part of a publishing initiative that, resembling the one in which the Palm Gryphius appeared, was devoted to the production of "reprints" of "literary-historical memorials," or monuments, as von Thurn calls them in his introduction (v–vii), to the literary and cultural heritage of the past.[40] While the use of the word is conventional in this context, that most such "monuments" were actually architectural objects suggests the nature of the impact that the publication of these volumes was intended to have.

The architectural analogy is also useful for understanding the details of these volumes. Even though von Thurn insists in his introduction, for example, that he has reproduced in his book the "difficult-to-decipher manuscripts" that he, like Weiß, had found in the Viennese Court Library (vii), in their original form "with

39. The absence from these volumes of the *Nepomuck* play, identified by Weiß as in all likelihood originally written by someone else, as noted above, is explained by reference to the more recent, revised edition of that text by Fritz Homeyer in 1907. I return to the Homeyer text below.

40. On the tradition of such reprints, albeit in a different context, in the series Neudrucke deutscher Literaturwerke des XVI. und XVII. Jahrhunderts (Reprints of Works of German Literature from the Sixteenth and Seventeenth Centuries) published by Max Niemeyer Verlag in Halle beginning in 1876 and continuing up through World War I, see Barner, "Literaturwissenschaft" 94–97.

all of their linguistic and orthographic peculiarities" (xxxvii–xxxviii), he also admits to having standardized the texts "following modern principles" (xxxviii), supplementing abbreviations, distinguishing between *das* and *daß,* which in the manuscripts are both rendered as *dz,* as he reports at the end of his introduction, and correcting "obvious" scribal errors as well. Von Thurn does not mention in his introduction the additional modernizations that he undertook, namely that in all fourteen of the plays as he prints them nouns are uniformly capitalized and modern punctuation used. No editorial commentary or any account of textual irregularities or variants at all is given at the bottom of each page of the play texts, as there is (although sparingly) in Weiß. The overall effect is to obscure what are actually the manifold editorial interventions that mark this edition of Stranitzky plays, and thus to present, indeed, perhaps even to substitute his early twentieth-century edition of the plays for the early eighteenth-century originals housed in the archive. Von Thurn's "preservation" strategy was, in other words, not to leave the textual monuments in the state of disrepair to which the passage of time had reduced them, but rather to render them capable of surviving by repairing and restoring them to an integral "modern" shape. There are similarities between von Thurn's efforts and those of Greve, for example, in the latter's "modernizing" edition of Hofmannswaldau, and with Benjamin's updating of the Palm Gryphius as well.

The physical differences and thus distance between von Thurn's collected plays of Stranitzky and Weiß's edition of *Nepomuck* are striking, and they would have been obvious in a comparison of the two volumes as they lay in front of Benjamin on the table in the reading room in the State Library in Berlin, suggesting that even this "folk" tradition was on the move in ways similar to the "high" Silesian plays he read in a variety of editions there. Even though updated, von Thurn's Stranitzky nevertheless continues the cultivation of the narrative of a "native" popular or folk tradition intersecting with the high (or at least higher) tradition of learned plays begun by Weiß, from whom von Thurn distinguishes himself in his introduction (viii), but whose overall project he follows. Von Thurn's Stranitzky edition does so somewhat counterintuitively by noting, first, on the occasion of mentioning the new and recent Homeyer edition of *Nepomuck* (1907), that Weiß's narrative of an "independent" and nonimitative folk origin for these plays may have to be revised. Homeyer had shown that at least five of the Stranitzky plays were based on Italian operas produced in Vienna; "the remaining plays" in all likelihood follow other "operatic texts" that have not survived (Von Thurn viii–ix). This more careful philological work nevertheless provides proof, according to von Thurn, that the Hans Wurst figure so often identified with Stranitzky himself, was genuinely "new" and "original" (ix), as there were no external or foreign models for it in the source texts that Homeyer and others had found. Here, philology serves identitarian ends, for the Stranitzky plays, as von Thurn represents them, can now conclusively be said to combine the popular and indigenous with the learned in ways of which Weiß would have been able to approve. Adducing a full complement of additional prior research, finally, von Thurn replaces Weiß's popularizing image of Stranitzky as a burlesque actor with an entirely different biography (xi–xxxvii), but one that does the reputation of the Viennese theater no harm. Based on a wide range of both archival sources, "fictional" autobiographical texts by "Hans Wurst," whom von Thurn takes to be Stranitzky himself, and official state documents, the life of Stranitzky as it emerges here is one of a successful wine dealer, canny entrepreneur, and owner of a hugely popular marionette theater, whom the editor thinks Vienna in the end must heartily thank for his efforts in establishing the city's first permanent German stage (xxviii). The two-volume edition of Stranitzky's (nearly) complete works in a series published by the custodial literary club of record in Vienna during these years is thus the appropriate monument to erect to this important literary native son.

Given the role that these volumes—editions, collections, and anthologies—played in confirming the narrative of a German-language dramatic tradition that could be understood as distinctly "native" because it could be shown to have roots in "ancient" German texts, on the one hand, and because it participated in a broadly conceived indigenous folk tradition, on the other, it is not surprising that Benjamin's consideration of "medieval" precursors for the Baroque tragic drama, as represented by Mone's volume, on the one hand, and of the plays about "affairs of state," as represented by the plays of Stranitzky collected by Weiß and von Thurn, on the other, for the most part occurs in the first and second sections of the second chapter of the *Tragic Drama* book. As suggested above in chapter 1, it is Benjamin's specific project in these sections to "redeem" both the genre and the Baroque by differentiating the plays that are his object of study from ancient tragedy, as well as from other forms of "Renaissance-ified poetry" (G: 1.1: 240; E: 60). The volumes edited by Mone, Weiß, and von Thurn help him in this project when they are cited snug up against the anti-Renaissance plays of the Silesian Baroque. It is also in these sections that Benjamin adduces further examples from the German Storm-and-Stress and Romantic playwrights (Zacharias Werner, 263 and 300; 84 and 121; Heinrich Wilhelm von Gerstenberg and Johann Anton Leisewitz, 300; 121; and Friedrich Schiller, 301; 122) and goes on to discuss the career of the "drama of fate" (307–16; 128–38), not only in various periods of German literature, but also with specific reference to Shakespeare and Calderón. All of these sources belong to the canon of "extreme" examples of the Baroque tragic drama that it is necessary to "collect" in order to develop a "concept" of the genre. Their ability to provide precisely a "wide material spectrum" is especially obvious in Benjamin's long lists of quotes taken from this broad tradition of texts, which resemble nothing so much as the stringing together of the note-card citations he had taken with him to Capri. Citations from both Gryphius and Stranitzky show their common interest in using source texts from the East in their plays (248–49; 68–69), for example, and lines from Lohenstein's, Gryphius's, and Stranitzky's dramas are quoted in a series and without differentiation to illustrate the famous "indecisiveness of the tyrant"

(250–51; 70–71), Most strikingly, extracts from works by Gryphius, Lohenstein, and Stranitzky, along with those from Shakespeare and Friedrich Schlegel, are lined up one after the other to demonstrate the commitment of the genre of the tragic drama across the ages to having important action take place at night (313–14; 134–35). To the reader, little if anything distinguishes these various generations of dramatic forms from one another in Benjamin's text, which thus quite literally patches together citational fragments from a wide range of texts so that the "constellation" of the German tragic drama may appear.

According to Benjamin, "the German drama of the Baroque" emerged out of the "situation of being caught between" the transcendent "mystery" indicated by the medieval texts, on the one hand, and the worldly "immanence" of the "profane drama" of the *Staatsaktionen*-plays, on the other (G: 1.1: 257–59; E: 78–80). More literally, it emerged out of the documents reproduced by Mone, Weiß, and von Thurn as they lay in front of him alongside the texts of the Silesians as he worked. Somewhat less literally, the epochal in-betweenness of the Baroque was something of an academic commonplace at the time. Both Paul Stachel and Herbert Cysarz had discussed the relationship between "popular drama" and "learned drama" in the seventeenth century in general (Stachel 364) and in the plays of Stranitzky in particular (Cysarz, *Deutsche Barockdichtung* 226), for example. Benjamin's argument about the difference of the Baroque from the ancient and Renaissance dramatic traditions, with its reliance on assertions about the "Passion play character" (G: 1.1: 255; E: 76) of the Baroque plays associated with Mone and about the fundamentally secular nature of the political plays as derived from Weiß and von Thurn, nevertheless stands out insofar as it produces another curious set of claims about the modern and "national" dramatic tradition he would define in his book. These claims have to do with the crucial place that the Spanish and English playwrights Calderón and Shakespeare and their plays occupy in the "origin of the German tragic drama." Calderón and Shakespeare are referenced specifically in the context of Benjamin's citations from the Mone, Weiß, and von Thurn texts and in connection with the "aesthetic aporias of the historical drama" (302; 123) that concern him in the final pages of the second section of the second chapter (304–7; 125–28) of the *Tragic Drama* book.

Benjamin's interest in these pages is famously the figure of the intriguing "minister," or adviser and courtly counselor. Given the Silesian playwrights' historical proximity to courtly power, and their interest in theories of sovereignty, it makes sense that the character of the courtly "intriguer" is ubiquitous in their plays and is thus also a frequent subject of commentary in Benjamin's book (G: 1.1: 274 and 277; E: 95 and 98). Relying on both Weiß and Mone, Benjamin's job here is nevertheless, first, to argue for the intimate connection between the medieval Passion play and the "affairs of state" plays in their common deployment of the devilish "clown" figure and the comic figure of the intriguing counselor often associated with Hans Wurst (304–5; 125–27). Even though the two traditions could be said to differ because of the increasingly secular nature of the later plays, Benjamin asserts that their juxtaposition is appropriate, for "the bureaucrat takes the place of the devil" as the result of this "secularization." Quotes from Mone and Weiß to the effect that the "clown" and the "fool of the following era" are related immediately follow this assertion. Citing Mone, Benjamin writes: "Just as now in the secular plays, so too already in the fifteenth century in the sacred plays, the clown took over the role of the comic figure in the play" (Mone, qtd. in Benjamin after Weiß, 305; 126). Benjamin confirms here that the association between the two anchors "the tragic drama, which often seems so elevated, in the native soil" (306; 127) of a deep German past. Although not stated explicitly, the argument intersects with the claim he borrows from Hübscher about the antithetical nature of the tragic drama: "Speculative aesthetics was seldom, indeed, probably never able to account for the proximity of the harsh joke and the atrocity" (305; 126). An extension of this tradition into the Silesian plays, with their own foregrounding of "ministerial intrigue" (304; 125), as well as the integration into a single tradition of all of the inventoried dramatic forms signaled by the homogenizing cascades of quotes noted above, would thus seem to be the logical—and unifying—next step.

It is here, however, that Benjamin seems to interrupt his narrative of a continuous "lineage of the Baroque tragic drama" (G: 1.1: 307; E: 128), which includes Mone's and Weiß's plays as well as those of the Second Silesian school, by noting that the "high" German "learned drama" (*Gelehrtendrama*) (304; 125) in fact does not feature the "cabal-producing adviser" nearly as effectively as the popular "folksy plays" of a Stranitzky. (That the term "learned drama" probably refers to the Silesians is suggested by Weiß's use of the term to designate their plays.) According to Benjamin, the Silesians (unlike Stranitzky) do not allow the "comedy" of the popular tradition, which is the necessary antithetical partner of "mourning," to penetrate onto the stage of the tragic drama. As a result, precisely those plays that are at the center of his discussion of the Baroque mysteriously appear to threaten to be exceptions to it. Yet Benjamin stays true to his method of measuring the "concept" by its "extremes" as he proceeds to argue that it is this "failure" that in fact defines these plays best: "Very little characterizes the limits of the art of the German Baroque drama so relentlessly as the fact that it gave over the expression of this significant relationship [between comedy and mourning] to the tradition of the popular play" (306; 127). The clarity of the "form" of the tragic drama as associated with the "lesser" plays of the Silesians is confirmed, in other words, by the claim that, in addition to Stranitzky, there are other playwrights in whose texts the figure of the buffoonish adviser makes a more successful appearance. These are the texts that display the all-important link to both the medieval and the popular traditions best.

It is this link that distinguishes the Baroque tragic drama from ancient tragedy once and for all. "In England," Benjamin writes, "it was Shakespeare who invested figures such as Iago and Polonius with the old scheme of the demonic fool, and with that, comedy entered into tragedy" (G: 1.1: 306; E: 127). Quoting Novalis, who well before him had already seen Shakespeare's wedding of the "comedy" and the "tragic drama" as a sign of just how different his plays were from "Greek tragic drama" (306–7; 127–28), Benjamin famously goes on to argue that precisely because Shakespeare—and Calderón—had in this respect written "more significant tragic dramas . . . than the seventeenth-century Germans," it was left to the Silesians to produce only a "static type" of the very genre alleged to represent the distinction between the antiquity-loving Renaissance and the "modern" and national German Baroque once and for all (306; 127). It is crucial to remember that Benjamin's claim here is not designed to dismiss the Germans in favor of their betters. Rather, to recall his explanation, from the opening of the chapter, regarding why he includes such a wide range of plays in his "development of the concept" of the Baroque tragic drama to begin with, only the Silesian plays, in combination with the "extremes" of the tradition represented in Mone, Weiß, and von Thurn, can display, "in the frail corpus of a feeble poetry," in the rigid "skeleton" of the imperfect example, that is, the true "form" of the German Baroque *Trauerspiel* (238; 58). That these extremes were quite literally not that far apart—and all necessary to indicate the "idea" of the tragic drama—is suggested by the fact that Benjamin would have discovered the Mone and Weiß texts in the folio volume of the Old Subject Catalog carrying the call number Y22a, just a few volumes to the left of volume Y24, in which the holdings of the Prussian State Library in the area of the Second Silesian school were listed, and where it is likely that the von Thurn books were listed as a newer edition of Weiß in turn.[41] That Shakespeare's plays might have been understood as a somewhat more distant example is possible; after all, the State Library holdings of editions of Shakespeare were listed in volume Z6b of the Old Subject Catalog, somewhat to the right and on the next shelf above Y24. Yet precisely their physical distance from the Silesians on the shelves of the Catalog Room suggests that Shakespeare's plays too could have counted as one of the "extremes" that made up the genre of the tragic drama that it was Benjamin's task to assess. The particular edition of Shakespeare that he cites confirms its membership in the "lineage of the German Baroque drama" in a number of ways, among them, that it was, quite literally, the Bard in German-language garb.

The Task of the Translator: Shakespeare as German Tragic Drama

The second chapter of Benjamin's *Tragic Drama* book contains two references to Shakespeare's *Hamlet*. The edition of *Hamlet* from which Benjamin quotes this most famous of "German" plays, and the related definition of Shakespeare as a

---

41. Again, volume Y22a no longer exists as Benjamin would have consulted it, as it was lost after the evacuation of the State Library holdings during the bombing of Berlin at the end of World War II.

"German" writer just before and during the years Benjamin was working on the *Habilitation,* help explain the place of the Danish prince's tale in the *Tragic Drama* book. Hamlet—both the character and the play that carries his name—had been explicitly identified with the fate of the German nation since the mid-nineteenth century, if not before.[42] The story of the various German-language editions of Shakespeare's plays available for Benjamin to read confirms how this identification came to be, indeed, how Shakespeare could have been said not only *not* to belong only to his birth culture of England, but also not to belong to the original (i.e., sixteenth- and early seventeenth-century) context of the so-called Elizabethan Renaissance at all. Such dislocations may have been what allowed *Hamlet* to be so easily absorbed into Benjamin's and others' studies of the German Baroque. One particular edition, namely the Schlegel-Tieck Shakespeare of 1825–33, is said to have been foundational for the German reception of the Bard up through World War I. This reception is best captured in the words of the famous playwright Gerhart Hauptmann, who wrote in 1915: "And even if [Shakespeare] was born and buried in England, Germany is the land where he truly lives."[43] Benjamin nevertheless did not use the 1825–33 Schlegel-Tieck edition when citing Shakespeare. Rather, he used—or claims in his footnotes to have used—an *updated* edition of Schlegel-Tieck prepared by Hermann Ulrici, who lived from 1806 to 1884. The distinction is important, for, as Kenneth Larson ("'Classical German Shakespeare'") explains, it was actually only with the republication of the Schlegel-Tieck translation in the second half of the nineteenth century under Ulrici's stewardship that the Schlegel-Tieck Shakespeare "achieved" its "canonical" status as *the* German Shakespeare. The world of Shakespeare studies into which Benjamin stepped when using the Ulrici edition clarifies how the Bard could so easily become part of the "lineage" of modern German Baroque tragic dramas that is at the center of Benjamin's book.

Ulrici was the first president of the German Shakespeare Society. Founded in the aftermath of the 1863 tercentenary celebrations of Shakespeare's birth, the society and its publishing organ, the *Shakespeare Jahrbuch* (Shakespeare Yearbook), played an important role in the consolidation of the "cult of Shakespeare" in Germany (Habicht, "Shakespeare Celebrations" 449), which had already begun much earlier with Lessing's well-known celebration of Shakespeare as the antidote to the allegedly poisonous influence of French classicism on the German dramatic tradition at the dawn of the so-called mythic period (1750–1815) of Shakespeare criticism in Germany (Habicht, "Shakespeare in Nineteenth-Century Germany" 142–43). This was the same period that not only saw the publication of Herder's

---

42. For the various claims that "Germany is Hamlet," see Habicht, "Shakespeare in Nineteenth-Century Germany" 151–54, and "Shakespeare Celebrations" 453.

43. Hauptmann xii.

and Goethe's famous essays on the Bard but also prepared the way for the famous translation endeavors of August Wilhelm Schlegel (1767–1845) and Ludwig Tieck (1773–1853). As noted above, Ulrici was also the general editor of the *revised* Schlegel-Tieck edition, which the society began publishing in 1867. It is the second edition (1876–77) of Schlegel-Tieck, which was revised under Ulrici's lead, that Benjamin cites as his source.

Ulrici's German Shakespeare was heavily indebted to research on Shakespeare by the English scholar John Payne Collier, whose publications on English sixteenth-century drama in general and on Shakespeare in particular had begun to appear in the early 1830s. Collier's well-known efforts on behalf of the playwright—and Ulrici's intersection with them—explain more about the Benjaminian notion of "origin" than has been understood to date. Ulrici's familiarity with Collier's work is clear in the former's *Ueber Shakspeare's dramatische Kunst und sein Verhältniß zu Calderon und Göthe* (On Shakespeare's Dramatic Art and His Relationship to Calderón and Goethe) of 1839, a book that Benjamin knew and had quoted from extensively in an earlier essay ("'El mayor monstruo, los celos' von Calderon und 'Herodes und Mariamne' von Hebbel: Bemerkungen zum Problem des historischen Dramas") that is assumed to have been written in 1923 (*Gesammelte Schriften* 2.1: 246–76, here 259).[44] The Collier texts that Ulrici cites in his 1839 book date from the period of Collier's early work, namely 1831–35. Collier then went on to publish an edition of Shakespeare in 1842–44, which was "supplemented" (Collier's word) by the publication in 1853 of emendations of that text based on Collier's infamous study of the annotations in the so-called Perkins copy of the 1632 Second Folio of Shakespeare's plays—infamous because these annotations were declared falsified, if not outright forgeries, by specialists at the British Museum in 1859 (Ioppolo 32). Nevertheless, not only Ulrici and Karl Elze (1821–89), who was the editor of the *Hamlet* volume in the Ulrici edition cited in Benjamin's notes, but also the German playwright and literary historian Julius Leopold Klein (1808–76), whose *Geschichte des englischen Drama's* (History of English Drama) (1876) is the source of a number of Benjamin's claims about *Hamlet* in the *Tragic Drama* book, continued to rely on Collier's work.[45]

Benjamin could have read *Hamlet* in the Ulrici edition in the Prussian State Library during his nearly year-and-a-half-long period of research there. As noted above, volume Z6b of the Old Subject Catalog (378–90) lists all of the editions of

---

44. Steiner, "Allegorie und Allergie" 684–85 n. 168, finds significant "prefigurations" of Benjamin's arguments about Calderón to be indebted to this book. I return to Ulrici's 1839 reading of *Hamlet* below.

45. Collier remained embroiled in controversy about possible forgeries of so-called Shakespearean documents for several decades thereafter. See Ioppolo 32–34 with notes there. Benjamin cites Klein in connection with *Hamlet* at G: 1.1: 368 and 402; E: 191 and 228. Collier is an important source for Klein throughout the second volume of his history of English drama, which is the volume from which Benjamin cites. On Benjamin's reliance on Klein for his theory of the afterlife of the medieval Vice figure in Shakespeare's plays, see Steiner, "Allegorie und Allergie" 690.

Shakespeare that would have been available there to Benjamin at the time. The State Library owned a large number of Shakespeare editions in both English and German, from a copy of the famous First Folio of 1623 and the original Schlegel translation from 1821–23, on the one hand, to numerous copies of both the subsequent Schlegel-Tieck version and the Ulrici revisions from 1867–71 and 1876–77 as well. The "panorama" (G: 1.1: 237; E: 56) of the continuous lineage of German Shakespeares, beginning with the original Schlegel and Schlegel-Tieck and extending into the time of both the revised text from which he claims he quotes and his own book, is visible in the tragic drama study itself as it was published in 1928. There, Benjamin's first *Hamlet* citation on pages 130 and 131 reads: "Dies ist die wahre Spükezeit der Nacht/Wo Grüfte gähnen, und die Hölle selbst / Pest haucht aus ihrer Welt." These famous lines are from the end of act 3, scene 2, and in the Arden Shakespeare read: "'Tis now the very witching time of night, When churchyards yawn and hell itself [breathes] out Contagion to this world." Benjamin's quote in the 1928 edition of the *Tragic Drama* book initially seems peculiar, not only because he appears to have preferred "breathes out" (*haucht*), which is the First Folio (1623) version of this line (contested, but nevertheless preferred over the Second Quarto of 1604's earlier "breakes" out[46]), but also because Benjamin's emendation changes the directionality of the "Contagion" (*Pest*). As indicated in the quote from the Arden edition above, that is, both the 1604 Quarto and the 1623 Folio of *Hamlet* read "to this world"; that is, the "Contagion" and the ghost of his father come "into this," Hamlet's, world. In the 1876–77 Ulrici edition of the Schlegel-Tieck translation of *Hamlet* that Benjamin had identified as the source of the quotation in his original note (*Ursprung des deutschen Trauerspiels* [1928] 248), this original (i.e., English-language) directionality is in fact maintained. There the lines read: "Nun ist die wahre Spükezeit der Nacht, / Wo Grüfte gähnen, und die Hölle selbst / Pest haucht in diese Welt," "to this world" (Ulrici, *Shakespeare's dramatische Werke* 98). The 1869 first edition of the Ulrici Schlegel-Tieck (also 98) also renders the line "to this world" (*in diese*), as do both the original Schlegel translation of *Hamlet* from 1798 and the Schlegel-Tieck translation of 1821–23.[47] Benjamin's version, however, as cited above, reads "aus ihrer Welt," "out of its world"; that is, it is out of the world of hell that the "Contagion" proceeds on its way to circulating in an open-ended set of possible places and times. The 1928 quote thus breaks with the continuity of the German tradition as figured in volume Z6b. "Origin"-like, Benjamin's version nevertheless gives the Shakespeare text a further afterlife in turn.

---

46. On the superiority of the quarto over the folio, still see Wilson, who nevertheless lists the "breakes/breathes" confusion under the heading "Misprints Not Yet Accounted For" (120).

47. Shakespeare, *Shakespeare's dramatische Werke* (1798) 263. I read the Schlegel-Tieck translation of *Hamlet* in its third edition: Shakespeare, *Shakespeare's dramatische Werke* (1844) here 95.

Even with its "correction," Benjamin's *Hamlet* quote allows his book to join the ranks of a German Shakespeare that not only stretches back through Ulrici to Schlegel-Tieck, but also brings that tradition "out of" these illustrious origins "into" his own time and text. It is not just that Benjamin could have read Shakespeare in any one of these translations that allows a German identity to emerge for the play. His desire to cast *Hamlet* as German may also be detected when, in the *Tragic Drama* book, the "witching time of night" quote is not identified as deriving from Shakespeare's play; rather, unattributed, it is sandwiched in between references to the German-language plays of Gryphius and Lohenstein, on the one hand, and of Stranitzky, on the other, at a point in Benjamin's argument (G: 1.1: 313–14; E: 134–35) where he is heaping citation on citation in support of an argument about the ongoing "origin" of the *German* tragic drama. That Benjamin cites *Hamlet* after the Ulrici edition offers an additionally precise window, then, on what it meant to offer the play as part of the German tradition. The background emerges, first, out of the story of the vexed tradition of English-language editions of Shakespeare on which some of the most famous German translators and editors, including Ulrici, relied in their work.

Edmond Malone's 1790 edition of Shakespeare's plays is the one on which the original Schlegel-Tieck edition appears to have been based (Habicht, "Shakespeare in Nineteenth-Century Germany" 143). According to Margreta de Grazia, the most important characteristic of Malone's Shakespeare was the innovation it represented in the editorial tradition. Emphasizing historical research and using documents and archives of materials from the sixteenth century to corroborate individual readings and emendations of orthography and diction in the text, Malone (1741–1812) had reversed the protocols that had become standard in seventeenth- and early to mid-eighteenth-century editorial practice. In these earlier traditions, "actual usage" in Shakespeare's day had been supplanted by stylistic, orthographic, and even moralistic catalogs of Shakespeare's "Beauties and Faults" (Pope, qtd. in de Grazia 63) developed according to the standards of the various editors' times. Malone sought, in his edition and textual apparatus, to "withstand" the "modern sophistications and foreign admixtures" that "history" (De Grazia 6) had introduced into the Bard's plays in this way. He did so by citing not post-1623 updated editions of Shakespeare by the likes of Nicholas Rowe (1709), Samuel Johnson (1765), and Alexander Pope (1723–25, 1747), but rather, only "Shakespeare's contemporaries to support his use of phraseology and metre" (De Grazia 119). By consulting, collecting, and referring only to the "written and spoken language of Shakespeare's period" (De Grazia 120), in other words, Malone's mission was to "expunge" the "contamination" of the texts by printers' blunders or editorial interpolations, or, indeed, by any interventions in the text subsequent to the 1623 Folio. Malone's very un-Benjaminian "work" was thus firmly rooted, indeed, immobilized, in the time of its original making, in the moment of the text's genesis, in other words.

Malone's method was nevertheless also constitutive of the invention of the canon of what is now considered sixteenth-century, Elizabethan, and Renaissance British literature, since "in the search for illuminating parallels to passages in Shakespeare's plays and poems, hundreds of formerly neglected contemporary literary materials were scrutinized," leading in the end, de Grazia writes, to the constitution of a "body of works" that became "characteristic" of a period with a "vocabulary, grammar, and poetics of its own" (122). The English Renaissance thus seems to have been created by editorial decree. Given this background, it is not surprising that Malone's was the edition that Schlegel and Tieck appear to have used as the basis of their translation, albeit in a much more complicated cooperative fashion than usually assumed, as Larson has shown. Tieck himself was quite interested, as suggested in the two volumes of *Altenglisches Theater* (Old English Theater) (1811) that appeared under his name and in his years of work on *Shakespeares Vorschule* (Shakespeare's Predecessors) (1823 and 1829), in the tradition of plays predating Shakespeare's (Larson, "Origins of the 'Schlegel-Tieck' Shakespeare" 24), and thus in an English Renaissance tradition assumed to have been all of a piece. Tieck seems to have understood, in other words, along with Malone, that Shakespeare belonged to the Renaissance, or at least to a bounded set of historical norms and a specific time.

By the high (or low) point of his career in the 1850s and 1860s, John Payne Collier (1789–1883), on whose work Ulrici, the general editor of the text from which Benjamin cites, relied, had a very different understanding from that of Malone of the authenticity of Shakespeare's plays and, indeed, of what the "original" of a text was. Again, it was Collier's research on Shakespeare on which Ulrici based his 1839 *Ueber Shakspeare's dramatische Kunst* (On Shakespeare's Dramatic Art), the book that Benjamin read and cited in an essay written at the same time as he was working on the *Tragic Drama* book. Ulrici writes: "Shakespeare and the history of English drama is mostly in debt to Payne Collier's efforts" (*Ueber Shakspeare's dramatische Kunst* v). He repeats the claim in the second, supplemented edition of the 1839 book, *Shakspeare's dramatische Kunst: Geschichte und Charakteristik* (Shakespeare's Dramatic Art: History and Characteristic) (1847) ("Vorwort," viii–ix). Not only had Collier, in his 1842–44 edition of Shakespeare's plays, put forth the maverick argument that "Shakespeare had chiefly employed his pen in the revival, alteration, and improvement of existing dramas" (Ioppolo 32), thus deauthorizing Shakespeare as the singular genius he had been alleged to be. He also subsequently and more spectacularly retracted "much of his editorial comment and criticism" originally published there (i.e., in the 1844 edition) in his updated *Notes and Emendations to the Text of Shakespeare's Plays,* published in 1853. In the *Notes and Emendations* volume, Collier offers textual readings of the plays based on his recent purchase and use of the controversial Perkins Folio. Allegedly a copy of the 1632 Second Folio, the Perkins text contained substantial corrections in its margins, which, according to Collier, had been "penned in" there by Thomas Perkins, a member of the acting company The King's Men, allegedly with Shakespeare's consent (Ioppolo 32). These were nevertheless the "corrections" that were subsequently found to have been tampered with, if not outright falsified and forged, by none other than Collier himself. Although Collier had earlier spent decades tracking down the sources of one of the earliest anthologies of memorable quotations extant from the period, the so-called *Englands Parnassus* of 1600, then, he is best remembered for his problematic association with this 1853 plagiarized or, if that is too strong, at least post-Shakespeare Shakespeare, whose texts were thus revealed to be by no means bound to the sixteenth century, the Renaissance, or any one edition of Shakespeare's plays.[48]

As noted above, Ulrici relied heavily on Collier in his 1839 study of Shakespeare, the book that Benjamin knew. It is Collier's work, according to Ulrici, that "in both public and private libraries all over England" had made it possible for "many an important document" to be found; thus, Ulrici writes, indirectly pointing to the subsequent fraud, "not only was [it possible] to confirm much that was once doubtful, but several entirely new and unexpected pieces of information were revealed" (*Ueber Shakspeare's dramatische Kunst* v). Of course Ulrici could not have known in 1839 that Collier would go on to forge materials in 1853. Nevertheless, what Ulrici liked about Collier's work in 1839 was that it in fact "confirms" many of the earlier "conjectures by Tieck," whose "contribution" it had in any case been to have used both the quartos and the folio to "[sweep] away the chaff of the arbitrary and highly prosaic emendations by the English editors" (vi). In Ulrici's eyes, the Englishman Collier's work thus only confirmed the earlier German translator's ability to understand the English playwright better than the latter's countrymen. Even in the much later general introduction to volume 1 of the first edition of Schlegel-Tieck (1867–71; vol. 1, 1867), in which Ulrici gives a thorough review of the editorial traditions in both English and German (83–113), Collier's earlier work, up through 1840, is still mentioned as having contributed in "significant" ways to "historical research" (96–97). Several pages later, the forgeries—"documents" that "he had fabricated himself with the intention to deceive" (99)—are mentioned, yet in an odd claim that appears to want to distinguish Collier's work as an editor from his work as a "critic." For Ulrici, it was the "critic" Collier who had engaged in forgery, not the editor, even though it is obvious, in Collier's own words, that the 1853 *Notes and Emendations* were as much of an editorial effort as the earlier edition itself. They contain proof, Collier writes there, of "the restored language of Shakespeare" himself (19). Even though Collier's "fabrication" of other documents is noted frequently elsewhere in Ulrici's introduction (e.g., 36, 39n, and 43), it is only mentioned in such a way as to show that, in the meantime, other, more

---

48. On the problematic "authenticity" of the *Englands Parnassus* anthology itself, see de Grazia 218–19.

respectable documents had demonstrated that Collier's fakes had not been so far off the mark.

Ulrici's apologetic attitude toward Collier and his perhaps problematic, but nevertheless decisively nongenealogical poetics of translation in the lengthy foreword to the edition of Shakespeare that Benjamin cites explain, at the level of editorial logic, how he can claim that it is a "commonly acknowledged fact" that August Wilhelm Schlegel's translation of Shakespeare had made "England's greatest dramatic poet into the spiritual property of the German nation" (Ulrici, "Allgemeine Einleitung" 110–11). After the Schlegel-Tieck translation, Shakespeare had become not only Germany's "adopted son" (114), according to Ulrici, but also, and perhaps more importantly, entirely "nationalized" (111) by the Germans. It was also Ulrici who, as president of the German Shakespeare Society, had called in his annual report for 1866, printed in the *Shakespeare Yearbook* of 1867, for the Germans to take complete ownership of the Bard: "We want to, as it were, de-Anglicize the Englishman Shakespeare" (*Shakespeare Jahrbuch* 2 [1867]: 2). In light of Ulrici's project to teutonify Shakespeare editorially, it is only ironic that Karl Elze (1821–89) of Dessau, who later became a professor of English philology at the University at Halle and who was the author of the individual "Annotations" and "Notes on *Hamlet*" that appeared in volume 6 of the Ulrici Schlegel-Tieck edition that Benjamin cites, should write that Schlegel "followed the quarto texts of *Hamlet* almost universally in the present play [i.e., *Hamlet*]" (Elze in Ulrici, *Shakespeare's dramatische Werke* 165). The word "breathes" (*haucht*), which appears just before the troublesome "into this world" (*in diese Welt*) phrase in all of the German editions, of course follows the "breathes" of the Folio rather than the "breakes" of the Quarto. Elze's claim about the affiliation of the updated Schlegel-Tieck *Hamlet* with the quartos, which, as he notes earlier in his introductory remarks, had in fact been discovered only fairly recently (Elze in Ulrici, *Shakespeare's Dramatische Werke* 10), is thus not quite correct. Moreover, in the context of an edition overseen by Ulrici, with his indebtedness to Collier, Elze's remark seems counterintuitive, since what he is suggesting is that the older and closer to the original English source the version of a text is, the better and more authentic it can be assumed to be. Collier's premise had been precisely the opposite, namely that an updated Shakespeare was inevitably the better one.

In his 1877 *Hamlet* introduction (Elze in Ulrici, *Shakespeare's dramatische Werke* 3–14), Elze actually refers to Collier on several occasions (4, 7, 9) in his discussion of various reputable commentators on Shakespeare and the British dramatic tradition without mentioning the forgeries, which were well known by this time. Elze's participation in the reediting of Schlegel-Tieck, and his claim at the end of his introduction that it had been "the leading minds of our nation," including Lessing, Schlegel, and Tieck, who had accomplished the "cleansing process" of the Bard's plays, which, having been so "deformed" over the years, were now restored "to their original purity" (14), suggest, in un-Malonian fashion, that it is only by moving away from the context of its particular historical and linguistic "genesis" (*Entstehung*) that an "original" text of *Hamlet* in the Benjaminian sense could be produced. In keeping with Ulrici's program of "de-Anglicization" of the Bard, the "purest" *Hamlet* would thus be the one that was the furthest removed from its historical moment of genesis—and thus both German and not necessarily tied to the English Renaissance at all.

Benjamin could have consulted the 1876–77 edition of the Ulrici Shakespeare in the State Library, as noted above. He had nevertheless already been reading Shakespeare for quite long time before he began his research for the *Tragic Drama* book; the editors of the Frankfurt edition describe "reading evenings" in Berlin beginning in 1908, for example, during which Shakespeare's works were read aloud in a small circle of friends (*Gesammelte Schriften* 2.3: 1420). Already by 1918, however, in notes on *As You Like It,* for example, even as Benjamin describes Shakespeare as living "at the time of the Renaissance" and as a playwright who had thoughts on "infinity" analogous to those of the great Renaissance figures of Nicolas of Cusa, Leonardo, and Michelangelo, he declares the Bard ultimately independent of the particular historical period. Indeed, Shakespeare is, according to Benjamin, "a Romantic poet," "the greatest Romantic" in fact (*Gesammelte Schriften* 2.2: 610). The claim is conventional and may have been indebted to Hegel's description of Shakespeare as "essentially romantic," as Werner Habicht suggests ("Shakespeare in Nineteenth-Century Germany" 146). Another link to a "Romantic" Shakespeare would have been the Schlegel-Tieck German-language edition that Benjamin appears to have been using, as the citation of the titles of the plays in German—*Wie es Euch Gefällt* and *Sturm*—in these notes suggests that it was. A Hegelian Shakespeare could also have emerged out of a reading of this edition, since in addition to his devotion to the Shakespeare cult, Ulrici was deeply involved in Hegelian debates, although perhaps somewhat differently than Habicht indicates. It was in fact via some of Ulrici's other work that by the time he wrote the *Tragic Drama* book Benjamin could have understood that Shakespeare was also something more than a "Romantic," indeed, that he was also the author and creator of a "Christian" Hamlet, who, "unique in the tragic drama[,] is the audience (*Zuschauer*) of God's grace." It was Shakespeare as the creator of this Hamlet who was, according to Benjamin, the only writer of tragic dramas who could "cause Christian sparks to arise out of the melancholy rigidity of the Baroque," something "the German tragic drama" had never been able to do (G: 1.1: 334–35; E: 158).

It is commonly assumed that Benjamin was indebted for his reading of a "Christian" Shakespeare to the man he considered the "most proper reader" (*Briefe* 1: 374) of the *Tragic Drama* book, namely Florens Christian Rang (1864–1924).[49] Benjamin writes to Hugo von Hofmannsthal in the winter of 1925, for example,

---

49. On Rang's and Benjamin's relationship, see Steiner, *Die Geburt der Kritik.*

after the withdrawal of his thesis from Frankfurt, that he had never "felt at home with Shakespeare, but, rather, could approach him only at a distance and periodically"; it was, moreover, only "in the company of Florens Christian Rang" that he had learned what it meant to be truly "comfortable with him [Shakespeare]" (*Briefe* 1: 406). Rang had commented on the figure of Hamlet as "the male version of the figure of Melancholy, that Dürer had modeled as female" (Rang, *Shakespeare der Christ* 166), for example, and the juxtaposition of Hamlet with Dürer's engraving is central to Benjamin's argument about the role of melancholy in a specifically Lutheran Baroque, as I show in chapter 3. But in the book in which Rang makes this claim, published posthumously as *Shakespeare der Christ* (Shakespeare the Christian) (1954), the focus is specifically on Shakespeare as a "poet of sonnets."[50] For an extended reading of the *plays* as "Christian," Benjamin may have had to turn to Ulrici instead.

The most relevant—and proximate—book on this topic was in fact by Ulrici. It was also a book that Benjamin had already read and cited in his earlier essay, "'El mayor monstruo, los celos' von Calderon und 'Herodes und Mariamne' von Hebbel," as noted above. In his 1839 *Ueber Shakspeare's dramatische Kunst* (On Shakespeare's Dramatic Art), Ulrici had already (and quite a bit earlier than Rang) claimed to be presenting "an assessment of Shakespeare's plays from the highest point of contemporary aesthetics, namely Christian aesthetics" (vii). The position was in line with his perhaps better-known scholarship; indeed, Ulrici's later critical assessment of Hegelian idealistic rationalism from the point of view of a more theistically informed position was the basis of his *Glauben und Wissen* (Faith and Knowledge) (1858), *Gott und die Natur* (God and Nature) (1862), and *Gott und der Mensch* (God and Man) (1866–73), all published during the same years that he was overseeing the new edition of Shakespeare's works based on Schlegel-Tieck.[51] But his position on religion is also apparent in the earlier, 1839 book, in which he offers a reading of the character Hamlet as a "Christ," a Christian, who, "still struggling with his human nature and its demand for revenge" (*Ueber Shakspeare's dramatische Kunst* 233) and "still caught in an earthly existence" (236) throughout the play, finally dies "in peaceful longing and transfiguration" (242). Ulrici's Hamlet dies believing in "the idea of a divine justice that is all-guiding" (241) and "with a firm trust in heaven's pardon and salvation" (242). The words are unmistakably audible in the eleventh-hour, Lutheran insight into God's grace that characterizes Benjamin's Hamlet too, and may also explain Benjamin's claim earlier in this section

---

50. For many years and especially after 1920, Rang had been deeply immersed in the sonnets as part of a translation project. See Jäger 119–45. It is fascinating that, according to Steiner, Rang placed "his translation of the sonnets in a historically parallel situation to the Schlegel-Tieck translation of the plays" (*Die Geburt der Kritik* 235). Jäger claims that Rang and Benjamin also corresponded about and discussed the plays.

51. See Habicht, "Shakespeare in Nineteenth-Century Germany" 146, for the suggestion that Ulrici may have written "under the influence of Hegel."

that "this, Hamlet's, word is philosophically Wittenbergian" (G: 1.1: 317; E: 138).[52] In any case, Ulrici was an author whose work Benjamin appears to have known perhaps as early as 1918–19, but certainly since 1923, when the Frankfurt editors suggest the Calderón-Hebbel essay was written (see *Gesammelte Schriften* 2.3: 998). Using Ulrici's edition of *Hamlet* may well have made sense, either in a copy of the Ulrici Schlegel-Tieck Benjamin could have owned as a student, or the copy he could have consulted during his months of research in the State Library in Berlin.

The German-language Shakespeare Benjamin cites in the *Tragic Drama* book was also more than the literal textual one discussed here, however. Another version of the Bard is visible in the appearance of other more figuratively updated German Shakespeares circulating widely in print at about this same time. Benjamin's writings from approximately these same years provide evidence that he was familiar with at least two of these additional versions. The profile of the playwright captured in Friedrich Gundolf's famous *Shakespeare und der deutsche Geist* (Shakespeare and the German Spirit) (1911), while controversial, was perhaps the most well known— or at least the one with the greatest popular impact—of the many literary-historical and critical versions of a German Shakespeare available in the early twentieth century. Gundolf's book gave the "myth of Shakespeare's role as a catalyst of classical-romantic German thinking . . . its quasi-definitive state" (Habicht, "Shakespeare in Nineteenth-Century Germany" 143).[53] Originally Gundolf's *Habilitation,* the book followed his own programmatic recommendations, registered in an essay from 1912, to produce cultural "heroes" by means of a "discerning transformation" of the past into a model for the present (qtd. in Osterkamp 164–65). Gundolf (1880–1931) had himself done just this in his own ten-volume translation of Shakespeare's plays. While he based his edition on Schlegel's translation as he had "reviewed" it (the volume contains "A. W. von Schlegels Uebersetzung durchgesehen," the elaborately decorative Jugendstil typeface of the edition's title page declares), it was also "in part newly translated" (*zum Teil neu uebersetzt*), as the title also makes clear.

This version of Shakespeare, reinvented for his own modern time, had been undertaken by the young Gundolf at the behest of the oracular poet-genius Stefan George (Osterkamp 164) and was published between 1908 and 1918 (second edition, 1920–21) as a more popular competitor for Ulrici's late nineteenth-century edition.[54] It was nevertheless the lengthy monograph *Shakespeare und der deutsche Geist* (Shakespeare and the German Spirit), which appeared in the midst of the

---

52. Benjamin goes on to claim that Hamlet is protesting the Lutheran position here. See Steiner, "Traurige Spiele" 35, on the role of Ulrici's work in Benjamin's understanding of Calderón; Steiner calls it a "productive utilization of materials he found in Ulrici" (36).

53. On the reaction to Gundolf in principle and to his Shakespeare book in particular in the context of Baroque scholarship, see H.-H. Müller, *Barockforschung* 136–47.

54. Steiner notes the intersection of Rang's and George's versions of Shakespeare's sonnets (*Die Geburt der Kritik* 251–52). On Benjamin's complicated intersection with Gundolf and George, see Brodersen, *Spinne im eigenen Netz* 123–25 and 219–22; and with abundant bibliography, Braungart.

publication of Gundolf's "translations" of the plays, that really made his reputation, for it represented an open challenge to what he perceived as the vacuous work of traditional philology of the sort that could have been associated with the Ulrici edition. Written by an author who, although an outsider in the academy, in fact became "the most famous scholar of German literature of his time,"[55] the book had gone through six editions by 1927. It had given Shakespeare an even newer profile as a "German" in ways that had very little to do with a traditional understanding of his origins, or of his identity as an English Renaissance playwright at all, by the time Benjamin included him among the other playwrights of the "German" tragic drama in his book. Gundolf's massive tome offers additional evidence of what Shakespeare signified in Germany at the time. Although based on a radically different scholarly method and trajectory than Ulrici's, Gundolf's book was aimed at a similar goal, namely the appropriation of Shakespeare as part of modern Germany's cultural heritage.

Gundolf's book "translates" Shakespeare into a German playwright by tracking his "penetration" "into German writing up through Romanticism," showing how his plays had made German poetry "fertile" (Gundolf, *Shakespeare und der deutsche Geist* vii) up through the time of Schlegel's and Tieck's work. This sexualized understanding of the English playwright's role in the "formation of the German spirit" (105) had begun, according to Gundolf, already in the seventeenth century (7–8), when versions of his plays traveled across the English Channel in the repertoires of the so-called English comedians, whose highly successful performances at a number of late sixteenth-century German courts were nevertheless geared to the lesser needs of a German audience caught in a process of cultural "decline" (4–5, 33, 56); the "Comoedianten" offered to these local consumers terrifying tragedy and grotesque farce in ways very much at odds with the culture of contemporaneous England, Gundolf writes, which was enjoying a true "Renaissance" of drama at the time (12; cf. also 35 and 56). While Gundolf's description of such early Shakespearean moments in Germany is entirely condemnatory, in substance it mirrors Ulrici's own descriptions of the "English actors" and the productions of their plays at German courts in his general introduction ("Allgemeine Einleitung" 101–2), where Ulrici specifically mentions their influence on the Silesian playwright Gryphius. Gundolf also devotes a lengthy early section of his *Shakespeare and the German Spirit* (71–82) to a comparative reading of Gryphius and Shakespeare, although not necessarily to Gryphius's benefit, in his project of assessing this early "stage of Shakespeare's impact on the German spirit" (71).[56] When Benjamin discussed the two

55. The career of the controversial Gundolf (originally Gundelfinger), first in association, then at odds with the George Circle, has received much scholarly attention. Osterkamp provides an excellent overview and gives a full bibliography. The quote here is from Osterkamp 162. Gundolf's monumental *Shakespeare: Sein Wesen und Werk* (Shakespeare: His Essence and Work) appeared in 1928, the same year as Benjamin's *Tragic Drama* book.

56. There are obvious continuities here with Weiß's discussions of the history of German-language drama (15–20).

playwrights together and in the context of both the popular dramatic tradition and "the German tragic drama," as he does, he thus found himself in good company.

Gundolf's story of the "rebirth" and Renaissance of Shakespeare "as a German linguistic unity," especially in Schlegel's translation (Gundolf, *Shakespeare und der deutsche Geist* 354), stops with the German Romantics at the outset of the nineteenth century. The chronology aligns his book with Ulrici's in indirect fashion, for, according to Gundolf, since then there had been no further versions of Shakespeare as an expression of the German "spirit" (355–56). It for this reason that both his and Ulrici's editions had to rely on Tieck's and Schlegel's work. The narrative of a post-Romantic literary void may well have been what prompted Gundolf to call for a further Renaissance, for a "new German spirit," to produce yet another "new image of Shakespeare" (358), one more in line with the grand achievements up through Schlegel, in Gundolf's own time. Gundolf's translation—based on Schlegel's and appearing simultaneously with the monograph—of course fits the bill, as it takes up the banner in ways not unlike Ulrici's Schlegel-Tieck, which had itself extended that original project.[57] Such literary-historical lineages, and the arc from the Baroque tragic drama up through the Storm and Stress and Romantic playwrights that Gundolf describes, mirror those articulated by Benjamin, as indicated above in chapter 1. It comes as no surprise, then, that in act 3, scene 2, of *Hamlet,* in Gundolf's translation, which appeared in the ninth volume of his 1914 edition of the plays, *Shakespeare in deutscher Sprache* (Shakespeare in German), as also in Benjamin's book, as noted above, we can read: "Nun ist die wahre Spükezeit der Nacht / Wo Grüfte gähnen, und die Hölle selbst / Pest haucht in diese Welt" (n.p.). Gundolf's Hamlet speaks his lines in the same German as Schlegel's, Schlegel-Tieck's, Ulrici's—and Benjamin's—Hamlets, in other words, and for good reason, as they are all evidence of the presence of Shakespeare moving not "out of hell," but rather "into" the "world" of "the German spirit."

Even though Gundolf's *Shakespeare and the German Spirit* does not appear among the volumes listed in Benjamin's account of the books he had read (*Gesammelte Schriften* 7: 437–76), the flood of copies in the book market—along with the reality of Gundolf's academic notoriety (he was famously considered, but ultimately rejected as the successor not only to the famous Erich Schmidt in Berlin [Osterkamp 166–70; Höppner "Eine Institution wehrt sich" 362–80], but also to countless other well-known professorial chairs)—would have made it difficult for anyone interested in Shakespeare not to know it or its author at the time.[58]

---

57. According to Gundolf in the merciless critiques that fill his pages, it would be difficult to overlook that most of the earlier German Shakespeares had actually for the most part failed to grasp the "power" and "will to realism" that was Shakespeare's "deepest instinct" (*Shakespeare und der deutsche Geist* 358), a task that Gundolf's own "new" German Shakespeare will clearly fulfill.

58. Since Benjamin's list begins only after 1916–17, according to the Frankfurt editors, it is possible that Gundolf's 1911 book might have been among the 461 some titles read before that point in time.

Benjamin nevertheless does list a number of other Gundolf titles—on Opitz, Gryphius, and Annette von Droste-Hülshoff, for example—as books that he had read (*Gesammelte Schriften* 7: 454, 459, 464). He also reviewed Gundolf's 1927 book on the Silesian playwright Andreas Gryphius for the feuilleton of the *Frankfurter Zeitung,* dated 1 January 1928 (3: 86–88)—albeit in decidedly unfriendly terms. That much of the review recalls arguments from Benjamin's own *Tragic Drama* book, fashioned here as critiques of Gundolf's failure to understand the "formal world" of Gryphius's work (87), is not surprising, as Benjamin's book had just appeared. In this brief little book on the Silesian poet, which Gundolf claims is based on lectures given a decade before, he declares he wants to comment on Gryphius's status against the background of the "fashionable frenzy that is accompanying the desired scholarly reappraisal of German Baroque poetry" (*Andreas Gryphius,* Vorwort, n.p.). The timing suggests that it may well have been in the aftermath of and in reaction to approaches such as Fritz Strich's in 1916 that Gundolf originally gave these lectures, which he then some years later turned into the book that Benjamin read. Gundolf's remark nevertheless also suggests that the "frenzy" for the Baroque had not yet settled down.[59] And even though Gundolf is at least as ungenerous to the Silesian playwright in *Andreas Gryphius* as he had been in the earlier Shakespeare book—"Gryphius has nothing to do with Shakespeare," he writes (*Andreas Gryphius* 6)—his repeated juxtapositions of the two (17, 20, 22, 26, 29–30, 38, 51, 57–58, 62) suggest that it would be fair to ask the question whether for Gundolf, Gryphius had not been, like Shakespeare, a man of the Renaissance (as Shakespeare had been in his *Shakespeare and the German Spirit*), or whether, perhaps, as Gundolf writes here, he had been a playwright whose work "makes quite clear for us what distinguishes the Baroque from [the Gothic and the Rococo]" (17). For Gundolf, as for Benjamin, then, it is Gryphius in juxtaposition to Shakespeare who defines the Baroque.

In this respect, it is only confusing when Benjamin writes in his review of Gundolf's *Andreas Gryphius* that Gundolf's reading of the Baroque playwright is "completely at odds" with "the paths of [current] research on the Baroque" (*Gesammelte Schriften* 3: 87), by which he presumably means his own book. For Benjamin, Gryphius emerges as a quintessentially Baroque writer and as an author not of tragedies, but rather of tragic dramas, and this precisely in juxtaposition to Shakespeare. In the *Tragic Drama* book, it is in *Hamlet* that one can best observe those elements of the tragic drama that Shakespeare's plays embodied but the German texts did not reflect. Benjamin famously writes: "At least once the period succeeded in calling up a figure that corresponded to the split between the neo-antique and the medieval in which the Baroque had seen the melancholic man. Germany was not able to do it,

---

59. Gundolf had studied with Wölfflin in Berlin in the years after his *Renaissance and Baroque* book had made the art historian famous (Osterkamp 163), and thus was directly familiar with debates about the Baroque as well.

however. This figure was Hamlet" (G: 1.1: 334; E: 157). Here, in a comparative turn that, again, does not differ substantially from Gundolf's, it is Shakespeare's *Hamlet* that confirms where the *German* Baroque tragic drama stands. *Hamlet* was thus a German text in both the Ulrici edition of Shakespeare and in the edition circulating under Gundolf's name (which was not significantly different from Ulrici's). The Bard can thus quite legitimately be, for Benjamin, "the foundation of the new form of drama" (*Gesammelte Schriften* 1.3: 915).

Gundolf's person and his work on Shakespeare were highly visible in the years Benjamin was working on the *Tragic Drama* book. There was, however, another literary-historical and critical version of Shakespeare that competed with Gundolf's during these years, one that brought the Bard even closer to the fold of the German Baroque poets than the parallels drawn between his work and Gryphius's by Ulrici and Gundolf might suggest. Already by 1916, Oskar Walzel (1864–1944) had published his now famous essay "Shakespeares dramatische Baukunst" (Shakespeare's Dramatic Architecture), in which an explicitly Baroque Shakespeare is described. Walzel, whose literary-historical project Walter Schmitz describes as "nationally oriented," was well known as a mediator not only between academe and a broader bourgeois literate public, but also to contemporary writers and artists alike.[60] The piece nevertheless originally appeared in the academically very respectable *Shakespeare Yearbook* 52 (1916) and was then reprinted in Walzel's 1926 *Das Wortkunstwerk* (The Linguistic Work of Art), which appeared after Walzel had accepted a distinguished professorship in Bonn. In Walzel's essay on Shakespeare, which originally appeared in the same year, and thus at the very birth hour of German Baroque studies, as Fritz Strich's essay on the "Baroque lyric style," the English playwright was—if not for the first time, then certainly with the most resonance, given the place of publication—labeled a "Baroque" playwright.[61]

Benjamin reviewed Walzel's *Linguistic Work of Art* in the feuilleton of the *Frankfurter Zeitung* on 7 November 1926 (*Gesammelte Schriften* 3: 50–51); that he was aware in 1926 of the context in which Walzel's article had originally appeared in 1916 is clear there when he discusses Walzel's place in a tradition of "formal analysis" (50) that takes as its anchors the work of Alois Riegl and Heinrich Wölfflin, for example, so prominent the decade before. Benjamin's commentary on Walzel's *Linguistic Work of Art,* which was a collection of sixteen essays published over the course of the previous two decades, focuses on the essays' relationship to the "recent trends in aesthetics" associated with the two art theorists; Benjamin

---

60. See Schmitz 124 and 119–20 also on the shape this nationalism took during the National Socialist years.

61. Hans-Harald Müller ("Die Übertragung des Barockbegriffs" 112) argues, and Rosenberg (117) agrees, that even though Strich's and Walzel's arguments on behalf of the Baroque succeeded in creating the period as the object of literary-historical study, they did not actually contribute to the discussion of the German literature of the seventeenth century. Neither addresses the question of Shakespeare's place in this discussion.

ultimately laments, by the end of the review, that Walzel has strayed too far into generalized statements about the "'synthetic' gesture" of art and thus away from fidelity to "the radical singularity of the work of art" (51) so important to Wölfflin, Riegl, and himself. Benjamin's location of Walzel in this company is not surprising, since Walzel himself knew the work of both Riegl and Wölfflin well; indeed, it was between their two methodologies that he had sought to negotiate in one of his early and most well-known works, *Wechselseitige Erhellung der Künste: Ein Beitrag zur Würdigung kunstgeschichtlicher Begriffe* (Reciprocal Illumination of the Arts: A Contribution to the Evaluation of Art Historical Concepts) (1917), the book to which Benjamin appears to be referring in his review. The essay on Shakespeare may well have been a kind of dry run for the *Reciprocal Illumination* book; indeed, there are often exact repetitions of arguments made in the essay in both that book and in Walzel's next work, *Gehalt und Gestalt im Kunstwerk des Dichters* (Content and Form in the Poetic Work of Art) (1923), which appeared just after he had moved to Bonn. According to Hans-Harald Müller, Walzel was "without a doubt one of the most versatile minds of German literary studies between 1900 and 1933" ("Die Übertragung des Barockbegriffs" 95), at which point permission to lecture at Bonn was summarily withdrawn and Walzel was forced into retirement because of his marriage to the half-Jewish Hedwig Karo.[62] Benjamin could not have been aware of this future when in his review he critiqued Walzel precisely in terms of his reputation for interdisciplinary, indeed, comparative intermedial methods due to the latter's interest in the "synthetical gesture."

The echo of the title of Wölfflin's 1915 *Principles of Art History* in the subtitle of Walzel's 1917 book situates the latter's work—and thus his take on Shakespeare—squarely within the Renaissance-Baroque debate. The original version of Walzel's essay "Shakespeare's Dramatic Architecture," as it appeared in the *Shakespeare Yearbook,* lists and explains Wölfflin's famous five categories, linear versus painterly, closed and open form, and so on, in the context of Walzel's interest in adapting to an analysis of "Shakespeare's form" the terms of the "transformation that took place in the fine arts between the sixteenth and the seventeenth century on the way from the Renaissance to the Baroque" ("Shakespeares dramatische Baukunst" 25). In 1916, it could perhaps not yet have been assumed that every reader of the *Shakespeare Yearbook* would be familiar with Wölfflin's terms; thus the detailed inventory of terms and the explanation were necessary. The passage is omitted, however, in the 1926 version, which Benjamin read; by then, Walzel could have expected a greater familiarity with the art historical categories, a familiarity attested in Benjamin's ability to supply them in his review when he notes the links in Walzel's argument to Wölfflin's "schematics" (*Gesammelte Schriften* 3: 50).

---

62. Karo-Walzel was deported in 1944, at age seventy-four, to Theresienstadt. The eighty-year-old Walzel, who because of the marriage was also to be expelled from the city, was nevertheless given permission to stay; he died in a bombing attack on Bonn in December 1944. See Enders 347.

Not omitted in 1926, however, was Walzel's famously contradictory explanation of the usefulness of applying Wölfflinian vocabulary and categories, including that of the Baroque, to a reading of Shakespeare:

It should not be assumed that I want to adopt Shakespeare in the service of the fashionable term Baroque. And it has become a fashionable term. I am in fact extremely uninterested in the term Baroque. At the same time, it does help us see that, in drama, Shakespeare['s plays] signify exactly the same transformation that the fine arts were undergoing at approximately the same time. This kind of historical relation is not my main point in terms of the task I have set myself here, however. Something else is much more important, namely the distinction between two major groups of formal possibilities in art. These two groups stand opposed to one another, but each has the same right to a recognition of their internal intentions and formal patterns, namely, following Wölfflin, open and closed style, starkly architectonic and looser, unarchitectural. ("Shakespeares dramatische Baukunst" [1916] 27; [1926] 317–18)

Walzel's claim that he does not intend his Shakespeare to be a "fashionable" Baroque playwright in specifically Wölfflinian terms is not borne out by the rest of the essay, however, in which he takes pains to do close readings of several of the plays of the man he identifies as the author of "Baroque drama" and creator of "Baroque art" ("Shakespeares dramatische Baukunst" [1916] 32; [1926] 323) par excellence. A reader could easily be forgiven for associating Shakespeare with the Baroque after reading Walzel's essay to the end.

Walzel's claim here that his interests in understanding Shakespeare as a Baroque playwright were not "historical" points not only to his complicity in what he may have understood as a "stylistic," Wölfflinian approach, which he, like Fritz Strich, endorsed at the same time,[63] but also, and just as fundamentally, according to Hans-Harald Müller ("Die Übertragung des Barockbegriffs" 96), to Walzel's indebtedness to his student Wilhelm Worringer's interest in his *Formprobleme der Gotik* (Formal Problems of the Gothic) (1911) in the "will to form" of the Gothic. This version of the Rieglian "artistic will" was a type of primal, or essential, "Teutonic artistic will" not bound to specific epochs, but, again, intrinsic to "the German spirit" coming to fruition in modern times. Worringer's Baroque was decisively and thoroughly German; to make Shakespeare Baroque was thus to adopt him as a native son in ways that were in fashion at the time. That in *The Linguistic Work of Art,* Walzel deletes not only the longer explanation of Wölfflin's categories from the essay as it had appeared in 1916, but also even his name from the bibliography ("Shakespeares dramatische Baukunst" [1916] 35; [1926] 325) indicates just how

---

63. Both Walzel and Strich later claimed that they came to their readings independently of each other; see Rosenberg 114.

much Worringer had come to replace Wölfflin in Walzel's mind, as a somewhat later Walzel essay on Shakespeare (1921), not surprisingly entitled "Das Deutschtum unserer Klassiker" (The Germanness of Our Classical Authors), reveals.

It is important to note that already in 1916, and in the *Shakespeare Yearbook* in particular, it was no accident that Walzel's Shakespeare, who had already been considered the property of the Germans since at least Ulrici's term as president of the German Shakespeare Society and tenure as editor of its journal, as noted above, could be identified as essentially German. Volume 52 of the journal reveals why. Appearing at the height of World War I and with Walzel's essay as the lead scholarly item, the volume also contains considerable front matter, including such documents as the "Address and Annual Report" (v-xv) from the annual meeting of the Society, and the transcription of the remarks by the president at the time. This preliminary matter notes that there were no representatives from England in attendance at the annual meeting, as there had been in the past. The president comments on this absence as unremarkable, however, since the English are no longer scholars; rather, only an "inhumane chorus," shouting "vile fictions . . . of crucified prisoners and children's hands being amputated," can be heard from across the Channel (v). He then goes on to excoriate "those in power . . . and the benighted in England today |who| would love to change us from free human beings into slaves" (vi). Such men are incapable of tending to their own heritage, and especially to Shakespeare. The scholarly work of the German Shakespeare Society, whose members were gathered there, was thus all the more legitimate and indeed was to be equated with militaristically described patriotic work. The introduction ends with a rousing and patriotic wartime call to the assembled scholars: "We are all prepared to sacrifice our homes and lives for the Kaiser and for the *Reich*" (xiv).

The main evening address, by Professor Rudolf Brotanek of Prague, that year at the annual meeting is also reprinted in the front matter to volume 52 (xvi–xlviii). Entitled, appropriately enough, "Shakespeare über den Krieg" (Shakespeare on War), it leads the audience through the lessons of the great playwright about war and peace, which are described as more familiar to "*our* politicians" (xlviii, emphasis added) than to "the amateurish English politicians" (xvii) of the Bard's original home. In volume 52, Shakespeare is thus clearly being used as what Habicht calls a "cultural weapon" ("Shakespeare Celebrations" 449); his "special closeness" (451) to Germany was all the more important in this wartime three-hundredth anniversary year of the Bard's death. It is no wonder that Walzel's essay, with its association of Shakespeare with the Baroque, was the lead academic essay in this context. Not only would the editors of the *Shakespeare Yearbook* have been pleased to publish an essay by a well-known scholar who had already been active in what Walzel himself later calls "propaganda" activities associated with the Great War.[64] They also

---

64. Walzel was himself—reluctantly, he later claims—actively complicit in such nationalist agendas and held what he calls "propaganda lectures" during the Great War. He describes these lectures

would have approved of an essay whose premise was based on the suggestion of a Baroque Shakespeare, especially since the Baroque had already some years before been christened as a signifier of a kind of primal, yet also all-pervasive "Germanness" by none other than Walzel's student Wilhelm Worringer.

In his memoirs, Walzel states categorically that, even as a student in Bern (1897–1907), Worringer (1881–1965) was one of his closest intellectual colleagues; later, the impact of Worringer's work became more and more important to him, first supplementing, then displacing Wölfflin's both in Walzel's own distinctions between classical and nonclassical, or Gothic, art and in the conceptualization of the "reciprocal illumination of the arts" (Enders 227–28). This displacement seems to have not yet fully occurred either in the Shakespeare essay or in Walzel's book of that title.[65] Worringer's interest in his widely distributed *Formal Problems of the Gothic,* a book that Benjamin read (*Gesammelte Schriften* 7: 452), is in what Worringer calls the "rehabilitation of those non-classical epochs in Europe that to date have experienced a measured and even negative evaluation from the point of view of Classicism" (9). The "actual" (*eigentlich,* that is, historical) Gothic is his main focus, but he is also interested in its role as a "timeless aspect of the race" that reappears subsequently in the "secret Gothic" of later "Teutonic" epochs and styles (126–27).[66] Worringer's inclusion of the Baroque (28, 60, 79–80, and 127, for example) in his list of "non-classical" periods whose forms expressed the "secret Gothic" is significant in the jingoistic context of the original publication of Walzel's "Shakespeare's Dramatic Architecture," for in this context, as suggested above, Walzel's proposal to understand Shakespeare via the lens of Baroque art would in all likelihood have been not only acceptable, but indeed, deeply desired by its editors, and thus given pride of place as the lead article in the 1916 wartime number of the *Shakespeare Yearbook.*

Worringer's project to "rehabilitate" nonclassical epochs of art of course recalls not only Wölfflin on the Baroque, but also Riegl's interests in a different kind of nonjudgmental and nonhierarchical art history. Jennings suggests that it was Riegl's work that gave Worringer his direction in the first place (*Dialectical Images* 152 and

---

explicitly as some of his first attempts to apply Wölfflin's "principles" to "poetry" as a way of trying to excite "an understanding for German art and for its essential characteristics . . . that for many counted as inferior." See Enders 167, for example; and Schmitz 120.

65. In the talk, held on 3 January 1917, that became the book, the work of both art historians, Wölfflin and Worringer, is discussed as suggestive of the role that a theory and practice of intermedial comparison could play; nevertheless, even as Walzel accurately notes—and underscores—Worringer's devotion to definitions of "Teutonic art" (*Wechselseitige Erhellung* 27) in that book, he just as accurately recapitulates Wölfflin's method and arguments too (29–41), indeed, gives them priority as an approach to "the individual work of art" (38 and 86).

66. As odd as it might sound in this context, even as he focuses on the Gothic as a "specifically northern development" (27) and as suggestive of a "northern feeling for form" (76), Worringer's project is an explicitly anti-Eurocentric one; "we must not confuse Europe and its fiction of progress with the world," he writes (24), as he examines what he calls "primitive" and "oriental" art along with the art of the West. On Worringer and the Baroque, see H.-H. Müller, *Barockforschung* 59–74.

156); he thus places Benjamin, as an inheritor of Riegl's work, in line with Worringer, with his major influence on Walzel. Walzel himself points out Worringer's dependency on Riegl in his 1913 essay, "Wilhelm von Humboldt über Wert und Wesen der künstlerischen Form" (Wilhelm von Humboldt on the Value and Essence of Artistic Form), which was reprinted, along with "Shakespeare's Dramatic Architecture," in the 1926 volume *The Linguistic Work of Art,* which Benjamin reviewed (Walzer, *Das Wortkunstwerk* 72). Benjamin thus could have discovered the intersection of the two men's work there. Riegl's relevance for both Worringer and Benjamin is important not just because of a common methodology, however, on which Jennings comments. It is also their shared interest in the Baroque that finds an afterlife in Benjamin's work. That is, even though the pre-Renaissance "Gothic" is Worringer's master example in the *Formal Problems* book, it is precisely because the Gothic had been overwhelmed by the "Italian Renaissance, which had entirely different spiritual assumptions," that "the northern Baroque" as "the renewed flaring up of the suppressed Gothic will to form" of the north, the originary northern, indeed, "Arian" (28) Gothic, becomes crucial to Worringer's thesis about the survivability of more or less permanent "northern" "forms."

According to Worringer, the Baroque was the period and style that offered an alternative to the "invasion of the foreign artistic ideal of the Renaissance" (61), which had been privileged by art history to date (73). Indeed, "after the intermezzo of the Renaissance," it was precisely this new "Gothic" style, the "transcendental style, the Baroque" (79–80), that emerged to have a lasting influence in the north. Much more recently, he concludes, the "secret Gothic," the post-Gothic Gothic, had made itself felt yet again, "even up into our own time" (127). There is an echo here of Benjamin's juxtaposition of the Baroque and Expressionism in the *Tragic Drama* book (G: 1.1: 234–35; E: 54). It must be noted that Worringer takes great pains to dismiss arguments that the superiority of the "Germanic" and "northern" "will to form" is anchored in "differences between the races" (29, 126–27); indeed, in political protest, Worringer refused to publish during the National Socialist years. Nevertheless, beginning in 1911, his work became well known for its argument that "the disposition for the Gothic only emerges where Teutonic blood becomes mixed with the blood of the other European races" (29). That a German Shakespeare could be Baroque precisely in the "mixing" that occurs in translation might not have seemed odd in light of such claims. For Worringer, neither the "Gothic" nor its afterlife in the "Baroque" is necessarily to be associated any longer with strictly defined historical epochs, or, for that matter, with narrowly circumscribed cultural spaces at all, but was, rather, all German all the time, where- and whenever each appeared.[67] Against this background, it is, again, not surprising that Walzel's

---

67. See H.-H. Müller, "Die Übertragung des Barockbegriffs," on the nonhistorical use of the term Baroque in Walzel.

argument about Shakespeare, with its indebtedness to Worringer's concept of a Teutonic Gothic Baroque, found a favorable reading with the editors of the *Shakespeare Yearbook* in 1916, for—as in Ulrici and Benjamin—it allowed the English playwright to be celebrated in appropriately German terms.

By 1921 and in the aftermath of Germany's crushing defeat, Walzel's Shakespeare had become much more than the merely formal representative of the Baroque that he was in "Shakespeare's Dramatic Architecture." Indeed, he had become a full-blooded German "classic" explicitly in association with Worringer's "concept of the Teutonic" as articulated in his *Formal Problems of the Gothic* in 1911. Worringer's book had gone through twelve editions by 1919, and by 1930 it had been reissued a twenty-first time. In an essay entitled "Das Deutschtum unserer Klassiker" (The Germanness of Our Classical Writers), which appeared in 1921 in the *Zeitschrift für Deutschkunde* (Journal for German Studies), Walzel argues that precisely a post-Versailles Germany must begin to understand "what it is that we are actually calling the essence of the German" (85) in an age when, as in the age of German "Classicism," the German state was no longer capable of serving as a unifying force. Although Wölfflin's distinction between the Renaissance and the Baroque is occasionally mentioned in this essay (90–91), it is, rather, Worringer's category of "the Teutonic-Gothic" (86) that Walzel introduces early on as the most "unifying and distinguishing characteristic of the German," linked not only to the "Baroque of the seventeenth century," but also to Shakespeare as "related in essential ways to the German" (85–86) and as "the artist of the Teutonic-Gothic" (95) par excellence. Walzel also addresses the allegiances that more traditional representatives of "classical" German literature, namely Schiller and Goethe, as well as Lessing, Klopstock, and the medieval writers Wolfram and Gottfried too, do or do not owe to "the Gothic aspect of Germanness" (99) in various texts and at various times in their careers. But in this essay, it is Shakespeare—in combination with Lessing (86–87), Goethe (97), and even Nietzsche (94)—who provides the most consistent measuring stick of where the German "Gothic" did and did not emerge at various times.

"The Germanness of Our Classical Writers" is not included in the selection of Walzel's earlier essays reprinted in 1926 in *The Linguistic Work of Art*, the volume that Benjamin reviewed. Perhaps this was because of the essay's obvious links to the immediate historical-political conditions of its original year of publication (1921), and its corresponding disregard for questions of "synthetic" method or intermedial concerns for what Walzel calls the "essential characteristic of the work of art," concerns that by 1926 he wanted to claim—in the foreword to *The Linguistic Work of Art* at least—had been his primary concerns of the wartime and postwar years (viii–ix). The 1921 essay does not fit easily into this model and in any case might not have been the kind of "scholarly" approach that Walzel would have chosen to highlight as his trademark in a collection of essays that appeared after he had made a significant career move from Dresden to Bonn. He had in fact carefully distanced himself in the meantime from both the "fashionable motto" that Worringer's idea of the Gothic had become and from the easy assumption of the opposition of the Baroque to the Renaissance that his reception of Wölfflin's work in his 1924 essay, "Das Wesen des dichterischen Kunstwerks" (The Essence of the Poetic Work of Art), had underscored. Benjamin nevertheless would have been familiar with Worringer's claims about the "Gothic" in another way, namely via Burdach's essay "On the Origin of Humanism" (discussed in chapter 1) which Benjamin quotes in the "Epistemo-Critical Prologue." Although Benjamin quotes only that part of Burdach's original note in which Troeltsch is named as the main culprit in association with the essentializing concept of "'the Gothic Man', who plays such a confusing role today," along with the just as questionable notion of "the Baroque Man, in whose guise Shakespeare is introduced to us today" (G: 1.1: 220–21; E: 40), in the original, it is in fact, and understandably, Worringer and his 1911 book that Burdach names as the origin of the claim (Burdach, *Reformation, Renaissance, Humanismus* 213). It may well have been in Burdach, in other words, that Benjamin came across the possibility of a Baroque Shakespeare yet again, associated, first, with Worringer, whose importance to Riegl then emerged with additional clarity in Walzel's "Essence of the Poetic Work of Art" and in his essay on Wilhelm von Humboldt in *The Linguistic Work of Art,* which Benjamin reviewed. Walzel's "Shakespeare's Dramatic Architecture" essay, which also appears there, nevertheless identifies Wölfflin's—rather than Worringer's—work as providing the base line for this alignment. Together, the work of these two men, with which Benjamin was clearly familiar, confirmed for him that it was entirely possible to identify Shakespeare as "a Baroque poet" alongside the more intuitively *German* Baroque playwrights of the Second Silesian school.

The Palm edition in which Benjamin read Gryphius's plays, the religious drama of the German Middle Ages, the farces of the Viennese Stranitzky, and Shakespeare's *Hamlet* all contributed to defining the Baroque tragic drama as ideologically (and linguistically) German. These texts all appear, moreover, in a kind of shorthand, on the list of issues that Benjamin notes will be central to his argument in the "Baroque book," jotted down on a loose page now in the Benjamin archives and reproduced in the Frankfurt commentary volume for the *Tragic Drama* book. The list includes "the founding of the new dramatic form [of the tragic drama] by Shakespeare," on the one hand, and, under the heading "Types of Drama in the Sixteenth and Seventeenth Centuries," the "mystery and Passion plays, in their German popular form" and the "dramas of affairs of state. Vienna," on the other (*Gesammelte Schriften* 1.3: 915–18). This rough list functions as a kind of inventory of many of the books described in this chapter. Moreover, even though—or perhaps better, precisely because—the material versions in which Benjamin encountered most of these texts did not in fact belong to the "time of genesis" of the German Baroque of the seventeenth century, they were crucial to defining what he comes to call the "origin" of the genre. As noted above, Benjamin writes of "origin": "The category of origin is thus not, as Cohen suggests, a purely logical one, but, rather, historical." Taken in their historical "totality," all of these books testified to the origin of the German tragic drama as the sum of its "pre- and post-histories" in material form (G: 1.1: 226; E: 46).

Many critics, including John Pizer, Uwe Steiner, and Bernd Witte, have discussed Benjamin's notion of "origin" in terms of theological, eschatological, and historico-philosophical principles of "pre-lapsarian semiotic plenitude" and "messianic" idealism (Pizer 41, 45) and via reference to the theories of origin offered by Goethe and Georg Simmel, both of whom Benjamin cites. It is Steiner, however, who most compellingly links such explanations of the weighty term as it is used in the *Tragic Drama* book also to the "empirical historicity of the real," and does so in direct reference to the plays themselves, which are, according to Steiner, "the works of art" and "the media in which history successfully appears" ("'Zarte Empirie'" 30).[68] In the "Exposé," or summary, of his *Habilitation* that Benjamin wrote for Hans Cornelius at Frankfurt as Cornelius prepared to review it, Benjamin himself explains that the "digressions" about both "the later tragic drama and . . . the medieval tendencies that are linked to the Baroque tragic drama" (*Gesammelte Schriften* 1.3: 950) are intrinsic to his "concept of origin" as a "historical category" in the thesis. He then goes on to describe the "task of the scholar" as one that must demonstrate "the unmistakable relation" of the essence—"des Wesens"—of the tragic drama to these earlier and later forms (951). The volumes of the Old Subject Catalog in the State Library on Unter den Linden provided him with an image of just such a "series of historical instantiations" (G: 1.1: 227; E: 46) of the "German" tragic drama as they were available in the cases of both Gryphius and the Shakespeare editions; the Mone, Weiß, and von Thurn volumes supplemented these plays with "unmistakable" examples of earlier and later forms of drama in the same German tradition to which Ulrici's, Gundolf's and Walzel's Shakespeares likewise belonged.

---

68. See Pizer 41–70 for a critical review of the ways in which "origin" has been understood by readers of Benjamin.

3

Melancholy Germans

War Theology, Allegory, and the Lutheran Baroque

In the last prewar summer of 1913, Benjamin wrote to his friend Franz Sachs about a visit to the Basel art museum with his mother. The young university student describes, in somewhat puzzling fashion, his viewing there of the "originals of some of the most famous of Dürer's graphic oeuvre: The Knight, Death, and the Devil, Melancholy, Jerome and many others. . . . Now, for the first time, I understand Dürer's power, and the Melancholy above all is an inexpressibly deep and expressive piece." Benjamin also describes works by Holbein and Grünewald. It may well have been this sheer accumulation of great German art or, perhaps, the "inexpressibly . . . expressive" nature of Dürer's *Melencolia I* (1514) itself that caused Benjamin to conclude: "I am getting closer and closer to the German art of the Renaissance, just as I noticed, when I was in Paris, that I was moved by the Italian art of the early Renaissance too" (*Briefe* 1: 76).

Benjamin's association of the "Renaissance" with the triumvirate of fifteenth- and sixteenth-century German artists—Dürer, Holbein, and Grünewald—is interesting, as is their apparent capacity (in his mind) to rival the early Italian Renaissance for his attention. Celebrating Dürer in particular in this way was consonant with assessments of the artist in general during the prewar years. Along with Martin Luther (1483–1546), the famous Dürer (1471–1528) had long been understood as one of the great German "cultural heroes" and original "prince of artists," never more so in fact than after 1871.[1] Indeed, a veritable industry of Dürer scholarship had emerged in and directly after that quadricentennial jubilee year of his birth, the same year as the parallel birth of the unified German state (see Bialostocki). The Dürer jubilee was only to be rivaled by the Luther celebrations in 1883, which likewise feted the modern afterlife of Reformation-era achievements on the national stage. Dürer commemoration peaked with the appearance in 1905 of a monograph on the artist by the famous Heinrich Wölfflin, in which Dürer is celebrated as the one who, in his alleged progress from "primitive" woodcuts to "refined" (*Albrecht Dürer* 206–8) copper-plate engravings like the *Melencolia I*—the image that Benjamin saw—demonstrated how German "Renaissance" art could compete with its illustrious Italian twin. In the context of the debacle of the war, it is only logical that Wölfflin's 1905 book was already in its third printing thirteen years later (1918). Like the widespread Reformation-jubilee programs of 1917, which I discuss below, the republication of Wölfflin's book may have been meant to boost morale in those dark days. In any case, its popularity signaled that the nation needed a cultural heritage of which it could be proud, perhaps particularly vis-à-vis the Italians, who had abandoned their position in the Triple Alliance in 1915. Ten years later and thus in the same year that Benjamin's *Tragic Drama* book appeared—which was also the year of yet another anniversary, this time the four-hundredth anniversary of the great artist's death—Wölfflin was still as moved by Dürer's art as Benjamin had been in Basel, and described it as exemplifying a "German way of seeing the world" (Wölfflin 1918, qtd. in Bialostocki 313). By this time, Dürer's work—and specifically the *Melencolia I* engraving—had nevertheless come to represent a somewhat different "Renaissance" for Benjamin, one that "anticipated" (G: 1.1: 319; E: 140) the Baroque, to be sure, but also one that "bequeathed as inheritance" (320; 142) to it a version of German melancholy that could no longer be celebrated in so unconditional a way. This was the version of melancholy that the "images and figures" of the German Baroque tragic drama—with its "crude stage" (335; 158)—dedicated to "Dürer's winged spirit of melancholy," as Benjamin writes. Here, Dürer's image no longer figures as part of an equation linked to the Renaissance. Rather, it now belongs to the specifically German equivalent thereof, namely the Reformation.

In this chapter, I examine Benjamin's discussion of Baroque melancholy in the *Tragic Drama* book in dialogue with this other "Renaissance," the rebirth, that is, of several key figures and doctrines of the Lutheran Reformation in Germany in the late nineteenth and early twentieth centuries. The association is one that Benjamin himself indicates is worth pursuing, when he writes at the very beginning of the so-called melancholy chapter: "The great German dramatists of the baroque

1. Joachim von Sandrart (1606–88), one of the first German art historians and theorists, had labeled Dürer a "prince of artists" in an inscription he wrote for the artist's tomb in Nuremberg in 1681. See Hutchison 8 and 5.

were Lutherans" (G: 1.1: 317; E: 138). I argue that it is against the backdrop of a specifically "Lutheran" melancholy that his famously obscure observations on the allegorical logic of Baroque emblematics can be best understood, particularly as they offer a commentary on the (in)ability of a highly confessionalized, yet also militant German state—whose traditions the revival of the study of the Baroque had meant to celebrate—to redeem itself in the face of the dismal modernity it had created as it entered World War I. This most "modern" of wars had been undertaken under the banner of a Lutheran "war theology" (*Kriegstheologie*), which was the subject of much debate at the time. The destruction permitted by the absolute separation of the sacred and the profane realms into the "two kingdoms" of God and of Man, for which Luther had called, was difficult to honor in the postwar period as having contributed to anything that could be understood as the nation's rebirth. I explore first the late nineteenth- and early twentieth-century confessional "battle for civilization" (*Kulturkampf*) in Germany out of which war theology developed. I then turn to a short story about Shakespeare's *Hamlet* that was written and published during these same years. Benjamin used this story by the scholar Rochus von Liliencron in the *Tragic Drama* book as an additional source for his reading of the play about the melancholic Danish prince as the "best"—or at least most representative—example of the "Lutheran" tragic drama. Understanding Liliencron's version of *Hamlet* as part of a commentary on war theology explains how Benjamin could see Shakespeare's play in this light.

Confessionalization, conventionally understood as the creation of uniform social and political groupings in bounded territories, or states, with these normative identities based in the routinization and standardization of collective religious observance, had begun in the second half of the sixteenth century in the German-speaking central European territories. By the late nineteenth century, the characterization of socially, politically, and geographically homogeneous groups as either Catholic or Protestant had led to a "battle for civilization" between the two traditional branches of German Christianity, and thus to considerable unrest in a newly unified polity eager to identify itself as a harmonious nation-state. Many of those who identified heavily with the state apparatus in the hegemonic north were committed to a Pan-German confessional uniformity that favored Protestantism. Written during the first phase of this battle, Liliencron's Hamlet novella was entitled "Die siebente Todsünde" (The Seventh Deadly Sin) and had originally appeared in 1877 in *Über Land und Meer* (Across Land and Sea), one of the myriad literary feuilletons published in Germany at the time. Reissued at the beginning of the new century—and thus just as a second wave of the *Kulturkampf* was sweeping the nation—in the volume that Benjamin cites (1903), the story has Lutheran undertones that make clear its place in the confessionalization narrative and explain its resonance within Benjamin's identifiably Lutheran version of the melancholy Danish prince. Curiously, in the story, Liliencron has his characters tutored by a wizened old mage who instructs them in the dangerous economic and political, spiritual and artistic consequences of succumbing to indolence by referring to a volume on the seven deadly sins by the seventeenth-century *Jesuit* Aegidius Albertinus. The Protestant Liliencron would have been familiar with the Albertinus volume his character cites, as he had edited and reissued it in 1884 as part of a larger plan for creating a more or less ecumenical cultural history of the German nation in the direct aftermath of the unification of Germany in 1871. His critique of the Jesuit's stance as old-fashioned in his introduction to that volume nevertheless makes it clear which side Liliencron was on. In the first section of this chapter, I read both the Albertinus editorial project and the Hamlet novella as part of an effort to settle the differences caused by confessional tensions—even if they both ultimately encouraged the identification of Germany as solidly Lutheran. Benjamin bases his claims about Baroque melancholy in the *Tragic Drama* book on details from both of these Liliencron texts; the commentary he offers on the ways that sixteenth-century Lutheran doctrine had been "reborn" in the seventeenth century is colored by them and sheds light on his assessment of the implications for Germany of a further materialization of confessional doctrine in his own modern world.

Although Benjamin was an avid consumer of the German feuilletons and, after the failure of *Habilitation* project, in fact partially supported himself by publishing in them, it is unlikely that he read Liliencron's novella in the 1877 number of *Across Land and Sea*. Rather, he probably saw the reference to the story in its 1903 reissued version in an essay by the art and cultural historian Aby Warburg that was published in 1920. Benjamin appears to have encountered Warburg's essay, "Heidnisch-antike Weissagung in Wort und Bild zu Luthers Zeiten" (Pagan-Ancient Prognostication in Word and Image in Luther's Day), fairly late in his research for the *Tragic Drama* book. The essay was nevertheless decisive for his argument about the Renaissance of Lutheranism in both the seventeenth and early twentieth centuries, as his repeated citation of it makes clear. Benjamin ultimately differed, however, from Warburg on the ideological and political implications of the positions inherited from the Reformation era, an era conceived of by both scholars as the origin of German modernity. The relationship that Reformed astrological science created between the spiritual and profane "kingdoms," between the transcendent-divine and the immanent-secular worlds, is the subject of Warburg's essay; his argument there and Benjamin's response to it in the *Tragic Drama* book are the subject of the second section of this chapter. Benjamin was ultimately skeptical of Warburg's version of Luther's "two kingdoms doctrine" and of the art historian's somewhat desperate celebration of the Renaissance-like promise of a "heroic" German reason's power to save Man from his melancholic immersion in the detritus of this world. Warburg had first worked on his article at the low point of World War I. Benjamin's postwar response does not underestimate, indeed, is in part predicated on the same kind of logic. Yet the way to live with the chasm that Lutheran theology—and its rebirth in modern times—had created between this world and the next, and thus with the melancholy possibility of nonredemption in this life or, conversely, redemption only in the next, receives a very different reading in the *Tragic Drama* book. Which version of the Reformation-era doctrine of the two kingdoms had been revived in the texts of the Baroque, and how this doctrine related to understanding how Man was to live in the here and now of an even more modern German world, were the questions that concerned Benjamin most.

The obscure theory of allegory developed in the last chapter of *The Origin of the German Tragic Drama* may also be understood against the background of the issue of confessionalization, in terms of the question, that is, of whether or not Germany had in fact fulfilled its "ancient," Reformation-era politico-theological mission when it was reborn into secular modernity. According to Benjamin, this was the context in which to analyze the figurative economy that governed Baroque emblematics. Emblems were two- or multi-part visual texts designed to teach their beholders to read images and words, things and the more abstract significance embedded in and represented by them, together. As such (and even though there were surely as many Catholic as Protestant emblem books and emblematists), emblems figured the difficult relationship between the two Lutheran kingdoms of God and of Man when they culled fragments and "ruins" from the "creaturely" realm and asked readers to intuit their greater meaning. At stake was whether access to this meaning could be guaranteed in the here and now, and, if so, by what means? The emblems often had accompanying verse that pointed the reader in the correct direction; did this mean the reader could or could not, should or should not, come up with the relation on his or her own? At what price would the grace of insight into a larger purpose (understood in the originally Lutheran sense of the term) be bestowed on the melancholic German citizen and state in both early modern and modern times? The final section of this chapter takes up these questions as they drive the literalization of the politics of allegory visible in one of the crudest of the "crude" (G: 1.1: 335; E: 158) German tragic dramas that Benjamin discusses in his "Baroque book," namely Andreas Gryphius's *Catharina von Georgien* (Catharine of Georgia) (1657).

Gryphius's play tells the story of a woman ruler who gives up both her earthly crown and her life for the sake of redemption in God's kingdom; it stages in grim detail—and thus comments metatheatrically on—the situation that Benjamin describes when he writes that it is "martyrdom . . . [that] prepares the body of the living person for emblematic purposes" (G: 1.1: 391; E: 217). The scenes in which Catharine is described as being brutally tortured to death by a power-hungry, lust-driven, and ultimately raving mad tyrant, and yet is represented as exiting history peacefully and with her eyes trained on the beyond, explain Benjamin's surely ambivalent statement that the "allegorization of the physical" can take place only in terms of the corpse. He writes: "Only thus, as corpses," can the characters of the tragic drama "enter into the homeland of allegory" (391–92; 217). This is of course a bitter pill to swallow for those who must continue to live in the world—and yet also the lesson that the plays of the German Baroque seem to have taught Benjamin to acknowledge, namely that redemption, indeed, spiritual rebirth, can really happen only in some other place, if it happens at all. As much as the celebration of the Renaissance of the German nation in the Baroque was the underlying subtext of Benjamin's book, then, what becomes visible in the actual texts of the "Lutheran" tragic drama, to which he refers so often in the *Tragic Drama* book, is that there is ultimately no guarantee of an unambiguous sense of progress beyond tragedy in this world. Redemption and rebirth come only rarely. And if they were to come for post–World War I Germany, they would come unannounced and undeserved.

Benjamin's Hamlet in the Crosshairs of War Theology

In chapter 2, I argued that the volumes of the dramatic texts on the shelves of Benjamin's libraries were both literally and metaphorically arranged in such a way as to form a celebratory narrative about the stability of a national cultural heritage. They represented a continuous tradition and "lineage of the German tragic drama" (G: 1.1: 307; E: 128) that reached not only back to medieval texts, but also out to absorb a Shakespeare considered German since the nineteenth century and rebaptized as such during the war. Benjamin's claims that he is interested in what makes the tragic drama "specifically German" alongside his inclusion of both Shakespeare's and Calderón's plays as the best exemplars, "the perfected artistic form" (260; 81), of "the baroque tragic drama," can be understood in this light. The Shakespeare play that was the most "German" of them all was *Hamlet,* as I have explained, and it is perhaps for this reason that it is the most frequently cited of Shakespeare's plays in the *Tragic Drama* book. In addition to reading the play about the melancholic Danish prince in German translation in the Ulrici edition and alluding to the work of authors who had christened Shakespeare as both Baroque and part of Germany's cultural patrimony during the war, Benjamin's *Tragic Drama* book contains references to a further version of the Hamlet story that was caught up in debates about the rebirth of a particular brand of Lutheranism in German national politics during both the run-up to 1914 and the war itself.[2] It is the implications of this peculiarly German version of melancholic Protestantism for the prince—and in turn for the nation—that Benjamin underscores in his reading of the tale.

Benjamin cites Shakespeare's *Hamlet* twice in the second chapter of the *Tragic Drama* book. The first citation occurs in his discussion of the prevalence of "dream visions" and "the impact of ghosts" in the plays of the Baroque (G: 1.1: 313–14; E: 134–35); the second follows directly upon the claim about the Lutheran identity of the "great German playwrights of the Baroque" (317; 138). In both cases, the

---

2. Shakespeare scholars often associate with the play the Calvinism that was historically linked on the continent with its Swiss and French instantiations. They see in Hamlet's "fall of a sparrow" speech (5.2.219–24), for example, evidence of a dialogue with the English (Scottish) Calvinism of King James. For an excellent overview, see Curran; Hoff.

quotes play a cat-and-mouse game of logic at the level of the sentence with references to the specifically German dramatic traditions that are Benjamin's concern. In the first case, Hamlet's famous "'Tis now the very witching time of night" speech (3.2.380–91), rendered in German—"Nun ist die wahre Spükezeit der Nacht" (314; 135)—follows a series of references to plays by the German playwrights Gryphius and Lohenstein, as I have noted, whose names are given in association with the titles of their plays. The quote is then followed by a citation from the Viennese Stranitzky's *Die Gestürzte Tyrannay in der Person deß Messinischen Wütterichs Pelifonte* (Tyranny Overthrown in the Person of the Messinian Brute Pelifonte). Here neither play title nor the identity of the playwright is introduced in the text, although they are given in the notes. While accompanied by a footnote to the edition after which he cites Hamlet's speech, Benjamin's nonattribution of the unforgettable "witching time" lines to the Bard here, sandwiched in between quotes from and references to the "Germans," could perhaps be forgiven, because of their manifest fame. Yet their position—and also that they are quoted in German—suggests that the citations from *Hamlet* are meant to provide additional support for Benjamin's claims about "the drama of the *German* Protestants" (G: 1.1: 276; E: 98; emphasis added) in its "classical Baroque" form "in Germany" (312; 133). Like the Protestant German Baroque plays, in other words, Shakespeare's play is indebted to the world of spirits and thus signals the power of a providential kind of "fate" to rule this world. By means of such textual gymnastics, Shakespeare's hero takes on a confessionally German role.

The second citation from *Hamlet* plays a similar role. It follows hard upon the opening of the second section of the second chapter, at the beginning of which the Baroque playwrights are identified as "Lutheran." And it occurs in a series of claims about the evacuation of sacred meaning from the secular and profane world dictated by the great Reformer's doctrine of faith and grace: Benjamin writes: "Even in Luther himself, the last two decades of whose life were filled with an increasing heaviness of soul, there are signs of a reaction against the assault on good works" (G: 1.1: 317; E: 138). The description of Luther's heaviness of heart is immediately supported with an (again) only belatedly attributed quote from Shakespeare's play (4.4.33–39), once more quoted in German: "'What is a man, / If his chief good and market of his time / Be but to sleep and feed? A beast, no more'. . . . These words of Hamlet contain both the philosophy of Wittenberg and a protest against it" (G: 1.1: 317; E: 138). The strange ventriloquizing of Luther by the at least notionally English Hamlet in this sequence is repeated, finally, at a textually less visible level in Benjamin's famously puzzling argument at the very end of the melancholy section, where the figure of Hamlet is said to have been uniquely able to capture the "dichotomy between the neo-antique and the medieval light in which the baroque saw the melancholic." The very "Germany" that is at the center of the "Baroque book" "was not the country which was able to do this" (334; 157), however; Germany, in other words, was not able to either capture or transcend the essence of the

Baroque contradiction, or duality, between the medieval and the neoantique versions of melancholy, Benjamin claims. Rather—or, perhaps better, nevertheless—the Englishman's "Wittenbergian" version of a melancholic Christian Dane could: "Only Shakespeare was capable . . . of striking Christian sparks from the baroque rigidity of the melancholic." Coyly quoting the Bard in a further unattributed and diacritically unmarked line, Benjamin writes: "The rest is silence" (335; 158).

In spite of Benjamin's disavowal of the German Baroque here, the repeated centrality to his argument of a nationalized and confessionalized Hamlet testifies to the issues that were at the center of his interest in the period that he repeatedly calls the "century of religious wars" (G: 1.1: 245; E: 65) and the "age of the wars of religion" (256; 76). The 1877 German-language edition of Shakespeare after which Benjamin quotes Shakespeare's play, edited by Hermann Ulrici and discussed in chapter 2, itself arose out of a vexed context that makes it possible to understand these references to the "wars of religion" in more than one way, as referring, that is, to both the early modern and the modern ages of confessional conflict in Europe. Even more revealing of this later context is a further Protestant version of the Danish prince that is referenced in connection with his famous melancholy just a few sentences later, when Benjamin refers to an early twentieth-century novella, "Die siebente Todsünde" (The Seventh Deadly Sin), originally written and published in a popular feuilleton, *Über Land und Meer* (Across Land and Sea), by the eminent scholar Rochus von Liliencron in 1877, and reprinted in 1903 in book form: "If the profound insight with which Rochus von Liliencron recognized the ascendancy of Saturn and marks of *acedia* in Hamlet is not to be deprived of its finest object, then this drama will also be recognized as the unique spectacle in which these things are overcome in the spirit of Christianity" (335; 158). Serendipitously published in exactly the same year, both Ulrici's Shakespeare edition and Liliencron's Hamlet novella emerged out of a period of confessional controversy that was tearing the relatively young nation of Germany apart. The denial in the *Tragic Drama* book that the German tradition could deal effectively with religious discord of this more recent vintage alerts us to Benjamin's familiarity with these tensions. German cultural Protestantism (*Kulturprotestantismus*), liberal nationalist Protestantism, had gone a dangerously long way in helping to define a united Germany as a *Leitkultur* (dominant culture) by the time both Ulrici and Liliencron were active in the late nineteenth century. It was this Protestant Germany that had gone to war in 1914 in ways of which the young Benjamin had strongly disapproved.

The context out of which Ulrici's and Liliencron's—and thus Benjamin's—German Protestant versions of Hamlet arose was that of the extraordinarily complex politico-confessional situation in the Reich at the end and turn of the century, when the confessions and their relation to German identity were not casual topics. Benjamin's references to Reformation-era Protestantism and its afterlife in the Baroque were embedded in the late nineteenth-century struggle between the Christian denominations known as the "battle for civilization" (*Kulturkampf*, c. 1860–90) and in its early twentieth-century revival during the "second battle for civilization" (*zweiter Kulturkampf*, c. 1907–14) as well.[3] The main sentiments of those involved in these contests can be heard in 1862 in the words of a founding member of the liberal Association of Protestants, Daniel Schenkel, for example: "We say with the very deepest conviction: The entire cultural progress of the peoples of our century rests on the basis of religious, moral, and spiritual freedom, and for that very reason, on Protestantism" (12). Schenkel's position on the role in Germany's "progress" of Lutheran (rather than Reformed, or Calvinist) Protestantism in particular was made more precise several years later by Wilhelm Scherer, the first official holder of a university chair in German literary history, who wrote in 1874, just three years after the unification of Germany: "Luther's Bible was the decisive foundational act of a unified German culture and language. It was the act that created what we today call our nation. We associate our national unity with Luther just as Italy associates its national unity with Dante. Luther's Bible is our Divine Comedy."[4]

That the grand achievements of statist modernization in Germany were understood in the post-1871 unified nation as coterminous with a specific denomination of Protestantism and its foundational figures, doctrines, and texts is manifest in such words. The actions undertaken subsequently to ensure the necessary confessional "cleansing" of non-Protestants from Germany make it clear that these sentiments were more than mere talk. Laws were passed in the 1870s restricting the citizenship rights of Jesuit teachers and priests, for example, and bishops who did not comply with the so-called May Laws were imprisoned; in 1891 one Carl Fey even eerily writes of the "racial darkness" (*Rassendunkel*) of the Catholic peoples, who did not belong in the German land.[5] Although most of these laws were officially rescinded by the early twentieth century, the renewed energy of what one historian has called the "furor protestanticus" (H. Smith 151) of a still ideologically potent second "battle for civilization" can still be heard in the words of a position paper written for the Protestant Union in Berlin in 1913: "The spiritual and moral development of all of Germany, including her Catholics, rests upon . . . the German Christianity of the Bible and the Reformation."[6]

The nation-rending confessional conflicts of these "wars for civilization" during the preceding fifty years had to be subordinated to the patriotic need for an ideologically and militarily unified "fortress *Germania*" after the declaration of more literal hostilities in 1914 (see H. Smith 165; Brakelmann). Church support of the bellicose nation nevertheless often remained overtly affiliated with the Lutheran legacy, as the title of Wilhelm Walther's 1914 book, *Deutschlands Schwert durch*

---

3. See H. Smith 19–49 and 141–65. I am grateful to Professor Helmut Smith for providing me with the original German of some of his archival documents.

4. Scherer 45–70, here 55.

5. See H. Smith 41 and 54.

6. Cited in H. Smith 160.

Luther geweiht (Germany's Sword as Consecrated by Luther), indicates in no uncertain terms. In theory, it was the historical Lutheran doctrine of "cujus regio, ejus
religio" that in 1555 had yoked what theologian Paul Althaus calls "Christ's kingdom" and the "kingdom of the world"—and thus spiritual concerns and political
jurisdiction and power—together in the first place.[7] In practice, the war theology
of the modern and homogeneous confessional state only "amplif[ied] . . . themes
that were already well defined in Protestant thinking" by "framing" the actual
war "in light of divine will and German destiny" (Chickering 125). Some of the
best-known Protestant theologians went on to endorse the upsurge of militarism
across the nation, creating the fraught wartime and postwar debates about Lutheranism with which Benjamin would have been familiar, in all likelihood primarily
through his friend the Protestant theologian Florens Christian Rang.[8] One of the
most famous contemporary theologians, Karl Barth, writes of his "horror" at seeing "nearly all of my German teachers" as signatories of "the horrendous manifesto
of the 93 German intellectuals, who, before the entire world, closed ranks with
the wartime political agenda of Kaiser Wilhelm II and his Chancellor, Bethmann-
Hollweg" (see Barth 293). Barth's version of what he in fact seems to have been the
first to christen as Luther's "two kingdoms doctrine" (*zwei Reiche Lehre*) involved
a decisively antiliberal Protestant stance, a more or less radical refusal of the immanence of God in the world, and thus of the notion that one could ally God's will
or plan with any human (i.e., statist or military) agendas at all.[9] The position led
him later to help draft the so-called Declaration of Barmen of 1934, which rejected
the jurisdiction or influence of National Socialism on German Christianity—over
which God alone, in his absolute transcendence, ruled. Ninety-three prominent
intellectuals, among them the Protestant theologians Adolf von Harnack and Reinhold Seeberg, who saw the two kingdoms as more firmly bound together, nevertheless did sign on in support of the war in 1914, seeing in the nation's military efforts
the fulfillment of God's plan on the ground.[10]

The problem with Barth's version of the two kingdoms doctrine, based on his
so-called dialectical theology, was that the absolute separation between church and
state could—and did—quite easily tip over into its opposite, into a vexed logic of
accommodation that, practically speaking, if not in doctrinal terms, was not far
from that subtending war theology. It was this rendering of the two kingdoms

---

7. Walther explains the "divinely legitimated right" (1) that the Germans have to fight the war
with the claim "The war is God's will" (11). On the two kingdoms, see Althaus 40.

8. Rang initially supported the prowar conservative nationalist position but after 1920 turned
vehemently against the militarism of the German state. See his treatise *Deutsche Bauhütte*, with a
"Zuschrift" by Benjamin (185–86). For another reading of the relation of Rang's *Deutsche Bauhütte* to
Benjamin's *Tragic Drama* book, see Steiner, "Traurige Spiele" 46–47.

9. See Estes 38 on Barth's naming of the two kingdoms theory. I return to this Lutheran doctrine
below.

10. The signatories of the manifesto may be viewed at http://www.nernst.de/kulturwelt.htm.

theory that lurked beneath the surface of the thoughts of Barth's contemporary and sometime colleague and friend the German Lutheran theologian Friedrich Gogarten, for example. In 1924, Gogarten had maintained that "all institutions and functions of human life, such as marriage, school, the state, the economy, art, and science," must be recognized as ephemeral, as they are merely the products of the creaturely, human "subject," "the I." Only by "opening one's eyes" for the "Thou" of divine reality can the real "law of things" be recognized and the limited (un)reality of such institutions be "destroyed" (see Gogarten 371). That most modern Protestants had made their peace with the de facto reality and authority of the power of inauthentic "institutions" does indeed call for action, according to Gogarten, but only in terms of one's theological politics (rather than in terms of the state's political theology).[11] Above all, one's eyes must always be kept trained on the absolute otherness of God.

The consequence of this mystical optic was a turning away from the world; it by no means demanded activist resistance to the state (although it did result in such resistance in the case of Barth). Rather, it was premised, in good Lutheran fashion, on waiting for God to bridge the gap between his own transcendence and the human world by means of revelation, or grace. The position was well within the original logic of what Gogarten calls the "Protestantism of the Reformers" (346). Luther had acknowledged the rights of secular power in his (in)famous "Widder die stürmenden Bawren" (Against the Robbing and Murdering Hordes of Peasants) of 1525, for example. There, he condemns the peasants' struggles outright as so much "rebellion," reminding the perpetrators that they are absolutely subject, "with their bodies and goods," to the "law of this world," "for baptism does not make men free in body and property, but |only| in soul." Conversely, the ruler "sins" in the eyes of God if he "does not fulfill his duties," if he does not "immediately reach for his sword" to put down the rebels, in other words (Luther 70–72). It was statements like these that earned Luther—and the confession that went by his name—the reputation of encouraging blanket "subordination . . . to the state" (Van Dülmen 207). Applied to Germany's wartime adversaries, the idea that the nation's secular military machine could carry out God's will by any means necessary permitted atrocities like the infamous "Rape of Belgium," with its anti-Catholic, "battle-for-civilization" hue to occur. It was all part of God's plan for Germany's "Holy War" (Strachan 1116–17).

In his *Protestant Ethic,* Max Weber famously describes the disjunction between the two kingdoms that permits this kind of runaway autonomy of the secular as the doctrine of the "absolute transcendentality of God" (60–61). For him, as for Benjamin, Calvinism fills the vacuum with honest work. Early in the *Tragic Drama* book, Benjamin refers to a similar absence of any "eschatology" (G: 1.1: 246; E: 66)

---

11. Compare Gogarten 347, for example.

as characteristic of a specifically Lutheran Baroque, however, and distinguishes its world from that of its Reformed twin. For the Lutherans, he writes in a more or less historically accurate assessment that also resonates with Barthian-Gogartian themes, "the hereafter is emptied out of everything which contains the slightest breath of this world." It is this same "vacuum" (246; 66) that, in the later melancholy section, results from the "empty world" of Lutheranism's "desecularization" (or resacralization) of religion,[12] and thereby creates the challengingly "antinomic" relation of religious people to "the everyday" and "secular life." The challenge is less for the actual "people," Benjamin explains, who respond to life in a desacralized world with "a sense of obedience." Rather, the "melancholy" that wells up under this Lutheran sky occurs primarily "in the great" (317; 138). Turning to the melancholy figure of the most proximate "great" personage in a similar state of helpless nonage, namely Prince Hamlet, may well have seemed the natural next step for Benjamin, particularly if he considered Hamlet a Lutheran. That the entire discussion that follows is centered on the figure of Melancholy, who, as captured in Dürer's etching, is, in Rang's later words, the "female" model for Hamlet as the "male figure of melancholy," suggests that it was a Hamlet of just this Lutheran sort of which Benjamin was thinking.[13] Benjamin's citation of Hamlet's words after the Ulrici edition confirms that his Dane spoke German. The references to Lilencron's novella about Hamlet suggest the prince had been "reborn" as a Lutheran in additional ways too.

As noted above, directly after his claim that it was the orthodoxies of "Lutheranism" that led to the melancholy of "great men," Benjamin cites Hamlet's famous "What is a man . . . ?" speech (4.4.33–39), and does so after the German translation he found in an edition of the play that was the updated edition of the 1825–33 Schlegel-Tieck translation, edited by Hermann Ulrici in 1876–77. As I showed in chapter 2, the distinction is not negligible; the republication of the Schlegel-Tieck translation under Ulrici's wing occurred in the second—and nationalist—half of the nineteenth century, and thus also placed Ulrici's Shakespeare squarely in the path of the "battle for civilization," with its relentless endorsement of a Protestant identity for the nation. That the German Hamlet Benjamin inherited from him is specifically Lutheran also peeks out from between the nearly very last lines of the melancholy section, when Benjamin refers to Hamlet as a "child of Saturn" (G: 1.1: 335; E: 158). The astrological and humoral—rather than confessional— origins of his melancholy seem to be given priority here. According to ancient, medieval, and Renaissance lore, that is, about which Benjamin learned in the work of the Warburgian scholars Erwin Panofsky and Fritz Saxl, as well as in the work of Aby Warburg himself, those born under the sign of Saturn are constitutionally

---

12. On the "desecularization of religion," see Van Dülmen 219.
13. Cited in Steiner, "Traurige Spiele" 33.

predisposed to a debilitating melancholy (326; 148).[14] According to Benjamin, the Baroque inherited from these earlier periods their explanation of the origins of "melancholy" (320; 142). The melancholic is characterized by a soul only weakly illuminated by the cold light of the furthest planet and by a dry and heavy "earthiness" and depressive nature inherited from Saturn as the monstrous archaic golden age deity Cronus. The Saturnine individual mirrors the god; potentially fertile, he is nevertheless nearly fatally afflicted with an excess of heavy black bile in the spleen, with a tendency to cleave to the earth, and also, potentially, with the mortal sin of sloth (*acedia*) in the face of a cold, cruel, and unredeemable world. Saturnine and Lutheran melancholy intersect and overlap here, for Benjamin had earlier characterized this very same kind of "heavy" melancholy as the effect of "Wittenbergian philosophy" (317; 138), with the result being a specifically German humanity caught in the immanence of a mournful world.

For many German readers of Shakespeare, the premier "offspring of Saturn" had of course long been the melancholy prince, Hamlet. For Benjamin, however, Hamlet's best face as a German melancholic was precisely not the one famously described by the revolutionary poet Ferdinand Freiligrath, who coined the phrase "Germany is Hamlet" "to castigate the political inactivity of German intellectuals" in 1844 (Habicht, "Shakespeare Celebrations" 453). Rather, at this point, Benjamin appears to believe that the actions of another Hamlet represented better chances for the nation's figurative redemption, namely the Lutheran Hamlet that had been created by Rochus von Liliencron. Liliencron had more accurately read the "marks of *acedia* in Hamlet['s features]," Benjamin writes; this Hamlet breaks the chains of melancholy by which he is confined precisely by using them to hoist himself up into the "Christian" sphere (G: 1.1: 335; E: 158). A note leads to the source of this claim: Liliencron's 1877 novella, "Die siebente Todsünde" (The Seventh Deadly Sin).[15] The seventh deadly sin is the same *acedia*, melancholy, and sloth that Benjamin followed the Warburgians in describing. Liliencron's novella in fact turns out not to be about the actual Shakespearean character, but rather about a series of Hamlet surrogates, including the "comely melancholy young man" named Sir Arthur ("Die siebente Todsünde" 108) and his friend, the fictional Shakespeare, who is the protagonist of the tale. In the course of the novella, the Bard must shake Sir Arthur from a debilitating lethargy induced by any number of factors that drag him down into the world. His noble leisure, his humanistic studies, a lawsuit over his familial inheritance, and confusion about his love affair with "Miss Ellen Addington"— Sir Arthur is unable to master, or transcend, any of these creaturely challenges.

---

14. For Benjamin's citations of the Warburgians' work, see below.

15. Parenthetical references in the text are to Liliencron's novella "Die siebente Todsünde" in the Duncker und Humblot edition published in Leipzig in 1903. In that edition, Liliencron's novella is dated from 1876 on the title page. It was first published in the 1877 issue of *Über Land und Meer* (Across Land and Sea), number 38.

He initially avoids—in good Lutheran (rather than Calvinist) fashion—any "healthy activity" (109) at all in the world, as Liliencron's narrator has his Shakespeare observe. Yet he also does not yet have his eyes trained on the beyond in any redemptive way. This is not yet a dialectical theology that sees in the other kingdom a path to redemption from the woes of this world.

And indeed, Sir Arthur wastes away for most of Liliencron's story, storming in and out of both his beloved's garden and Shakespeare's atelier (where Shakespeare is working on rewriting *Hamlet,* the first version of which had flopped at the opening of the novella), fleeing both his beloved's attentions and his friend's ministrations in a series of tumultuous, melancholic scenes. Liliencron's Shakespeare, by contrast, first uses the figure of Sir Arthur as a model for a successful rewriting of his play and then deploys the rewrite and a command performance of the play, with Sir Arthur in attendance, to save his young friend's psyche and soul. In the novella, the diagnosis of Arthur as a melancholic—and, just as importantly, the solution to Shakespeare's own intellectual fatigue vis-à-vis his work on the *Hamlet* script—is based on the account of the seven deadly sins in a manuscript shown to Shakespeare by a character known as the "old Master," a wizened old scholar who feeds the Bard "material for learning" to make up for the "education" he feels he lacks ("Die siebente Todsünde" 119). This particular manuscript is by one of the "old Master's" former students, Aegidius Albertinus, and is entitled "Lucifer's Infernal Chase" (121–23). After the "old Master" recites long sections of the book about *acedia* and the distance of the melancholic from God's goodness and grace aloud to Shakespeare (158–61), the playwright proceeds to catch up his quill and in no time completes what turns out to be the spectacularly successful revision.

Excerpting Aegidius Albertinus's *Lucifers Königreich und Seelengejaidt* (Lucifer's Kingdom and Pursuit of Souls) (1616) for use in his novella would have been easy for Liliencron, as he was the editor of the Albertinus facsimile edition in Kürschner's series, Deutsche National-Litteratur (German National Literature), published in 1884. Liliencron cites his edition of the Baroque Albertinus text in the foreword to his 1903 republication of the Hamlet novella; numerous quotes from this foreword appear in Benjamin's *Tragic Drama* book as well. Liliencron was nevertheless much more famous as the founder and general editor of the multivolume *Allgemeine Deutsche Biographie* (General German Biography) than as a writer of novellas. Beginning in 1869, he was the prime mover behind this monumental collection of information about the cultural history of German arts, sciences, and letters under the sponsorship of the Bayerische Akademie der Wissenschaften (Bavarian Academy of Sciences). Although Liliencron retired in 1907 after fifty-three volumes of the *Biography* had been completed, the years of his engagement with the project, whose purview he describes in a letter to Leopold von Ranke as being "the entire history of the nation contained in its political, scientific, artistic, and industrial development," overlapped almost exactly with the decades of the "battle for civilization" described above.[16] It is probably significant that Liliencron came from a pro-Prussian German (rather than Danish) family in Schleswig-Holstein and was a good Protestant. Yet he saw it as his scholarly duty to be ecumenical and spent considerable time, his biographer, Anton Bettelheim, claims, working—in what Bettelheim calls the context of the "fateful turn" for the soon-to-be-unified nation in 1871—to have scholars from both sides of the confessional aisle (Catholic and Protestant) collaborate in their work on the *Biography*.[17] It is nevertheless difficult to consider that project as anything other than the attempt to create—by peaceful means in book form—the confessional unity, if not also homogeneous cultural tradition, for the young nation that the Protestant majority sought to impose by law.

The introduction of the Albertinus text from which Benjamin quotes supports this thesis. Even as Liliencron glosses over Albertinus's problematic identity as a "student of the Jesuits" (and thus as "a zealous representative of the reactionary Catholicism of that period"), for example, and emphasizes that the book is most importantly "the work of a popular [*volkstümlich*] writer," he also makes clear that the "learnedness" of this Ur-German "primitive" author stood diametrically opposed to "modern trends." Indeed, according to Liliencron, Albertinus had sought to cancel out the gains of humanism and the Reformation all at once by turning back "the clock of Man's spirit several centuries" (Liliencron, Einleitung, v, i, and xx–xxi). Given his dismissal of Albertinus and of the Jesuit's extraordinary emphasis in his book on the value of Catholic "penance" as a model for "modern" intellectual progress, it is significant that Liliencron has the perhaps more compelling of the two Hamlets of his novella—the charismatic character of Shakespeare— listen to the "old Master" quote Albertinus, to be sure, but also finally shake off his melancholy writer's block by means of a curious amalgamation of Calvinist hard work on the script and Lutheran belief in God's grace. "Feel the hand of God," Liliencron's Shakespeare thunders at Sir Arthur ("Die siebente Todsünde" 177), when Arthur morosely tells him he has lost the inheritance case and thus become more slothful than ever. In Sir Arthur's legal defeat and hard times in the world, Liliencron's Shakespeare sees the possibility of redemption for his friend, whom he encourages in the same breath to have an almost Lutheran faith in the unseen love of "Miss Ellen" (179), which emanates from a kingdom beyond.

A vocabulary of melancholy and divine grace, of faith in invisible love, and of "the light of wisdom" defeating "the night of madness" ("Die siebente Todsünde" 180) fills the final pages of the Liliencron novella to which Benjamin refers. By the end, the hold of the old Jesuit lore of melancholy—represented by the Albertinus citations—on both of the now more-or-less Lutheran Hamlet stand-ins has been broken for good. It is no wonder that Benjamin saw in (Liliencron's) Hamlet a "spectator of the grace of God," and it is more than possible that the Shakespeare

---

16. Liliencron's letter to Ranke is quoted in Bettelheim 157.
17. See Bettelheim 164–65.

to whom Benjamin attributes the ability to strike "a Christian spark" out of the Baroque "rigidity of the melancholic" (G: 1.1: 335; E: 158) was the Shakespeare of Liliencron's tale. Against this background, it may seem curious that Benjamin repeatedly denies that any German could see his way clear to this kind of "Christian" redemption, for both of the Shakespeares—Ulrici's and Liliencron's—whom he recruits to the cause of an ironically Lutheran rebellion against a Wittenbergian sense of resignation and hopelessness *were* "German." And in his novelistic German version of Hamlet, Liliencron has even created something like a hyper-Lutheran who defeats his confessionally induced melancholy by fleeing into it.

While depicted in a more or less redemptive scenario in Benjamin's *Tragic Drama* book, the intensification of the Lutheran stance visible in the actions of Liliencron's Hamlet may nevertheless have also had another side. For one thing, it sounds quite a bit like Gogarten's theory of commitment to the realm of the "Thou." As for Gogarten, so here too "rebellion" seems, in good Lutheran fashion, to remain a strictly spiritual affair. Enacted in the heart or, in Liliencron's novella, on a fictionalized stage and amid an intimate circle of friends in Shakespeare's workshop, the move beyond melancholy in any case occurs at a good distance from the consolidating secular powers of the nineteenth- and twentieth-century German state as they lurked beneath the cover of faith. The elision of any link between the individual's spiritual and creative redemption and the kingdom of Man may well have been precisely the problem a Lutheran Hamlet presented for Benjamin. Indeed, by distinguishing this version of the "overcom[ing]" of melancholy from the "crude theater" of the German playwrights (G: 1.1: 335; E: 158), he may have been suggesting that a better Germany—or at least the Germany prefigured in the world of the actual Baroque tragic dramas as opposed to these Shakespearean worlds—would or should stand firm and confront "existence" directly as "a rubbish heap of partial, inauthentic actions" (318; 139), rather than turning away from the very forces that created them.

Benjamin acknowledges the real "rubbish heap" produced by the Germans in post–World War I Europe in his "reply" to the more or less eirenic, and yet also deadly serious *Deutsche Bauhütte* (German Builders' Guild) text by his friend Rang in 1924. In that book, the Protestant theologian suggests that, as a way of saving its "spiritual life" and the soul of the nation, Germany must take responsibility for the "war damages" and "the destroyed lives of civilians" inflicted on France and Belgium by the German military during the war by paying reparations to those countries for the destruction (14–15). Benjamin had had doubts about Rang's "analysis" of the situation, he writes in his "reply," but these doubts had in large part been erased by the text that Rang wrote. Benjamin now (somewhat implausibly of course) has hopes that Rang's plan will have an "effect" (Zuschrift 185) and be made a reality. In this context, Benjamin's acknowledgment in the *Tragic Drama* book that the German playwrights of the Baroque, and Lohenstein and Gryphius in particular, had in fact had important "political duties" in their time (G: 1.1: 236;

E: 56) is significant. It may not be by chance that much of Benjamin's analysis of the German plays turns on just how engaged their princely protagonists do or do not stay with the detritus that surrounds them. In the distance Benjamin claims to find between (Liliencron's) Hamlet and the German Baroque tragic dramas, he may have been trying to locate the possibility of a different kind of Renaissance for the nation in the vision of a real "rebellion" against the "Wittenbergian philosophy" that had partially driven the war. Other intellectuals, whose work he admired, had endorsed a version of Lutheran melancholic thinking that had yoked the state and the divine realms together in fateful ways, however. This made Benjamin's task more difficult. In the *Tragic Drama* book, he seems to have settled for a position of critique.

Reforming the Baroque: Benjamin on Warburg on Luther

Among the holdings of the Warburg Institute Archives in London may be found five hand-drawn sketches by the famously eccentric art and cultural historian Aby Warburg (1866–1929), which suggest how he was to illustrate a lecture that he eventually held in 1918.[18] The topic of the talk is indicated by the heading scrawled at the top right of one of the drawings: "Luther's Birthday" (*Luthers Geburtsdatum,* or "Luther's date of birth"). Originally planned for early 1917 as part of the four-hundred-year jubilee of the Reformation organized by the Gesellschaft für Hamburgische Geschichte (Society for the History of Hamburg), the talk was postponed several times, not only because of Warburg's ongoing research into his topic, but also because of the lack of coal to heat the venue (Wedepohl 351). Jubilee celebrations of the Reformation in Germany had been highly political, secular affairs since as early as 1617 (Burkhardt 276–77). This celebration, during the "turnip winter" of 1916–17, one of the coldest winters in Germany on record, was no exception; it presented an obvious opportunity, in the face of hunger and disillusionment both in the trenches and on the home front, to engage in a rousing (if compensatory) wartime celebration of the Rankean "Luther-to-Bismarck" "hegemonic narrative" of "how [the] modern German [state] came to be" (Brady, "Protestant Reformation" 11)—the very same narrative that war theology sought to tell.

Like Benjamin's later work in the *Tragic Drama* book, the Jewish Warburg's interest in 1917 in a topic related to Luther and to Germany's "national" religion was neither new nor idiosyncratic for more or less assimilated members of his faith. In two essays entitled "Deutschtum und Judentum" (Germanness and Jewishness) (1915 and 1916), Hermann Cohen, for example, argues—in a far more localized form of Jacob Burckhardt's assessment of the birth of "modern" Europe in the

---

18. The sketches may be found in the holdings of the Warburg Institute Archive (WIA), III.90.2, F. 63–67. The title and date are on F. 63.

Renaissance—that with the Reformation, Germany had entered on the "world historical" stage.[19] Warburg's choice of subjects for his lecture was thus as politically loaded as Benjamin's investigation of the "Lutheran" plays of the German Baroque.[20] The essay Warburg went on to publish based on the talk "Heidnisch-antike Weissagung in Wort und Bild zu Luthers Zeiten" (Pagan-Ancient Prognostication in Word and Image in Luther's Day) (1920)—and Benjamin's fascination with it in the *Tragic Drama* book—makes sense when read against the background of the intersecting logics of Protestant war theology and the perhaps peculiar, but also logical upsurge in astrological thinking that occurred during the war. I discuss Warburg's interest in Reformation-era astrology and its historical link to the two kingdoms theory first in order to explain his commitment to the idea that Germany's future promise originated during the Reformation and could be reborn in his own time. I then turn to Benjamin's parallel interests, but also to his more hesitant response.

The bulk of Warburg's argument in the "prognostication" essay addresses the visual and literal rhetorics of astral determinism in both learned and popular materials from the Reformation period. According to these materials, the starry conjunctions dominant at the time of Luther's birth could be read as either challenging or supporting the Reformation's theological and, just as important, its political aims. Technically speaking, the historical two kingdoms theory was as implicated in this argument as it was in the war theological debates described above, particularly insofar as the astrological teachings of the learned Philip Melanchthon, the *praeceptor Germaniae* and friend and companion of Luther, were concerned. These teachings are at the center of the first part of the Warburg essay to which Benjamin so often refers, where Warburg addresses the impact of these same astral forces on the world as it is visible in the work of the equally celebrated early modern symbol of Germanness, Albrecht Dürer. Warburg's reading of Dürer's *Melencolia I* here reminds us of Benjamin's interest in the image as a part of the "German Renaissance" in art.[21] Warburg's preliminary "Luther's Birthday" sketch of

---

19. Cohen 242. The Jewish support for this reading of the Lutheran era may make Benjamin's interest in it equally understandable. On the "dialectics of assimilation" of Protestantism by the early twentieth-century Jewish intelligentsia, including Cohen and Cassirer, see Liebeschütz 230–31.

20. Gombrich indicates in his famous "intellectual biography" of the art historian that Warburg had in fact sought to get involved in the "patriotic" war as early as 1914 by traveling to Italy to meet with Italian art historical colleagues and found a journal designed to encourage them to support staying the course as part of the Triple Alliance. In 1915, when the Italians broke with the alliance, Warburg symbolically broke with them, turning away from his interest in Italian art to the art of another "period of crisis" for the nation, namely the Reformation, finding Germany's Renaissance in it (Gombrich, *Aby Warburg* 207). See Strachan 142 on the "war enthusiasm" of urban intellectuals.

21. The so-called German Renaissance in art that the "Dürerzeit" (time of Dürer's activity) was said to represent was celebrated in nationalistic terms during the war just as enthusiastically as was Luther's Reformation era. See Kaufmann on the "nationalist sentiments" (30) and the deployment of the idea of a "German Renaissance" for "national unification in the nineteenth century" and for "purposes of political propaganda . . . during the 1914–18 war" (192).

how he intended to illustrate the lecture seems to offer a direct theorization of how he—and subsequently, Benjamin—would have the parallelisms between his Reformation-era subject and the "rebirth" of its significance in the wartime context of his presentation understood. The hasty drawing indicates that he intends to display all of his multiple and mutually illuminating visual materials (astrological nativity charts, prognostication pamphlets, the Dürer engraving) simultaneously rather than as a sequence; this way the web of both literal and figurative citations, of parallels and similarities between and among them, could be recognized by the viewing audience all at once. The technique is at the conceptual heart of what subsequently became known as Warburg's signature concept of the "Wanderstraßen" (highways or itineraries), along which a globe-trotting pictorial unconscious traveled from east to west and back again, as well as between and among the regimes of high visual culture and its more quotidian equivalents.[22] In the Luther lecture, the "highway" in question is also the one that ran from the early modern into the modern wartime years, in which the politico-theological issues on which Warburg wanted to focus were as intimately involved with a culture of astrology as they had been in Reformation times.

Recent scholarship has shown that beginning in 1914, Warburg began to be consumed, almost to the exclusion of his earlier academic work, with the compilation of what has come to be known as his *Kriegskartothek* (war card catalog), his wartime collection of citations of newspaper and magazine articles from the German and foreign press. The seventy-two file boxes into which the citations were carefully sorted were ordered by topic—"Aberglaube, Prophezeiungen" (Superstition, Prophecies), "Verhalten im Kampf" (Behavior during Battle), "De figuris coelis metereologiisque" (On Meteorological Events), "Deutschland: Religion, Ethik" (Germany: Religion and Ethics)—and track the resurgence of various kinds of magical thinking in association with war-related themes in the World War I years. The rise in astrological thought in particular—as well as in occultism, spiritualism, and other "irrational" belief systems—may have been represented after the end of hostilities as a kind of desperate response to the horrible and horribly uncontrollable rationalization of the means of destruction.[23] But the note cards in the "war card catalog" confirm that there was a widespread conviction at the time that such beliefs and practices were effective, as when it was reported that soldiers were carrying amulets into battle, hoping to be protected by them from the industrially enabled carnage of the trenches, and that troops were being made—and had requested—to march through or near the village where a notorious female visionary

---

22. On the "Wanderstraßen" concept, see McEwan 15–16.

23. According to Carl Christian Bry in his 1924 book, *Verkappte Religionen: Kritik des kollektiven Wahns* (Hidden Religions: A Critique of Collective Delusion), for example, myriad forms of such beliefs abounded. Arnold F. Stolzenberg agreed in a 1928 issue of the journal *Das evangelische Deutschland* (Protestant Germany). Everything and anything seems to have been acceptable leading up to and during the war, Stolzenberg writes, as long as it could "bridge the abyss that has opened up between the Here and the Beyond." Bry and Stolzenberg are quoted in Winkle 262–63.

claimed to have spoken with the Virgin Mary and several saints.[24] Warburg's collection also included references to articles in the press about the emergence of an active medium industry, with practitioners promising those left behind the possibility of renewed contact with their war dead, as well as about numerous prophecies of possible dates for successful military engagements and even the end of the war, based on readings of favorable or malevolent conjunctions of the stars. By 1918, there are said to have been over ninety thousand items in the war catalog, an indication of the "frenzy" with which Warburg pursued his task (Schwartz 50–51). He considered collecting these materials a way of charting "seismograph[icall]y" the various forms of religio-magical thinking rampant at the time of the "catastrophe for Germany" of the war.[25]

Both the categories into which Warburg sorted his evidence and the popular provenance of the materials he was assembling were not unlike those associated with many of the Reformation-era documents at the heart of his "Luther's Birthday" talk, the research for which was consuming him at exactly the same time. In the article based on the lecture, he investigates the response of Luther and his coterie to the huge numbers of popular polemical pamphlets about astrology and single-sheet imprints, with their prognostications and prophecies, primarily of imminent disasters, both naturally and divinely caused, that were circulating throughout the tense years of the "pamphlet wars" of the early Reformation (1521–25).[26] Warburg's interest in pursuing the historical origins of the logic behind the parallel practices he could observe in his own time is clear. Because, moreover, these practices belonged to the same highly confessionalized culture, Warburg is able to link materials associated with the very focused topic of his occasional lecture, namely the manipulation of Luther's nativity charts by his enemies and friends (hence, "Luther's birthday"), with these larger prognosticatory trends and expand on their relevance for understanding the role of astrological thinking in both the early modern and the modern worlds. The "headline images" (513) in which Warburg was interested were part of a larger culture of early modern print and news, indeed, of the flood of "politico-intellectual propaganda texts" (490), he writes, which fed the hungry market of the "sensational press" (510–11) during the Reformation years. Like the contemporary materials assembled in the war catalog, the documents that Warburg examines in his lecture emanated from a highly politicized landscape in which the religio-magical and the confessional-secular were closely intertwined.[27]

---

24. On the immense popularity of the female seer Barbara Weigand and her visions, see Schlager.
25. See Carl Georg Heise's 1945 report on Warburg's activities during World War I, cited in Schwartz 42.
26. On the pamphlet wars, see Hammerstein; Köhler.
27. Wedepohl (328–34) argues that Warburg's interest in the role of popular print culture was piqued by reports in the German press of the impact on the Italian "masses" of Gabriele D'Annunzio's jingoistic political "orations," which was similar to the effect of the popular astrological pamphlets of the Reformation that were said to have incited the peasants to revolt in the mid-1520s.

First among the many texts and images that Warburg discusses in his essay is what was, in 1917–18, an unknown 1531 letter from Melanchthon to the astrologer Johann Carion. According to Warburg, Melanchthon's letter reveals that he believed in the legitimacy of on-the-ground political reasoning based on the appearance of a "comet that appears to be in Cancer," as well as on a variety of prophecies by "a wench from Kitzingen," "a citizen from Schmalkalden," and "a Belgian virgin" (494), all of which Melanchthon then relates in the letter to a discussion of the Danish king Christian's and the emperor Charles V's impending military moves and the even more local and pressing issue of the support of some of the German princes and electors for the anti-imperial League of Schmalkalden. The discourses of the allegedly supernatural and magical and a highly rationalized calculus of state are clearly cozy bedfellows here, the intimate exchange between them made easier by a reading of wondrous signs of various sorts. The role of the divine is, however, in no way downplayed. For example, Warburg quotes Melanchthon as concluding with regard to the prophecies in particular: "Overall I think that there is some great movement in the offing and I pray to God that he influences this event to turn out well, such that both the church and the state are well served" (494). The belief that the astrologically determined and the political-secular realms intersect is captured in these words, which thus testify not to a superstitious "primitive" culture, but rather to what Robert Scribner has called the "one-way" Lutheran logic of "sacred action," which "flows from the divine to the human" spheres (268) rather than the other way around. The transcendental divine causality and kingdom behind the movement of heavenly bodies may well be something that men, as fallen creatures on earth, can only imperfectly understand. But if the border between the two realms represented by the starry canopy, for example, is recognized as connecting rather than setting them apart, then trained astrologers and prophecy readers can see God's political intentions for the profane Protestant world in his signs.

As transparent as this kind of political instrumentalization of astrological thinking may appear, it was not unrelated to doctrinal issues central to both historical Lutheranism and to battle-for-civilization contests over "denominational ideology" that had been and continued to be fought over the soul of the modern German state (Graf 31). Luther's two kingdoms theory is again of special interest in this regard. Its terms make clear the intimate relationship between only notionally transcendent religious forces and Man's sociopolitical life, which allowed divinely mandated and controlled events to unfold with regularity in the "kingdom" of the here and now.[28] The Reformer's own thinking on the topic was notoriously complex, and desperate attempts to clarify which phase of his thoughts on the issue related most aptly to any number of the "fateful" events of subsequent German

---

28. Luther uses at least two German terms to refer to these two "kingdoms" in his work: *Reich* (realm, kingdom) and *Regiment* (ruled jurisdiction, government). See Thompson 164 and 165–73.

history have abounded over the years.[29] But the fundamental parameters of the two kingdoms theory have always been clear. They articulate a model of two "orders of government through which God exercises his lordship over mankind," the "kingdom" and "government of God" and "Christ," on the one hand, and the "worldly," or secular, government, on the other (Thompson 166–67). Luther himself seems to have believed that, even though they were by definition separate, a certain kind of traffic between the two kingdoms was a binding norm. In the still pastorally inflected "Von weltlicher Obrigkeit, wie weit man ihr Gehorsam schuldig sei" (Temporal Authority: To What Extent It Should Be Obeyed) (1523), for example, he argues that, for the "real Christian," Man's salvation lies in the hands of God alone; in this respect, his "government" has jurisdiction over the most important of Man's duties, namely "righteousness." The "kingdom of this world" plays no small role in the achievement of this singular purpose, however. For one thing, the worldly kingdom's agents—kings, princes, earthly magistrates—always already exist in the world only "by God's will and ordinance." They thus in effect function semiautonomously as guarantors of the "external peace" that permits the pursuit of the "teachings of Christ." While the key point here is the interlocking and parallel logic of the two systems, with the divine kingdom on top, it is not surprising that Luther's original argument, namely that the "civil law and sword" represented crucial forms of "divine service," later emerged to support claims about wartime Germany's sacred Protestant mission.[30]

It is in this context that we may understand the role of a "Lutheran" astrology in the Reformation era. Beginning already in the 1520s, when Luther and Melanchthon began formulating their ideas, insight into astral patterns functioned as one of the ways in which the *ordinatio divina* (divine order, or government) that transcended human understanding could in fact be discerned by denizens of the earthly realm (Althaus 44). In Melanchthon's mind in particular, the two orders were actually linked via the stars; astrology could thus help "reveal, by decoding signs, the original design of God's providence" in the realm above.[31] Melanchthon's related interest in astronomy belonged, in turn, to a "Lutheran" natural philosophy, whereby knowledge of the celestial bodies, for example, could give "insight into God's intended order for the world" (Methuen 394). God's kingdom may thus be invisible, otherworldly, and transcendent. But by the logic of a Lutheran "sidereal speculation," the "inner worldly" realm was not irrevocably cut off from God's blueprint for mankind, etched as it was into—and thus visible in—the starry patterns above.[32] Like their early twentieth-century avatars, rulers of early modern

---

29. Althaus, referring in 1957 to the role the two kingdoms theory played in the National Socialist period, suggests that the doctrine has had a "fateful" impact on German history for "centuries" (40).

30. Luther, "Temporal Authority" 275–93; "Von weltlicher Obrigkeit" 362–76.

31. See Caroti; Kusukawa; Methuen; and Fink-Jensen. The quote here is from Caroti 113.

32. On the various forms of "sideral speculation" that abounded in the Reformation era, see Barnes, here 132.

confessionalizing territories had had good reason to be invested in maintaining belief in (and yet also themselves managing) the dissemination of confessionalized lore about the role of the astral forces, as it helped these rulers control how the populace negotiated their economic, social, and political lives. Lutheran princes and cities have in fact been characterized as particularly "hospitable" to astrological thinking.[33] In turn, reliance among their subjects on astrological almanacs and calendars belonged to a "set of [all-consuming, meaningful] coherent practices," including recourse to such "sacrally potent objects" as "church bells" as "apotropaic[ally]" capable of "protect[ing] against storms and lightning," and "hymnals" and "prayers books" treated as containers of "healing . . . power" that could also help produce a good crop.[34] The phenomenon of infantrymen carrying amulets into the trenches and making pilgrimages to local blessed sites four hundred years later does not seem so very different from such early modern practices. Warburg's interest in such behaviors thus makes a kind of historical sense. In both cases, the "worldly" kingdom was endowed with a "highly charged sacrality" emanating from some higher will. As in the Reformation era, so too in the early twentieth century, "all secular events, social, political, and economic, could have cosmic significance" (Scribner 269). The outbreak of interest in astrology and the occult at the height of World War I coincides logically, in other words, with the Protestant war theology officially associated with it. Warburg's wartime interest in Lutheran astrology—and Benjamin's interest in Warburg's essay in turn—should be read in this context.

In the first part of the "prognostication" essay, Warburg takes Melanchthon's letter to Carion, on the one hand, and, more importantly for his argument, the struggles that Melanchthon had with Luther over the nativity chart drawn by the Italian (and Catholic) astrologer Lucas Gauricus, on the other, as a sign of the penetration of astrological thinking deep into the heart of Reformation politics. In the Gauricus chart (Warburg fig. 123)—the only version of which we have dates from 1552, but which Warburg surmises is from around 1532, when Gauricus visited Wittenberg—the date of Luther's birth is postponed until 1484 (instead of the conventionally agreed-on year of 1483), and his nativity placed on a day and at an exact time when the conjunction of the planets Mars, Jupiter, and Saturn had occurred. The year 1484 had long been predicted by astrologers to be a year in which, according to Warburg, "a new era in the development of western religion [would] begin" (500). The most widely disseminated version of this prediction had been in one Johann Lichtenberger's prognostication pamphlet, which, first published in Latin

33. Lutheranism's reception of astrological thinking has been called particularly "hospitable" (Calvin disdained it for both theological and sociopolitical reasons), and astrology described as "integral to the formation of a Lutheran confessional culture," part and parcel of the "evangelical movement['s]" "mass exercise in propaganda . . . for the faith." See Dixon; the quotes here are from Barnes 131; and Dixon 413 and 416. On Calvin's concerns that astrological prognostication of disastrous events could lead to rampant social unrest, see Barnes 135.

34. See Brady, "'Confessionalization'" 12, on the abundance of "coherent practices." For the examples of Protestant "sacred" objects and rituals, see Scribner 269–70.

in 1490, had circulated widely before being translated into German and printed in Wittenberg in 1527. According to Warburg, Lichtenberger was following an earlier pamphlet of the Dutch Paulus von Middelburg in predicting "the appearance of a religious man, who [would] provoke an ecclesiastical revolution" (514) in the fall of 1484. Moving Luther's birth to that year thus made a great deal of sense. That many agreed at the time is quite clear in the names "Luther" and "Melanchthon" scrawled above the monk figures in a 1492 illustrated edition of Lichtenberger that Warburg consulted in the Hamburg State and University Library (Warburg fig. 137). Warburg identifies the words as "written in an old hand that most likely belonged to the sixteenth century" (516).

The details of the Latin text that accompanied the Catholic Gauricus's early sixteenth-century nativity chart for Luther invested the changed date with a more profoundly threatening significance: the man born on that day would be a "sacrilegious heretic," "a most bitter enemy to the Christian religion" (Warburg fig. 123). The much predicted "revolution" is cast negatively here as a way of stirring up opposition to the Reformer by focusing on the intersection of the heavy planet, Saturn, with that of the dangerous planet, Mars, on his day of birth. This particular conjunction of other planets with Saturn was especially problematic in Warburg's reasoning because of the legacy of *Saturnfürchtigkeit* ("fear of Saturnine influences," 505–8), identified with both the homophagic god of antiquity and the planet whose great distance from earth, flat light, and slow movement led it to be identified, in the discourses of medieval humoral psychology and theology alike, not only with both literal and spiritual lethargy, sluggishness, and sin (*acedia*), but also, in the sixteenth-century mass media, with threatening meteorological disasters of all kinds, including the torrential rainfall and flooding predicted for 1524. It was this same "fear of Saturn" that had afflicted Liliencron's Hamlet.

Warburg is fascinated by the way a wide selection of visual print culture fed the astrological hysteria associated with this particular prediction during the early modern period, and includes numerous examples in his text (Warburg figs. 131, 132, 133). Here again, parallels to his work in the war catalog abound. In response to Gauricus's chart, he explains, the position of the stars at the time of Luther's birth was—at Melanchthon's prompting—analyzed and recalculated, recalculated and analyzed, over and over again by several scholars belonging to the Reformer's inner circle; a series of carefully drawn alternatives to it was produced by Carion, Johann Pfeyl, and the "official" Wittenberg astrologer, Erasmus Reinhold (Warburg fig. 124). (Warburg reports that Melanchthon even went so far as to interview Luther's mother to get the exact details of the hour and minute at which her by-then famous son first saw the light, 501.) These charts acknowledge and adopt the new year and date (namely 22 October 1484) of Luther's birth from Gauricus but tamper with the exact time of day in order to place Jupiter and Saturn at a careful remove from the sphere of Mars at the time of the Reformer's birth (502–4). In this way, Luther's nativity is deftly pushed out of the path of a potentially threatening astral conjunction even as his association with the now optimistically interpreted prediction about the birth of a "religious revolutionary" in 1484 (502) is preserved. Because God's plans for German reform were understood to be everywhere legible in the heavens, Melanchthon and company were able to work deftly—and devoutly—with the lore of astral enchantment to ensure a correct reading that supported and celebrated their confessional program on the ground.

Warburg notes that Luther initially thought very little of this kind of magical thinking; "Es ist ein dreck mit irer kunst," he writes in the earthy vernacular of *Table Talk,* loosely translated: "Your [astrological] art is a load of crap" (500). He claims that his birth date and time were exclusively of God's doing: "That which occurs by virtue of God's will and is his work we ought not to attribute to the power of the stars" (504–5). This is a nearly willful misreading of Melanchthon's efforts of course, which were in fact designed to use astrology to have Luther's reforms represent the fulfillment of God's plan. Warburg indicates that he sees what must have nevertheless ultimately been a secret accord between the two men on the point when he quotes the obviously astrologically informed Reformer, again in *Table Talk,* commenting on his own "identity as a child of Saturn": "Ego Martinus Luther sum infelicissimis astris natus, fortassis sub Saturno" (I Martin Luther was born under the most unlucky stars, perhaps even under Saturn) (505). In a cunning foreword to the 1527 German edition of Lichtenberger's prognostication pamphlet attributed to Luther, moreover, which Warburg reproduces in full in an appendix (545–50), Luther is allowed to unpack at length his own understanding of "the natural 'art', or science, of the stars" (546) as a kind of sacred astrology along Melanchthonian lines. There Luther recommends that people attend to the prophecies contained in the booklet not because Lichtenberger has issued them, but rather because "the signs in the sky and on earth are surely not mistaken. They are God's and His angels' work" (549). With such citations, Warburg establishes the links between the otherworldly and the mundane embedded in Luther's thinking, as well as his perhaps politically canny complicity with his partner's logic of a confessionally enchanted world (both above and below) that Melanchthon's brand of Protestant astrology could explain and shape.

The other iconically German figure of this same period in whom Warburg is interested, Albrecht Dürer, responded to the pressures of a world permeated by what Warburg calls the multiple "creaturely" determinisms associated with this kind of astrological thinking (528, 530) with even greater clarity and force than the former monk.[35] According to Warburg, Dürer likewise believed that the world was enchanted, but that astrological knowledge could help negotiate redemption in it. In a reading of Dürer's *Melencolia I* that is heavily indebted to a densely researched

---

35. The German term *Kreatur,* "the world of the flesh," refers to Man's world; Max Weber (60, for example) and, more famously, Benjamin (see below) use the same term as Warburg to refer to Man's life in the world.

article on the engraving published in 1903–4 by "my late friend Carl [*sic*] Giehlow[,]
who left us too early" (526) (an article that Benjamin also cites at great length),
Warburg tracks how ancient astral theories distinguished between good and bad
Saturnine influences on the body, and argues that the struggle between them informed Dürer's planning of the image.[36] That these ancient theories had migrated,
via Marsilio Ficino and the so-called Picatrix text, into the northern humanist court
context of Maximilian I (526–28) and become accessible to "northern" humanists
and artists there, was the thrust of Karl Giehlow's learned piece. The argument is
important at a submerged level for Warburg's wartime claims about the specifically
German provenance of these elements of the great artist's work. Warburg also—
and not surprisingly—gives his reading of Dürer's image a specifically "Lutheran"
twist, noting that Melanchthon himself acknowledged Dürer's achievement in the
engraving in two places in his *De anima* text (529).

According to Warburg, Dürer's Melancholy resists the power of the stars to
determine what Warburg calls Man's "creaturely sublunar fate" (528), a fate that
could cause Melancholy to lay aside the tools of any activity at all, such as those visible at her feet. Her ability to do so, indeed, to become a "thinking, working human
being" (528) not unlike Liliencron's Shakespeare, is enabled precisely by Lutheran
astrologics; she looks up (as she is shown to be doing in the Dürer etching) into and
is inspired by God's plan, whose light illuminates the world below by means of the
comet shown in the upper left-hand corner of the image. Protected by a belief in the
legibility of God's will in the stars, this Melancholy becomes "heroic" for Warburg
as an agent of her own redemption. Following Melanchthon's original extension
of astrology into astronomy, Warburg then goes on to claim that astrology works
hand in hand with mathematical reasoning (indicated by the compass in Melancholy's hand) to guarantee an accurate reading of the divine signs. The comet with
a rising not falling tail, in the upper left, simulates the grace that links God's world
with that of an autonomous Man. Lutheran astral magic thus functions here as an
efficient conduit between the two kingdoms, and Warburg celebrates the fact in no
uncertain terms.

For Warburg, both Luther's and Dürer's legacies for Germany lie in the renaissance of the ability of the nation to fulfill a sacrally endorsed mission as it was inherited from the Reformation. It is thus not surprising that at the end of the section on
Dürer, Warburg designates both the monk and the artist as "liberators," heroes in
the "battle for the inner intellectual and religious liberation of modern man" (531)
that the Germans, on behalf of all of modernity, seem poised to win. Like the ultimate accord between Melanchthon and Luther on the divine nature of astrology,

---

36. Karl Giehlow, "Dürers Stich 'Melencolia I' und der maximilianische Humanistenkreis." The
near simultaneity of the dates of Giehlow's essay and Max Weber's *Protestant Ethic* is uncanny and may
not have gone unnoticed by, among others, Walter Benjamin. See below.

but even more so, Dürer's image is a document of the gradual victory, Warburg writes, "of Germanness" (the grammar here is peculiar—"des Deutschen") "in the battle against a pagan-cosmological fatalism" (529), a victory that finds its high point in the divinely "magical" force-field of the stars capable of acting as a kind of road map of God's purpose. There has been much debate about the politically opportunistic or otherwise reactive shifts discernible in Melanchthon's original stance on the two kingdoms doctrine; he has been accused of being at an unpardonable distance from a more Barthian version when, "bowing to the state," he articulated his ideas about the *cura religionis,* the "oversight of the church," being placed more firmly in the secular magistrates' hands.[37] His astrological theory would nevertheless suggest that, with Luther, Melanchthon in fact believed deeply in the need to preserve continuity between the two realms so that the sublunar world could continue to be understood as controlled by the divine. In a beleaguered wartime Germany, Warburg seems willing to settle for the rebirth of something like this kind of connection between God's will and the nation in the here and now.

Even if he does not explicitly rely on war theological claims, Warburg's celebration of Lutheran and Reformation-era logic in his lecture reveals his conviction that in Germany the secular and the spiritual realms are sutured firmly together. That he believed in the cohabitation of modernity with something like divine magic at a kind of primordial level in the German unconscious is clear when he concludes his argument with a quote from that other great German, Goethe. In his "Materialien zur Geschichte der Farbenlehre" (Documents on the History of the Science of Color), Goethe had written (Warburg quotes him) that the intertwined nature of a rational science like mathematics with astrology, and thus the collaboration (rather than the contest) between noble reason and bleak fatalism, explain why "superstition" is in fact not at all uncommon "in the so-called enlightened centuries" (535). Warburg may strain, in other words, to offer Luther's initial resistance to efforts to alter his date of birth, along with Dürer's use of astrological symbols in *Melencolia I,* as testimony to the "history of the intellectual freedom of the modern European" (534). But it is really the Protestant Melanchthon and the great Goethe (who seems to be drafted here into service as an "enlightened" interpreter of Reformation thought to the modern world) who use reason to locate the astrological path that leads from God's other-worldly kingdom to the human world of science in Man's. Melanchthon and Goethe are thus the actual heroes for Germany in this jubilee-year talk.

It would be dishonest not to note that, as much in sync with the wartime celebrations of the German Protestant tradition as Warburg's lecture may have been, in the published version he lets slip at the end that this history may ultimately have to be read as "tragic" (534), even doomed. What may be a postwar admission

---

37. Estes reviews the controversies (xii–xiv).

of this fact may not be by chance. In closing, Warburg refers to a figure from an-other Goethe text, namely Faust (534). In a talk planned for and given in the bleak years of 1917–18, when the German defeat was basically clear, this reference to the early modern conjurer is as legible as a commentary on contemporary events as Warburg's overall interest in political astrologics was. For Warburg, Faust is "the modern scientist" par excellence, who struggled valiantly, yet ultimately in vain, to conquer "an intellectual space of reason" (534) between magic and rationality. (This failure may be why Warburg writes at the very beginning of the article that his remarks about the Reformation period could function as the first chapter of the "handbook" on "the un-freedom of modern superstitious man" that had yet to be written; 490). Why did Faust fail where Luther, Melanchthon, and Dürer did not? Perhaps it was because he mistakenly wagered with the devil instead of with God. Warburg does not give this reason, however, but closes, rather, with his famous claim: "Athens will of course always and repeatedly desire to be won back from Alexandria" (534). The peculiarly recursive grammar of this sentence—which suggests that an inborn German reason somehow takes pleasure in repeat-edly experiencing itself in the dangerous embrace of astrological "magic," even as it also repeatedly does battle with the irrational in an effort to wrest itself free—nevertheless suggests that the struggle on the part of the "modern" nation's early modern surrogates, Luther, Dürer, and now Faust, to find a better link between God's plan and the here and now may ultimately turn out to have this same kind of tragic end.

Benjamin's version of these debates in the *Tragic Drama* book can be most com-pactly observed in his opening salvo in the melancholy chapter noted above: "The great German dramatists of the baroque were Lutherans" (G: 1.1: 317; E: 138). Klaus Garber has remarked on the implications of this claim (*Rezeption und Ret-tung* 81–120). Benjamin's active correspondence about early modern religious his-tory and doctrine with his close friend Rang during these years (indeed, Rang's death in 1924 meant, according to Benjamin, that the book had lost its only "real reader," *Gesammelte Schriften* 1.3: 883) suggests the context in which the implica-tions of the volatile theopolitical conflicts of the early modern period for German modernity might have been presented to him.[38] Benjamin's assertion of the "Lu-theran" identity of the playwrights whose works are the main subject of his book is nevertheless curious, since it could be debated whether it is even true. After all, the lower nobility and patrician sponsors of the Baroque dramas about which he was writing may not have even been Lutherans, but rather crypto-Calvinists, leaving

---

38. On Rang as a "collaborator" on the book, see the detailed inventory of exchanges between him and Benjamin, including letters from Rang, portions of which Benjamin included nearly verbatim in the book itself, in the notes to the German edition of the *Tragic Drama* book in volume 1.3 of *Gesam-melte Schriften*, 884–95, here 887.

us to wonder about the confessional affiliation of the playwrights in their employ.[39] Benjamin may not have been aware of this wrinkle. Had he been, it would help explain the Weberian echoes in the passage that follows the opening statement quoted above, in which, without identifying it as such, it is the problem of how Lutheranism configured the two kingdoms theory that concerns Benjamin most. He writes:

> Whereas in the decades of the Counter-Reformation[,] Catholicism had penetrated secular life with all the power of its discipline, the relationship of Lutheranism to the everyday had always been antinomic. The rigorous morality of its teaching in respect of civic conduct stood in sharp contrast to its renunciation of 'good works'. By denying the latter any special miraculous spiritual effect, making the soul dependent on grace through faith, and making the secular-political sphere a testing ground for a life that was only indirectly religious ... it did, it is true, instill into people a strict sense of obedience to duty, but in its great men it produced [only] melancholy. ... Human actions were deprived of all value. Something new arose: an empty world ... a rubbish heap of ... inauthentic actions. (G: 1.1: 317; E: 138–19)[40]

The "Lutheran faith," Benjamin continues in the *Tragic Drama* book, refused what he understood as the Calvinist solution to the gap between the transcendent and the mundane that a theological doctrine like the two kingdoms theory had to a certain extent itself opened up. Continuing to stare "the rubbish heap" of their "existence" directly in the face, and frozen in an "emptied world" (318; 139), Lutherans have to wait—and wait and wait—for God's intervention through grace. Hence the "bleak rule of [their] melancholic distaste for life" (319; 140).

As a commentary on the disastrous economic and political situation in and for Germany, both on the home front and on the postwar world stage, after the promise that the nation was fulfilling the work of God has been irreparably broken, Benjamin's words ring true. Instead of glorying in the possibility of a divine plan being revealed in the victories of war, Benjamin writes, the Lutheran Baroque of the post–Thirty Years' War period was paralyzed by the same kind of "satanic ensnarement" in history (G: 1.1: 320; E: 141–42) to which Germany had fallen victim at the outset of World War I. When he quotes Arthur Hübscher's comments here that this is the reason that seventeenth-century "'baroque nationalism' was never associated with political action" and could never express itself as the "revolutionary will of *Sturm und Drang* or the Romantic war against the philistinism of state and public life" (320; 141) had done, Benjamin's critique of both aggressive war theology

---

39. On the confessional identity of the noble family that sponsored one of the major German Baroque playwrights about whom Benjamin writes, namely Daniel Casper von Lohenstein, see Newman, *Intervention of Philology* 30 and 122.

40. Max Weber writes in a similar way about an "inhumane" and "harsh" Calvinism that creates in Man a profound "inner loneliness" and "deep spiritual isolation" (60–61).

and the passivity of official Lutheranism, and its failure to do what was right for the nation, can be heard. Warburg's "prognostication" essay is quoted (sometimes footnoted, but sometimes not) countless times in this and the final chapter of Benjamin's book. It may have been what gave Benjamin the idea to understand the "empty world" (317; 139) as a Lutheran rather than a Calvinist dilemma, and then to use that sixteenth-century world to investigate the seventeenth-century interest in astrology as a way of tracking the more recent failure in Germany to develop a religious program in any more than a merely instrumental way.

Benjamin's ideas about the implications of an astrally organized early modern world linked to a Lutheran tradition differ significantly from Warburg's, then, and resemble more the precarious approach of a Barthian-Gogartian type, just as his more downbeat Baroque differs from the heroic German Renaissance that Warburg saw emerging out of the Reformation era. Benjamin continues: "The heritage of the Renaissance" from which "this age [the Baroque] derive[d its] material" concerned the "only indirectly religious life" and deepened the "contemplative paralysis" of its "great men" (G: 1.1: 317–20; E: 138–40). Benjamin is clearly referring here to the Dürer engraving that Warburg discussed, and the image in fact immediately makes an appearance, albeit in refashioned form: "It accords with this [i.e., the claim about the contemplative paralysis of great men caught in a Lutheran world] that in the proximity of Albrecht Dürer's figure, *Melencolia,* the utensils of active life are lying around unused on the floor, as objects of contemplation. This engraving anticipates the Baroque in many respects" (319; 140). And yet, it does so, antithetically to Warburg's version, primarily in its indication that the melancholy Baroque man is imprisoned in the "satanic" melancholic paralysis mentioned above. Benjamin writes, for example, that the "vain activity of the [courtly] intriguer[s]" who populated the Baroque plays must actually be understood as "the worthless antithesis of passionate contemplation" (320; 141); the sovereign and his lackeys are similarly trapped in the "depths of the creaturely realm" (324; 146), as are the "despots" and "tyrants" (322; 144) who crowd the stages of the German Baroque plays. For Benjamin, their access to the "absolute transcendentality" via grace that Warburg found in Melanchthon's and Dürer's Lutheran worlds is denied. There are very few heroic "liberators" here, in other words.

Given that they reverse Warburg's claims in nearly every respect, it is perhaps surprising that these pages of Benjamin's work (G: 1.1: 323–29; E: 145–51) are primarily a tissue of extensive citations from both Warburg and Giehlow (on whom Warburg too had depended), as well as from Erwin Panofsky's and Fritz Saxl's 1923 book on Dürer's *Melencolia,* in which they had taken it as their mission to complete Warburg's work. Benjamin lifts the substance of his argument directly out of these texts, interweaving long quotes from them (again, sometimes footnoted, often not) on astrology and the development of humoral psychology out of its "science" (326; 148), for example, as well as some of the lengthy passages from the medieval and Renaissance texts his scholarly contemporaries had included as quotes in their texts, with his own citations on melancholic astral-humoral issues from additional seventeenth-century texts. (The Warburgians did not respond entirely positively when Benjamin sent them this semiplagiarized text, as Sigrid Weigel notes.)[41] Yet he does so, in the end, only to refute them. By dwelling on the radical separation of Man from God's world, that is, and Man's incapacitating "immersion in the life of creaturely things" (330; 152), Benjamin tracks how the afterlives of Lutheran melancholia in the Baroque era in fact diverge from the optimism of Warburg's theory of "sublime melancholy" (329; 151).

The key moments in the *Tragic Drama* book that signal Benjamin's reversal of Warburg's upbeat reading of Lutheranism's afterlives are, ironically, marked by a return to the Albertinus text that he had encountered in Liliencron's Hamlet novella (to which he had probably been led by a footnote in Warburg's essay). Stitching together quotes from Liliencron's 1884 Albertinus edition with references to plays by the Baroque dramatists, Gryphius, Lohenstein, and Hallmann (G: 1.1: 322–23, 326, 331; E: 144–45, 148, 154), Benjamin describes how the Baroque melancholic, instead of "escap[ing] madness" by means of the "Melancholia 'illa heroica'" that Warburg describes (329; 151), for example, "'goes mad and fades into despair'" (323; 145). Missing from the "inventory" of "symbols of melancholy embodied in [Dürer's] engraving" (331; 154) drawn up by Giehlow and the "other scholars" is, Benjamin writes, Albertinus's "stone," the "weighty mass," that Benjamin indicates is the heavier "theological concept of the melancholic" (332; 155) of the Baroque. It is revealing that it is the Jesuit Albertinus's understanding of sloth, *acedia,* that Benjamin uses here to describe the personnel of the "Lutheran" tragic drama as "dismal[ly]" and "hopeless[ly]" loyal only to the "creaturely" realm and the "world of things" (333; 156). The strongly Barthian refusal of commerce between the kingdom of Man and the kingdom of God he describes seems to be the equivalent of a kind of theological backsliding into the "old-fashioned" Jesuit and thus anti- or pre-Reformation mode. Yet there is also no hope for redemption, at least for the Germans. Their world "knows no higher law" (333; 157), Benjamin explains. Even the most pious of his Baroque Lutherans is not touched by "the sound of revelation" (330; 152) in the secular world.

Benjamin's understanding of how to live with the melancholy reality of a Lutheran two kingdoms theory reborn in both early modern and modern Germany is thus quite distinct from Warburg's. The postwar date of Benjamin's text suggests that it may have been only after the national defeat of 1918 that he could produce his depressingly accurate account of the loss of a Lutheran Germany's soul. Benjamin's famously opaque insights into Baroque melancholy in the *Tragic*

---

41. Warburg's assistant, Saxl, did read the chapter of the *Tragic Drama* book that Benjamin sent to Hamburg, and sent it on to Panofsky, who apparently sent Benjamin a "cool" response to it. Saxl remarks that, although "interesting," the essay was "not easy to read." See Weigel 122–24.

Drama book may have derived from his own personal melancholic nature, as some scholars have claimed. But these insights also suggest Benjamin's stance on the devastating effects of the confessional logic that subtended the nation's actions in the war. If the failure to be able to believe in Warburg's perhaps desperately optimistic, salutary understanding of the link between God's purpose for Man and life on the ground is clear in Benjamin's case, his final argument in this chapter nevertheless does target a figure whose creaturely life was successfully illuminated by the "reflection of a distant light, shining back from the depths of self absorption" (we obviously think of the Dürer image here). As we know, however, "Germany" was not the country that was able to have imagined it. Rather, this "figure" was "Hamlet" (334; 157).

The tragedy of Benjamin's Hamlet is, however, that, as Benjamin writes, it is only briefly "before its extinction" that Hamlet's life, as the "object . . . of his mourning," can be redeemed by moving "into a blessed existence." The notion is perverse insofar as "self awareness" (G: 1.1: 335; E: 158) thus in no way guarantees a "heroic" redeemed life, as it does for Warburg, but rather only a front-row seat at the spectacle of destruction and death. Here again, the prince seems to figure forth wartime Germany in spite of Benjamin's denials. The description in the third and final chapter of the *Tragic Drama* book of a theory of Baroque allegory that, in mysterious fashion, can in fact redeem the "comfortless confusion" and "desert of all human existence" in which the tragedy of Germany was caught (405; 232) sounds curiously similar. The passages in which this theory is developed are some of the most arcane and difficult to understand in this arcane and difficult book. They involve a series of metaphors that indicate that when such a redemption occurs, it is mostly by chance, as when "those who lose their footing turn somersaults in their fall" and, in an abrupt "about turn," "rediscover themselves," no longer in "the earthly world of things," but rather "under the eyes of heaven" (405–6; 232). The exchange of the heavenly for the earthly kingdom comes here without warning and, indeed, entirely without work. It is an agentless redemption, in other words, that recalls the Lutheran doctrine of grace developed by some of the early twentieth-century dialectical theologians mentioned above. That one can only clumsily stumble into such redemption, if at all, suggests the rareness of its occurrence. Indeed, it seems more likely that, even if there is a brief glimpse of heaven, the somersault will end in a fall, or, as in the case of Hamlet, in "extinction" and death. It may have been from the other tragic dramas, namely the German Baroque plays themselves, that Benjamin learned that this moment of insight might in fact not coincide with a fall simply by chance but rather literally *require* the loss of the world. The absolute fall out of immanence into transcendence, and thus out of Man's world into God's, often occurs in those plays only via the stage property of an allegorized corpse, as Benjamin understood. Only so could the "transitoriness of things" be "rescue[d] into eternity" (397; 223).

Allegory, Emblems, and Gryphius's *Catharina von Georgien*

Andreas Gryphius's Baroque tragic drama *Catharina von Georgien Oder Beweh-rete Beständigkeit* (Catharine of Georgia; or, Constancy Defended) (1657) takes as its subject the story of a Christian queen who, according to at least one source, was a canny military strategist and formidable political force in the complex world of early modern western central Asia, where Orthodox Georgia was sandwiched between Persia and the powerful Ottoman Empire. Catharine led her people effectively but was ultimately taken captive and held by the shah of Persia for seven years. During that time, she was subject to his demands to both marry him and convert to Islam, both of which kinds of importuning she steadfastly refused. As punishment for what is taken to be this otherwise highly laudable conduct, and also as a result of local political maneuverings on the part of the shah's diplomatic advisers, she was first brutally tortured and then ultimately burned alive, a martyr to her chastity, religious faith, and strength of will. These are the historical events that form the tense subject of Gryphius's play, which, while underscoring Catharine's this-worldly constraints, also bills itself as a display of a constancy (*constantia, Beständigkeit*) that, even as it beggars restriction to the material realm, is what endows Catharine's politically brutal sojourn on this earth with higher meaning. The play has been called a "Protestant version of the [genre] of the martyr-tragedy," at the center of which lies a "genuinely Lutheran opposition of secular and spiritual power" (Borgstedt 61 and 49). The tension the play stages between political-historical contingencies and a transcendent sphere defined by Christian ethico-moral codes is thus not unrelated to the two kingdoms theory I have discussed. Its "two-part title" (G: 1.1: 371; E: 193)—with the case of the queen's creaturely individuality used as a pointer to indicate her nearly other-worldly constancy and thus to intimate the necessity of her earthly doom as the sole conduit to that realm beyond—is an example of the kind of emblematic logic that Benjamin saw governing the Baroque's response to this theory and out of which he developed his own ambivalent conception of allegory in the *Tragic Drama* book.

Gryphius's play was written around 1647 and first published a decade later; the historical events of 1624 it depicts were thus not so very far in the past for either its author or its audiences, which were several. The issue of audience, indeed, of how to be a good reader of either plays or emblems, or, indeed, of a Lutheran world emptied of (or at least absolutely separate from) the world beyond, is key to understanding what Benjamin describes as the "violent" "dialectical movement" (G: 1.1: 342; E: 166) of allegory. On the one side lies the "frozen, primordial landscape" of "secular" history, he writes, and, on the other, the "unfolding" of the "significance" of the "creaturely" in "death" (343; 166). How to judge her fit with one or the other of these worlds is precisely Queen Catharine's challenge in Gryphius's play, the grim details of which are proof of the accuracy of Benjamin's claim that "the German tragic drama was never able to use allegory inconspicuously" (368; 191). Indeed, his

most pressing question about the Baroque plays that are his subject comes toward
the end of the *Tragic Drama* book: "What is the significance of those scenes of horrible martyrdom in which the baroque drama wallows?" (390; 216). Gryphius's
play is not unusual in the vivid brutality of such scenes, which anchor not only the
characters who experience it, but also its audience and readers, in the violent ruins
of the secular political world. The challenges of finding redemption beyond this
world are great. It may thus not be by chance that, in his introductory examination
of allegory, Benjamin highlights the reference to Herder's understanding of emblems in Friedrich Creuzer's early nineteenth-century history of symbols, *Symbolik
und Mythologie der alten Völker, besonders der Griechen* (Symbolics and Mythology of
the Ancient Peoples, Particularly the Greeks) (1819); emblems are expressions of a
specifically "German power" that emerged with particular prominence in the para-
digmatically "emblematic age" of the Reformation (G: 1.1: 345; E: 168), he notes.
Gryphius's play must have seemed extremely "Lutheran" to Benjamin in its display
of the difficult relation between the travails of this world and God's will, as that
relation determined its highly emblematic texture and themes. It certainly invited
him to consider allegory in Protestant terms.

From the outset Gryphius's *Catharine of Georgia* calls attention to the challenges
inherent in the allegorical culture of the Baroque. At the opening of act 1, the queen
narrates to her companion, Salome, a dream she has had the previous night. In
the dream, in which she was the protagonist, Catharine observed how, clothed in
the magnificent garb of her royal station, she had begun to feel on her temples the
pressure of her diamond-studded crown as it shrank. "In a flash" (l. 330), the crown
transformed itself into a wreath of thorns; piercing and then penetrating deep into
her skull, it caused streams of blood to run down her face (l. 335).[42] The more
she and others struggle in the dream to free her from this "most horrible agony"
(l. 342), the more firmly the thorny crown takes hold, resulting, finally, in the gory
disfiguration of the queen. Catharine goes on to describe how in the dream, even
as she suffered the torturous embrace of her crown, "a stranger" assaulted her by
grabbing her breasts "not without pain" (l. 344), causing her, finally, to faint. Even
though the account ends with the queen's explanation that, still in the dream, she
comes to be enveloped in a sense of well-being and is able to observe her tormentor,
who turns out to be the shah, trembling with fear at her feet (ll. 345–50), the extended, nightmarish account can leave both viewer and reader only with a queasy
memory of the sadistic crown and the queen's mutilated breasts.

If daylight sometimes helps to dull one's memories in such cases, Gryphius reso-
lutely refuses to allow dramatic time to erase the details of Catharine's lurid vision. In act 5, the dream comes to life, albeit offstage, as the actual tormenting of
the queen is described in even more gruesome detail by a serving woman, Serena,

---

42. Line references are to Gryphius, *Catharina von Georgien*. All translations of this play are my own.

whose name belies her emotional state (ll. 61–100). Serena reports the progress of the torture step by step and with an attention to anatomical specifics made possible, one might argue, by the playwright's participation in the public dissecting of human corpses in the famous anatomical theater in Leiden, where he spent the years 1638 through 1644. The textual particulars involve a painstaking description of Catharine's internal organs, which are revealed as the flesh is methodically stripped away from her torso and her breasts ripped to shreds. Gryphius mercilessly has the queen survive this brutality only to have her thrust, still living, into the flames (ll. 104–25). In a particularly macabre twist, her charred head is ultimately rescued from the ashes and appears, relic-like, on stage (ll. 209–20) to be handed over to her son, Tamaras, by the Russian ambassador, who had been the one who had pleaded with the shah for the queen's release—obviously to no good effect. Gryphius's dedication to the gruesome theatrics of martyrdom, which in any case followed with care the "script" established in his French source, Claude Malingres, Sieur de S. Lazare's *Histoires Tragiques de nostre Temps* (Tragic Histories of Our Times) (1635), is rivaled only by that of his fellow Silesian playwright Daniel Casper von Lohenstein, who, some years later, called for the actual staging (rather than mere reporting) of the grizzly torture of the eponymous heroine of his tragic drama *Epicharis* at the hands of the Roman emperor Nero as punishment for her involvement in the Pisonian conspiracy. In 1655, a series of engravings was printed in connection with what some scholars claim was a planned performance of Gryphius's *Catharine of Georgia* play, somewhat perversely dedicated to the reigning duchess, Luise, at the small Silesian court of Ohlau, a female head of state and probably, like Catharine, a member of a religious minority too (see Zielske). In these engravings by Johann Using, the image of the woman's tortured body, while repugnant, captures the viewer's attention and is hard to dismiss.[43] One must wonder how Duchess Luise, as Gryphius's patron and sponsor, reacted to the play.

Given that any number of the tragic-drama plots of the plays of the German Baroque culminated in macabre scenes like the ones described here, it is no wonder that Benjamin refers to them as "crude theater" (G: 1.1: 335; E: 158). The "creaturely" dimension of human existence in which he is especially interested is nowhere more obvious than when the interiors of the broken bodies of their characters are displayed prominently for audiences to see. Benjamin develops his theory of allegory out of readings of the significance of the maimed corpses, stage props, and ruins that littered the seventeenth-century stage of which he writes. When he claims, then, that "norms of emblematics" (391; 216) may be understood on the basis of such scenes of cruelty and martyrdom, we may be forgiven for thinking that he may have had in mind the dream narration scene with which Gryphius's play begins

---

43. The Using engravings are reproduced in Zielske, as well as in volume 3 of Hugh Powell's edition of Gryphius's *Trauerspiele*.

(Benjamin refers to it several times in the book), since the gory dream did in fact have precedents in actual emblems. The competing interpretations the characters in the play give of Catharine's nightmare vision, and the significance for them of the scene of torture that it appears to predict, stage a moment of emblematic representation that calls attention to the tension between the *Realpolitik* necessary to negotiate the contingent and brutal political realities of both early modern and modern life, on the one hand, and the possibility of leading a life of "moral autonomy" that transcends these constraints by following the mandates of an other-worldly sphere, on the other (Koepnick 279). The play's performance of early modern practices of emblem making and reading may well have helped Benjamin see allegory as a way of understanding the fatal crossroads at which a modern Lutheran Germany stood, but also as a commentary on the fact that the road to spiritual rebirth might be a slippery and precarious one with many false turns.

Queen Catharine's dream recounts the transformation of her crown into an instrument of torture. The image to which the dream refers can be found in any number of seventeenth-century emblem books, which Benjamin refers to as the "authentic documents of the modern allegorical way of looking at things, the literary and visual emblem-texts of the Baroque" (G: 1.1: 339; E: 162). These widely circulated collections of conventional wisdom provided opportunities for the witty combination of elements from nature, history, and myth and were designed to reveal—or to provoke readers into construing—the coherence of the phenomenal and noumenal worlds. A particularly fine example of the thorny-crown emblem was included in Guillaume de La Perrière's *La Morosophie* of 1553, for example, which describes itself as a collection of one hundred "emblemes moraux" (moral emblems). The *pictura,* the actual illustration, which emblem theorists refer to as the "body" of the emblem, is of an opulent crown thick on its inside with thorns; it is accompanied by French verses, the "soul" or *scriptura,* that gloss the image by telling the reader its greater meaning, namely that the "fine gold" of the crown means only "great pain" for its wearer. In another rendering of the same image by the Spanish political theorist Diego de Saavedra Fajardo, first published in 1640 but reprinted numerous times throughout the seventeenth century and all over Europe, the explanatory motto under the image is compact; it reads, *Bonum fallax* (loosely translated "The Good That Betrays" or "Fake Goods").[44] Combined, the "body" and the "soul" of the emblem are meant to guarantee insight into a previously obscure, but now clear moral, political, religious, or natural-historical message about, in this case, the realities of sovereignty's dangerous burdens. The very fact of this emblem's inclusion in these two exceedingly popular and widely available print inventories of early modern commonplaces about the lives of the

---

44. The La Perrière image and verse are reproduced in Henkel and Schöne 1259, as are the Saavedra verses.

powerful, together with the consistency of the message expressed about its significance in two volumes first published some one hundred years apart, suggests a
certain hermeneutic stability, a guarantee of interpretive orthodoxy apparently surrounding the statement that the powerful suffer precisely when they are powerful.
Another emblem, whose motto reads, *Tollat qui te non noverit* (Only he who is
unfamiliar with the heavy weight of ruler will take it up), would appear to confirm
the rule. This emblem, as familiar to consumers of early modern emblem books as
the thorny-crown emblem to which Catharine's dream refers, is rendered exquisitely in Julius Wilhelm Zincgref's *Emblematum Ethico-Politicorum Centuria* (One
Hundred Ethical-Political Emblems) of 1619. The Zincgref emblem distinguishes
itself by being one of the very few actual emblems that Benjamin discusses in the
Tragic Drama book (G: 1.1: 252; E: 73).

The scarcity of historical examples of emblems in Benjamin's argument does
not suggest, however, that he was unfamiliar with what he calls "the more original
works" (G: 1.1: 339; E: 162) of Baroque emblematics. Nor, indeed, are his claims
about their significance for the allegorical logic of the period inaccurate, as the
reception of the thorny-crown emblem in Gryphius's play attests. Benjamin famously, yet perhaps somewhat counterintuitively (given the apparent stability of
meaning in the emblem collections), describes "the antinomies of the allegorical"
as dictating that "any person, any object, any relationship can mean absolutely
anything else" (350; 174–75). He claims, in other words, that one of Baroque allegory's primary tasks was to reveal that the significance of its images—and thus,
of the fragmentary "ruins" of the sublunary, or "creaturely," realm of (in this case)
real-world courtly manipulation and intrigue they both represented and "bodied
forth"—were not stable, or, at least, that there was no guaranteed relation between
suffering in the this-worldly realm, and redemption in the next. The claim may
seem perverse in the context of a play that seems to celebrate Catharine's nearly
Christ-like acceptance of her martyrdom as the avenue to the world of the divine.
Gryphius's play nevertheless not only shows the horrible price the body must pay
for its removal into God's kingdom. It also thematizes the difficulty of knowing for
sure whether that redemption will or can occur by showing that the thorny-crown
emblem's meaning is at best ambiguous in the play; it is thus of problematic value,
especially for those, who, like Duchess Luise, belonged to the very political world
whose opacity the emblems were designed to clarify. The hope that there is something more must be almost literally a leap of faith.

The interpretive conundrum surrounding the thorny-crown emblem that arises
in Gryphius's play—and its exemplification of Benjamin's claims about the antinomies of Baroque emblematics—points to the ambiguity of living in a ruined world
and to the attendant possibility of a profoundly "unheroic" relation to the realm
of contingency. Indeed, after Catharine ends her description of the dream in act
1, her serving maid, Salome, takes up the role of early modern reader of emblems
by providing a gloss of the dream image. The dream is "too true" (l. 355), Salome

says; the queen had indeed suffered mightily in earlier times precisely because of the heavy burdens of majesty represented by the crown. Salome's reading seems to accord with the general understanding of the often painful obligations of power indicated by the glosses in the emblem books. The sense of relief Catharine feels at the end of the dream is nevertheless a premonition, according to Salome, of the aid, indeed the "freedom" (l. 357), that is imminent, especially since she then proceeds to reveal to the queen that she has a message from the queen's son, Tamaras, that will be delivered to the queen by the secret emissaries from Georgia, who are then immediately brought on stage. In a nearly uninterrupted—and thus in performance terms necessarily show-stopping—speech of some three hundred lines, the queen's countrymen inform her of the complex political events roiling her realm. Salome glosses the fact of the message from the prince—and the presence of Demetrius and Procopius as his envoys—as the future promise signified by "the beautiful crown shown to her by the night" (ll. 364–65). Salome's reading of the queen's dream is odd, first of all, because emblem theory in principle suggests that the gloss, or "soul," of the specifics of an emblem's image is meant to lead the reader of the emblem up the ladder of meaning, so to speak, to the more general insight hidden in the "body" of the illustration, and not back down to another individual or merely historical occasion, such as the arrival of the prince's message or the ambassadors' presence, which might or might not embody that wisdom. Moreover, the crown in the dream is anything but "beautiful." Nevertheless, although admittedly a bit unorthodox in these ways, Salome's initial reading does seem to fit with what was clearly accepted at the time as the way in which the thorny-crown emblem should be read, namely to indicate the reality of the material (i.e., political and military) burdens of those in power.

Yet, what is odd about Gryphius's attribution to Salome of knowledge of well-known emblems is not that this clearly recognizable emblem is invoked in the play. Rather, that Gryphius offers not just one—namely Salome's—apparently conventional gloss, but later, also a second reading of the crown dream that turns out to be at odds with the first is what gives one pause. This second gloss occurs toward the end of act 4, after Catharine has learned that she will be tortured (ll. 353–70). By this time, the queen has been challenged—in return for her freedom—to both abjure her faith and yield her chastity to the shah by his minion, Imanculi. She has refused and accepted a martyr's fate instead, with the explanation that Christ too had to suffer before entering his kingdom (l. 238). Over the earthly crown the shah offers her Catharine will thus choose the "eternal crown" (l. 262), she says. The reference is to, among other things, the opening allegorical scene of the play in act 1, in which an allegorical figure of Eternity has indicated the transitory nature of earthly power represented by the detritus of power strewn about her on the stage (ll. 1–88), a scene that is also illustrated by Using. In the Using engraving, the earthly crown that Salome had taken the dream crown to signify actually lies neglected in the foreground of the image. This is the same crown that adorns the title page of the

Using illustrations, the one that the shah offers the queen. The "eternal crown" she prefers can be seen up above, proffered to her by an angelic figure. This literally superior crown is also the well-known symbol of martyrdom, the "corona Martyris," as described in tomes such as Filippo Picinelli's *Mundus symbolicus* of 1687, for example, and is accompanied by the palm frond of suffering (see Zielske 12 n. 17). "Martyrdom . . . prepares the body of the living person for emblematic purposes," Benjamin writes (G: 1.1: 391; E: 217). In the play itself, the dream emblem does prepare Catharine for the martyrdom of her body. The clear choice of the one crown over the other in the Using image, which accurately illustrates Catharine's ultimate preference, nevertheless downplays the fact that there is a sustained struggle in the play over the actual significance of the crown emblem—and thus over the substance of her choice.

In the competing readings of Catharine's dream, Gryphius's play offers a judiciously skeptical commentary on the plausibility of making the right choice, indeed, on the difficulty of choosing the heavenly over the profane crown and path—and thus of *constantia* over political manipulation and duplicity. Or, if that is too strong, it reveals that that choice will occur only when there is no other way out. This difficulty emerges with greatest clarity in act 4, where the competing regimes of earthly politics and divine glory, and thus the dueling kingdoms of Man and God, are under constant pressure. The queen clearly seeks to remove all ambiguity about the meaning of the crown by engaging at the very end of the act in a moment of emblematic reading herself; just before she is led away from her women to the torture chamber, she recalls her dream and explains: "Now the dream that last night, when I was overcome with sleep and fear, pointed to this outcome, is fulfilled" (ll. 353–55). The crown of thorns signifies the martyrdom God has bestowed on her, she explains: "God makes me a gift of this crown when I die as he did" (l. 370). The sadistic man of the dream is, in turn, her imminent death. The shah's henchmen proceed to more or less enact her reading in the carefully orchestrated torture sequence described in act 5 that deliberately echoes the details of Catharine's nightmare vision. In allowing the queen's gloss, which endows the crown, as a symbol of earthly power, with divine significance, to follow and thus literally supersede Salome's earlier, more pragmatic and "applied" reading, Gryphius's play would seem to stage an example of how to read emblems correctly by indicating how to move through the external appearance of the image "up" to the greater "redeemed" truth to which it points. Salome, who saw the crown only as an image of earthly power, is in the process cast as a bad reader of emblems, and it is Catharine who, by glossing the crown "properly," that is, figuratively and within the frame of the world beyond, succeeds in merging with what has conventionally been taken to be the allegory of the play that bears her name. That is, the drama's double title sees the suffering of the queen first and foremost as a way to examine the abstract concept, probably neo-Stoic in nature, of spiritual steadfastness and Christian fortitude, rather than as the occasion for a history lesson about the hazards of a harsh political life in western central Asia—or in Silesia—in the first decades of the seventeenth century.

Yet the availability of two possible readings of the emblem in Gryphius's play, and the somewhat troubling fact that Salome's apparently discarded gloss actually appears to have been more in line than Catharine's with early modern *doxa* about sovereignty, as represented by the emblem books, might have created the real need expressed in Benjamin's reflections on allegory to understand how emblems work. What could Gryphius's staging of the two readings in conflict mean? Is the play primarily about early modern political or early modern spiritual life? What is the connection between them? Is it, moreover, about clear choices on the part of princes and all political actors faced with difficult decisions, or about the impossibility of making such decisions correctly? Stefanie Arend has argued that a careful reading of the characters of Salome and Imanculi, the shah's messenger to Catharine, reveals them as proponents of a perhaps more Machiavellian, but nevertheless more commonly accepted early modern political calculus than the queen. It is Salome, after all, who arranges for the secret visit of the Georgian messengers and who reminds Catharine in act 1 of her obligation to secure the succession of her son, Tamaras, to the throne (ll. 169–226). In similar fashion, Imanculi, even as he brings her his master's offer of marriage and conversion in act 4, engages in a lively political debate with Catharine, pointing out to the queen, for example, that, according to a logic of *ratio status* that transcends national and confessional differences, it is her duty, precisely as sovereign, to act rationally by looking beyond the irrelevant details of chastity and religious faith to the future welfare of her kingdom (ll. 80–264). Catharine's evolving commitment to martyrdom and to an unearthly kingdom and glory begins to look somewhat unorthodox, even a bit overwrought, when considered in the context of these kinds of more pragmatic political positions. Such positions are nevertheless intermittently, but also steadily promoted both throughout and also at the conclusion of the play, when Seinel Can, the shah's other minister, succeeds in act 5 in manipulating the Russian ambassador into not blowing Catharine's death out of proportion (ll. 257–344); doing so would only create a major diplomatic incident and endanger the public face of both Russian foreign policy and the Persian throne. In these ways, the play suggests the early modern lesson that those in power ought to act pragmatically and amorally and without a clear sense of—or concern for—the beyond.

Arend's suggestion that what is driving Gryphius's text is an examination of the tense relationship between a doctrine of moral absolutes, on the one hand, and the exigencies of early modern political life, on the other, explains a certain formal unevenness in the play. The text oscillates between often energetic dramatic dialogues and at least two lengthy, soliloquy-like narrations of political background, lifted, to all appearances, directly from Claude Malingres's prose narrative, which again has been said to be Gryphius's main source. This formal tension is not the result of the author's inexperience, however; rather, it mirrors the rhetorical and ideological struggle in which the play engages between foregrounding the historical details of Catharine's fight for political survival before her capture, as evidenced in the informative, but long-winded speeches, on the one hand, and downplaying the horrifying realities of her case as subordinate to and merely an example, albeit a spectacular one, of Christian devotion to virtue and God, on the other. In the end, the question of how to read this play is really the same question as the one concerning the crown: When is a thorny crown a crown, indicative of lessons about the vexed nature of sovereignty and burdens of earthly rule, and when, pointing beyond itself, is it a more or less religious symbol of the earthly suffering that afflicts all of mankind prior to its redemption at the hands of God? Put another way, when is a historical queen historical, subject to the demands of real time to which she must respond in kind, and when is she merely the illustrative part of an emblem, a prop, in an extended allegory of transcendence that leaves the world behind? How, finally, can we, how could Gryphius guarantee a "progression" from one to the other reading, when, as Arend points out, Catharine herself has a difficult time in the play leaving her successful, if sometimes duplicitous political history behind? How much, finally, would the suggestion of Catharine's patient endurance of torture and her allegorical significance as a Mankind redeemed have helped a literal early modern head of state, such as Duchess Luise, get through her or his politically hazardous day? Conversely, how much would it help the state if that sovereign were to conclude that, given the realities of early modern political life, earthly dominion should best be put aside in order to make room for the kind of perhaps devout, yet also profoundly melancholic withdrawal opted for in two spectacular early modern cases, namely Emperor Charles V and Queen Christina of Sweden, retirements that, if chosen in the smaller principalities of Silesia, where Gryphius was born, lived, and wrote, would have exposed these small polities to incredible dangers at the hands of greater confessional regimes? Perhaps it is best in such cases not to choose faith or the divine realm. Questions of this nature about what could be considered "good" and responsible, politically and morally defensible behavior on the part of sovereigns in politically and religiously fraught times were certainly ones the duchess might have asked herself, had she attended Gryphius's play—if it was indeed staged for her at her residence in Ohlau in 1655, as the Using illustrations suggest.

Given these questions, it is important to remember that Gryphius himself did not require that the queen's torture be staged; indeed, he makes a point of having the splaying open of her body and the gory amputation of her breasts "merely" narrated in act 5 by the serving woman, Serena, who is herself said to have fainted at the sight of Catharine's agony, unable, like the audience of the play, to actually contemplate it at length (ll. 10–13 and 96–100). The text indicates that the shah was present in the torture chamber (l. 45), however; his ghoulish presence is accurately depicted by Using in one of his illustrations. The shah's inability to turn away from the sight of the queen's tormented body is significant, and yet also calls attention to the play's bizarre conclusion, in which he also experiences some kind of vision (ll. 345–48). In a replaying of the sequence of the original thorny-crown emblem dream, an apparition of the battered queen is spectacularly transformed into an angel in front of his eyes (ll. 375–400). It is not clear how this scene might actually have been staged. Using's engraving mistakenly shows the shah staring only at the posttransformation Catharine, and thus captures neither his horrified contemplation of her mutilated body, as it is called for in ten lines of explosive terror and lament (ll. 375–84), nor its (for him) equally terrifying transmutation into angelic form, which has the collateral effect of translating his earthly survival into a living psychic hell. The queen's transformation is reproduced, in other words, in him, yet in reverse, as her realistically implausible elevation into a state of eternal bliss in front of his eyes triggers his visible fall into madness and a lifetime of creaturely suffering not so very different from either the martyrdom she has endured or what Benjamin calls the "ensnarement of history" (G: 1.1: 320; E: 141–42) that marks her character. In other words, Using's image does not show the possible link between the state of both characters' existential realities and the state of their souls. Nor, perhaps more importantly, does it allow us to wonder, as Nicola Kaminski has done (104), what we are to make of the fact that the only character in this play able to complete a proper emblematic reading by seeing beyond the maimed body to its greater significance in a transcendent realm— namely the shah—does so only in a state of intense confusion, even insanity. Using's image thus supplies for the viewer what the reader or audience of Gryphius's play is prevented by the play itself from seeing, namely the redemption of the queen, which in the play text appears only as part of unreliable hallucination on the part of the shah.

Gryphius's play thematizes several times over the question of how the bodies of emblems and allegories, of queens and earthly suffering, are to be read properly, and, just as importantly, whether they can or cannot be used to point beyond or signify anything other than the realm of history on which they rely. Using's illustration of the torture scene, with the queen's body as the center of visual attention, runs counter to Gryphius's decision to have that body, in its most creaturely moment, indicated only in words, as if, emblematically speaking, Using thought it possible to supply only the *pictura*, the image, assuming that the audience would produce the "correct" *scriptura*, or motto, itself. Gryphius appears not to have been so sure. It is impossible to know why Using's illustrations supplied scenes not present in the play. (There has been no scholarly proof that the play was actually staged in Ohlau in any way that followed these prints.) Nevertheless, Using's supplements call attention to an important moment in Gryphius's play, namely the veering away of the text from having its audience actually contemplate the queen at her most creaturely, and thus from having to consider the depressing reality of her fall into despair as a formerly successful, but now dispossessed political animal and head of state. This is the lesson that Benjamin's remarks about emblematics in the *Tragic Drama* book indicate he may have learned from Gryphius's decision not to stage the torture scene. While it is clear, in other words, that Gryphius envelops the issue of the queen's body and its attendant historicity in the fulsome emblematic apparatus for which the play is so well known, this does not mean that he does not also subtly acknowledge in the serial glossing of the thorny-crown emblem precisely the difficulty, if not also the ultimate arbitrariness, of reading—and living—history allegorically in a Lutheran world, the very difficulty that Benjamin's discussion of Baroque emblematics reveals.

Benjamin attempts in the third chapter of the *Tragic Drama* book to distinguish between the much-prized symbolic thinking of German Classicism, the "idea" and its "appearance" as one, on the one hand; and what he calls the "movement between extremes," here the extremes of the "material" and the "transcendent," in the form of "expression" that was Baroque allegory as it was most "authentically" available in Baroque emblem books (G: 1.1: 339; E: 162), on the other. As arcane as Benjamin's distinction between symbol and allegory here may appear, what is at stake in this chapter emerges quite clearly when read through the lens of Gryphius's play, in which the "idea" of the concept of *constantia* is thrust up against the "appearance" of the historical example of the Georgian queen's suffering. Benjamin's theory of allegory also becomes clear when read in light of several of the scholarly sources from which he derived his understanding of emblematics, most prominently, Karl Giehlow's monumental study, "Die Hieroglyphenkunde des Humanismus in der Allegorie der Renaissance" (The Humanistic Study of Hieroglyphics in Renaissance Allegory), published in 1915. Warburg's "prognostication" essay, discussed above, was also important. Benjamin cites liberally from Giehlow's monograph-length essay, in which the scholar examines primary sources documenting the theories of Marsilio Ficino and others about hieroglyphic writing in the Renaissance, and tracks these theories as they migrated into the practice of the coterie of scholars and artists around Holy Roman Emperor Maximilian I, which included Albrecht Dürer. Giehlow is particularly interested in understanding the mostly Lutheran afterlives of the earlier Italian theories. We in turn see the afterlife of his work in other work on Dürer by the Warburgians that Benjamin knew, including Warburg's essay, as well as Panofsky's and Saxl's 1923 book on Dürer. Benjamin also cites two late seventeenth-century Latin-language reviews of Claude François Menestrier's 1682 *La philosophie des images* (The Philosophy of Images) in this section. His knowledge of both sixteenth- and seventeenth-century theoretical treatments of emblems derives from these sources, all with their respective confessional inflections (Lutheran and Jesuit). His deployment of them in his theory of allegory helps illuminate the choice that the Lutheran, Gryphius, made not to show the vivid image of the queen's broken body in his play, first of all because Gryphius was deeply knowledgeable about the tradition of Jesuit martyr plays, which prided themselves on the actual display of suffering, and second because of the precarious and unpredictable reactions real human beings might have when actually confronting such suffering in the world, as indicated by Giehlow and others.

As noted above, Benjamin's emblematic reading of the Lutheran Baroque begins with the claim with which he opens this chapter, that the "antinomies of the allegorical" dictate the "dialectical" character [of allegory], whereby "every person, every thing, every relation can mean absolutely anything else" (G: 1.1: 350; E: 174–75). That an object can mean something else is of course the essence of the *pictura-scriptura* relation in the emblem. In the process, "the profane world" can be "both elevated and devalued" (351; 175), Benjamin writes, since the *pictura* is necessary to, yet must ultimately be dissociated from its gloss if the greater insight is to be attained. Benjamin is primarily concerned here to explain what he calls the "Christian origin of the allegorical outlook" (394; 220). Yet he relies heavily on extensive quotations from Giehlow as well as his successors, Warburg, Panofsky, and Saxl, to explain the power, residually pagan and even demonic, that can accrue to "the material," "the physical," and "the elemental . . . creaturely" (400–2; 226–29) in the process of allegorization, a power that represents a potentially threatening force capable of blocking—even as it provokes and is necessary to—the Christian allegorist's project to move beyond the realm of facticity. The allegorist must do all he can to resist and triumph over precisely this creaturely force, in other words, precisely by submitting matter and the profane to signification. He does so, however, according to Benjamin, only via a process of brooding contemplation in dangerous imitation of the "rebellious, intense gaze of Satan" (403; 229).

This claim makes sense, first of all, since emblems were often used as part of the furniture of contemplative, and particularly religious, activity in the early modern period. More important, however, are the implications of Benjamin's claim that without "patient . . . meditation" the allegorist may be satanically tempted by the allurements of this life and thus not be able to get beyond the "things" that "in the simplicity of their essence . . . as enigmatic allegorical references . . . continue to be dust" (G: 1.1: 403; E: 229). If we consider Benjamin's words here in the light of the two kingdoms theory, they suggest how difficult it is to get beyond the parameters of Man's world. In the context of a Lutheran theory of emblems, what we see is the threatening suggestion that successful allegorical reading, which involves seeing beyond this world to God's, is in fact terribly difficult to perform, since "spiritual" meaning is often so deeply intertwined with "the material as its counterpart," a material facticity that can be "concretely experienced [only] through evil" (403; 230). The reader of emblems must first confront the emblematic *pictura* directly, allowing the possibility of being seduced by it; only after "patiently contemplating" it in this way can she couple the *pictura* with the signifying *scriptura,* or motto, that might redeem it. Referencing Gryphius's frame, the queen must first confront and perhaps even lament her (lost) crown as a sign of worldly sovereignty and accept that her creaturely life is a life that ultimately promises only death. Only after deep consideration can the crown and her life—and death—be left behind as objects of a redemptive reading. That this act of contemplation may be short-circuited or go awry triggers anxiety in Benjamin, which is clear from his association of it with the "satanic." The reasons for this anxiety are most fully expressed in the last several pages of the *Tragic Drama* book.

In order to avoid being seduced by the thingness of the profane, Benjamin writes, the allegorist must first engage deeply—and dangerously, as it turns out—with the world precisely in its "unashamed crudity" (G: 1.1: 405; E: 231) as "dust" (403; 229). This is the world as a "heap of ruins" he so famously describes as the "bleak confusion of Golgotha" (405; 232). It is only then, Benjamin asserts in the obscure locution noted above (its obscurity nods toward the shift in Benjamin's rhetoric and the emergence of his own anxiety here), that, like "those who stumble turn somersaults as they fall" (405; 232), readers of allegories (and emblems) may "in the most extreme . . . so . . . turn about that all . . . darkness, vainglory, and godlessness seems to be nothing but self-deception" (405; 232). Golgotha will only then be seen no longer as Golgotha, but rather as an "allegory of resurrection" (406; 232). It is by virtue—and yet, only by virtue—of this single and unexpected "about-turn," Benjamin writes, that "the immersion of allegory has to clear away the final phantasmagoria of the objective . . . [and] rediscovers itself . . . under heaven" (406; 232). He concludes: "This is the essence of melancholy immersion: that its ultimate objects, in which it believes it can most fully secure for itself that which is vile, turn into allegories, and these allegories fill out and deny the void in which they are represented, just as, ultimately, the intention does not faithfully rest in the contemplation of bones, but faithlessly leaps forward to the idea of resurrection" (406; 232–33). The unpredictability of this ironically "faithless" leap signals the ultimate helplessness of the melancholic Lutheran allegorist who, if he (or she) is radical enough, will see no way to gain any sure footing at all on any bridge between Man's and God's worlds.

Benjamin's allegorical theory, with the slippery connections between a profane world capable of being both "elevated" and "devalued" and that world's final meaning, echoes the way emblems function in Baroque tragic dramas like Gryphius's *Catharine of Georgia*. The "good allegorist," like the queen, will immerse herself deeply, like Warburg's Saturnine man, in objects, in the image, historical matter, and the world, yet have enough Jovian wherewithal to suddenly "turn about" to look at, but also beyond, the heavy matter of the creaturely, the object, the thing, beyond her kingdom and her maimed body, in other words, for its "soul," its "redemption" and significance, thus "denying the void," as Benjamin writes, of the "earthly world of things" (406; 232–33). The danger, however, and the threat—nearly inaudibly, yet persistently evident especially at the end of the *Tragic Drama* book—are that not everyone, and especially not all princes, will "turn around," but will remain gripped, rather, by this earthly world, by both its access to power and its corpses and creatureliness, and by the historical tragedy they repeatedly create and enact. This is precisely the realm that most consumed the playwrights of the Lutheran Baroque, as Benjamin clearly recognized, with their focus on not only the always prominent figure of the intriguer, but also the treacherous realm of the court, where the logic of the (in)famous state of exception rules, the space, that is, where the action of the Silesian plays inevitably transpires. Seen from the point of view of emblems, such a dwelling in the realm of the creature and the day-to-day would suggest a kind of short circuit of or at least resistance to the synergistic dialectic of allegory, a moment when it becomes difficult, if not impossible, for the reader or viewer to supply an effectively redeeming and world-transcending gloss to the all-absorbing realm of the *pictura*.

Salome's first reading of the thorny-crown emblem is itself somewhat paradoxically suggestive of this kind of short-circuited reading, since she glosses the crown of the dream as signifying no more than itself, namely earthly power, the pragmatics of which dominate the play. Salome reads for signification, but only in such a way as to lead back to the concrete "body" of the queen as it resides in the world of duplicitous advisers and pragmatic diplomats, rather than to a "beyond" of its more lofty significance and the redemption of Catharine's soul. This is an insight that only the crazed shah—and not the spectators of the play—is ultimately guaranteed. And if it is only the madman who actually sees the road to redemption, the rest of the world is trapped. Gryphius may have realized that he could not underscore any more vehemently the dominance of the realm of history, whose appeal was already obvious in the extended narrations of the queen's own pride in her political past, on the one hand, and in the odd dialogue between the Russian ambassador and the shah's lackey in act 5, on the other, which seems to culminate in the dismissal of the importance of the queen's ultimate sacrifice for the political players who survive her (ll. 341–44). If he displayed, in other words, the power of history to both break the queen's body and discount her suffering to viewers of the play like Duchess Luise, they might have found it too difficult to tear their eyes away from the spectacle of Catharine's creaturely defeat and thus too hard to continue believing in the possibility of the "turn" that would enable them to see the higher realm to which such suffering could lead. The sheer difficulty of allegorizing in the face of the pressures of the political world may have been the reason that Gryphius decided against showing the queen's torture on stage. Benjamin seems to have grasped this reasoning in his reading of the emblematics of broken bodies in the Baroque *Trauerspiel*.

Benjamin indicates quite clearly the extent to which controversies over religious dogma during the early modern period were a determining element of his understanding of allegorical theory. Gryphius was a devout Lutheran, all the more so as his birth family and place were decimated and destroyed early in the century by the forces of the Catholic Counter-Reformation. His appointment later in life as city advocate for Glogau, one of the main cities in what had been the predominantly Protestant area of Silesia, meant that he was primarily responsible for leading the tense negotiations with the central authority of the Catholic Habsburgs on behalf of the city. He was exceedingly active, in other words, in precisely the dangerous and bleak secular world of which Benjamin writes, defending local interests as the pressures of the greater power of the empire put a Counter-Reformation pincer grip on Silesia—an actor on a real-life political stage, in other words, not unlike the one depicted in his play *Catharine of Georgia*, in which the minority religion of the Christian queen is thrust into crass and unequal contact with the surrounding Muslim powers and crushed by them. Scholars have noted that Gryphius was heavily influenced, as were many of the "Lutheran" playwrights about whom Benjamin writes, by the Jesuit theater tradition and, in the case of Gryphius in particular, who spent his young adulthood in the multicultural city of Danzig, by the legacy of the order's spectacular martyr dramas (see Parente). At a very young age, for example, Gryphius translated one of the *Tragoediae sacrae* (Sacred Tragedies) of the French Jesuit Nicolaus Caussinus, *Felicitas,* whose near-martyr plot anticipates that of his own later, independent Catharine play. *Catharine of Georgia* captures just this rich, yet also highly combustible cultural and confessional mix in, among other things, the way it just barely swerves away from requiring a display of Catharine's ruined body in the text. It thus problematizes the question of how representations—and in this case, literal stagings—of martyrdom might be received in a melancholic Lutheran world. Was one to believe in the higher meaning of such a death as a matter of faith, or realize that only madmen dare to make such a leap?

Gryphius's play draws attention to the vexed status of what Benjamin calls the "norms of emblematics" (G: 1.1: 391; E: 217) and whether or not it was possible to live with and by them in a Lutheran world. In the French source text, for example, Catharine undergoes an eleventh-hour conversion from an icon-loving Orthodox Christian to a good Catholic, since only an Augustinian monk is there to give her death rites. The charred head, which is referenced in Gryphius's play, as noted above, goes on to become, in the French source, a relic and the cause for the founding of an Augustinian church in predominantly Orthodox Georgia. In Gryphius's version, which otherwise follows its source in excruciating detail, the head survives, but it is understandably not elevated into a relic in this "Lutheran" play. The power of the body part to either perform or provoke an act of conversion may have been strategically suppressed, or, if that is too strong, then avoided precisely because of the Lutheran Gryphius's doubt that "things" should be taken so easily to stand in for, to signify, or to coexist, in some kind of symbolic embrace, with higher versions of themselves. In spite of the emblematic cocoon that surrounds the Catharine play, then, and on which most scholars have focused, there remains the nagging suspicion that the extremes to which the playwright must go to show, or not to show, that her cruel suffering has a point, indicate—after the fashion of the nonresolution of the two readings of the emblem of the thorny crown—that the jury was still out on the possibility of reading the allegory of suffering on the queen's part in any ultimately (self-) redeeming way. Benjamin seems to have understood and accepted this possibility. His reading of the "brutal stage" of "Lutheran" Baroque drama in any case itself functions well as an allegory of modern Germany's blocked path to redemption.

CONCLUSION

Baroque Legacies: National Socialism's Benjamin

The preface to *Benjamin's Library* began with a quote from Benjamin's essay "Literary History and the Study of Literature" (1931). I repeat that quote below because of its aptness as an introduction to the discordant image called up by the title of my conclusion, in which I discuss a particularly uncanny afterlife for Benjamin's Baroque. This post-Benjaminian version of the Baroque resonates uneasily, however, with some of the same issues that he addresses in the *Tragic Drama* book, namely the ability of "works," both literal Baroque texts and the ideas associated with them, to play a role in arguments about modernity and the nation. As for Benjamin, so also in this example, the story told about the Baroque relies on narratives about national cultural renewal that are deployed in a context that may seem counterintuitive to some. The invocation of Benjamin in direct association with the political and social movement of National Socialism, which might well be said to have caused his death, nevertheless reveals a great deal about the importance of taking periodization claims seriously whenever they occur.

In the essay "Literary History and the Study of Literature," we will remember, Benjamin describes contemporary literary historians as mercenary soldiers, who, entering a house full of treasures and claiming to admire its contents, in fact "do not give a damn for the order and inventory of the house," for they "have moved in [only] because it is strategically situated and because it is a convenient vantage point from which to bombard a railway or bridgehead whose defense is important in the civil war" (Benjamin, *Selected Writings* 2: 461–62). The jarring thought that there was a "National Socialist Benjamin" may appear to be no more than a further strategic maneuver of this sort. It is designed, however, to be deliberately provocative, indeed, to disrupt the history of Benjamin reception with which we have become familiar, by tracing the ghostly presence of Benjamin's "Baroque book" in Nazi-sponsored texts. In these texts, Benjamin's ideas are neatly, although sometimes quite covertly, inscribed in both the footnotes and otherwise apparently marginal places in the textual apparatus, such as bibliographies and notes, as well as in the very terminology (Bollenbeck's "semantic stockpiles," 5) and methodologies deployed. The discovery of the subterranean presence of the work of a German Jew, who killed himself on the Spanish border in 1940 rather than be taken prisoner by the Gestapo, in Party-approved and, in some cases, even Party-sponsored scholarship beginning in the 1930s and as late as 1941, is nevertheless not overtly opportunistic in the ways Benjamin's original image suggests. All the same, it is revealing of how books create their own histories in the ways I have been suggesting throughout.

One might explain—or explain away—the afterlife of Benjamin's Baroque in Nazi-era scholarship by asserting that this scholarship merely kidnapped occasional Benjaminian insights, and, discarding their Jewish author as an inconvenience, integrated snippets of his ideas into the nationalist and often anti-Semitic rewritings of German literary history that flowed from the presses of the Reich after 1933. But there may have been something more than sporadic pilfering at work here. Indeed, what the labyrinth of direct and indirect citations of Benjamin's work in post-1933 German texts reveals is that there seems to have been something quite acceptable in Benjamin's thought to at least some Party-identified scholars, which, like many involved in intellectual labor from the late 1920s through the early 1940s in German literary studies (*Germanistik*) in general and in German Baroque literary studies in particular, had its origins in the late nineteenth-century and early twentieth-century academic and disciplinary debates that I have traced here. That Benjamin's ideas about the Baroque are present in texts identified with National Socialism at some important methodological and ideological as well as semantic levels serves as an illustration of what Wilhelm Voßkamp ("Deutsche Barockforschung"), building on the important work of Hans-Harald Müller (*Barockforschung*), has designated as precisely the *absence* of a "break in continuity" between studies of the Baroque of this earlier period and those of the Nazi years. Voßkamp argues that while some of the "institutional assumptions" of German literary studies of course changed after 1933 ("Deutsche Barockforschung" 699), certain methodological and "theoretical academic" premises did not (702).[1] The discovery in post-1933 Nazi

---

1. Voßkamp's claims about "continuity" need to be assessed carefully against the work of Jaumann, on which Voßkamp relies. Jaumann (*Die deutsche Barockliteratur*) argues that Baroque studies in the 1920s and 1930s experienced a significant "re-evaluation," which is particularly visible in the work of Benjamin on the Baroque tragic drama.

scholarship on the Baroque of both Benjamin's work and ideas that it shared with work on the Baroque from the 1910s and 1920s confirms Voßkamp's point—which was indirectly Benjamin's point too when he defined "origin" as a combination of pre- and posthistories caught in the complex eddies of history. The Nazi contributions to Baroque studies in which his work appears thus themselves function as "witnesses" to the survival of Benjamin's ideas in material form—in spite of the efforts of the Party, to which their authors had in many cases declared outright allegiance, to silence him and other German-Jewish scholars once and for all.

Disrupting the specific claim that has insinuated itself with great vigor into most understandings of Benjamin's work—a claim that the dean of the original generation of Benjamin scholars, T. W. Adorno, was perhaps the first to make in his 1955 edition of some of Benjamin's essays, namely that Benjamin's "name had been repressed in and by the public German consciousness since 1933" (ix)—allows us, first of all, to see that Adorno's assertion was quite simply not true. In addition to some eight reviews of the *Tragic Drama* book between 1928 and 1936, which Uwe Steiner first noted in his 1989 essay, "Allegorie und Allergie," Benjamin's work on the Baroque drama also made its way discretely, yet unmistakably, into the textual interstices of several high-profile, Party-approved texts in subsequent years.[2] This reception was possible because some of what Benjamin claimed to be doing in his book, including his celebration of a specifically German tradition of Baroque texts, accorded methodologically and substantively quite well with Nazi-inflected literary-historical claims. The overlaps are thus understandable, as they frequently drank from the same sources. Indeed, it is part of the broader irony of what some might consider the disturbing proximity of Benjamin's and National Socialism's Baroques that precisely that which they shared also seems to have allowed Party-identified scholars to dedicate considerable effort to finding a place in the literary-historical canon for a period that may have seemed to have been as odd a candidate for absorption into a National Socialist literary-historical agenda as Benjamin himself. Showing not only where Benjamin appeared, but also what in the "inventory" of the shared domain of his and National Socialism's assessments of the Baroque allowed for this apparently alarming cohabitation, is my subject here. The effect that listening more closely to Nazi-sponsored texts as unexpected "witnesses" to an odd afterlife for Benjamin's Baroque might have in recuperating a more nuanced genealogy and history of the reception of his work in general should be obvious. Instead of continuing the hagiographic enterprise begun by Adorno, we can reinsert Benjamin into the continuum of the time out of which his work emerged. Just as importantly, examining the afterlives of Benjamin's book in

---

2. For an earlier discussion of the reception of Benjamin's book, see Jaumann, *Die deutsche Barock-literatur* 570–76. Jaumann (576) nevertheless agrees with Adorno that the *Tragic Drama* book failed to get a "critical" reception until after Adorno's 1955 publication of the two-volume Benjamin edition. See also Garber, *Rezeption und Rettung* 59–81.

National Socialist work on the Baroque opens a window onto the politics of literary history and periodization during the Nazi years by asking us to track not just how illustrious single authors, such as Goethe and even Shakespeare, were translated into figures of National Socialist pride, but also the extent to which period theorization often accommodates itself to political pressure, circumstance, and change.[3]

In his fascinating history of the footnote, Tony Grafton points to a serious consideration of footnotes as one way to begin to reclaim "those parts of history which lie beneath ground level," the "hidden cracks and forgotten conduits" of historical and political knowledge transmission (6). While this observation has lain at the heart of my discussion of Benjamin's *Tragic Drama* book throughout this book, here it is a short footnote in a post-1945 book about German Baroque drama by the well-known Germanist and scholar of the Baroque Albrecht Schöne that is particularly interesting in this respect. At the end of the brief introductory chapter of his now famous 1964 book, *Emblematik und Drama im Zeitalter des Barock* (Emblematics and Drama in the Age of the Baroque), Schöne notes that Baroque emblematics is "a nearly submerged continent, concerning which only a very few specialists have engaged in reconnaissance" (14). While Schöne is the coauthor of the spectacular encyclopedia of early modern emblems that he compiled with Arthur Henkel in 1967, it was his earlier, 1964 *Emblematics and Drama* that first took up the challenge of exploring this "Atlantis" of Baroque figures and texts, a challenge unaddressed, Schöne claims in the footnote that accompanies his claim, since the 1946 review of the literature by Henri Stegemeier; "since that time," the note reads, "hardly anything has changed." The main text above then proceeds to outline the dimensions of the mid-twentieth-century voyage of discovery that Schöne will undertake. A second, final footnote to these opening remarks stands out for both its content and its placement as the last word on the page. It reads: "Walter Benjamin was the first to draw our attention to these kinds of connections; let me especially underscore here [the importance of] his treatise on the 'origin of the mourning play' (1928; cf. bibliography, no. 99)."

There is much to ponder about Schöne's notes. For one thing, why does he get the title of Benjamin's book wrong—leaving out the crucial adjective "German"? Just as substantively, what is the significance of the literal subordination of Benjamin's inaugural study of emblematics in 1928 to Schöne's own 1964 project on this page? Placed so as to seem quite literally marginal to the main argument, one might overlook that, as Baroque scholar Gerhard Spellerberg observed just six years later, Schöne's understanding of the significance of emblematics throughout

---

3. Barner ("Literaturgeschichtsschreibung") provides excellent data about the persistence of a variety of literary-historical schemas from the Nazi period well into the post-1945 period. Schools and introductory university curricula were particularly impacted by the discourses of literary history as they were formulated in overview volumes and handbooks, which in many cases found their origins in the 1933–45 years.

his book is heavily indebted to, indeed literally supported by, Benjamin's prior work (see below). Of greater interest, however, than Schöne's curious masking in 1964 of his reliance on Benjamin's earlier insights into Baroque emblematics is the implicit historical location that Schöne wants to give his own book by placing it, in the first note, in relationship to texts that appeared in 1928 (Benjamin) and 1946 (Stegemeier), respectively, for these dates silently mark—even as they elide—the very fact of World War II and the impact it had on the scholarly community in Germany. By refusing to mention National Socialism—and indeed, that the author of the "first" treatment of Baroque emblematics and drama had in fact died as a result of the Nazi regime—Schöne effectively disappears the location and historical context of Benjamin's book along with its focus on that which was decidedly "German." Schöne thus fails to take a stance here—as he actually did in subsequent publications—on the relationship between the disciplinary history of German literary studies and the National Socialist machine (see Schöne, *Göttinger Bücherverbrennung*).

Spellerberg, who was the one to point out Schöne's reliance on Benjamin, nevertheless himself engaged in a similar politics of elision several years later in a footnote in *Verhängnis und Geschichte* (Fate and History) (1970), his monumental study of the work of one of the Silesian Baroque playwrights, Daniel Casper von Lohenstein. Like the plays of Gryphius, Lohenstein's dramas figured prominently in Benjamin's *Tragic Drama* book, to which Spellerberg explicitly refers in his study. His reception of Benjamin nevertheless distorts the context in a way similar to Schöne's. As he works his way through the secondary literature on Lohenstein, for example, Spellerberg refers approvingly to "modern and very contemporary Baroque Studies" (12–13), among which he includes the work of both Benjamin and Schöne, as well as of one Erik Lunding, who had published an important book on Silesian Baroque drama in 1940. By setting these three scholars, publishing in 1928, 1940, and 1964, and thus during the prewar, wartime, and postwar periods respectively, into a kind of timeless dialogue with one another in an unglossed way, Spellerberg silences the astounding differences between them and between the various epochs of scholarship on the Baroque they represent. In the process, he seems, like Schöne, and perhaps for some of the same complex reasons, to forget history, specifically the history of Germany and German Baroque studies between 1928 and 1967, particularly when he refers to the Benjamin of the 1928 *Tragic Drama* book as a contemporary of Erik Lunding. Lunding's book on Silesian drama was published, ironically, in the very same year that Benjamin took his own life. In Spellerberg's mind, Benjamin is a contemporary of Lunding as well as of Schöne in a kind of timeless and ideologically uninvested academic realm.[4]

---

4. For a similar politics of historical elision in the annotational and dedicatory apparatus of a 1953 edition of Lohenstein's plays, see Newman, *Intervention of Philology* 167–69.

This constellation of footnotes and of the scholarship to which they refer is not at all timeless or neutral, however. Rather, it is part of the discourse of Baroque studies in postwar, indeed, Cold War West Germany that, like much of the rest of German literary studies, relied for survival on eliding the years between 1933 and 1945.[5] The Schöne-Spellerberg examples do allow access to the world of National Socialism indirectly, however, via Spellerberg's reference to the "third man" and other interlocutor in these only superficially marginal conversations about Benjamin—namely Erik Lunding. Lunding may or may not have been something of an academic anomaly in war-torn Europe. A Dane who earned his doctoral degree in Copenhagen in 1939 with the thesis version of his book on the Silesian Baroque, Lunding did the research for his dissertation in Germany and greater Germany, so to speak, between 1936 and 1939, specifically in Munich, Berlin, and Graz. He would probably not have been immune to National Socialist propaganda or to the winds of anti-Semitism either in Germany or in Denmark, which was finally occupied in the fall of 1940. It may have been for this reason that he does not discuss the work of a Jewish scholar, namely Benjamin, directly in his book on the very same plays that had so fascinated Benjamin a little over a decade earlier.

Despite the overt absence of Benjamin in Lunding's 1940 book, he *is* nevertheless there, both literally and somewhat more abstractly, buried deep in Lunding's bibliography (207), for example, but also and more importantly, woven throughout the argument and texture of the book. The uncanny resemblances between Lunding's and Benjamin's arguments about the Baroque tragic drama include chapter epigraphs in Lunding from Calderón and from London's Globe Theater, traditionally associated with Shakespeare; as noted above, these two non-German playwrights figure prominently in Benjamin's book as, ironically, the authors of the best examples of the Baroque *Trauerspiel*. Lunding is fascinated, moreover, with the concepts and genres of the "martyr drama" (14) and the "drama of fate" (78), which are likewise central to Benjamin's study. Finally, Lunding discusses the indebtedness of the German tragic drama not to ancient Greek tragedy, but to medieval forms and ideas (passim), and highlights the figures of the tyrant (96) and the courtly intriguer that fills the plays (127–28) too. He also taxonomizes the world of the Baroque according to its investments in competing visions of immanence and transcendence (61 and 161). It is difficult not to hear echoes of Benjamin's 1928 *Tragic Drama* book here as well. Indeed, looking at Lunding's bibliography, one could be forgiven for thinking that he may have begun researching his thesis in the footnotes to Benjamin's earlier study of precisely the same plays. In much the same way, then, as Benjamin seems to have been reborn in the post–World War II era in the interstices of Albrecht Schöne's 1964 study of the emblem, Benjamin spoke

---

5. On the tendency of post-1945 work to reach back for its own origins to the pre-1933 period, see Barner, "Literaturgeschichtsschreibung" passim, but esp. 125.

to Germanists in wartime Europe from between the lines of Lunding's text. As it turns out, Lunding's 1940 study of the Second Silesian school of drama was quite highly regarded by Nazi-identified Baroque scholars in subsequent years.

In 1941, an immense five-volume German literary history was issued by the Kohlhammer Publishing House in Stuttgart and Berlin. Entitled *Von deutscher Art in Sprache und Dichtung* (The German Way in Language and Poetry), the project had been developed the year before in Weimar at the "Kriegseinsatztagung deutscher Hochschulgermanisten" (Wartime Mobilization Conference of German University Germanists), a meeting called by three prominent professors of German literary studies. One of these scholars, Gerhard Fricke of Kiel University, is especially central to understanding the startling presence of Benjamin's book on the tragic drama in work written or approved of by Nazi-identified scholars. The volumes of *The German Way* contain some forty essays, most of them written specially for the collection, by leading scholars of German literature from the medieval period to the present. The project was dedicated, according to an announcement in *Zeitschrift für deutsche Bildung* (Journal for German Education) 16 (1940), to promoting the "cultural and political ethos of National Socialism."[6] In volume 3 of *The German Way,* Professor Willi Flemming of Rostock weighs in with an essay entitled "Die deutsche Seele des Barocks" (The German Soul of the Baroque) that drips with National Socialist rhetoric about "the German man" of the period and about the "drive" or "will" of Germans to "create" and "achieve" (173).

If we listen carefully to Flemming's analysis, we hear a curious dialogue going on between the lines of the Party-sponsored harangue. Like Lunding, Flemming develops a series of arguments that appear to be nothing short of a kind of commentary on Benjamin's theses about the Baroque. This ghostly debate includes Flemming's interest, again, so similar to Benjamin's, in the courtly "intriguer" (190) and the "feeling of fate" (186), as well as in "Shakespeare" and "the Spanish" (198), albeit in order to highlight—as was appropriate for the volume in which the essay appeared—the "specifically German realization of a more general European phenomenon" (175). (It should be noted here that in his article on Grimmelshausen's Simplicissimus "as a German persona," also in volume 3 of *The German Way,* the well-known Germanist Julius Petersen makes a similar argument on behalf of German exceptionalism; Petersen's contribution also dialogues eerily with Benjamin's book, especially when he examines the place of eschatology, "creatureliness," and an Ulrician Christian redemptionist frame in the worldview of the Baroque.)[7] The covert conversation with Benjamin in which Flemming appears to be most engaged finds further articulation in a polemic against seeing the period of the German Baroque as a period of "decadence," a period "devalued as a degenerate

---

6. As cited in Barner, "Literaturgeschichtsschreibung" 144 n. 12.
7. See Petersen, esp. 213.

Renaissance" (171). These are of course the very terms in which Benjamin, follow-ing both Heinrich Wölfflin and Alois Riegl, discusses the period of the Baroque both at the end of the "Epistemo-Critical Prologue" and throughout the beginning of the second chapter of his book, as discussed in chapter 1.[8] It would be nearly im-possible to do more than conjecture about what access Flemming might have had to Benjamin's 1928 book, since, like other contributors to the 1941 Party-sponsored volume, Flemming apparently recognized that the purpose of the project was not to make a substantial scholarly contribution, but rather to co-opt literary history in the name of the *Volk*. He thus did not annotate his article in any detail. Neverthe-less, it could be argued that, in an odd kind of call-and-response format, it was Benjamin's readings that gave shape to Flemming's claims. Moreover, at the very end of the essay, in something that *looks* like a footnote, even if it is not one, Flem-ming remarks: "There is no need for a bibliography here, as Erich Trunz recently published a reliable overview of most of the important publications since 1924 in *Deutsche Vierteljahrsschrift für Literaturwissenschaft und Geistesgeschichte* [The Ger-man Quarterly for Literary Studies and *Geistesgeschichte*], number 18, 1940, Essay Volume, pages 1–100" (199). Here, in the margins of Flemming's article and in the reference to Trunz, more hidden conduits of National Socialism's access to Benja-min come into view.

Erich Trunz's 1940 overview of scholarship on the German Baroque, "Die Er-forschung der deutschen Barockdichtung: Ein Bericht über Ergebnisse und Auf-gaben" (The Study of German Baroque Poetry: A Report on [Scholarly] Results and Tasks Still to Be Done), is one hundred pages long, too long for an article pub-lication today, and extreme even for the time. Perhaps its overt investment in the rhetoric and ideology of National Socialism guaranteed its appearance. As embar-rassing as it apparently had been for them, the editors of the *German Quarterly* had already begun in 1935 to follow Nazi cultural policy by encouraging their authors to "eliminate *Jew.* authors as much as possible."[9] In his piece, Trunz, now remem-bered as a major scholar of German Classicism, does the editors of the journal one better and in fact mentions the work of one important "Jewish" scholar, Arnold Hirsch, by name, but only in order to condemn it. Hirsch's work is contaminated by "the old materialist class theory," Trunz reports ("Die Erforschung" 79), a meth-odological (and indeed, political) failing perhaps typical of his race. The bulk of the essay goes on to endorse a National Socialist platform, reporting in exhaustive and exhausting detail on all scholarship on the period published since 1924, and

---

8. Flemming's description of the place of melancholy in the Baroque ("Die deutsche Seele" 185) nevertheless casts it specifically not as part of a Stoic inheritance, nor as "ataraxia as a kind of phlegmatic behavior," which is how Benjamin had characterized the melancholics of the Baroque in his chapter on melancholy in the *Tragic Drama* book. Rather, Warburg-like, Flemming sees in Baroque melancholy a curious kind of "self assertion" (185).

9. Qtd. in Dainat, "Wir müssen ja trotzdem weiter arbeiten" 78.

cataloging the various treatments of the Baroque primarily on the basis of whether or not they demonstrate that "a striving of an essentially German kind" (2) was essential to the period. Good poetry, such as that to be found in Baroque hymns, for example, is good because it is the forerunner of trends that are emerging "today in poetry, particularly in hymnic poetry," that, like traditional hymns, deals with set themes such as "the *Führer,* soldiers, the war dead, the blessing of the farmers, the symphony of work, mothers, youth, the festivals of the *Volk,* etc." (45). There can obviously be no overt place for Benjamin's work here. Yet Trunz does refer to a somewhat earlier bibliographic study of scholarship on the Baroque as "an indispensable aid" for his own study (25). Hans Pyritz's "Bibliographie zur deutschen Barockliteratur" (Bibliography of Work on German Baroque Literature), which was published as an appendix to Paul Hankamer's *Deutsche Gegenreformation und deutsches Barock* (The German Counter-Reformation and the German Baroque) (1935), is "fundamental for all research." Pyritz's bibliography was some thirty pages in length and is far more schematic than Trunz's, although not as "entirely independent of Hankamer's account, which appeared at the same time" as Trunz would have liked ("Die Erforschung" 25).[10] In the present context, what is crucial to note is that Benjamin's *Tragic Drama* book *is* listed by Pyritz with little fanfare (499), and yet also in a somewhat prominent place as the first entry under "The Individual Forms: *Mourning Play.*" In the margins of the margins, then, Benjamin makes a center-stage appearance in Trunz's Party-line work.

Earlier on in Trunz's article, moreover, one of the founders of the "new" Baroque studies is named (5–7). He is Herbert Cysarz, who, as Peter Becher has shown, by 1938 had become "a leader [*Führer*] of the folk-ishly predisposed intelligentsia of the Sudetenland and [thus] a supporter of National Socialism" (292) at the German University in Prague (the Czech Charles University was closed soon thereafter on 17 November 1939, some eight months after the occupation of the city).[11] It is no surprise that Trunz spotlights Cysarz as the inaugurator of the new way in his review, for Trunz had been named as Cysarz's successor in Prague after the latter had departed to take over the chair of his doctoral adviser, Walter Brecht, at the university in Munich in 1938–39. Trunz was already at Prague when his piece in the *German Quarterly* appeared in 1940.[12] Cysarz, whose work Benjamin of course also knew and cited no fewer than eleven times in the *Tragic Drama* book (see chapter 1), is one of the central figures in Trunz's nationalist argument in his "Study of German Baroque Poetry." Cysarz was the author not only of the 1924 *Deutsche*

---

10. Pyritz's bibliographic inventory follows Hankamer's chapter headings exactly. By 1940, Trunz was clearly attempting to downplay Party member Pyritz's earlier relationship to his doctoral adviser, Hankamer, who had been relieved of his position in 1935–36. On Hankamer's political "crime" of "un-German Catholicism," see Harms.

11. See Glettler 15.

12. On Trunz, see Kunisch.

Barockdichtung (German Baroque Poetry), on which Benjamin relies quite heavily
in places, but also of a plethora of works reeking of the kind of localist boosterism
presaged by the early twentieth-century work of Josef Nadler, who had discussed
the Baroque in the third volume of his *Literaturgeschichte der deutschen Stämme und
Landschaften* (Literary History of the German Tribes and Regions), published in
1918; Nadler is showcased along with Cysarz by Trunz ("Die Erforschung" 5–7)
in 1940, and had been cited by Benjamin as well.[13] Cysarz's 1938 *Deutsche Front im
Südosten: Fünf sudetendeutsche Reden* (The German Front in the Southeast: Five
Sudeten-German Speeches) was published, as Cysarz notes in the foreword, in "the
first year of the Sudeten-German era, the year of the birth of Greater Germany";
in his subsequent book, *Das deutsche Schicksal im deutschen Schrifttum* (German
Fate in German Literature) (1942), Cysarz gives this same "Greater Germany" top
billing as having been "Europe's wartime stage," also in an earlier era of conflict,
namely the seventeenth century of the Baroque (25).

Along with Cysarz, Trunz highlights the contributions to recent Baroque
studies of two additional scholars, namely Gerhard Fricke, lead editor of the
five-volume *The German Way in Language and Poetry* (Trunz, "Die Erforschung"
55–57), and the Dane Erik Lunding. Trunz laments in a footnote-like addendum
at the very end of his article (99–100) that Lunding's 1940 book had become available to him too late to be dealt with in detail; the study is nevertheless incredibly
"fresh" (100) and clearly presented. Indeed, in its promise for the future of German
Baroque studies, Trunz concludes, Lunding's book resembles no work so much as
Fricke's 1933 *Die Bildlichkeit in der Dichtung des Andreas Gryphius* (Pictorial Language in the Work of Andreas Gryphius), a book that Trunz had already described
as "one of the best pieces of research in Baroque Studies overall" (57). Trunz notes
that Fricke's book is especially useful because of its treatment of the subject of emblematics, which is, Trunz writes, "a vast and still entirely unresearched field" (43).
The irony of this claim could not be more apparent, appearing as it does in an
article published in 1940, the very year in which the author of the "first" (or at least
a very early) study of the emblematic culture of the Baroque, namely Benjamin,
committed suicide. Trunz's specialist readers at the time surely would have noticed
the oversight, since Fricke, in the 1933 book so celebrated in Trunz's essay, writes
at great length about the relationship of symbol to allegory, of martyrs and melancholy, and of tragedy and the tragic drama, as well as about emblems, mysticism,
and the Kabbalah. Here, he echoes no one so clearly as Benjamin, whose "Baroque
book" dealing with precisely these issues had appeared five years earlier. The parallels are not surprising, since, in his 1933 book, Fricke, not yet practicing the ex-
clusionary scholarly methods that were to become so popular in the coming years,

13. On Nadler, see Jaumann 401–5. Benjamin cites Nadler in the *Tragic Drama* book, albeit volume 2 rather than volume 3 of the work.

actually cites Benjamin's 1928 work quite straightforwardly, just as Pyritz was to do in 1935. Had Trunz read Fricke, as he surely did, it would have been difficult to claim that Baroque allegory and emblematics were still completely "unresearched," for, according to Fricke's footnote on pages 264–65 (n. 3), Benjamin has done the pathbreaking work on the topic in his "energetic, smart, and stimulating work," which, although unfortunately written in a "sibylline" language and style, shows "very emphatically" that allegory is the "constitutive factor of Baroque aesthetics." Although present by name only here and in one other footnote (Fricke 199 n. 7), Benjamin is thus one of the important ghosts in the machine of Fricke's much-lauded book.

In the same fateful year that Fricke's study of Gryphius was published, namely 1933, he also made a major speech at the Nazi book-burning in the university town of Göttingen and was much feted for it. This speech, along with the *Pictorial Language* book, which contained such high praise of Benjamin's work, ironically appears to have created enough visibility for Fricke to make him a candidate for the lead editor spot on the Party-sponsored project of *The German Way* that appeared eight years hence. Gudrun Schnabel has described the extent of Fricke's "devotion to the Party" during the National Socialist period, yet also his successful "de-Nazification" (73) and "confession" of his Nazi-identified past in front of his students in Cologne in 1965. Schnabel's remark that Fricke never fails to be mentioned as "an exemplary case of National Socialist literary criticism" (84) nevertheless highlights the ways in which the historiography of the disciplines under National Socialism tends to underestimate the complexities of the practice of scholarship at the time. In 1941, and thus at the height of the "wartime mobilization" of literary-historical scholarship, Willi Flemming was able to cite Erich Trunz, who in turn celebrated Pyritz, Cysarz, Lunding, and Fricke, as completely acceptable. Fricke, Lunding, and Pyritz nevertheless had all endorsed Benjamin's work and cited it in both discrete and overt ways between 1933 and 1940. Cysarz and Benjamin appeared in their publications from 1924 and 1928, respectively, to have been devoting attention to many of the same ideas and to have cited similar sources, and Lunding, in 1940, seems to have relied on Benjamin's earlier readings of the Silesian tradition as well. Upon closer examination, uneasy continuity after uneasy continuity emerges into view.

At first sight, it might seem surprising that, in 1933, the soon-to-be enthusiastic Party-men Fricke and Pyritz could openly cite the Jewish Walter Benjamin's "energetic" work on the Baroque, and that Lunding in 1940 could more discretely and Trunz perhaps even inadvertently follow their lead. Yet we must consider that, even though Benjamin withdrew the manuscript from consideration as his *Habilitation* by the academic authorities at Frankfurt in 1925, he quickly went on to make arrangements to publish it; the appearance of *The Origin of the German Tragic Drama* in Berlin in 1928 was, as few scholars have noted, facilitated first and foremost by Walter Brecht, the Germanist in Vienna, who had been the doctoral adviser of Herbert Cysarz, whose work was so celebrated by Trunz. Brecht read Benjamin's manuscript and forwarded it to Hugo von Hofmannsthal, who published parts of it in his journal, *Neue deutsche Beiträge* (New German Essays), in 1927. Hofmannsthal subsequently recommended Benjamin's thesis to the publishing house of Rowohlt in Berlin, where it was finally published the following year. Thereafter, although Benjamin complained about the failure of anyone from the Warburg circle, for example, to review the *Tragic Drama* book, it was reviewed prominently at least nine times. There is therefore good reason to suspect that other scholars of the Baroque would have at least known about it, if not also read it with care. Of these nine reviews, only seven are listed by the editors of the Frankfurt edition of Benjamin's works on which most scholars rely. The omissions are significant, for as lukewarm as several of the seven are about the complex work, thus allowing for an argument to be made about the rejection of Benjamin's ideas by an either already or incipiently anti-Semitic (or perhaps merely uninspired) academy, the two other reviews appeared in reputable and widely circulated professional journals and signal a positive reception of Benjamin's work. They also reveal what kinds of discursive and methodological factors might have allowed his approach to fit well with subsequent Nazi approaches to the Baroque.

In 1930, Günther Müller, a prominent scholar of German literature and subsequent Nazi Party member, captures the significance of Benjamin's book quite precisely in his review entitled "Neue Arbeiten zur deutschen Barockliteratur" (Recent Works on German Baroque Literature) in the *Zeitschrift für deutsche Bildung* (Journal for German Education). Müller notes that the *Tragic Drama* book is more of a "philosophical treatise" (332) than a book of scholarship and writes that a "critical assessment" of Benjamin's contribution to the field of Baroque studies would exceed the review genre, indeed, would itself require "a second book." Nevertheless, Müller states that it is "without question" that Benjamin "could enrich German Baroque Studies with important categories" (332). Readers of the review in 1930 would have thus clearly been steered in the direction of Benjamin's work. Six years later, Robert Petsch of Hamburg is able, in his review article entitled "Drama und Theater: Ein Forschungsbericht, 1920–1935" (Drama and Theater: The State of Research, 1920–1935), which appeared in the *Deutsche Vierteljahrsschrift für Literaturwissenschaft und Geistesgeschichte* (German Quarterly for Literary Scholarship and *Geistesgeschichte*) (1936), to devote nearly half a page to Benjamin's "challenging" book, with its analyses of allegory, emblematics, treatment of "fortuna," and so on (613–14). The half-page summary may seem worth the oblivion into which it then fell; that Benjamin's book finds a place at all in an article that ranges for more than a hundred pages over the terrain of Aristotle studies, production studies, and much, much more, is astounding nevertheless. As interesting as he finds Benjamin's work, however, what Petsch does not like in the book is significant, namely that it tends to wander over disciplinary lines into the neighboring discourse of "art criticism" (614). Petsch's and Müller's reviews signal that there is no question that Benjamin's book on the Baroque could still be read and openly cited as late as 1936. Because of this reception, it is not surprising that he appears in the margins of Nazi-sponsored work up through 1941. Moreover, it may have been precisely the discipline-related and methodological factors to which Petsch objected that allowed it to survive when its author did not.

Petsch's comment about Benjamin's *Tragic Drama* book in his article in the *German Quarterly* in 1936 points the way to an initial understanding of the acceptability of Benjamin's ideas, if not of his person, to Baroque studies in the Nazi period. As "challenging" as Petsch finds Benjamin's work, he does not like it when Benjamin strays into the domain of "art criticism." Petsch's objection to this kind of scholarly interdisciplinarity opens a window onto the conceptual world in which we have already seen that Benjamin moved, a world in which his ideas and those of subsequent Nazi academic elites appear to have been able to coexist when they shared, in the first place, a vocabulary and an approach to the Baroque still indebted to the originally Wölfflinian distinction between the Renaissance and the Baroque. In the *Tragic Drama* book, Benjamin found himself in agreement about this issue with Riegl, who had been one of the first to defend the radically historicist position that "artistic value was relative," and thus that the Baroque was as worthy of consideration as the Renaissance or classicism or, indeed, any period not traditionally defined as having "attained artistic supremacy" over others.[14] For a discipline like literary history in its National Socialist form, such relativism was crucial, as it allowed the German "will" to have found continuous expression in literature over time. Indeed, it was this very logic of continuity that drove the five-volume project of *The German Way* in 1941. Concepts like Riegl's on periodization, which Benjamin shared, were thus fundamental to Nazi literary history.

But it was also Riegl's contribution to the related art historical and methodological debate about what Michael Jennings has described as "a coherent theory of the historical determination of the cultural object" that was meaningful for both parties ("Walter Benjamin" 77). In his curriculum vitae of 1928, the same year in which the *Tragic Drama* book appeared, Benjamin describes his debt in his study of the dramas of the Second Silesian school to Riegl as well as to another and very problematic thinker, namely the legal theorist Carl Schmitt, in the following way:

> This task, one that I had already undertaken on a larger scale in *The Origin of the German Tragic Drama,* was linked on the one hand to the methodological ideas of Alois Riegl, especially his doctrine of the "artistic will" [*Kunstwollen*], and on the other hand to the contemporary work done by Carl Schmitt, who in his analysis of political

---

14. One of the earliest articles on Riegl's significance is Zerner's. The quotes here are from Zerner 179.

phenomena has made a similar attempt to integrate phenomena whose apparent ter-
ritorial distinctness is an illusion. (*Gesammelte Schriften* 6.1: 219)[15]

Benjamin's relation to Schmitt has been the subject of much debate. In the present
context, however, it is the methodological parallels between Schmitt's "philosophical studies of the state" and Benjamin's own "art philosophical manner of research"
(parallels that Benjamin underscores in a letter to Schmitt in December 1930)
rather than the invocation of Schmitt's theory of sovereignty that are significant.[16]

The curriculum vitae suggests that Benjamin, like Schmitt and Riegl, was interested in undertaking an intense study of diverse individual "artifacts" in order
to see how "the structure and proper experience of an epoch," indeed, the "artistic
will" (*Kunstwollen*) of a period, is "inscribed" in them. In an earlier essay that treats
some of the same textual artifacts as the 1928 book, Benjamin writes: "Thus, in
the face of history, the task of the poet is absolutely clear; it is to allow the unity of
history to emerge in his reproduction [of it, i.e., of history]" (*Gesammelte Schriften*
2.1: 249). An intensive analysis of works thus permits the unified "artistic volition"
and "character of an age" to emerge.[17] Margaret Iversen has written of Riegl that
he "recognized . . . that in order for a particular work of art to have meaning, it
must be couched in something comparable to a public language" of its time (13).
Benjamin articulates his version of this thesis about the imbrication of artistic form
and specific historical periods in his essay "The Rigorous Study of Art": "The new
type of research," whose patron saint and founder is Riegl, Benjamin claims, "is
concerned with the correlation that gives rise to reciprocal illumination between,
on the one hand, the historical process and radical change and, on the other, the
accidental, external, and even strange aspects of the work of art" (*Selected Writings*
2: 669). Such claims echo both Riegl's belief in the "cultural unity," the "basic inten-
tional unity of a social group" (Zerner 184), and Schmitt's belief in the integration
of phenomena with their times.

Jennings, Henri Zerner, and others have pointed out that Riegl's ideas were all
the rage in late nineteenth- and early twentieth-century Europe. What they have
not noted, however, is that Benjamin, along with Erwin Panofsky and Wilhelm
Worringer, for example, were not the only ones influenced by Riegl's vocabulary
and ideas. According to Jennings, the significance of Riegl's work for even the

---

15. Bredekamp makes a fascinating argument for reading Benjamin's reliance on Schmitt for his
definition of the "state of emergency" as also indebted to the status of the exception in his art critical
methodology; the individual, phenomenal "exception" and the "borderline concept" are likewise reminiscent of Riegl's concept of the "unique extreme" that is the "origin" of the idea.

16. For the letter and a reading of Benjamin's relation to Schmitt, see S. Weber, "Taking Exception
to Decision"; Bredekamp.

17. Jennings, "Walter Benjamin" 79–80. See Olin xxii for "artistic volition" as the translation of
the *Kunstwollen* that "informs all artistic manifestations of a given period, and relates artistic form to a
wide cultural context."

pre-Marxist Benjamin can best be assessed in terms of their common interest in "collective forms of experience"; Riegl wanted to understand the concept of "artistic will" in an anti-Romantic, anti-subjectivist way, as a mode of commentary on how "art intensively reflected major shifts in the structure and attitudes of collectives: societies, races, [and] ethnic groups," Jennings writes ("Walter Benjamin" 84–85). This appeal to the "superindividual," collective forces of an era or place allows the critic and/or historian of culture to "extrapolate from the individual, concrete detail to the culture at large" (88) and to "overthrow the supremacy of the individual creator" (Zerner 179). But Riegl's claim for a kind of seamless continuity between the individual and the collective, as well as between the work of art and the "cultural unity" of its origin, may have more troubling afterlives too. Riegl writes: "When we consider not just the arts, but rather any of the other cultural activities and domains of mankind—the state, religion, science—we will conclude that in all of these spheres there exists a relationship between individual and collective unity. But if we were to follow the direction of the will that certain peoples in certain times expressed in these same cultural domains and spheres, it will become unmistakably evident that this direction is fundamentally entirely identical with that of the 'artistic will' of that same people" (*Gesammelte Aufsätze* 63). Thus, although he struggled to define what he meant by "artistic will" over and over again, as noted in chapter 1, it seems clear that Riegl's claims for organicity and for the relationship between the work of art and the "will" of a particular *Volk* could have had other implications as well. That it was Hans Sedlmayr of the University of Vienna who wrote the introduction to a volume of Riegl's essays in 1928–29 may well have enhanced a particular reading of Riegl among the National Socialist crowd. Sedlmayr held the chair in art history at Vienna from 1936 through 1945 and is reported to have been an "ardent supporter" of the Nazi regime (Iversen 14–15).

To assess the similarity of Benjamin's reliance on Riegl to Riegl's reception in National Socialist Baroque studies and then extrapolate from it that it was these elements that allowed Benjamin's ideas to be heard by Nazi ears, we can turn—or return—to some of the best-known theorists and scholars of the German Baroque, whose work has already been cited for its curious inclusion of Benjaminian ideas. In their work, we find additional echoes of Riegl's ideas. Although neither scholar quotes or cites him by name, the vocabulary of "artistic will" and of the subordination of the individual artist or artistic artifact to the superindividual unity of the *Volk* is unmistakable in both Gerhard Fricke's 1933 book on Gryphius, for example, and in the 1940 review article by Erich Trunz. Fricke underscores the importance of the image for an "analysis of the poetic artistic will" (195), and Trunz writes that the charge to the current generation of Germanists studying the Baroque is to discern the period's "formal will of its own" (2) in its texts; now is the time for "us" to "undertake the task of overcoming the modern, insofar as it is [merely] subjective, and of finding a new supra-individual order" ("Die Erforschung" 87), Trunz writes. In the final note, moreover, of the article in which he praises the Danish Baroque scholar Erik Lunding, Trunz indicates that Lunding's argument usefully echoes that of Heinrich Hildebrandt, "whose book, which appeared at approximately the same time, was unknown to Lunding" (100). Trunz had summarized Hildebrandt's 1939 *Die Staatsauffassung der schlesischen Barock-dramatiker im Rahmen ihrer Zeit* (The Concept of the State of the Silesian Baroque Dramatists in the Context of Their Time) already earlier in his review essay (57–58) as a study that helped "the new Baroque Studies" make visible "the actual will of this art" (58). Hildebrandt's learned study, which had been his 1938 dissertation at Rostock, works to demonstrate the mutual "inter-penetration of life and thought, politics and ideas, the state and culture" (164) in the Silesian example; the formulation sounds Rieglian in its claim for the embeddedness of the artwork in a larger political and ideological domain.[18] That Hildebrandt's interests were in harmony with other aspects of their time is not surprising, for his doctoral adviser was none other than Willi Flemming, whose essay "The German Soul of the Baroque" was soon to appear in volume 3 of the 1941 Party-sponsored *The German Way*.

Flemming's early work is praised fulsomely by Trunz in Rieglian terms in his review essay of 1940. The introduction to Flemming's edited volume of the Silesian plays, which is volume 1 in his six-volume *Barockdrama* (Baroque Drama) (1930–33), is especially "illuminating," for example, on "the particular artistic will" of the Baroque poets, Trunz claims ("Die Erforschung" 7). Flemming devotes considerable space in his introduction to that volume (*Das schlesische Kunstdrama* 15–19) to explaining exactly what the fundamental values and desires of the period were. Not surprisingly, the section is entitled "The Artistic Will" ("Das Kunstwollen") (15). Although Flemming does not cite Riegl here, he does devote the section to describing the turbulent and emotional period that produced plays designed to disturb and overwhelm their audiences in decidedly unclassical ways. The use of Riegl's term in the heading of the section, without any commentary or note regarding its provenance, suggests that, by this time, readers would understand and approve of the methodology on which a section on "the artistic will" of the Baroque would be based.

As Hans-Harald Müller has effectively shown (*Barockforschung* 169–77), Willi Flemming later used the culture of the German Baroque as a field on which to play out the ideological positions of National Socialism via a methodology that sought to locate an emphatically nationalistic "artistic will" (*Kunstwollen*) in all literary artifacts in even crasser ways than he had done in his "German Soul" essay. Flemming's *Wesen und Aufgaben volkhafter Literaturgeschichtsschreibung* (The Essence and Tasks of Folkish Literary-Historical Scholarship) (1944) has as its main thesis, for example, that the new literary history can be based only on a "folkish view of

---

18. Hildebrandt does not cite Benjamin in his notes, but his bibliography, like Lunding's, is nearly a mirror image of Benjamin's sources; one cannot help but wonder if Hildebrandt did not also know that Benjamin's book, like his own, was intimately concerned with the question of the theory of sovereignty.

history" (20) and that a *Volk* can be defined only in terms of its "racial . . . compo-nents" (8). The method of such a history, Flemming writes, will be the "examina-tion of the artistic will" that "lives unconsciously in the heart of the poet and directs his hand" (47). And elsewhere: "The artistic will is native to its time at an uncon-scious level" (52). Riegl's term, the "artistic will," which appears to have been so widely understood already a decade earlier as to not need further explanation, is thus in ample evidence here, but in a far more deliberately politicized way. Flem-ming's constant references in the 1944 volume, written and published at the height of the war, to an earlier publication, namely a coffee-table book entitled *Deutsche Kultur im Zeitalter des Barock* (German Culture in the Age of the Baroque) (1937), reveal that he had been making arguments about the necessity of studying the "ra-cial characteristics of style" (*Deutsche Kultur* 19) of the period as well as its "Ger-manic sensibility" (82) already for quite some time.

Flemming's tendency to indulge in a liberal sprinkling of Riegl's term "artis-tic will" around the overtly propagandistic 1944 *Essence and Tasks* volume never-theless predated the Nazi rise to power. It already underlies his methodology in the very much earlier *Andreas Gryphius und die Bühne* (Andreas Gryphius and the Stage) (1921), for example, which was his doctoral dissertation. In the section en-titled "Kunst und Kultur" (Art and Culture) in that book, Flemming develops an argument that could be straight out of Riegl, especially insofar as it polemicizes against a strictly "materialist" understanding of the origin of the work of art in a way reminiscent of Riegl's attacks on Gottfried Semper's explanation of aesthetic evolution in terms of the material conditions of its production. Flemming argues instead that a kind of totalizing agenda will characterize all artworks of a given time and place.[19] He writes:

> Relatively favorable economic conditions are the precondition that must in fact be present. We can nevertheless not measure what emerges out of them with any exact mathematical formulae. Since the human will—if perhaps unconsciously—lies at the foundations of the relations of production, it is not only understandable, but also even necessary, that a certain total spiritual [*geistig*] character emerge together with the economic relations, a spiritual character that is not determined by economic condi-tions, but rather springs out of the fertile soil of the conditions of willing at the time. The determining power of the will cannot be mistaken in the history of the arts. That works of art are produced of course does not depend on this collective will; yet, its im-pact is to be seen in the individual field of art to which the interests of the majority of the younger artists turn. Every epoch depends on a single artistic problematic, on the representation of space, for example, on the painterly, on drama or lyric. All hands lay hold of a single oar in the ship of art to propel it forward. (*Andreas Gryphius* 2)

---

19. On Riegl versus Semper, see Zerner 178; Iversen 22.

Flemming's argument here that it is in the artwork that the collective will is expressed allows the work its aesthetic autonomy to be sure, yet also links it to the "total character" of the epoch. In a kind of reversal of the argument I have been making, it should come as no surprise that Walter Benjamin himself cites this book, Flemming's 1921 study of the plays of Andreas Gryphius, four times in his *Origin of the German Tragic Drama* of 1928, since he too was trying to develop a method whereby one could gain an understanding of the "meaning of this epoch" (i.e., the Baroque) through an analysis of its works.

For Benjamin, it is next to impossible to grasp the full "prospect of the totality" of the Baroque; this goal must initially be shunned or at least approached only indirectly through a disciplined analysis of its "details" and "extremes." The reversal—and the parallels between the two men's work—only proves the point, however. Both Flemming and Benjamin were speaking similar-enough "dialects" of a common Rieglian language of the "artistic will" in the 1920s that one can see how Benjamin could cite Flemming and then how Flemming, in a later variation, could be cited by the likes of Trunz, who also cited Fricke, Lunding, and Pyritz, all of whom, coming around full circle, had relied on and, in the case of Pyritz, even praised Benjamin in turn. There are nuances, to be sure, in the respective deployments of Riegl's ideas in Benjamin's book and in the work of these National Socialist scholars. It is nevertheless clear that his vocabulary and historical-critical method were appealing enough for them to work their way out of the late nineteenth- and early twentieth-century contexts and discussions on which both sets of individuals cut their intellectual and theoretical teeth, so to speak, and into two sets of writings: the writings, that is, of the Jew, Walter Benjamin, soon to be victim of the Gestapo, and of men like Fricke, Trunz, and Flemming, whose university careers took off between 1933 and 1945. Richard Wolin has written eloquently about Benjamin's conservatism and its relation to right-wing ideologies in the interwar years. The uneven legacies of Riegl's approach to the concept of the "artistic will" of a people and period suggest an additional genealogy for the acceptability of Benjamin's ideas about the Baroque to an academy operating under the National Socialist regime.

*   *   *

In René Wellek's encyclopedic article, "The Concept of Baroque in Literary Scholarship," published in the *Journal of Aesthetics and Art Criticism* in 1946, the hugely learned Czech émigré gives an account of the debates about the Baroque that begins with Wölfflin in 1888 and extends up through 1946. The article covers the research in six European languages over the course of twenty pages of densely documented prose. Even though Benjamin's *Tragic Drama* book is—oddly—not included in Wellek's review, the earlier parts of Wellek's bibliography read much like an inventory of Benjamin's own "library" of studies of the Baroque—Strich, Nadler, Walzel, Hübscher, and Cysarz, among others. The famous statement with which Wellek's piece opens—"All students of English will realize that the use of the term 'baroque' in literature is a recent importation from the continent of Europe" (77)—acknowledges the provenance of these debates while also depicting the Baroque as a "general European movement" (87), "a general European phenomenon," which "was not confined to a single profession of faith" nor "limited to one national spirit or one social class." "It seems to me . . . impossible," Wellek muses, "to claim one nation as the radiating center of the baroque or to consider the baroque a specific national style" (92–93). Wellek's desire in 1946 to imagine a time when at least aesthetically the continent was not either subdivided into nationalist domains or split against itself (as it was to be in the post-Potsdam era), indeed, when the "European" heritage was whole, is reminiscent of Erich Auerbach's project in *Mimesis* (also first published in 1946) to create an integral Europe out of the shards of the national civilization that he, like Wellek (whose colleague at Yale he would become in 1950), had had to leave behind.[20] Wellek was of course aware that the seventeenth century on the European continent had been nothing if not a dry run for future, modern eras of conflict and catastrophe, and notes that the vogue for studying the Baroque in Germany in the 1920s was driven by perceived similarities between the seventeenth century and the "aftermath" of the Great War (79–80). It was probably for this reason that Wellek insisted that *his* version of the Baroque would differ from the heretofore "frankly ideological" (92) ways in which the period has been understood, as the origin, that is, of an alternative modernity to the one that had torn Europe apart, both in the seventeenth century and more recently as well. Benjamin's claim that "works" contain in themselves both their pre- and their posthistories, histories that make up the "origin" of the work in constellated form, echoes here. Benjamin's Baroque was perhaps not "frankly" ideological, but it was unmistakably the "origin" of a peculiarly German modernity all the same. Because of their common cause in discerning the fundamentals of the German "artistic will," National Socialism–era Baroque scholars could thus both directly and indirectly reference Benjamin's work. The Baroque that existed in these several early to mid-twentieth-century iterations of the period across two world wars in Germany may well be the one to which Wellek wanted to imagine his as an alternative. Future versions of the Baroque may provide other afterlives as well.

---

20. On Auerbach's view of Europe, first from Istanbul and then from the United States, see Damrosch; Said; Landauer; Newman, "Nicht am 'falschen Ort.'"

BIBLIOGRAPHY

Ackerman, James S. "Toward a New Social Theory of Art." *New Literary History* 4.2 (1973): 315–30.

Adam, Wolfgang. *"Dichtung und Volkstum* und erneuerter *Euphorion:* Überlegungen zur Namensänderung und Programmatik einer germanistischen Fachzeitschrift." *Zeitenwechsel: Germanistische Literaturwissenschaft vor und nach 1945.* Ed. Wilfried Barner and Christoph König. Frankfurt: Fischer, 1996. 60–75.

Adel, Kurt. "Rudolf Payer von Thurn und seine Faustnovelle." *Jahrbuch des Wiener Goethe-Vereins* N.F. 73 (1969): 67–82.

Adelung, Johann Christoph. *Versuch eines vollständigen grammatisch-kritischen Wörterbuches Der Hochdeutschen Mundart, mit beständiger Vergleichung der übrigen Mundarten, besonders aber der Oberdeutschen.* Leipzig: Johann Gottlieb Immanuel Breitkopf, 1774–86.

Adorno, Theodor W. "Der mißbrauchte Barock." *Ohne Leitbild: Parva aesthetica.* Frankfurt: Suhrkamp, 1967. 133–57.

———. Einleitung. Walter Benjamin, *Schriften.* Ed. Theodor W. Adorno and Gretel Adorno with Friedrich Podszus. Vol. 1. Frankfurt: Suhrkamp, 1955. ix–xxvii.

Albertinus, Aegidius. *Lucifers Königreich und Seelengejaidt.* 1616. Ed. Rochus Freiherr von Liliencron. Berlin and Stuttgart: W. Spemann, 1884.

Alewyn, Richard. *Vorbarocker Klassizismus und griechische Tragödie: Analyse der 'Antigone'-Übersetzung des Martin Opitz.* Heidelberg: G. Köster, 1926.

———. Vorwort. *Deutsche Barockforschung: Dokumentation einer Epoche.* Ed. Richard Alewyn. Cologne and Berlin: Kiepenheuer und Witsch, 1965. 9–13.

Allgemeine Deutsche Biographie. 50 vols. Berlin: Duncker und Humblot, 1967–71.

Alpers, Svetlana. "Style Is What You Make It: The Visual Arts Once Again." *The Concept of Style*. Ed. Berel Lang. Philadelphia: University of Pennsylvania Press, 1979. 95–117.

Altenhofer, Norbert. "Die zerstörte Überlieferung: Geschichtsphilosophie der Diskontinuität und Traditionsbewußtsein zwischen Anarchismus und konservativer Revolution." *Weimars Ende: Prognosen und Diagnosen in der deutschen Literatur und politischen Publizistik 1930–1933*. Ed. Thomas Koebner. Frankfurt: Suhrkamp, 1982. 330–47.

Althaus, Paul. "Luthers Lehre von den beiden Reichen im Feuer der Kritik." *Luther-Jahrbuch* (1957): 40–68.

Arend, Stefanie. *Rastlose Weltgestaltung: Senecaische Kulturkritik in den Tragödien Gryphius' und Lohensteins*. Tübingen: Niemeyer, 2003.

Barner, Wilfried. "Das europäische 17. Jahrhundert bei Lessing und Herder." *Europäische Barock-Rezeption*. Ed. Klaus Garber et al. Vol. 1. Wiesbaden: Harrassowitz, 1991. 397–417.

———. "Literaturgeschichtsschreibung vor und nach 1945: Alt, neu, alt/neu." *Zeitenwechsel: Germanistische Literaturwissenschaft vor und nach 1945*. Ed. Wilfried Barner and Christoph König. Frankfurt: Fischer, 1996. 119–49.

———. "Literaturwissenschaft." *Beiträge zur Methodengeschichte der neueren Philologien: Zum 125jährigen Bestehen des Max Niemeyer Verlages*. Ed. Robert Harsch-Niemeyer. Tübingen: Max Niemeyer Verlag, 1995. 91–110.

———. "Nietzsches literarischer Barockbegriff." *Der literarische Barockbegriff*. Ed. Wilfried Barner. Darmstadt: Wissenschaftliche Buchgesellschaft, 1975. 568–91.

Barner, Wilfried, and Christoph König, eds. *Zeitenwechsel: Germanistische Literaturwissenschaft vor und nach 1945*. Frankfurt: Fischer, 1996.

Barnes, Robin B. "Astrology and the Confessions in the Empire, c. 1550–1620." *Confessionalization in Europe, 1555–1700*. Ed. John M. Headley, Hans J. Hillerbrand, and Anthony J. Papalas. Aldershot, UK: Ashgate, 2004. 131–53.

Barth, Karl. Nachwort. Friedrich Schleiermacher, *Schleiermacher-Auswahl*. Munich and Hamburg: Siebenstern Taschenbuch Verlag, 1968. 290–312.

Barthes, Roland. "Myth Today." 1957. *Mythologies*. Ed. and trans. Annette Lavers. New York: Noonday Press, 1991. 109–59.

Bathrick, David. "Reading Walter Benjamin from East to West." *Colloquia Germanica* 12.3 (1979): 246–55.

Becher, Peter. "Herbert Cysarz (1896–1985) Germanist: Seine Prager Universitätsjahre." *Prager Professoren 1938–1948: Zwischen Wissenschaft und Politik*. Ed. Monika Glettler and Alena Miskova. Essen: Klartext, 2001. 277–97.

Benjamin, Walter. *Briefe*. 1966. Ed. Gershom Scholem and Theodor W. Adorno. Rev. Rolf Tiedemann, 1978. 2 vols. Frankfurt: Suhrkamp, 1993.

———. "Eduard Fuchs, der Sammler und der Historiker." Walter Benjamin, *Gesammelte Schriften*. Ed. Rolf Tiedemann and Hermann Schweppenhäuser. Vol. 2.2. Frankfurt: Suhrkamp, 1977. 465–505.

———. "Goethe's Elective Affinities." 1924–25. Walter Benjamin, *Selected Writings*. Ed. Marcus Bullock and Michael W. Jennings. Vol. 1. Cambridge, MA: Harvard University Press, 1996. 297–360.

———. "Ich packe meine Bibliothek aus." Benjamin, *Gesammelte Schriften*. Vol. 4.1. Frankfurt: Suhrkamp, 1972. 388–96.

———. "Literary History and the Study of Literature." Benjamin, *Selected Writings*. Ed. Michael W. Jennings, Howard Eiland, and Gary Smith. Vol. 2. Cambridge, MA: Harvard University Press, 1999. 459–65.

———. "Literaturgeschichte und Literaturwissenschaft." 1931. Benjamin, *Gesammelte Schriften*. Vol. 3. Frankfurt: Suhrkamp, 1972. 283–90.

———. *The Origin of the German Tragic Drama*. Trans. John Osborne. London and New York: Verso, 1977.

———. "The Rigorous Study of Art." Benjamin, *Selected Writings*. Ed. Michael W. Jennings, Howard Eiland, and Gary Smith. Vol. 2. Cambridge, MA: Harvard University Press, 1999. 666–72.

———. "Strenge Kunstwissenschaft." Benjamin, *Gesammelte Schriften*. Vol. 3. Frankfurt: Suhrkamp, 1972. 363–74.

———. *Ursprung des deutschen Trauerspiels*. Berlin: Rowohlt, 1928.

———. *Ursprung des deutschen Trauerspiels*. Walter Benjamin, *Schriften*. Ed. Theodor W. Adorno and Gretel Adorno with Friedrich Podszus. Vol. 1. Frankfurt: Suhrkamp, 1955. 143–365.

———. *Ursprung des deutschen Trauerspiels*. Benjamin, *Gesammelte Schriften*. Ed. Rolf Tiedemann and Hermann Schweppenhäuser. Vol. 1.1. Frankfurt: Suhrkamp, 1974. 203–430.

———. Zuschrift. Florens Christian Rang, *Deutsche Bauhütte*. Sannerz and Leipzig: Gemeinschaftsverlag Eberhard Arnold, 1924. 185–86.

Berens, Peter. "Calderons Schicksalstragödien." *Romanische Forschungen* 39 (1926): 1–66.

Bettelheim, Anton. *Leben und Wirken des Freiherrn Rochus von Liliencron, mit Beiträgen zur Geschichte der Allgemeinen Deutschen Biographie*. Berlin: G. Reimer, 1917.

Beverley, John. "Going Baroque?" *boundary 2* 15.3 (1988): 27–39.

Bialostocki, Jan. "Dürer in the Agony of German Ideologies." *Dürer and His Critics*. Saecula Spiritalia 7. Baden-Baden: V. Koerner, 1986. 219–63.

Biddick, Kathleen. *The Typological Imaginary: Circumcision, Technology, History*. Philadelphia: University of Pennsylvania Press, 2003.

Bloch, Marc. *The Historian's Craft*. 1949. Trans. Peter Putnam. New York: Knopf, 1953.

Bobertag, Felix. *Zweite schlesische Schule*. Vol. 1. Deutsche National-Litteratur: Historisch-kritische Ausgabe 36. Berlin and Stuttgart: M. Spemann, 1885.

Boden, Petra. "Julius Petersen: Ein Wissenschaftsmanager auf dem Philologenthron." *Euphorion* 88 (1994): 82–102.

———. "Stamm—Geist—Gesellschaft: Deutsche Literaturwissenschaft auf der Suche nach einer integrativen Theorie." *Literaturwissenschaft und Nationalsozialismus*. Ed. Holger Dainat and Lutz Dannenberg. Tübingen: Niemeyer, 2003. 215–61.

———. "Zur Entwicklung der literaturhistorischen Konzeption Julius Petersens." *Zeitschrift für Germanistik* 9.5 (1988): 572–86.

Bollenbeck, Georg. "The Humanities in Germany after 1933: Semantic Transformations and the Nazification of the Disciplines." *Nazi Germany and the Humanities*. Ed. Wolfgang Bialas and Anson Rabinbach. Oxford: Oneworld Press, 2007. 1–20.

Borchardt, Frank L. "Petrarch: The German Connection." *Francis Petrarch Six Centuries Later: A Symposium*. Ed. Aldo Scaglione. Chapel Hill: University of North Carolina Press, 1975. 418–31.

Borgstedt, Thomas. "Gryphius: *Catharina von Georgien;* Poetische Sakralisierung und Horror des Politischen." *Interpretationen: Dramen vom Barock bis zur Aufklärung*. Stuttgart: Reclam, 2000. 37–66.

Borinski, Karl. *Die Antike in Poetik und Kunsttheorie von Ausgang des klassischen Altertums bis auf Goethe und Wilhelm von Humboldt*. Leipzig: Dieterich, 1914–24.

——. *Die Weltwiedergeburtsidee in den neueren Zeiten.* Munich: Verlag der Bayerischen Akademie der Wissenschaften in Kommission des G. Franzschen Verlags (J. Roth), 1919. Originally presented as a lecture, 2 November 1918.

Borst, Arno. *Der Turmbau von Babel: Geschichte der Meinungen über Ursprung und Vielfalt der Sprachen und Völker.* Stuttgart: A. Hiersemann, 1957–63.

Boureau, Alain. *Kantorowicz: Stories of a Historian.* 1990. Trans. Stephen G. Nichols and Gabrielle M. Spiegel. Baltimore and London: Johns Hopkins University Press, 2001.

Brady, Thomas A. "'Confessionalization'—The Career of a Concept." *Confessionalization in Europe, 1555–1700: Essays in Honor and Memory of Bodo Nischan.* Ed. John M. Headley et al. Burlington, VT: Ashgate, 2004. 1–20.

——. "The Protestant Reformation in German History." German Historical Institute, Occasional Paper 22. Washington, D.C.: German Historical Institute, 1988. 9–32.

Brakelmann, Günter. *Der deutsche Protestantismus im Epochenjahr 1917.* Witten: Luther-Verlag, 1974.

Braudel, Fernand. "The Situation of History in 1950." 1950. *On History.* Trans. Sarah Matthews. Chicago: University of Chicago Press, 1980. 6–22.

Braungart, Wolfgang. "Walter Benjamin, Stefan George und die Frühgeschichte des Begriffs der Aura." *Castrum peregrini* 46.230 (1997): 38–51.

Bredekamp, Horst. "From Walter Benjamin to Carl Schmitt, via Thomas Hobbes." Trans. Melissa Thorson Hause and Jackson Bond. *Critical Inquiry* 25 (1999): 247–66.

Breslau, Ralf, ed. *Verlagert, Verschollen, Vernichtet: Das Schicksal der im 2. Weltkrieg ausgelagerten Bestände der Preußischen Staatsbibliothek.* Berlin: Staatsbibliothek zu Berlin Preußischer Kulturbesitz, 1995.

Brodersen, Momme. *Spinne im eigenen Netz: Walter Benjamin; Leben und Werk.* Bühl-Moos: Elster Verlag, 1990.

——. *Walter Benjamin.* Frankfurt: Suhrkamp, 2005.

Brown, Marshall. "The Classic Is the Baroque: On the Principle of Wölfflin's Art History." *Critical Inquiry* 9.2 (1982): 379–404.

Buci-Glucksmann, Christine. *Baroque Reason: The Aesthetics of Modernity.* Trans. Patrick Camiller, with an introduction by Bryan S. Turner. London and Thousand Oaks, CA: Sage Publications, 1994.

Buck-Morss, Susan. *The Dialectics of Seeing: Walter Benjamin and the Arcades Project.* Cambridge, MA: Harvard University Press, 1989.

Burckhardt, Jacob. *The Civilization of the Renaissance in Europe.* 1860. Trans. S. G. C. Middlemore. London: Phaidon, 1995.

Burdach, Konrad. *Reformation, Renaissance, Humanismus: Zwei Abhandlungen über die Grundlage moderner Bildung und Sprachkunst.* Berlin: Verlag von Gebrüder Paetel, 1918.

Burkhardt, Johannes. "The Thirty Years' War." *A Companion to the Reformation World.* Ed. R. Po-chia Hsia. Oxford: Blackwell, 2004. 272–90.

Caroti, Stefano. "Melanchthon's Astrology." *'Astrologi hallucinati': Stars and the End of the World in Luther's Time.* Ed. Paola Zambelli. Berlin and New York: Walter de Gruyter, 1986. 109–21.

Carrard, Philippe. *Poetics of the New History: French Historical Discourse from Braudel to Chartier.* Baltimore and London: Johns Hopkins University Press, 1992.

Chartier, Roger. *The Order of Books: Readers, Authors, and Libraries in Europe between the Fourteenth and Eighteenth Centuries.* 1992. Stanford, CA: Stanford University Press, 1994.

Chickering, Roger. *Imperial Germany and the Great War, 1914–1918.* Cambridge: Cambridge University Press, 1998.

Clark, Stuart, ed. *The Annales School: Critical Assessments.* 4 vols. New York and London: Routledge, 1999.

Cohen, Hermann. "Deutschtum und Judentum." 1915. *Hermann Cohens Jüdische Schriften.* Vol. 1. Berlin: C. A. Schwetschke und Sohn, 1924. 237–301.

Collier, J. Payne. *Notes and Emendations to the Text of Shakespeare's Plays from Early Manuscript Corrections in a Copy of the Folio, 1632.* New York: Redfield, 1853.

Curran, John E., Jr. *Hamlet, Protestantism, and the Mourning of Contingency: Not to Be.* Aldershot, UK: Ashgate, 2006.

Curtius, Ernst Robert. "Mittelalterlicher und Barocker Dichtungsstil." *Modern Philology* 38.3 (1941): 325–33.

Cysarz, Herbert. *Das deutsche Schicksal im deutschen Schrifttum.* Leipzig: P. Reclam, 1942.

———. *Deutsche Barockdichtung: Renaissance, Barock, Rokoko.* Leipzig: H. Haessel, 1924.

———. *Deutsche Front im Südosten: Fünf sudetendeutsche Reden.* Karlsbad: A. Kraft, 1938.

———. "Vom Geist des deutschen Literatur-Barocks." *Deutsche Vierteljahresschrift für Literaturwissenschaft und Geistesgeschichte* 1.2 (1923): 243–68.

Dainat, Holger. "Von der neueren deutschen Literaturgeschichte zur Literaturwissenschaft: Die Fachentwicklung von 1890 bis 1913/14." *Wissenschaftsgeschichte der Germanistik im 19. Jahrhundert.* Ed. Jürgen Fohrmann and Wilhelm Voßkamp. Stuttgart and Weimar: Metzler, 1994. 495–537.

———. "Wir müssen ja trotzdem weiter arbeiten." *Zeitenwechsel: Germanistische Literaturwissenschaft vor und nach 1945.* Ed. Wilfried Barner and Christoph König. Frankfurt: Fischer, 1996. 76–100.

Damrosch, David. "Auerbach in Exile." *Comparative Literature* 47.2 (1995): 97–117.

Daviau, Donald G. "Hermann Bahr, Josef Nadler und das Barock." *Adalbert-Stifter Institut des Landes Oberösterreich Vierteljahresschrift* 35.3/4 (1986): 171–90.

Davis, Kathleen. *Periodization and Sovereignty: How Ideas of Feudalism and Secularization Govern the Politics of Time.* Philadelphia: University of Pennsylvania Press, 2008.

Davis, Natalie Zemon. "Rabelais among the Censors (1940s, 1540s)." *Representations* 32 (1990): 1–32.

De Certeau, Michel. *The Writing of History.* Trans. Tom Conley. New York: Columbia University Press, 1988.

De Grazia, Margreta. *Shakespeare Verbatim: The Reproduction of Authenticity and the 1790 Apparatus.* Oxford: Oxford University Press, 1991.

Deleuze, Gilles. *The Fold: Leibniz and the Baroque.* Foreword and trans. Tom Conley. Minneapolis: University of Minnesota Press, 1993.

Derrida, Jacques. "Interpretations at War: Kant, the Jew, and the German." *New Literary History* 22.1 (1991): 39–95.

Didi-Huberman, Georges. "Obscures survivances, petits retours et grande Renaissance: Remarque sur les modèles de temps chez Warburg et Panofsky." *The Italian Renaissance in the Twentieth Century.* Ed. Allen J. Grieco, Michael Rokke, and Fiorella Gioffredi Superbi. Acts of an International Conference, Florence, Villa I Tatti, 9–11 June 1999. Florence: Leo S. Olschki, 2002. 207–22.

Dilly, Heinrich. "Heinrich Wölfflin und Fritz Strich." *Literaturwissenschaft und Geistesgeschichte 1910 bis 1925.* Ed. Christoph König and Eberhard Lämmert. Frankfurt: Fischer, 1993. 265–85.

Dittmann, Lorenz. *Stil, Symbol, Struktur: Studien zu Kategorien der Kunstgeschichte.* Munich: Fink, 1967.

Dixon, C. Scott. "Popular Astrology and Lutheran Propaganda in Reformation Germany." *History* 84 (1999): 403–18.

D'Ors, Eugenio. *Du baroque.* Paris: Gallimard, 1935.

Eagleton, Terry. "Macherey and Marxist Literary Theory." *Against the Grain: Selected Essays, 1975–1985.* London: Verso, 1986. 9–22.

Enders, Carl, ed. *Wachstum und Wandel: Lebenserinnerungen von Oskar Walzel.* Berlin: Erich Schmidt Verlag, 1956.

Estes, James M. *Peace, Order, and the Glory of God: Secular Authority and the Church in the Thought of Luther and Melanchthon, 1518–1559.* Leiden and Boston: Brill, 2005.

Ewald, Petra, and Dieter Nerius. "Zur Entwicklung der Großschreibung im Deutschen." *Die Groß- und Kleinschreibung im Deutschen.* 2nd ed. Leipzig: VEB Bibliographisches Institut, 1990. 15–21.

Faber du Faur, Curt. "Eine Sammlung deutscher Literatur des Barock in der Bibliothek der Yale-Universität in New Haven." *Philobiblon: Eine Vierteljahrsschrift für Buch- und Graphik-Sammler* 2.1 (1958): 8–30.

———. "The Faber du Faur Library: The Collector and His Collection." *The Yale University Library Gazette* 20.1 (1945): 1–6.

Faerber, Sigfrid. *Ich bin ein Chinese: Der Wiener Literarhistoriker Jakob Minor und seine Briefe an August Sauer.* Hamburger Beiträge zur Germanistik 39. Frankfurt: Peter Lang, 2004.

Febvre, Lucien. *Combats pour l'histoire.* Paris: Armand Colin, 1992.

———. "De 1892 à 1933: Examen de conscience d'une histoire et d'un historien." 1933. *Combats pour l'histoire.* Paris: Armand Colin, 1992. 3–17.

———. "History and Psychology." 1938. *A New Kind of History and Other Essays.* Ed. Peter Burke. New York: Harper Torchbooks, 1973. 1–11.

———. "A New Kind of History." 1949. *A New Kind of History and Other Essays.* Ed. Peter Burke. New York: Harper Torchbooks, 1973. 27–43.

———. *The Problem of Unbelief in the Sixteenth Century: The Religion of Rabelais.* 1942. Trans. Beatrice Gottlieb. Cambridge, MA: Harvard University Press, 1982.

Ferguson, Wallace K. *The Renaissance in Historical Thought: Five Centuries of Interpretation.* Boston and New York: Houghton Mifflin, 1948.

Fink, Carole. "Marc Bloch: L'historien et la résistance." *Marc Bloch aujourd'hui: Histoire comparée et sciences sociales.* Ed. Hartmut Atsma and André Burguière. Paris: Éditions de l'École des Hautes Études en Sciences Sociales, 1990. 51–64.

Fink-Jensen, Morten. "Medicine, Natural Philosophy, and the Influence of Melanchthon in Reformation Denmark and Norway." *Bulletin of the History of Medicine* 80 (2006): 439–64.

Flemming, Willi. *Andreas Gryphius und die Bühne.* Halle: Niemeyer, 1921.

———. *Das schlesische Kunstdrama.* Deutsche Literatur: Sammlung literarischer Kunst- und Kulturdenkmäler in Entwicklungsreihen 13: Barock: Barockdrama, vol. 1. Leipzig: P. Reclam, 1930.

———. *Deutsche Kultur im Zeitalter des Barock.* Potsdam: Akademische Verlagsgesellschaft, 1937.

———. "Die deutsche Seele des Barocks." *Von deutscher Art in Sprache und Dichtung.* Ed. Franz Koch et al. Vol. 3. Stuttgart and Berlin: W. Kohlhammer Verlag, 1941. 171–99.

———. *Wesen und Aufgaben volkhafter Literaturgeschichtsschreibung.* Breslau: F. Hirt, 1944.

Fohrmann, Jürgen. "Das Bild des 17. Jahrhunderts in der Literaturgeschichte nach 1848." *Europäische Barock-Rezeption.* Ed. Klaus Garber et al. Vol. 1. Wiesbaden: Harrassowitz, 1991. 576–92.

———. *Das Projekt der deutschen Literaturgeschichte: Entstehung und Scheitern einer nationalen Poesiegeschichtsschreibung zwischen Humanismus und Deutschem Kaiserreich.* Stuttgart: J. B. Metzler, 1989.

Fricke, Gerhard. *Die Bildlichkeit in der Dichtung des Andreas Gryphius: Materialien und Studien zum Formproblem des deutschen Literaturbarock.* Berlin: Junker und Dünnhaupt, 1933.

Fubini, Riccardo. "Renaissance Historian: The Career of Hans Baron." *Journal of Modern History* 64 (1992): 541–74.

Fumaroli, Marc. Préface. *Baroque et classicisme.* Ed. Victor Tapié. Paris: Livre de Poche, 1980. 7–42.

Garber, Klaus. *Martin Opitz, der Vater der deutschen Dichtung: Eine kritische Studie zur Wissenschaftsgeschichte der Germanistik.* Stuttgart: J. B. Metzler, 1976.

———. *Rezeption und Rettung: Drei Studien zu Walter Benjamin.* Tübingen: M. Niemeyer, 1987.

———. "Richard Alewyn." *Richard Alewyn, mit unveröffentlichten Dokumenten und Fragmenten aus dem Nachlass: Ausstellungskatalog der Universitätsbibliothek der Freien Universität Berlin, 24. Februar bis 17. April 1982.* Berlin: Universitätsbibliothek der Freien Universität, 1982. 3–10.

Garber, Klaus, et al., eds. *Europäische Barock-Rezeption.* 2 vols. Wolfenbüttler Arbeiten zur Barockforschung 20. Wiesbaden: Harrassowitz, 1991.

Garber, Klaus, and Ludger Rehm. *Global Benjamin: Internationaler Kongress zum Hundertsten Geburtstag Walter Benjamin.* Munich: Fink, 1992.

Giehlow, Karl. "Dürers Stich 'Melencolia I' und der maximilianische Humanistenkreis." *Mitteilungen der Gesellschaft für Vervielfältigende Kunst: Beilage der "graphischen Künste"* 262 (1903): 29–41, 3[?] (1903): 6–18, 4 (1904): 57–78.

Gilloch, Graeme. *Walter Benjamin: Critical Constellations.* Cambridge: Polity Press, 2002.

Ginzburg, Carlo. "Mentalität und Ereignis: Über die Methode bei Marc Bloch." 1965. *Spurensicherung: Über verborgene Geschichte, Kunst und soziales Gedächtnis.* Trans. Karl F. Hauber. Frankfurt: DTV, 1988. 126–48.

Giuriato, Davide. "Löschblatt: Vom Umgang mit Walter Benjamins Handschriften." *Modern Language Notes* 117 (2002): 560–75.

Glettler, Monika. "Tschechische, jüdische und deutsche Professoren in Prag. Möglichkeiten und Grenzen biographischer Zugänge." *Prager Professoren 1938–1948: Zwischen Wissenschaft und Politik.* Ed. Monika Glettler and Alena Miskova. Essen: Klartext, 2001. 13–25.

Gogarten, Friedrich. Nachwort. Martin Luther, *Vom unfreien Willen.* Munich: Chr. Kaiser Verlag, 1924. 344–71.

Goldmann, Lucien. "Structure: Human Reality and Methodological Concept." *The Structuralist Controversy: The Languages of Criticism and the Sciences of Man.* Ed. Richard Macksey and Eugenio Donato. Baltimore and London: Johns Hopkins University Press, 1970. 98–124.

Gombrich, Ernst. *Aby Warburg: An Intellectual Biography.* Chicago: University of Chicago Press, 1986.

———. "Hegel und die Kunstgeschichte." *Hegel-Preis-Reden 1977.* Stuttgart: Belser Verlag, 1977. 7–28.

———. *In Search of Cultural History.* Oxford: Clarendon Press, 1967.

Gossman, Lionel. "Burckhardt in der anglo-amerikanischen Geisteswelt." *Begegnungen mit Jacob Burckhardt/Encounters with Jacob Burckhardt.* Ed. Andreas Cesana and Lionel Gossman. Basel, Schwabe, and Munich: C. H. Beck, 2004. 113–48.

——. "Jacob Burckhardt: Cold War Liberal?" *Journal of Modern History* 74 (2002): 538–72.

Graf, Friedrich Wilhelm. "The German Theological Sources and Protestant Church Politics." *Weber's Protestant Ethic: Origins, Evidence, Context.* Ed. Hartmut Lehmann and Guenther Roth. Cambridge: Cambridge University Press, 1987. 27–49.

Grafton, Anthony. *The Footnote: A Curious History.* Cambridge, MA: Harvard University Press, 1997.

Grimm, Jacob, and Wilhelm Grimm. *Deutsches Wörterbuch.* Leipzig: Verlag von S. Hirzel, 1854–.

Grossman, Jeffrey. "The Reception of Walter Benjamin in the Anglo-American Literary Institution." *German Quarterly* 65.3–4 (1992): 414–28.

Gryphius, Andreas. *Catharina von Georgien, Trauerspiel.* Ed. Alois M. Haas. Stuttgart: Reclam, 1975.

——. *Das verliebte gespenst gesangspiel, und die geliebte Dornrose, scherzspiel.* Ed. Hermann Palm. Breslau: Trewendt und Granier, 1855.

——. *Freuden und Trauer-Spiele auch Oden und Sonnette.* Breslau: Veit Jacob Treschern; Leipzig: Johann Erich Hahn, 1663.

——. *Großmüttiger Rechts-Gelehrter / Oder Sterbender Aemilius Paulus Papinianus: Trauer-Spil.* Breslau: Gottfried Gründern, [1659].

——. *Lustspiele.* Ed. Hermann Palm. Bibliothek des Litterarischen Vereins 138. Tübingen: H. Laupp, 1878.

——. *Trauerspiele.* Ed. Hermann Palm. Bibliothek des Litterarischen Vereins 162. Tübingen: H. Laupp, 1882.

Gundolf, Friedrich. *Andreas Gryphius.* Heidelberg: Weiss'sche Universitätsbuchhandlung, 1927.

——. *Martin Opitz.* Munich and Leipzig: Duncker und Humblot, 1923.

——. *Shakespeare und der deutsche Geist.* 1911. 4th ed. Berlin: Georg Bondi, 1920.

Habicht, Werner. "Shakespeare Celebrations in Times of War." *Shakespeare Quarterly* 52.4 (2001): 441–55.

——. "Shakespeare in Nineteenth-Century Germany: The Making of a Myth." *Nineteenth-Century Germany: A Symposium.* Ed. Modris Eksteins and Hildegard Hammerschmidt. Tübingen: Narr, 1983. 141–57.

Hallmann, Johann Christian. *Leich-Reden/Todten-Gedichte und Aus dem Italiänischen übersetzte Grab-Schrifften.* Frankfurt und Leipzig. In Verlegung Jeremiae Schrey und Heinrich Johann Meyer, 1682.

——. *Trauer- Freuden- und Schäffer-Spiele.* Breslau: In Verlegung Jesaiae Fellgiebels Buchhändler, n.d. [1684].

Hammerstein, Helga Robinson. "The Battle of the Booklets: Prognostic Tradition and Proclamation of the Word in Early Sixteenth-Century Germany." *'Astrologici hallucinati': Stars and the End of the World in Luther's Time.* Ed. Paola Zambelli. Berlin and New York: Walter de Gruyter, 1986. 129–50.

Hampton, Timothy. "Introduction: Baroque Topographies." *Yale French Studies* 80 (1991): 1–9.

Hanssen, Beatrice. *Walter Benjamin's Other History: Of Stones, Animals, Human Beings, and Angels.* Berkeley: University of California Press, 1998.

Harms, Wolfgang. "Die studentische Gegenwehr gegen Angriffe auf Paul Hankamer an der Universität Königsberg 1935/36: Ein Versuch der Verteidigung einer Geisteswissenschaft." *Nach der Sozialgeschichte: Konzepte für eine Literaturwissenschaft zwischen Historischer Anthropologie, Kulturgeschichte und Medientheorie.* Ed. Martin Huber and Gerhard Lauer. Tübingen: Niemeyer, 2000. 281–301.

Hauptmann, Gerhart. "Deutschland und Shakespeare." *Jahrbuch der deutschen Shakespeare-Gesellschaft* 51 (1915): vii–xii.

Hausenstein, Wilhelm. *Vom Geist des Barock.* Munich: R. Piper und Co., 1924.

Hauser, Arnold. *Philosophie der Kunstgeschichte.* Munich: Beck, 1958.

Heinsius, Theodor. *Vollständiges Wörterbuch der deutschen Sprache.* Vienna: Christian Friedrich Schad, 1828–30.

Henkel, Arthur, and Albrecht Schöne. *Emblemata: Handbuch zur Sinnbildkunst des XVI. und XVII. Jahrhunderts.* Stuttgart: J. B. Metzler, 1967.

Henne, Helmut. *Hochsprache und Mundart im schlesischen Barock: Studien zum literarischen Wortschatz in der ersten Hälfte des 17. Jahrhunderts.* Cologne and Graz: Böhlau Verlag, 1966.

Hermand, Jost. *Literaturwissenschaft und Kunstwissenschaft.* Stuttgart: Metzler, 1965.

Hildebrandt, Heinrich. *Die Staatsauffassung der schlesischen Barockdramatiker im Rahmen ihrer Zeit.* Rostock: Carl Hinstorffs Buchdruckerei, 1939.

Hoff, Linda Kay. *Hamlet's Choice: A Reformation Allegory.* Lewiston, NY: E. Mellen, 1988.

Hohendahl, Peter Uwe. "Gervinus als Historiker des Barockzeitalters." *Europäische Barock-Rezeption.* Ed. Klaus Garber et al. Vol. 2. Wiesbaden: Harrassowitz, 1991. 561–76.

Holly, Michael Ann. "Cultural History, Connoisseurship, and Melancholy." *The Italian Renaissance in the Twentieth Century.* Ed. Allen J. Grieco, Michael Rokke, and Fiorella Gioffredi Superbi. Acts of an International Conference, Florence, Villa I Tatti, 9–11 June 1999. Florence: Leo S. Olschki, 2002. 195–206.

——. *Panofsky and the Foundations of Art History.* Ithaca, NY: Cornell University Press, 1984.

——. "Wölfflin and the Imagining of the Baroque." *Visual Culture: Images and Interpretations.* Ed. Norman Bryson et al. Hanover, NH and London: University Press of New England, 1994. 347–64.

Holsinger, Bruce. *Neomedievalism, Neoconservatism, and the War on Terror.* Chicago: Prickly Paradigm Press, 2007.

——. *The Pre-Modern Condition, Medievalism, and the Making of Theory.* Chicago: University of Chicago Press, 2005.

Honold, Alexander. "Julius Petersens Berliner Barock-Seminar 1927/28 zwischen den Schulen und Zeiten." *Berliner Universität und deutsche Literaturgeschichte.* Ed. Gesine Bey. Frankfurt: Peter Lang, 1998. 89–104.

Höppner, Wolfgang. "Die Mode des Barock und der preußische Zopf: Die deutsche Literatur des 17. Jahrhunderts im Wissenschaftskonzept Wilhelm Scherers." *Europäische Barock-Rezeption.* Ed. Klaus Garber et al. Vol. 1. Wiesbaden: Harrassowitz, 1991. 593–604.

——. "Eine Institution wehrt sich: Das Berliner Germanische Seminar und die deutsche Geistesgeschichte." *Literaturwissenschaft und Geistesgeschichte 1910 bis 1925.* Ed. Christoph König and Eberhard Lämmert. Frankfurt: Fischer, 1993. 362–80.

——. "Wilhelm Scherer, Erich Schmidt und die Gründung des Germanischen Seminars an der Berliner Universität." *Zeitschrift für Germanistik* 9.5 (1988): 545–57.

Horn, Franz. *Die Poesie und Beredsamkeit der Deutschen, von Luthers Zeit bis zur Gegenwart.* 4 vols. Berlin: Enslin, 1822–29.

Hübscher, Arthur. "Barock als Gestaltung antithetischen Lebensgefühls: Grundlegung einer Phaseologie der Geistesgeschichte." *Euphorion* 24 (1922): 517–62 and 759–805.

Hutchison, Jane Campbell. "'Ehrlich gehalten nah und feren': Five Centuries of Dürer Reception; Albrecht Dürer (1471–1528) in German History." *Albrecht Dürer: A Guide to Research.* New York and London: Garland, 2000. 1–24.

Ioppolo, Grace. *Revising Shakespeare.* Cambridge, MA: Harvard University Press, 1991.

Iversen, Margaret. *Alois Riegl: Art History and Theory.* Cambridge, MA: MIT Press, 1993.

Jäger, Lorenz. *Messianische Kritik: Studien zu Leben und Werk von Florens Christian Rang.* Europäische Kulturstudien 8. Cologne, Weimar, and Vienna: Böhlau, 1998.

Jahrbuch der Bücherpreise und Ergebnisse der Versteigerungen in Deutschland, Deutsch-Oesterreich, der Tchecko-Slovakei, Ungarn, Holland 22 (1927). Ed. Gertrud Hebbeler. Leipzig: Harrassowitz, 1928.

Jahrbuch der deutschen Shakespeare-Gesellschaft 52 (1916). Ed. Alois Brandl and Max Förster. Berlin: Verlag von Georg Reimer, 1916.

Janz, Rolf-Peter. "Das Ende Weimars—aus der Perspektive Walter Benjamins." *Weimars Ende: Prognosen und Diagnosen in der deutschen Literatur und politischen Publizistik 1930–1933.* Ed. Thomas Koebner. Frankfurt: Suhrkamp, 1982. 260–70.

Jaumann, Herbert. "Der Barockbegriff in der nichtwissenschaftlichen Literatur- und Kunstpublizistik." *Europäische Barock-Rezeption.* Ed. Klaus Garber et al. Vol. 1. Wiesbaden: Harrassowitz, 1991. 619–33.

———. *Die deutsche Barockliteratur: Wertung-Umwertung.* Bonn: Bouvier Verlag, 1975.

Jay, Martin. Preface. Alain Boureau, *Kantorowicz: Stories of a Historian.* Trans. Stephen G. Nichols and Gabrielle M. Spiegel. 1990. Baltimore and London: Johns Hopkins University Press, 2001. vii–xi.

Jennings, Michael W. *Dialectical Images: Walter Benjamin's Theory of Literary Criticism.* Ithaca, NY: Cornell University Press, 1987.

———. "Walter Benjamin and the Theory of Art History." *Walter Benjamin, 1892–1940: Zum 100. Geburtstag.* Ed. Uwe Steiner. Bern and New York: Peter Lang, 1992. 77–102.

Kaminski, Nicola. *Andreas Gryphius.* Stuttgart: Reclam, 1998.

Kany, Roland. *Mnemosyne als Programm: Geschichte, Erinnerung und die Andacht zum Unbedeutenden im Werk von Usener, Warburg und Benjamin.* Tübingen: Niemeyer, 1987.

Kaufmann, Thomas DaCosta. *Toward a Geography of Art.* Chicago and London: University of Chicago Press, 2004.

Kemp, Wolfgang. "Fernbilder: Benjamin und die Kunstwissenschaft." *"Links hatte noch alles sich zu enträtseln . . .": Walter Benjamin im Kontext.* Ed. Burkhardt Lindner. Frankfurt: Syndikat, 1978. 224–57.

———. Nachwort. Alois Riegl, *Spätrömische Kunstindustrie.* 1901. Berlin: Gebr. Mann Verlag, 2000. 1–19.

Kiesant, Knut. "Die Wiederentdeckung der Barockliteratur: Leistungen und Grenzen der Barockbegeisterung der zwanziger Jahre." *Literaturwissenschaft und Geistesgeschichte 1910 bis 1925.* Ed. Christoph König and Eberhard Lämmert. Frankfurt: Fischer, 1993. 77–91.

King, Katie. *Theory in Its Feminist Travels: Conversations in U.S. Women's Movements.* Bloomington: Indiana University Press, 1994.

Kittel, Peter. *Die Staatsbibliothek zu Berlin Preußischer Kulturbesitz und ihr Alter Realkatalog.* Berlin: Staatsbibliothek zu Berlin—Preußischer Kulturbesitz, 1994.

Kittsteiner, Heinz-Dieter. "Walter Benjamins Historismus." *Passagen: Walter Benjamins Urgeschichte des XIX. Jahrhunderts.* Ed. Norbert Bolz and Bernd Witte. Munich: Fink Verlag, 1984. 163–97.

Klein, J[ulius] L[eopold]. *Geschichte des Englischen Drama's [sic]*. 2 vols. Leipzig: T. O. Weigel, 1876.

Koch, Franz, et al., eds. *Von deutscher Art in Sprache und Dichtung*. 5 vols. Stuttgart and Berlin: W. Kohlhammer Verlag, 1941.

Koepnick, Lutz P. "The Spectacle, the *Trauerspiel*, and the Politics of Resolution: Benjamin Reading the Baroque Reading Weimar." *Critical Inquiry* 22 (1996): 268–91.

Köhler, Hans-Joachim. "The 'Flugschriften' and Their Importance in Religious Debate: A Quantitative Approach." *'Astrologici hallucinati': Stars and the End of the World in Luther's Time*. Ed. Paola Zambelli. Berlin and New York: Walter de Gruyter, 1986. 153–75.

Köhn, Eckhardt. "Sammler." *Benjamins Begriffe*. Ed. Michael Opitz and Erdmut Wizisla. Vol. 1. Frankfurt: Suhrkamp, 2000. 695–724.

König, Christoph. "'Geistige, private Verbündung': Brecht, Nadler, Benjamin und Hugo von Hofmannsthal." *Literaturwissenschaft und Geistesgeschichte 1910 bis 1925*. Ed. Christoph König and Eberhard Lämmert. Frankfurt: Fischer, 1993. 156–71.

Körner, Josef. "Barocke Barockforschung." *Historische Zeitschrift* 133 (1926): 455–64.

Kunisch, Hans-Peter. "Erich Trunz (*1905) Germanist: Von Lobwasser über das Gegenwartsschrifttum zu Goethe." *Prager Professoren 1938–1948: Zwischen Wissenschaft und Politik*. Ed. Monika Glettler and Alena Miskova. Essen: Klartext, 2001. 299–311.

Kusukawa, Sachiko. *The Transformation of Natural Philosophy: The Case of Melanchthon*. Cambridge: Cambridge University Press, 1995.

Landauer, Carl. "Auerbach's Performance and the American Academy, or How New Haven Stole the Idea of *Mimesis*." *Literary History and the Challenge of Philology*. Ed. Seth Lerer. Stanford, CA: Stanford University Press, 1996. 179–94.

Larson, Kenneth E. "'The Classical German Shakespeare' as Emblem of Germany as a 'geistige Weltmacht': Validating National Power through Cultural Prefiguration." Paper presented at the Annual Meeting of the Modern Language Association, 1991. Available at http://aurora.wells.edu/-klarson/.

———. "The Origins of the 'Schlegel-Tieck' Shakespeare in the 1820s." *German Quarterly* 60 (1987): 19–37.

Lepsky, Klaus. *Ernst H. Gombrich: Theorie und Methode*. Vienna and Cologne: Böhlau Verlag, 1991.

Leyh, Georg. *Die deutschen wissenschaftlichen Bibliotheken nach dem Krieg*. Tübingen: J. C. B. Mohr (Paul Siebeck), 1947.

Liebeschütz, Hans. "Aby Warburg (1866–1929) as Interpreter of Civilisation." *Leo Baeck Institute Yearbook* 14 (1971): 225–36.

Liliencron, Rochus Freiherr von. "Die siebente Todsünde." *Über Land und Meer: Allgemeine Illustrierte Zeitung* 38 (1877): 629–31, 649–51, 670–74, 690–94.

———. Einleitung. Aegidius Albertinus, *Lucifers Königreich und Seelengejaidt*. 1616. Berlin and Stuttgart: W. Spemann, 1884. i–xxi.

———. *Wie man in Amwald Musik macht, Die siebente Todsünde: Zwei Novellen*. Leipzig: Duncker und Humblot, 1903.

Lindner, Burkhardt. "Habilitationsakte Benjamin: Über ein 'akademisches Trauerspiel' und über ein Vorkapitel der 'Frankfurter Schule' (Horkheimer, Adorno)." *Zeitschrift für Literaturwissenschaft und Linguistik* 53–54 (1984): 147–65.

———, ed. *"Links hatte noch alles sich zu enträtseln . . .": Walter Benjamin im Kontext*. Frankfurt: Syndikat, 1978.

Link-Heer, Ursula. "Manier/Manieristisch/Manierismus." *Ästhetische Grundbegriffe: Historisches Wörterbuch in sieben Bänden*. Ed. Karlheinz Barck et al. Vol. 3. Stuttgart and Weimar: Metzler, 2000. 790–846.

——. "Zur Kanonisierung antiklassischer Stile: Manierismus und Barock." *Kanon Macht Kultur: DFG-Symposium, 1996*. Ed. Renate von Heydebrand. Stuttgart and Weimar: Metzler, 1998. 156–76.

Lohenstein, Daniel Caspers von. *Sophonisbe: Trauerspiel*. Breslau: Auf unkosten Jesaiae Fellgibel, 1680.

——. *Sophonisbe, Trauer = Spiel*. Frankfurt and Leipzig: Zu finden bey Joh. Herbord Kloßen, 1724.

Löwy, Michael. "Walter Benjamins Kritik des Fortschritts: Auf der Suche nach der verlorenen Erfahrung." *Antike und Moderne: Zu Walter Benjamins 'Passagen.'* Ed. Norbert W. Bolz and Richard Faber. Würzburg: Königshausen und Neumann, 1986. 214–23.

Lunding, Erik. *Das schlesische Kunstdrama: Eine Darstellung und Deutung*. Copenhagen: P. Haase & Sons Forlag, 1940.

Lupton, Julia Reinhard. *Afterlives of the Saints: Hagiography, Typology, and Renaissance Literature*. Stanford, CA: Stanford University Press, 1996.

Luther, Martin. "Against the Robbing and Murdering Hordes of Peasants." *Selected Writings of Martin Luther*. Ed. Theodore G. Tappert. Vol. 3. Philadelphia: Fortress Press, 1967. 347–55.

——. "Temporal Authority: To What Extent It Should Be Obeyed." *Selected Writings of Martin Luther*. Ed. Theodore G. Tappert. Vol. 2. Philadelphia: Fortress Press, 1967. 267–319.

——. "Von weltlicher Obrigkeit, wie weit man ihr Gehorsam schuldig sei." *Luthers Werke: Studienausgabe*. Ed. Otto Clemen. Vol. 2. 6th ed. Berlin: de Gruyter, 1967. 360–94.

——. "Widder die stürmenden bawren." *Luthers Werke: Studienausgabe*. Ed. Otto Clemen. Vol. 3. 6th ed. Berlin: de Gruyter, 1967. 69–74.

Macherey, Pierre. "For a Theory of Literary Reproduction." *In a Materialist Way: Selected Essays by Pierre Macherey*. Ed. Warren Montag. Trans. Ted Stolze. New York: Verso, 1998. 42–51.

Malgarini, Alessandra Bertini. "Werner Jaeger in the United States: One among Many Others." *Werner Jaeger Reconsidered*. Ed. William M. Calder III. Atlanta: Scholars Press, 1992. 107–23.

Mannack, Eberhard. *Andreas Gryphius*. Stuttgart: Metzler, 1986.

Marcus, Leah. "Renaissance/Early Modern Studies." *Redrawing the Boundaries*. Ed. Stephen Greenblatt and Giles Gunn. New York: MLA, 1992. 41–63.

McEwan, Dorothea. *"Wanderstrassen der Kultur": Die Aby Warburg-Fritz Saxl Korrespondenz 1920 bis 1929*. Munich and Hamburg: Dölling und Galitz Verlag, 2004.

Menninghaus, Winfried. *Walter Benjamins Theorie der Sprachmagie*. Frankfurt: Suhrkamp, 1980.

Mentrup, Wolfgang, ed. *Materialien zur historischen Entwicklung der Gross- und Kleinschreibungsregeln*. Tübingen: Max Niemeyer, 1980.

Mentrup, Wolfgang, et al. *Duden: Wann schreibt man gross, wann schreibt man klein? Regeln und ausführliches Wörterverzeichnis*. Mannheim and Zurich: Bibliographisches Institut/Dudenverlag, 1969.

Methuen, Charlotte. "The Role of the Heavens in the Thought of Philip Melanchthon." *Journal of the History of Ideas* 57.3 (1996): 385–403.

Meves, Uwe. "Das Fach deutsche Sprache und Literatur an den deutschen Universitäten im Jahre 1846." *Ausgewählte Beiträge zur Geschichte der Germanistik und des Deutschunterrichts im 19. und 20. Jahrhundert.* Hildesheim: Weidmann, 2004. 651–72.

Migge, Walther, ed. *Wilhelm Hausenstein: Wege eines Europäers; Katalog einer Ausstellung.* Sonderausstellung des Schiller Nationalmuseums, Marbach, Katalog 18. Munich: Kösel Verlag, 1967.

Mignolo, Walter. *The Darker Side of the Renaissance: Literacy, Territoriality, and Colonization.* Ann Arbor: University of Michigan Press, 1995.

Milch, Werner. "Deutsches Literaturbarock: Der Stand der Forschung." *German Quarterly* 13.3 (1940): 131–36.

Minor, Jacob. *Die Schicksals-Tragödie in ihren Hauptvertretern.* Frankfurt: Rütten und Loening, 1883.

Mohlo, Anthony. "Burckhardtian Legacies." *Medievalia et humanistica* 17 (1991): 133–39.

Mone, Franz Josef. *Schauspiele des Mittelalters.* Karlsruhe: Druck und Verlag von C. Macklot, 1846.

Moser, Walter. "Barock." *Ästhetische Grundbegriffe: Historisches Wörterbuch in sieben Bänden.* Ed. Karlheinz Barck et al. Vol. 1. Stuttgart and Weimar: Metzler, 2000. 578–618.

Müller, Günther. *Deutsche Dichtung von der Renaissance bis zum Ausgang des Barock.* Wildpark and Potsdam: Akademische Verlagsgesellschaft Athenaion, 1930.

——. "Neue Arbeiten zur deutschen Barockliteratur." *Zeitschrift für deutsche Bildung* 6 (1930): 325–33.

Müller, Hans-Harald. *Barockforschung: Ideologie und Methode; Ein Kapitel deutscher Wissenschaftsgeschichte 1870–1930.* Darmstadt: Thesen Verlag, 1973.

——. "Die Übertragung des Barockbegriffs von der Kunstwissenschaft auf die Literaturwissenschaft und ihre Konsequenzen bei Fritz Strich und Oskar Walzel." *Europäische Barock-Rezeption.* Ed. Klaus Garber et al. Vol. 1. Wiesbaden: Harrassowitz, 1991. 95–112.

Nägele, Rainer, ed. *Benjamin's Ground: New Readings of Walter Benjamin.* Detroit: Wayne State University Press, 1991.

Nerius, Dieter. "Position und Rolle von Konrad Duden in der Entwicklung der deutschen Orthographie." *Studien zur Geschichte der deutschen Orthographie.* Ed. Dieter Nerius and Jürgen Scharnhorst. Hildesheim and Zurich: Georg Olms Verlag, 1992. 239–75.

Nerius, Dieter, and Jürgen Scharnhorst, eds. "Einführung." *Studien zur Geschichte der deutschen Orthographie.* Hildesheim and Zurich: Georg Olms Verlag, 1992. 1–21.

Neumann, Carl. "Ist Wirklich Barock und Deutsch das Nämliche?" *Historische Zeitschrift* 138.3 (1928): 544–49.

Newman, Jane O. "*Aus dem (Jerusalemer) Archiv:* Fritz Strich to Judah Magnes on Walter Benjamin, 26 March 1928." *Trajekte: Zeitschrift des Zentrums für Literaturforschung Berlin* 13 (2006): 4–7.

——. *The Intervention of Philology: Gender, Learning, and Power in Lohenstein's Roman Plays.* Chapel Hill and London: University of North Carolina Press, 2000.

——. "Nicht am 'falschen Ort': Saids Auerbach und die 'neue Komparatistik.'" *Erich Auerbach: Geschichte und Aktualität eines europäischen Philologen.* Ed. Karlheinz Barck and Martin Treml. Berlin: Kulturverlag Kadmos, 2007. 341–56.

——. *Pastoral Conventions: Poetry, Language, and Thought in Seventeenth-Century Nuremberg.* Baltimore: Johns Hopkins University Press, 1990.

———. "'The Present Confusion Concerning the Renaissance': Burckhardtian Legacies in the Cold War United States." *Other Renaissances.* Ed. Brenda Deen Schildgen, Gang Zhou, and Sander Gilman. New York: Palgrave-MacMillan, 2006. 243–68.

———. "Rosenzweig and the 'Modern' Baroque State." *Rosenzweig Jahrbuch/Rosenzweig Yearbook* 5 (2011): 235–63.

Ngugi wa Thiong'o. *Something Torn and New: An African Renaissance.* New York: Basic Civitas Books, 2009.

Olin, Margaret. *Forms of Representation in Alois Riegl's Theory of Art.* University Park: Pennsylvania State University Press, 1992.

Osterkamp, Ernst. "Friedrich Gundolf (1880–1931)." *Wissenschaftsgeschichte der Germanistik in Porträts.* Ed. Christoph König et al. Berlin and New York: de Gruyter, 2000. 162–75.

Palm, Hermann, ed. *Acta publica: Verhandlungen und Correspondenzen der schlesischen Fürsten und Stände.* Im Namen des Vereins für Geschichte und Alterthum Schlesiens. 4 vols. Breslau: Josef Max und Komp., 1865–75.

———. *Beitraege zur Geschichte der deutschen Literatur des XVI. und XVII. Jahrhunderts, mit einem Bildnisse von M. Opitz.* Breslau: Verlag von E. Morgenstern, 1877.

———. *Martin Opitz von Boberfeld: Zwei beiträge zur lebensgeschichte des dichters.* Breslau: Verlag von E. Morgenstern, 1862.

Panofsky, Erwin. "Der Begriff des Kunstwollens." 1920. Panofsky, *Deutschsprachige Aufsätze.* Ed. Karen Michels and Martin Warnke. Vol. 1. Berlin: Akademie Verlag, 1998. 1019–34.

Panofsky, Erwin, and Fritz Saxl. *Dürers 'Melencolia I': Eine Quellen- und Typengeschichtliche Untersuchung.* Berlin and Leipzig: B.G. Teubner, 1923.

Parente, James A., Jr. "Andreas Gryphius and Jesuit Theater." *Daphnis: Zeitschrift für Mittlere Deutsche Literatur* 13.3 (1984): 525–51.

Parkes, M. B. *Pause and Effect: A History of Punctuation in the West.* Berkeley: University of California Press, 1993.

Pensky, Max. *Melancholy Dialectics: Walter Benjamin and the Play of Mourning.* Amherst: University of Massachusetts Press, 1993.

Petersen, Julius. "Grimmelshausens Simplicissimus als deutscher Charakter." *Von deutscher Art in Sprache und Dichtung.* Ed. Franz Koch et al. Vol. 3. Stuttgart and Berlin: W. Kohlhammer Verlag, 1941. 201–39.

Petsch, Robert. "Drama und Theater: Ein Forschungsbericht (1920–35)." *Deutsche Vierteljahrsschrift für Literaturwissenschaft und Geistesgeschichte* 14.14 (1936): 563–653.

Pettazzi, Carlo. "Studien zu Leben und Werk Adornos bis 1938." *Theodor W. Adorno.* Ed. Heinz Ludwig Arnold. Munich: Text und Kritik, 1977. 22–43.

Pietrzak, Ewa. "Andreas Gryphius und die schlesischen Piasten." *Andreas Gryphius: Weltgeschick und Lebenszeit; Ein schlesischer Barockdichter aus deutscher und polnischer Sicht.* Ed. Stiftung Gerhart-Hauptmann-Haus. Düsseldorf: Droste Verlag, 1993. 229–42.

Piterberg, Gabriel. *The Returns of Zionism: Myths, Politics, and Scholarship in Israel.* New York and London: Verso, 2008.

Pizer, John. *Toward a Theory of Radical Origin: Essays on Modern German Thought.* Lincoln: University of Nebraska Press, 1995.

Podro, Michael. *The Critical Historians of Art.* New Haven, CT and London: Yale University Press, 1982.

Podszus, Friedrich. "Biographische Notiz." Walter Benjamin, *Schriften.* Ed. Theodor W. Adorno and Gretel Adorno with Friedrich Podszus. Vol. 2. Frankfurt: Suhrkamp, 1955. 530–36.

Pongs, Hermann. "Wieland und Shakespeare." *Festschrift zum 200. Geburtstag des Dichters Christoph Martin Wieland, geb. 5. September 1733–gest. 26. Januar 1813.* Biberach an der Riß: Stadtgemeinde und Kunst- und Altertumsverein, 1933. 177–80.

Pyritz, Hans. "Bibliographie zur deutschen Barockliteratur." Paul Hankamer, *Deutsche Gegenreformation und deutsches Barock: Die deutsche Literatur im Zeitraum des 17. Jahrhunderts.* Stuttgart: Metzler, 1935. 478–512.

Rabinbach, Anson. *In the Shadow of Catastrophe: German Intellectuals between Apocalypse and Enlightenment.* Berkeley: University of California Press, 1997.

Rampley, Matthew. "From Symbol to Allegory: Aby Warburg's Theory of Art." *Art Bulletin* 79.1 (1997): 41–55.

———. *The Remembrance of Things Past: On Aby M. Warburg and Walter Benjamin.* Wiesbaden: Harrassowitz, 2000.

Rang, Florens Christian. *Deutsche Bauhütte.* Sannerz and Leipzig: Gemeinschaftsverlag Eberhard Arnold, 1924.

———. *Shakespeare der Christ: Eine Deutung der Sonette.* Ed. Bernhard Rang. Heidelberg: Verlag Lambert Schneider, 1954.

Raulet, Gérard. "Benjamins Historismus-Kritik." *Walter Benjamin, 1892–1940: Zum 100. Geburtstag.* Ed. Uwe Steiner. Bern and New York: Peter Lang, 1992. 103–22.

Raulff, Ulrich. *Ein Historiker im 20. Jahrhundert: Marc Bloch.* Frankfurt: Fischer, 1995.

Richter, Gerhard. *Walter Benjamin and the Corpus of Autobiography.* Detroit: Wayne State University Press, 2000.

Riegl, Alois. *Die Entstehung der Barockkunst in Rom.* 1908. Munich: Mäander, 1987.

———. *Gesammelte Aufsätze.* Augsburg and Vienna: Benno Filser Verlag, 1928–29.

———. *Spätrömische Kunstindustrie.* 1901. Berlin: Gebr. Mann Verlag, 2000.

———. *Stilfragen: Grundlegungen zu einer Geschichte der Ornamentik.* Berlin: R. C. Schmidt & Co., 1923.

Roloff, Heinrich. "Aufstellung und Katalogisierung der Bestände." *Deutsche Staatsbibliothek 1661–1961.* Vol. 1, *Geschichte und Gegenwart.* Ed. Horst Kunze et al. Leipzig: VEB Verlag für Buch- und Bibliothekswesen, 1961. 131–74.

Rosenberg, Rainer. "Über den Erfolg des Barockbegriffs in der Literaturgeschichte: Oskar Walzel und Fritz Strich." *Europäische Barock-Rezeption.* Ed. Klaus Garber et al. Vol. 1. Wiesbaden: Harrassowitz, 1991. 113–27.

Rumpf, Michael. *Spekulative Literaturtheorie: Zu Walter Benjamins Trauerspielbuch.* Königstein/Ts.: Athenäum, 1980.

Said, Edward W. "Secular Criticism." *The World, the Text, and the Critic.* Cambridge, MA: Harvard University Press, 1983. 1–30.

Scharnhorst, Jürgen. "Jakob Grimm und die Orthographie." *Studien zur Geschichte der deutschen Orthographie.* Ed. Dieter Nerius and Jürgen Scharnhorst. Hildesheim and Zurich: Georg Olms Verlag, 1992. 91–131.

Schenkel, Daniel. *Die kirchliche Frage und ihre protestantische Lösung.* Elberfeld: R. L. Friedrichs, 1862.

Scherer, Wilhelm. "Die deutsche Spracheinheit." *Vorträge und Aufsätze zur Geschichte des geistigen Lebens in Deutschland und Oesterreich.* Berlin: Weidmannsche Buchhandlung, 1874. 45–70.

Schildgen, Brenda Deen, et al., eds. *Other Renaissances.* New York: Palgrave-MacMillan, 2006.

Schlager, Claudia. "Seherinnen und Seismographen: Ausschnitthaftes zur Trouvaille 'Barbara Weigand' aus Aby Warburgs Kriegskartothek." *Kasten 117: Aby Warburg und der*

Aberglaube im Grossen Krieg. Ed. Gottfried Korff. Tübingen: Tübinger Vereinigung für Volkskunde, 2008. 215–43.

Schmitt, Carl. *Political Theology: Four Chapters on the Concept of Sovereignty.* Trans. George Schwab. Cambridge, MA: MIT Press, 1985.

Schmitz, Walter. "Oskar Walzel (1864–1944)." *Wissenschaftsgeschichte der Germanistik in Porträts.* Ed. Christoph König et al. Berlin and New York: de Gruyter, 2000. 115–27.

Schnabel, Gudrun. "Gerhard Fricke: Karriereverlauf eines Literaturwissenschaftlers nach 1945." *Deutsche Literaturwissenschaft 1945–1965: Fallstudien zu Institutionen, Diskursen, Personen.* Ed. Petra Boden and Rainer Rosenberg. Berlin: Akademie Verlag, 1997. 61–95.

Schöne, Albrecht. *Emblematik und Drama im Zeitalter des Barock.* Munich: Beck, 1964.

——. *Göttinger Bücherverbrennung 1933: Rede am 10. Mai 1983 zur Erinnerung an die 'Aktion wider den undeutschen Geist.'* Göttingen: Vandenhoeck und Ruprecht, 1983.

Schoolfield, George C. "Nadler, Hofmannsthal und 'Barock.'" *Adalbert-Stifter Institut des Landes Oberösterreich Vierteljahresschrift* 35.3/4 (1986): 157–70.

Schöttker, Detlev. *Konstruktiver Fragmentarismus: Form und Rezeption der Schriften Walter Benjamins.* Frankfurt: Suhrkamp, 1999.

——. "Walter Benjamin und seine Rezeption: Überlegungen zur Wirkungsgeschichte (aus Anlaß des 100. Geburtstags am 15. Juli 1992)." *Leviathan: Zeitschrift für Sozialwissenschaft* 2 (1992): 268–80.

Schulin, Ernst. "German 'Geistesgeschichte,' American 'Intellectual History', and French 'Histoire des Mentalités' since 1900: A Comparison." *History of European Ideas* 1.3 (1981): 195–214.

Schwartz, Peter. "Aby Warburgs Kriegskartothek: Vorbericht einer Rekonstruktion." *Kasten 117: Aby Warburg und der Aberglaube im Grossen Krieg.* Ed. Gottfried Korff. Tübingen: Tübinger Vereinigung für Volkskunde, 2008. 39–69.

Scribner, Robert W. "The Reformation, Popular Magic, and the 'Disenchantment of the World.'" 1993. *The German Reformation: The Essential Readings.* Ed. C. Scott Dixon. Oxford: Blackwell, 1999. 262–79.

Sedlmayr, Hans. "Einleitung: Die Quintessenz der Lehren Riegls." Riegl, *Gesammelte Aufsätze.* Augsburg and Vienna: Benno Filser Verlag, 1928–29. xi–xxxiv.

Shakespeare, William. *Shakespeare's dramatische Werke, übersetzt von August Wilhelm Schlegel.* Berlin: Johann Friedrich Unger, 1798.

——. *Shakespeare's dramatische Werke, übersetzt von August Wilhelm Schlegel und Ludwig Tieck.* 3rd ed. Berlin: G. Reimer, 1844.

——. *Shakespeare's dramatische Werke, nach der Uebersetzung von August Wilhelm Schlegel und Ludwig Tieck, sorgfältig revidirt und theilweise neu bearbeitet, mit Einleitungen und Noten versehen, unter Redaction von H. Ulrici.* Berlin: Georg Reimer, 1867–71.

——. *Shakespeare's dramatische Werke, nach der Uebersetzung von August Wilhelm Schlegel und Ludwig Tieck, sorgfältig revidirt und theilweise neu bearbeitet, mit Einleitungen und Noten versehen, unter Redaction von H. Ulrici.* 2nd rev. ed. Berlin: Georg Reimer, 1876–77.

——. *Shakespeare in deutscher Sprache, herausgegeben zum Teil neu Uebersetzt von Friedrich Gundolf.* Berlin: Georg Bondi, 1908–18.

Smith, Anthony D. *Nationalism: Theory, Ideology, History.* Cambridge: Polity Press, 2001.

Smith, Helmut Walser. *German Nationalism and Religious Conflict: Culture, Ideology, and Politics, 1870–1914.* Princeton, NJ: Princeton University Press, 1995.

Spellerberg, Gerhard. *Verhängnis und Geschichte: Untersuchungen zu den Trauerspielen und dem "Arminius"—Roman Daniel Caspers von Lohenstein.* Bad Homburg: Gehlen, 1970.

Sprinker, Michael. Foreword. Pierre Macherey, *The Object of Literature*. 1990. Trans. David Macey. New York: Cambridge University Press, 1995. ix–xiii.

Stachel, Paul. *Seneca und das deutsche Renaissancedrama: Studien zur Literatur- und Stilgeschichte des 16. und 17. Jahrhunderts*. Berlin: Mayer und Müller, 1907.

Steiner, Uwe. "Allegorie und Allergie: Bemerkungen zur Diskussion um Benjamins Trauerspielbuch in der Barockforschung." *Daphnis* 18.4 (1989): 641–701.

———. *Die Geburt der Kritik aus dem Geiste der Kunst*. Würzburg: Königshausen und Neumann, 1989.

———. "Traurige Spiele—Spiele vor Traurigen: Zu Walter Benjamins Theorie des barocken Trauerspiels." *Allegorie und Melancholie*. Ed. Willem van Reijen. Frankfurt: Suhrkamp, 1992. 32–63.

———. *Walter Benjamin*. Stuttgart and Weimar: Metzler, 2004.

———. "'Zarte Empirie': Überlegungen zum Verhältnis von Urphänomen und Ursprung im Früh- und Spätwerk Walter Benjamins." *Antike und Moderne: Zu Walter Benjamins 'Passagen.'* Ed. Norbert W. Bolz and Richard Faber. Würzburg: Königshausen und Neumann, 1986. 20–40.

Strachan, Hew. *The First World War*. Vol. 1, *To Arms*. Oxford: Oxford University Press, 2001.

Strayer, Joseph R. Introduction. Bloch, *The Historian's Craft*. New York: Knopf, 1953. vii–xii.

Strich, Fritz. "Der literarische Barock." 1956. *Kunst und Leben: Vorträge und Abhandlungen zur deutschen Literatur*. Bern and Munich: Francke Verlag, 1960. 42–58.

———. "Der lyrische Stil des siebzehnten Jahrhunderts." *Abhandlungen zur deutschen Literaturgeschichte: Franz Muncker zum 60. Geburtstag*. Ed. Eduard Berend et al. Munich: Beck, 1916. 21–53.

———. "Deutsche Barocklyrik." *Genius, Bilder und Aufsätze zu alter und neuer Kunst*. Ed. Carl Georg Heise and Hans Mardersteig. Leipzig: Kurt Wolff Verlag, 1920. 106–18.

———. "Die Übertragung des Barockbegriffs von der bildenden Kunst auf die Dichtung." 1956. *Der literarische Barockbegriff*. Ed. Wilfried Barner. Darmstadt: Wissenschaftliche Buchgesellschaft, 1975. 307–28.

———. "Renaissance und Reformation." *Deutsche Vierteljahrsschrift für Literaturwissenschaft und Geistesgeschichte* 1.4 (1923): 582–612.

———. "Zu Heinrich Wölfflins Gedächtnis." 1956. *Kunst und Leben: Vorträge und Abhandlungen zur deutschen Literatur*. Bern and Munich: Francke Verlag, 1960. 222–41.

Thompson, W. D. J. C. "The 'Two Kingdoms' and the 'Two Regiments': Some Problems of Luther's *Zwei-Reiche-Lehre*." *Journal of Theological Studies* n.s. 20.1 (1969): 164–85.

Trunz, Erich. "Die Erforschung der deutschen Barockdichtung: Ein Bericht über Ergebnisse und Aufgaben." *Deutsche Vierteljahrsschrift für Literaturwissenschaft und Geistesgeschichte* 18 (1940), Referatenheft: 1–100.

———. "Erinnerungen an Julius Petersens Seminar 'Deutsche Barocklyrik' im Wintersemester 1927/28 an der Universität Berlin." *Wolfenbüttler Barocknachrichten* 5 (1978): 123–31.

Ulrici, Hermann. "Allgemeine Einleitung: Geschichte Shakespeare's und seiner Dichtung." *Shakespeare's dramatische Werke nach der Übersetzung von August Wilhelm Schlegel und Ludwig Tieck, sorgfältig revidirt und theilweise neu bearbeitet*. 2nd rev. ed. Berlin: Georg Reimer, 1876–77. 3–114.

———. *Shakspeare's [sic] dramatische Kunst: Geschichte und Charakteristik des Shakspeareschen Dramas*. 1839. 2nd ed. Leipzig: T. O. Weigel, 1847.

———. *Ueber Shakspeare's [sic] dramatische Kunst und sein Verhältniß zu Calderon und Göthe*. Halle: Eduard Anton, 1839.

Van Dülmen, Richard. "The Reformation and the Modern Age." 1987. *The German Reformation*. Ed. C. Scott Dixon. Oxford: Blackwell, 1999. 193–219.

Von Martin, Alfred. *Soziologie der Renaissance*. 1932. Munich: C. H. Beck, 1974.

Von Thurn, Rudolf Payer. *Wiener Haupt- und Staatsaktionen*. Vienna: Verlag des Literarischen Vereins in Wien, 1908.

Voßkamp, Wilhelm. "Deutsche Barockforschung in den zwanziger und dreißiger Jahren." *Europäische Barock-Rezeption*. Ed. Klaus Garber et al. Vol. 1. Wiesbaden: Harrassowitz, 1991. 683–703.

Walther, Wilhelm. *Deutschlands Schwert durch Luther geweiht*. Leipzig: Dörffling und Franke Verlag, 1914.

Walzel, Oskar. "Das Deutschtum unserer Klassiker." *Zeitschrift für Deutschkunde* (=*Zeitschrift für den deutschen Unterricht*) 35.2 (1921): 81–100.

———. "Das Wesen des dichterischen Kunstwerks." 1924. *Das Wortkunstwerk: Mittel seiner Erforschung*. Leipzig: Quelle und Meyer, 1926. 100–122.

———. "Shakespeares dramatische Baukunst." 1916. *Das Wortkunstwerk: Mittel seiner Erforschung*. Leipzig: Quelle und Meyer, 1926. 302–25.

———. "Shakespeares dramatische Baukunst." *Jahrbuch der deutschen Shakespeare-Gesellschaft* 52 (1916): 3–35.

———. *Wechselseitige Erhellung der Künste: Ein Beitrag zur Würdigung kunstgeschichtlicher Begriffe*. Berlin: Reuther und Reichard, 1917.

Warburg, Aby. "Heidnisch-antike Weissagung in Wort und Bild zu Luthers Zeiten." 1920. Warburg, *Gesammelte Schriften*. Ed. Horst Bredekamp et al. Vol. 1.2. Berlin: Akademie Verlag, 1998. 487–558.

Warnke, Martin. "Die Entstehung des Barockbegriffs." *Europäische Barock-Rezeption*. Ed. Klaus Garber et al. Vol. 2. Wiesbaden: Harrassowitz, 1991. 1207–23.

———. "On Heinrich Wölfflin." *Representations* 27 (1989): 172–87.

Weber, Max. *The Protestant Ethic and the Spirit of Capitalism*. Trans. Talcott Parsons. 1930. London and New York: Routledge, 1992.

Weber, Samuel. "Genealogy of Modernity: History, Myth, and Allegory in Benjamin's *Origin of the German Mourning Play*." *Modern Language Notes* 106.3 (1991): 465–500.

———. "Taking Exception to Decision: Theatrical-Theological Politics; Walter Benjamin and Carl Schmitt." *Walter Benjamin, 1892–1940: Zum 100. Geburtstag*. Ed. Uwe Steiner. Bern and New York: Peter Lang, 1992. 123–38.

Wedepohl, Claudia. "'Agitationsmittel für die Bearbeitung der Ungelehrten': Warburgs Reformationsstudien zwischen Kriegsbeobachtung, historisch-kritischer Forschung und Verfolgungswahn." *Kasten 117: Aby Warburg und der Aberglaube im Grossen Krieg*. Ed. Gottfried Korff. Tübingen: Tübinger Vereinigung für Volkskunde, 2008. 325–68.

Weidner, Daniel. "Kreatürlichkeit: Benjamins Trauerspielbuch und das Leben des Barock." *Profanes Leben: Walter Benjamins Dialektik der Säkularisierung*. Ed. Daniel Weidner. Frankfurt: Suhrkamp, 2010. 120–38.

Weigel, Sigrid. "Bildwissenschaft aus dem 'Geiste wahrer Philologie': Benjamins Wahlverwandtschaft mit der 'neuen Kunstwissenschaft' und der Warburg-Schule." *Schrift-Bilder-Denken: Walter Benjamin und die Künste*. Ed. Detlev Schöttker. Frankfurt: Suhrkamp, 2004. 112–27.

Weinhold, Karl. *Rede bei Antritt des Rectorats. Gehalten in der Aula der Königlichen Friedrich Wilhelms-Universität in Berlin, 15 October 1893*. Berlin: Julius Becker, 1893.

Weiß, Karl. *Wiener Haupt- und Staatsactionen: Ein Beitrag zur Geschichte des deutschen Theaters.* Vienna: Carl Gerold, 1854.

Wellek, René. "The Concept of Baroque in Literary Scholarship." *Journal of Aesthetics and Art Criticism* 5.2 (1946): 77–109.

Werner, Karl Ferdinand. "Marc Bloch et la recherche historique allemande." *Marc Bloch aujourd'hui: Histoire comparée et sciences sociales.* Ed. Hartmut Atsma and André Burguière. Paris: Éditions de l'École des Hautes Études en Sciences Sociales, 1990. 125–33.

Wiedemann, Conrad. "Andreas Gryphius." *Deutsche Dichter des 17. Jahrhunderts.* Ed. Harald Steinhagen and Benno von Wiese. Berlin: Erich Schmidt Verlag, 1984. 435–72.

Wild, Christopher J. *Theater der Keuschheit, Keuschheit des Theaters: Zu einer Geschichte der (Anti-)Theatralität von Gryphius bis Kleist.* Freiburg: Rombach, 2003.

Wilson, J. Dover. *The Manuscript of Shakespeare's "Hamlet" and the Problems of Its Transmission.* 2 vols. Cambridge: Cambridge University Press, 1934.

Winkle, Ralph. "Masse und Magie: Anmerkungen zu einem Interpretament der Aberglaubensforschung während des Ersten Weltkrieges." *Kasten 117: Aby Warburg und der Aberglaube im Grossen Krieg.* Ed. Gottfried Korff. Tübingen: Tübinger Vereinigung für Volkskunde, 2008. 261–99.

Wittfogel, Karl August. *Geschichte der bürgerlichen Gesellschaft.* Berlin: Malik Verlag, 1924.

Wölfflin, Heinrich. *Albrecht Dürer.* Darmstadt: O. Reichl, 1922.

———. *Kunstgeschichtliche Grundbegriffe.* 1915. 7th ed. Munich: F. Bruckmann, 1929.

———. "'Kunstgeschichtliche Grundbegriffe': Eine Revision." *Logos: Internationale Zeitschrift für Philosophie der Kultur* 22 (1933): 210–18.

———. *Renaissance und Barock: Eine Untersuchung über Wesen und Entstehung des Barockstils in Italien.* 1888. 3rd ed. Munich: F. Bruckmann, 1908.

Wolfskehl, Karl. Einleitung. *Sammlung Victor Manheimer: Deutsche Barockliteratur von Opitz bis Brockes* (auction catalog). Munich: Karl und Faber, 1927. 1–4.

———. *Sammlung Victor Manheimer: Deutsche Barockliteratur von Opitz bis Brockes* (auction catalog). Munich: Karl und Faber, 1927.

Wolin, Richard. *Walter Benjamin: An Aesthetic of Redemption.* 2nd ed. with new intro. Berkeley and Los Angeles: University of California Press, 1994.

Worringer, Wilhelm. *Formprobleme der Gotik.* 1911. Munich: R. Piper und Co. Verlag, 1922.

Zerner, Henri. "Alois Riegl: Art, Value, and Historicism." *Daedalus* 105 (1976): 177–88.

Zielske, Harald. "Andreas Gryphius' Trauerspiel 'Catharina von Georgien' als Politische 'Festa Teatrale' des Barock-Absolutismus." *Funde und Befunde zur schlesischen Theatergeschichte.* Ed. Bärbel Rudin. Dortmund: Veröffentlichungen der Forschungsstelle Ostmitteleuropa, 1983. 1–32.

INDEX